MAKING URBAN REVOLUTION IN CHINA

To: Mr. Daniel Trenholm,
With best wishes.

Joseph Yick
7-8-96

The end of the Sino-Japanese War in 1945 brought not peace but renewed confrontation between Mao Zedong's Chinese Communist Party and Chiang Kai-shek's Guomindang. The ensuing Civil War, at the threshold of the Cold War, held enormous significance for international strategic alliances, and in particular the interests of the United States in East Asia, and has been the subject of intense research and debate ever since. Joseph Yick's **Making Urban Revolution in China: The CCP-GMD Struggle for Beiping–Tianjin, 1945–1949,** based partly on the rich new sources available in the PRC since 1978, rethinks the traditional interpretations of the Chinese Communist Party's victory in 1949 and makes a major contribution to the historiography of this period.

Studies on Contemporary China

Studies on Contemporary China

MAKING URBAN REVOLUTION IN CHINA

THE CCP-GMD STRUGGLE FOR BEIPING–TIANJIN, 1945–1949

JOSEPH K.S. YICK

An East Gate Book

M.E. Sharpe
Armonk, New York
London, England

An East Gate Book

Copyright © 1995 by M. E. Sharpe, Inc.

Library of Congress Cataloging-in-Publication Data

Yick, Joseph K. S., 1953–
Making urban revolution in China : the CCP-GMD struggle for
Beiping–Tianjin, 1945–1949 / Joseph K. S. Yick.
p. cm. — (The studies on contemporary China)
"An East Gate book."
Includes bibliographical references (p.   ) and index.
ISBN 1-56324-605-8 (hardcover : acid-free paper).
ISBN 1-56324-606-6 (pbk. : acid-free paper)
1. China—History—Civil war, 1945–1949.
2. Peking (China)—History. 3. Tientsin (China)—History.
I. Title. II. Series.
DS777.542.Y53   1995
951.40'2—dc20   95-5921
CIP

Printed in the United States of America

BM (c)   10   9   8   7   6   5   4   3   2   1
BM (p)   10   9   8   7   6   5   4   3   2   1

To the memory of my mother, Lau Sin Kai

Contents

List of Maps

Abbreviations

For complete authors' names, titles, and publication data for the works cited here in short form, see the Bibliography. The following abbreviations are used in the Notes and the Bibliography.

BDDS Zhongguo Renmin Zhengzhi Xieshang Huiyi Beijingshi Weiyuanhui, *Beiping dixiadang douzheng shiliao*

BDJ Chen Shaochou, Teng Wenzao, and Lin Jianbo, *Baiqu douzheng jishi*

BDL Zhongguo Renmin Zhengzhi Xieshang Huiyi Beijingshi Weiyuanhui, *Beijing de liming*

BDS Pu Yuhuo and Xu Shuangmi, *Baiqu douzheng shihua*

BDYW Zhonggong Beijing Shiwei Dangshi Yanjiushi, *Beijing dangshi yanjiu wenji*

BDZW Zhonggong Beijing Shiwei Dangshi Yanjiushi, *Beijing dangshi zhuanti wenxuan*

BGD Zhonggong Beijing Shiwei Dangshi Yanjiushi, *Beijing gemingshi dashiji*

BGJC Zhonggong Beijing Shiwei Dangshi Yanjiushi, *Beijing gemingshi jianming cidian*

BHJQ Beijingshi Dang'anguan, *Beiping heping jiefang qianhou*

BXG Song Bo, *Beijing xiandai gemingshi*

JSBX Beijingshi Dang'anguan, *Jiefang zhanzheng shiqi Beiping xuesheng yundong*

LSX Liu Shaoqi, *Liu Shaoqi xuanji*

MZJ Mao Zedong, *Mao Zedong ji*

MZX Mao Zedong, *Mao Zedong xuanji*

SWLS Liu Shaoqi, *Selected Works of Liu Shaoqi*

SWMT Mao Tse-tung, *Selected Works of Mao Tse-tung*

SWZE Zhou Enlai, *Selected Works of Zhou Enlai*

TJ Tianjin Shehui Kexueyuan Lishi Yanjiuzuo, *Tianjin jianshi*

TJJ Zhonggong Tianjin Shiwei Dangshi Ziliao Zhengji Weiyuanhui, *Tianjin jiefang jishi*

TLZ Zhongguo Renmin Zhengzhi Xieshang Huiyi Tianjinshi Weiyuanhui, *Tianjin lishi de zhuanzhe*

TWZX Zhongguo Renmin Zhengzhi Xieshang Huiyi Tianjinshi Weiyuanhui, *Tianjin wenshi ziliao xuanji*

TXGY Liao Yongwu, *Tianjin xiandai geming yundongshi*

WZXB Zhongguo Renmin Zhengzhi Xieshang Huiyi Beijingshi Weiyuanhui, *Wenshi ziliao xuanbian*

WZXJ Zhongguo Renmin Zhengzhi Xieshang Huiyi Quanguo Weiyuanhui, *Wenshi ziliao xuanji*

ZDCZ Zhongguo Renmin Jiefangjun Zhengzhi Xueyuan Dangshi Jianyanshi, *Zhonggong dangshi cankao ziliao*

ZEX Zhou Enlai, *Zhou Enlai xuanji*

ZMZS Zhongguo Guomindang Zhongyang Weiyuanhui Dangshi Weiyuanhui, *Zhonghua minguo zhongyao shiliao chubian*

ZZQY Tuanzhongyang Qingyunshi Yanjiushi, *Zhonggong zhongyang qingnian yundong wenjian xuanbian*

ZZWX Zhongyang Dang'anguan, *Zhonggong zhongyang wenjian xuanji*

Acknowledgments

This book began as research for my doctoral dissertation, completed in 1988 at the University of California at Santa Barbara.

My Southwest Texas State colleague Dennis Dunn commented on an early version of the introduction and chapter 1. Another colleague, Frank De la Teja, provided technical assistance.

I am grateful to the thoughtful suggestions of Professors Gail Hershatter, Lincoln Li, Alan Liu, Edward Rhoads, and Patricia Stranahan. Professor David Strand improved the manuscript with his insightful comments on many parts of it. My greatest debt is to Professor Steven Levine, who painstakingly helped me revise the whole manuscript.

I thank *Asian Studies in the Southwest* for permission to quote from my "1939–1949, A Decade of Significance: The Ascendancy of the Urban Strategy over the Rural Strategy in the Chinese Communist Movement" (vol. II [April 1994], pp. 18–25). I also thank Mr. David Kidd and Professor Lucian Pye for permission to quote from their letters.

Mrs. Muriel Pilley and Mr. Gary Rice kindly edited the various drafts. A Stanford East Asia National Resource Center Travel Grant enabled me to find research materials at the Hoover Institution's East Asian Collection in 1991. I also appreciate the assistance of Mrs. Mabel Lee-Luk and Ms. Rowena Tsang in the purchase and mailing of Chinese books.

Although the book has greatly benefited from the constructive advice of my colleagues and friends, the responsibility for any errors or omissions in the book is mine.

Above all, this book would not have been written without the spiritual support of my family and my wife, Hideko.

Introduction

The end of the Sino-Japanese War in August 1945 brought not peace but a renewed confrontation between the Chinese Communist Party (CCP) and the Guomindang (GMD), historic rivals each convinced that China's destiny lay in its hands. A virtual civil war was initiated as both parties rushed to reclaim territories occupied by the defeated Japanese. The Communists believed that they had to face a long and difficult struggle, for the Nationalists surpassed them in military power, political authority, and external support. At the time the GMD controlled 2.7 million regular troops, compared with a CCP force of about one million soldiers. John K. Fairbank commented: "The Nationalist armed forces were at least twice the size of the CCP's and moreover had the advantage of American equipment and supplies plus the assistance of the U.S. Navy in transporting troops and the U.S. Marines in the Tianjin–Beijing Area."[1]

In the early stages of the Civil War, the Communists were indeed on the defensive as Nationalists pursued their advantage, but by late 1948 the situation had reversed itself. CCP forces had surrounded the urban-based GMD and were closing in on final victory. The Nationalist armies suffered serious defeats, which soon led to the loss of Manchuria and North China. Why was there such a dramatic turnaround for the CCP in just three years?

One dominant explanation of the Communist victory focuses on the CCP's effective mobilization of peasants, especially in North China, during the Sino-Japanese War (1937–45), and sees the Communist victory as a species of peasant revolution. A second popular explanation focuses on the military dimension of the Civil War, and argues that the GMD was simply overpowered by the CCP militarily in the Civil War period (1945–49). As summations of the sources of CCP triumph and GMD failure in mainland China, both the "peasant revolution" and "armed struggle" theses are certainly important components of an overall explanation. In order to construct a complete interpretative framework, however, the CCP-GMD political conflict in urban areas must also be studied.

The central purpose of this study is to examine the struggle in North China. The focus is on Beiping (Beijing)* and Tianjin. These cities were the GMD's central strongholds in North China. In mid-November 1948, however, thousands of GMD troops who survived the Battle of Liaoxi–Shenyang (12 September–2 November 1948) escaped to Tianjin. These defeated soldiers looted Chinese homes and heightened the level of tension in the city and in the Beiping–Tianjin area, which was anxiously awaiting the massive attack from Communist armies. Although *Huabei ribao* (North China daily), the major official newspaper of the GMD authorities in Beiping, had published earlier (6 November) an editorial entitled, "The Future of North China Is Absolutely Bright,"[2] few Chinese expected the Nationalists to be able to expel the Communists. Even the United States ambassador to China, J. Leighton Stuart, shared the same gloomy prediction.[3]

Without any hope of strong military support from the south as the Nationalists were beaten in the Battle of Huai-Hai (6 November 1948–10 January 1949), the GMD authorities in Beiping–Tianjin and North China were engulfed in a military and political crisis. The dilemma of Fu Zuoyi, commander-in-chief of the GMD North China Bandit-Suppression General Headquarters in Beiping, best illustrated the critical situation of the GMD regime in the region.

A capable regional general, to whom Chiang Kai-shek presented one of his private planes for personal use as a token of trust, Fu Zuoyi could not control all the "Central" troops in North China. ("Central" troops referred to those armies commanded by the graduates of the Whampoa Military Academy.) When Fu's crack units were destroyed by Communist forces in early December 1948, his plan for the defense of the Beiping–Tianjin area collapsed. Communist troops moved to tighten their encirclement of the cities. Fu could only sit helplessly and wait in Beiping. His own military force was gone, and the troops of the "Central" armies could not be depended on to follow his command. Factional divisions were weak points in the GMD power structure.

Communist agents operated in Beiping–Tianjin. Fu's own daughter (Fu Dongju) and her fiancé (Zhou Fucheng) were members of the Chinese Communist Underground Party (hereafter CCUP) (*Zhonggong dixiadang*).[4] During the Sino-Japanese War, she studied at the Southwest Associated University in Kunming and was a member of the Democratic Youth Alliance—a major front organization of the CCP. In 1947 Zhou, a Nankai University student in Tianjin, was ordered by the CCUP to recruit Fu Dongju, who became a full Party mem-

---

*On 28 June 1928, the GMD government in Nanjing renamed Beijing ("northern capital") as Beiping ("northern peace"). During their occupation of Beiping from late July 1937 to August 1945, the Japanese called it Beijing. In the Civil War period, both the Nationalists and the Communists called the city Beiping. On 27 September 1949, the Communists restored its old name—Beijing.

ber. She worked as a reporter at the *Dagong bao* (The impartial) in Tianjin and later transferred to Beiping, giving the CCUP access to sensitive information from General Fu's own family.[5] Fu Dongju could not convince her father to defect. However, her reports through Zhou Fucheng to the Beiping CCUP on the activities and anxieties of her father proved immensely useful to the Communists in the Battle of Beiping–Tianjin (29 November 1948–31 January 1949).

In late 1948, Fu Zuoyi secretly negotiated peace with the CCUP. Among the negotiators was Zhang Dongsun, a professor at Yanjing University and deputy chairman of the Democratic League. Fu also secretly endorsed a number of prominent local GMD and social leaders (including the speaker of the Beiping Municipal Council, a former mayor of Beiping, and the daughter of Kang Youwei) who were engaged in an open drive for peace. However, Fu did not inform his subordinate commanding general in Tianjin, Chen Changjie, of his real intentions and the details of the negotiation process. Instead, Fu asked Chen to fight to the end. Ultimately, the Communists conquered Tianjin and captured Chen. Beiping was "liberated" peacefully when Fu surrendered.

On one level, the GMD lost the cities because of the military factor. Since Chen Changjie refused to surrender, Tianjin was seized by the superior Communist forces. The "uprising" (that is, the surrender or defection to the enemy) of Fu Zuoyi and the "peaceful liberation" of Beiping were caused by the Nationalist military weakness, the Communist siege of the city, the threat of a forthcoming massive assault from outside, and the loss of Tianjin. The Communists themselves, however, did not view the Battle of Beiping–Tianjin as a purely military affair. At the Second Plenum of the Seventh CCP Central Committee (CC) (5–13 March 1949), Chairman Mao Zedong glorified Beiping and Tianjin as two dominant patterns of Communist conquest—Tianjin for the defeat of GMD armies, Beiping for the peaceful incorporation of GMD troops into the People's Liberation Army (PLA).[6]

The "Tianjin pattern" (*Tianjin fangshi*) and the "Beiping pattern" (*Beiping fangshi*) permeated the whole Civil War period. Tianjin was not the first city to fall after fierce fighting, and Fu Zuoyi was not the first GMD general to accept a peaceful military reorganization (that is, to surrender). But Tianjin was a CCP-conquered major metropolis; Beiping remained the first model of so-called peaceful liberation in the Civil War and paved the way for similar conquests in Hunan, Sichuan, Xikang, Yunnan, and Xinjiang.[7] Besides, Fu Zuoyi's "uprising" ended the Battle of Beiping–Tianjin, and his surrender of Beiping with more than two hundred thousand troops was the most important example of the Communist united-front activities among GMD officers and soldiers.[8] In short, the Tianjin and Beiping patterns demonstrated the military and political solutions for the conclusion of the Civil War in (urban) China.

Furthermore, the Battle of Beiping–Tianjin, the last of the three decisive campaigns in the Civil War, prompted the official shift of the CCP's work from the countryside to the city. At the Second Plenum in 1949, Chairman Mao issued his historic statement about shifting the center of gravity of Party work from the countryside to the city. He appealed to the Party to do its utmost to learn how to administer and build the cities. He warned that if it could not learn how to manage the cities and win the struggle against its urban enemies, the Party would fail.[9] In addition, ten days after this plenary meeting, the CCP CC and other central organizations showed their urban orientation by leaving their headquarters in Xibaipo Village, Pingshan County, Hebei Province, and entering Beiping on 25 March 1949.

Chairman Mao pinpointed the political importance of the Battle of Beiping–Tianjin and the cities in the CCP's overall strategy and victory. But he did not elaborate on what actually happened within Beiping and Tianjin from 1945 to 1949. To many students of the Chinese Communist revolution (1919–49), the political activity of the CCP in the GMD-controlled areas—the so-called White areas (*Baiqu*)—also remains terra incognita.[10] This fact is odd, since in Communist theory the city, not the countryside, should always be the focus of the revolution, because it is the source of historical progress and of the creative forces of revolution. Besides, the CCP-GMD political struggle during the Civil War period was concentrated in urban areas.

From 1945 to 1949 the GMD was predominantly urban-based; Tianjin and Beiping were GMD urban islands in a CCP-dominated rural ocean. On the one hand, the GMD did not have resources to reoccupy the vast countryside. On the other hand, the CCP did not operate in rural areas alone. It carried on open legal activities until mid-1947 and thereafter clandestine illegal activities in GMD areas. There can be no doubt that the CCP aimed to conquer urban China. The Party's conquest of Beiping and Tianjin was an appropriate symbolic conclusion to the Communist revolution in North China.

It is thus important to reevaluate the salience of the urban sector in the CCP victory even though Yan'an's rustic leaders (particularly Mao Zedong) prevailed over sophisticated urban (underground) veterans (especially Liu Shaoqi and Zhou Enlai) to control the CCP until at least 1976.[11] Jiang Zemin, Zhu Rongji, Chen Xitong, Wang Hanbin, Ren Jianxin, and other current Communist leaders were underground veterans during the 1940s.[12] It seems that since the Third Plenum of the Eleventh CCP CC (December 1978), the urban cadres have become more prominent in Chinese Communist politics and national reconstruction.

Although urban activities are a critical part of the Chinese Communist movement, there have been comparatively few Western scholarly publications on them in the past four decades.[13] In recent years mainland Chinese scholars have published steadily on the general political and military dimensions of the Civil War.[14] Further, the convening of a large-scale academic conference on CCP history during the Civil War period, at Tianjin Normal University from 12 June to 15 June 1990, signaled the growing importance of this subject in CCP research in mainland China.[15] The Communist authorities have also published primary and secondary sources on their underground activities and the conquest of major Chinese cities such as Nanjing, Shanghai, Beiping, and Tianjin.[16] In view of the abundance of new sources, it is now time to study the Communist revolution in a specific urban area during the Civil War period.

Beiping–Tianjin was the strategic focus of the CCP-GMD struggle for North China. Tianjin and Beiping were the only two metropolises in the region with populations of over a million each; they were also the second and the third largest Chinese cities from 1945 to 1949.

In the Civil War era, the CCP was ready to leave its rural headquarters in Northwest China. In the wake of the strategic retreat from Yan'an in March 1947, the Party's leadership was split into three separate groups. Chairman Mao, Zhou Enlai, the Party Central, and the PLA Headquarters stayed behind in North Shaanxi to direct the Civil War and to play hide-and-seek with the weary GMD troops. Mao simultaneously delegated authority to the Central Work Committee led by Liu Shaoqi and Zhu De to manage important Party Central assignments. This work committee settled down in Xibaipo Village, Hebei Province. The Shanxi-based Central Rear Committee, led by Ye Jianying and Yang Shangkun, took charge of the security of the Communist rear areas. Mao, Zhou, the Party and PLA Headquarters, and the Rear Committee were united with the Central Work Committee at Xibaipo in May 1948.

This kind of operational flexibility of the Communists certainly showed the regional dispersion of the central decision-making apparatus of the CCP and PLA.[17] But it can be argued that from mid-1947 to mid-1948, the center of the Communist movement had gradually shifted to North China (particularly Hebei), where the Communists had created base areas such as the Jin-Cha-Ji (Shanxi–Chahar–Hebei) Border Region through social reform, revolution, and anti-Japanese nationalism during the Sino-Japanese War period. The physical relocation of the CCP and PLA Headquarters from remote and rural Northwest China to an area closer to the major GMD cities can also signify the Communist city-bound mentality. While Yan'an was "the cradle of revolution," the city was where the revolution intended to settle on reaching maturity.

Furthermore, it was from North China that the CCP dispatched large contingents of political cadres and troops to build a "structure of power" in the Northeast.[18] Militarily, during the Sino-Japanese War Lin Biao and other Communist leaders sharpened tactics in North China and then used them against the Nationalists in the postwar Northeast China. Lin's and other Communist armies were responsible for the siege of Beiping in late 1948, and they destroyed the GMD Tianjin defense. After that, Lin marched southward to mop up the remnant GMD troops. The Liaoxi–Shenyang and Beiping–Tianjin campaigns were thus closely related.

When the Sino-Japanese War ended in 1945, it would have made sense for the GMD to have focused its pacification program on North China—the center of Communist power. In 1943 and 1944, the *Dagong bao* in Chongqing organized a debate on the issue of the postwar capital. Most politicians and scholars favored Beiping as the capital. In the wake of the Japanese surrender, there were two groups within the GMD arguing over the takeover program. One suggested the establishment of Beiping as the capital with North China being the focus of the takeover process. The other wanted the capital returned to Nanjing and the area south of the Yangzi River marked for takeover. Because of the insistence of several high-level GMD members from Jiangsu and Zhejiang, Nanjing finally remained the capital. This decision not only influenced the takeover measures in North China, but might have been a factor in the collapse of the GMD.[19] On 14 January 1948, the GMD government proclaimed Beiping the "accompanying capital" (*peidu*). The new title did not bring any material benefit to the city or lessen the Communist threat to Beiping.

The Nationalist strength in North China immediately after the Sino-Japanese War was so negligible that the GMD had to rely on the defeated Japanese, the triumphant Americans, and Japan's puppet armies in China to regain its authority. For the GMD, the restoration of such authority in North China should have been the key to eliminating the Communist threat. But before a consolidation of military and political power in North China materialized, Chiang Kai-shek committed his best-equipped troops to recover the Northeast. This disastrous Northeast Campaign was the beginning of the end for the Nationalist cause. But it was the loss of Northeast *and* North China that signaled the forthcoming collapse of the GMD.

The Beiping–Tianjin area was unique in several other aspects. The diffusion of Marxism as ideology and the organizational emergence of the CCP were carried out by Beijing intellectuals and students. Beijing was the point of origin of Chinese Marxism and also of Chinese Communism, although the CCP headquarters was established in Shanghai. Besides, intellectuals and students in Beijing–Tianjin have always played a significant historical role in China's intellectual and political movements: the May Fourth Movement of 1919, the December Ninth Movement of 1935, the student movement from October 1945 to 1948, the democratic demonstrations of 1986, and the People's Movement of 1989.

Beiping and Tianjin, therefore, are excellent case studies of how the cities were lost by the GMD and won by the CCP. They can demonstrate the extent of Communist urban activity and the crucial importance of political struggle attached to military struggle. The Communists could not hope to win simply by moving troops into position. The GMD might not have lost if it had built secure bases with public support in the cities.

Urban Revolution

This is a study of the Communists making urban revolution when the GMD state was breaking down in Beiping and Tianjin. These cities were strategic places in

North China for the Communists to hide out, consolidate power, and strike against the ruling GMD. These areas were complex examples of urban-centered *moderate* revolutionary activities under the general guidance of the small and elitist CCUP. Their mission was to mobilize urban social forces to achieve *political-military* ends. In short, this study explores the contestation of two competing forces; it centers on Communist urban power and policy but also includes the Nationalist rival program and activity.

This study indicates that student protests, or "student tides" (*xuechao*), were at the center of Communist political struggles in Beiping–Tianjin. In these cities, the student movements, coupled with significant work among GMD officers and soldiers, were the most important part of the Communist urban united front and party-building—their two "magic weapons." Accordingly, CCUP's mobilization of students and its underground student work committees in Tianjin and particularly in Beiping take precedence over other Communist activities in this study. A survey of the approach of the CCP toward student and other movements will show how they mobilized urban dwellers for political-military struggle. This study also shows that while the CCP was ideologically proletarian-based and had an urban strategy, that strategy did not target the proletariat. This debunks the view that the Communist support in the cities during the Civil War period was based among proletarian workers.[20] On the contrary, the working class was largely untouched by the Communist political movement; it was the students who provided the thrust of CCP political success, though indirectly. Students acted as spokesmen and leaders for the interests of workers, although they lacked the power base and effective means of coercion for actually toppling the GMD regime.

While organization, strategy, and mobilization were important to the building of the CCUP's power, these factors alone could not guarantee the undermining of the GMD's power. The CCUP also sought to extend its control beyond the reach of close organization (via cells and the like). The Communists were more skillful than the Nationalists in using context—partly the result of their movement of armies and partly the product of forces they had no control over like inflation— to influence the decisions of individuals and groups who were not under their control. Predisposition and mood (such as discontent) of various groups and other potentialities could be converted into political power for the CCUP and into political liability for the GMD in the cities. The spaces between the two political forces could also be influenced by such seemingly amorphous factors as public opinion (on the GMD's postwar takeover and nationalism, for example), filiality (Fu Dongju toward her father), and anxieties about personal and family interest and security (Fu Zuoyi's and those of others).

The Chinese Communist revolution was "a military struggle for the political power of the nation."[21] The military confrontation, like the moderate revolution inside Beiping–Tianjin, was a means of gaining national power. While the revolution was won mainly on the battleground, not in the streets of Beiping and

Tianjin and other cities, the Communist urban activity should not be down-played. In other words, Mao Zedong's "political power grows out of the barrel of a gun" aphorism does not mean that political power cannot grow from other sources. One should not dismiss the achievement of Communist open and under-ground work and the urban united front and party-building in consolidating power and coordinating the military attack from outside.

Furthermore, it is my contention that the outcome of the Civil War (1945–49) was determined mainly by domestic issues. Its origin was the struggle for power between the CCP and the GMD, their divergent land and urban policies, and their unwillingness to reach a political settlement. In light of their military con-flicts in the pre-1945 years and their bitter mutual enmity, it is doubtful whether a coalition government, if ever established because of Chiang Kai-shek's mo-nopolization of both American and Soviet support, would have lasted long or guaranteed genuine peace. More important, the GMD might have had a chance to defeat the CCP if the former had successfully and simultaneously monopo-lized American support, suppressed anti-American sentiment, intensified the anti-Soviet (anti-Communist) movement, and secured the urban bases. Therefore, the American intervention in North China and the anti-Americanism within GMD areas deserve analysis because they affected the Nationalists' political fortunes.

In brief, this is a local study of the Communist political struggles in Beiping–Tianjin within the context of the Civil War itself. It presents a civil war reality that superimposes international, national, and regional levels of activity upon the level of urban conflict that concerns me most.

Besides, this study demonstrates that during the last phase of the Communists' national conquest, their urban underground cadres and supporters became the backbone of the forthcoming national reconstruction and played a key role in the administration of cities and the stabilization of post-1949 China.

Last but not least, this study helps downgrade the Mao Zedong–centered CCP history. While Mao played a preeminent role in the rural revolution and created a so-called Sixteen-Character Guideline (*Shiliuzi fangzhen*) for underground work in White areas, his involvement in the urban struggle in the 1930s and 1940s was comparatively small.[22] This book sheds light on the theoretical and practical contributions of other Communist leaders (particularly Zhou Enlai) and lesser-known local cadres (particularly Liu Ren). It helps reevaluate the relative import-ance of the urban areas in the Chinese Communist movement.

By focusing on Communist activities in the cities, we have a more broadly based understanding of the Communist revolution. In Beiping–Tianjin, the CCUP built and consolidated power. It fought and escalated the struggle against the GMD authorities by exploiting the latter's blunders and accumulating strength through student mobilization. I hope this book will enhance our knowl-edge of the major actors and events in the urban power struggle between the CCP and the GMD, and will reveal significant regional and local variations in the pattern of Communist victory.

Format

In this book, chapter 1 shows the experiences of the Communists: the strategic and tactical considerations and behavior of the Beijing–Tianjin CCP from 1921 to 1945, when it targeted workers and students for mobilization. After the debacle of 1927, however, the Communists gradually realized the crucial importance of student politics and cultural struggle. This revolutionary legacy and emphasis on students and intellectuals are essential for understanding the Communist struggles in the cities during the Civil War period. Chapter 2 is a brief survey of the military history and the national and international levels of the Chinese Civil War. It includes a discussion of the national strategies of the CCP and the GMD. Chapter 3 analyzes the North China dimension of the GMD-CCP conflict. It discusses GMD and CCP military and political organizations in the region, and the strategy and tactics that each side pursued with respect to the urban areas. It also describes the urban-policy prescriptions of major Communist leaders like Mao Zedong, Zhou Enlai, Liu Ren, and others. Chapter 4 is a profile of Beiping and Tianjin as urban environments for political struggle. It shows the abnormal urban conditions at the time, and their effect on the CCUP's strategic calculations of what in the cities needed to be grasped in order to achieve political-military control. It also details the organization and leadership of the CCUP in the cities, including the key leaders' backgrounds and earlier careers. Chapter 5 is the core of the study: the university and school setting where the CCUP from 1945 to 1948 effectively battled for the support of this key urban constituency through a series of student protests and other activities. Chapter 6 is concerned with other urban arenas, primarily the labor movement, and secondarily sectors such as government, business, and telecommunications. Chapter 7 is a chronological narrative of the last six months of the CCP-GMD struggle. It conveys the sense of excitement as the Communists scented victory and assigned their urban cadres a series of tasks involving the protection of organizational assets and urban infrastructure to facilitate their takeover and the establishment of their new administration. The conclusion is a discussion on the significance of the cities in the Chinese Communist movement, and the relationships among the urban, rural, and military aspects of the Chinese Communist victory.

Notes

1. John King Fairbank, *China*, p. 331.
2. See *Huabei ribao*, Beiping, 6 Nov. 1948.
3. See Steven I. Levine, *Anvil of Victory*, pp. 1–2.
4. There is no official definition of *Zhonggong dixiadang* in Communist literature. For example, Zhonggong Zhongyang Dangxiao Lilunbu's nine-volume *Zhongguo gongchandang jianshe quanshu* fails to define the term. It seems that the concept of an "underground party" was Leninist in origin and emerged out of the CCP's Sixth Congress (June 1928) in Moscow. See Wang Zhangling, "Gongdang tewu zuzhi de fenxi," pp.

1–6. In general, *Zhonggong dixiadang* referred to all the underground Communist organizations and personnel in the enemy-controlled (urban) areas from 1927 or 1928 to 1949. The CCP often claimed that their *dixiadang* operated "in the heart of the enemy." See Zhang Zhiyi, "Zai diren xinzang nei," pp. 9–39; *Mianhuai Liu Ren tongzhi*, p. 9. For a general survey of the work experiences of the CCUP, see Ma Shitu's *Zai dixia*. For a Nationalist analysis of the CCUP activities, see Sifa Xingzhengbu Tianchaju, *Gongfei shentou zhanshu zhi yanjiu*, esp. ch. 1. See also Xiong Xianghui et al., *Zhonggong dixiadang xianxingji*.

5. See Sha Xiaoquan and Liu Yan, "Jiefang qianxi Nankai Daxue de tongzhan gongzuo," pp. 247–48.

6. See *SWMT*, vol. IV, pp. 361–62, 374f.

7. See Wang Piji, " 'Beiping fanshi' de chansheng ji lishi yiyi," p. 19; Wang Piji and Xiao Chi, "Beiping heping jiefang," pp. 40–41. One may argue that the fall of Changchun (a city of half a million residents) without fighting after a long siege (May–October 1948)—a part of the Battle of Liaoxi–Shenyang—should have been the first model. In Changchun, Zheng Dongguo, deputy commander-in-chief of the GMD Northeast China Bandit-Suppression General Headquarters, was actually forced to give up the city because of the defection of a subordinate general and the starving garrison troops. Worst of all, 150,000 civilians were starved to death because the PLA under Mao Zedong's order forbade them to evacuate the city. See Zhang Zhenglong, *Xuebai xuehong*, ch. 31. It was Mao's horrible *political* tactic to break the morale of GMD troops by forcing them to fight for food with the civilians. In short, the Changchun case was not a peaceful conquest and incorporation of GMD armies in the manner of the "Beiping pattern"; moreover, Changchun was much less strategically important than Beiping.

8. In light of the high honors (particularly the first-class Liberation Medal and ministership of water conservancy and electric power) bestowed on him after the establishment of the People's Republic of China, Fu's surrender was more important to the CCP than these other Nationalist "uprisings": Zheng Dongguo in Changchun, Cheng Qian and Chen Mingren in Hunan, Liu Wenhui, Deng Xihou, Guo Rugui, and Pan Wenhua in Sichuan and Xikang, Lu Han in Yunnan, Tao Zhiyue in Xinjiang, and Zhang Zhizhong—the GMD's principal peace negotiator with the Communists—in Beiping (April 1949).

9. See *SWMT*, vol. IV, pp. 363–64; Kenneth Lieberthal, *Revolution and Tradition in Tientsin*, p. 10 (note that, different from Lieberthal, I take the 1945–49 period as one of "revolution"). Before the capture of Tianjin and Beiping, the CCP had already conquered a number of towns and lesser cities. Kalgan (Zhangjiakou), the political center of Chahar, was the first strategic city seized by the Communists in North China. Nonetheless, it was the occupation of Tianjin and Beiping, not of Kalgan or Shenyang (the only metropolis with a population of over one million in Northeast China), that signified the genuine Communist return to the urban areas.

10. The GMD-controlled areas were also known as Chiang Kai-shek–controlled areas. In Chinese Communist terminology, the GMD areas in the period 1927–49 were the "White [i.e., enemy-controlled and counterrevolutionary] areas," as opposed to the "Red [i.e., CCP-controlled and revolutionary] areas" (*Hongqu*). The White areas also included the territories occupied by the Japanese and their collaborators in China during the wartime period (1937–45). Furthermore, the White areas mainly referred to the enemy-controlled *urban* areas, not the countryside.

11. Of course, Liu and Zhou also operated in the countryside before 1949. During the Cultural Revolution (1966–76), the so-called Gang of Four launched a smear campaign against the contributions of the underground Communist cadres in White areas. Many underground veterans were denounced and purged as traitors or GMD special agents. See *BDS*, p. 3.

12. Jiang is currently the general secretary of the CCP and chairman of the People's Republic of China. He was a member of the Shanghai CCUP. Zhu is currently one of the seven members of the Standing Committee of the 14th CCP Politburo. He was a member of the New Democratic Youth League (1947–51), a front organization of the Beiping CCP. Chen is currently a regular member of the 14th CCP Politburo. He was a member of the Democratic Youth Alliance in Beiping. Wang is currently an alternate member of the 14th CCP Politburo. He was a leading member of the Student Committee of the Beiping CCUP during the Civil War period. Ren is currently one of the six secretaries of the CCP CC Secretariat. He was a Beijing University student and joined the CCUP in June 1948.

13. For a sampling of the important literature on the urban dimension, see Lyman P. Van Slyke's *Enemies and Friends*, Tetsuya Kataoka's *Resistance and Revolution in China*, Suzanne Pepper's *Civil War in China*, Angus W. McDonald, Jr.'s *The Urban Origins of Rural Revolution*, and Steven Levine's *Anvil of Victory*.

14. For example, see Jie Lifu, *Jiefang zhanzheng shilu*, 2 vols.

15. See Guo Xiaoping, "Quanguo jiefang zhanzheng shiqi dangshi," pp. 54–59, 40.

16. On Beiping and Tianjin, see *BDDS, BDL, BDYW, BDZW, BGD, BGJC, BHJQ*, and *BXG; TJJ, TLZ*, and *TXGY*.

17. See Levine, *Anvil of Victory*, p. 6.

18. See ibid., ch. 3.

19. See Wang Yuting, "Huabei zhi shoufu yu xianluo," part II, p. 120; Tan Zhilan, *Cangsang qishi nian*, pp. 203, 208–9.

20. Even in Shanghai, the Communist labor movement was based on artisan, rather than proletarian, workers during the Civil War period. Besides, the cooperation of turncoat gangsters was of first importance to the CCP in its efforts to gain leverage over Shanghai labor. See Elizabeth J. Perry, *Shanghai on Strike*, pp. 117–29. While the Chinese working class has been capable of influential political action and helped prepare the way for the Communist accession to power, the workers did not play the dominant role in the urban revolution from 1945 to 1949.

21. Pepper, *Civil War in China*, p. 4; see also Jack Gray, *Rebellions and Revolutions*, p. 286.

22. Just before the 7th CCP National Congress (1945), Dong Biwu (CC regular member and the Communist representative to the People's Political Council in Chongqing) reported to Mao Zedong the activities of the CCP CC Southern Bureau (January 1939–November 1944, August–December 1945). Mao admitted that he operated in Soviet (i.e., Communist) areas and was engaged in warfare; he did not understand the work in White areas. Dong's report made Mao understand that most of the Communist organizations functioned well in GMD areas. See *BDS*, pp. 2–3. See ch. 3 for the "Sixteen-Character Guideline."

MAKING URBAN REVOLUTION IN CHINA

1

Beijing–Tianjin: Communist Organizations, 1921–1945

It is essential to understand the legacy of the Communist intellectual/student–led organizations, key personalities, and revolutionary experiences in Beijing–Tianjin prior to the Japanese surrender in August 1945. In the 1920s the Communists were unable to create powerful organizations and an effective united-front approach in the cities. Through better strategies and tactics that accorded with the realities in the 1930s and 1940s, and aided by the Nationalist weakness, the Japanese aggression, and the anti-Japanese national sentiment, the Beiping–Tianjin CCUP had survived and prepared for new challenges by the time of the Japanese surrender.

Beijing–Tianjin CCP, 1921–27

The Beijing–Tianjin CCP was a key Communist organization in urban China.[1] In the wake of the First CCP Congress in 1921, a Beijing Local Committee under Li Dazhao's leadership was established to work among students and workers. After the Second Party Congress in 1922, the CCP Central established a Beijing Area Committee under Li. It was in charge of the work in Beijing–Tianjin and northern China. This Committee also managed the work of the Beijing Local Committee. Actually these committees were staffed by the same personnel. As the Communists say, "two brand names, one set of personnel" (*liangkuai paizi, yitao yima*). This odd organizational arrangement could signify the central importance of Beijing in northern China from the Communist standpoint. It could also be a tactic to confuse the enemy. The Communists continued this organizational practice in the Civil War period.

3

A number of Communist Party reorganizations emerged during 1924–27 to facilitate the First GMD-CCP United Front. In March 1924 there were forty-six Communists in the reorganized Beijing Area Committee; only one of them was a worker. By September 1925, the Committee had recruited several hundred converts from Beijing University and other institutions; only thirty-one of them were workers. In October 1925 a Northern Area Committee was created to replace the Beijing Area Committee and to supervise a new Beijing Local Committee. In May 1926 there were 1,700 Communists in northern China. In February 1927 there were three thousand CCP members in the area; a thousand of them operated in the Beijing area.[2]

The Beijing Communists' activity among the proletariat, which was a small part of the work force dominated by crafts, commerce, and traditional services (for example, rickshaw men), was unremarkable. The Communists performed poorly in their first attempts to mobilize the lower class, and they were inept at playing the local political game.[3] Even the work report issued by the Labor Department of the GMD Beijing Committee (dominated by the CCP and the GMD Left) (February 1927) admitted that there had been little activity except among the thousand-strong railway men in Changxindian in the suburb of Beijing, and among them only 320 had joined the labor union. The vast majority of Beijing workers in municipal administration, such as electric service, cable service, mail service, and water supply, were not organized by the CCP.[4] For strategic reasons, however, the CCUP would return in the 1940s to operate among the workers, especially those in municipal administration and railway service.

In Tianjin the Communists established a Local Committee in the spring of 1924. Yu Fangzhou, a Nankai University student, was the leading cadre of the Committee. As late as 1927 there were 459 CCP members in Tianjin; a large proportion of them were workers.[5]

While the Communists were much more active in labor work in Tianjin from 1919 to 1927, the Party leadership there remained intellectual/student–led. As in Beijing, the CCP Tianjin Local Committee centered work on students. The Communists assigned cadres with an intellectual background to organize among railroad workers, printers, dockworkers, and mill operatives. Initial contact was made with mill workers by Yu Shude and An Ticheng, two returned students from Japan who founded the earliest workers' school.

The Tianjin Local Committee also established a Tianjin General Labor Union in August 1925. Its membership rose from 17,900 in late 1925 to 32,280 in late 1926. The Communist labor movement was led by intellectuals, however. Zhao Shiyan was the secretary of the Committee for the Workers' Movement of the Northern Area Committee. Li Jida—like Zhao, a student returned from France—was the secretary of the Tianjin Local Committee.[6]

In April 1927 there were 57,967 Communist Party members in China. Workers comprised 50.8 percent, peasants 18.7 percent, intellectuals 19.1 percent, military men 3.1 percent, middle-level and lower-level traders 0.5 percent, and other social groups 7.8 percent. Altogether, 3,109 Communists operated in northern China; half of them worked in Beijing–Tianjin.[7] Overall, the CCP was quite proletarian in Party membership during 1921–27, but intellectuals and students were the leading force.

In brief, the CCP, under the united-front leadership of the GMD and the strongly repressive warlord regimes, was a minority in the national revolution. By 1927 the urban-based and intellectual/student–led CCP had failed in its proletarian-oriented revolution. Worst of all, the Party was almost destroyed by the Nationalists and the warlord authorities, who killed the Beijing–Tianjin Communist leaders, including Li Dazhao, Yu Fangzhou (died in January 1928), Zhao Shiyan, Li Jida, and An Ticheng.

In Beijing–Tianjin the Communist activity among the railway and textile workers was just a modest beginning and their labor activity in Tianjin was politically insignificant. The CCP, influenced by the Comintern's unrealistic conception of the united front in China, had failed to make "correct" distinctions between friend and enemy. Nonetheless, during the period 1919–27 the intellectuals and students had played the major role in establishing the Beijing–Tianjin CCP. Afterward they performed the same role in rebuilding the Party.

Beijing–Tianjin CCUP, 1927–37

Only ten thousand Communists survived the GMD purge in 1927. The decade from 1927 to 1937, however, was important in the Communist movement because it was the beginning of the CCUP history while its main forces retreated from the cities.

From 1927 to 1934 external attack, confusion, and factional strife plagued the urban CCP organizations in the area. The CCP Northern Area Committee and the Beijing Local Committee were destroyed by the warlord authorities in April 1927. In order to recoup its losses, the CCP established a Beijing–Hebei Provincial Committee in Tianjin on 1 August 1927. On the same day the Beijing Local Committee was reorganized as the Beijing City Committee, and the Tianjin Local Committee became the Tianjin City Committee. Six days later, the CCP convened an emergency meeting at Hankou; afterward the Party Central decided to establish a Northern Bureau to supervise the Provincial Committee. The Northern Bureau convened an enlarged meeting in Tianjin in September and expelled the Communists who had affiliated with Chen Duxiu or were blamed for the urban debacle by the Provincial Committee and the Beijing and Tianjin City Committees. By then the Provincial Committee controlled only 1,024 members.[8]

In October 1927 the Communists launched "adventurist" revolts against the warlord authorities in Beijing–Tianjin. As a result, the Northern Bureau and the Beijing and Tianjin City Committees were decimated. The Party Central had to reorganize the City Committees in November and to abolish the Bureau in December 1927. Although the August Seventh Emergency Conference of the CCP had emphasized the task of creating a solid secret fighting organization against the enemy,[9] the events of October proved that the CCUP was not effectively clandestine.

By February 1928 a reorganized Provincial Committee had control of a reorganized Beijing City Committee and had registered only 433 Communist members inside Beijing. Among them, students comprised 60 percent, workers 20 percent, peasants 5 percent, "professional revolutionaries" 5 percent, other urban residents and professionals 10 percent.[10] By January 1928 there were only 190 surviving Communist members in Tianjin; most of them were workers.[11]

In December 1928 the Beiping–Tianjin Provincial Committee held an enlarged meeting in Tianjin. This conference abolished the City Committee and ordered the Provincial Committee to take charge of the work in Tianjin. The Beiping City Committee was reorganized.

In late February of 1929, there were 120 Communists in Beiping. In March 1929 the reorganized Beiping City Committee increased its membership to 150. (This figure held firm until the end of the Beijing–Hebei Provincial Committee in December 1930, when a new Hebei Provincial Committee was established to supersede the Beijing–Hebei Committee and the Northern Bureau.) In April 1929 there were 120 Communists in Tianjin.[12]

From late 1929 to the end of 1934, the Beiping CCUP was demolished at least nine times by the GMD authorities. In February 1931 there were 160 Communists in Beiping. In late September of 1931, there were 74 Party members. In July 1932 the Communist membership was 139. In May 1933 the membership was up to 218; 10 percent of them were workers, 5 percent were peasants. But by late 1934 the Communist organizations had been so devastated by the enemy that the total Party membership in Hebei was only 600 (as contrasted with 1,900 in June 1929). The Beiping Party leadership could contact only 7 members; and there were only 30 Communists in Tianjin.[13]

Between 1928 and 1934 Communist traitors (those who defected to the enemy after capture or were purged in various Party reorganizations) helped the GMD authorities arrest a large number of Communists including Peng Zhen,[14] the director of the Organization Department of the Tianjin Local Committee and the Beijing–Hebei Committee. He was arrested in Tianjin in 1929 and released in 1935. Liu Ren, a member of the Tianjin City Committee and the secretary of its Textile Action Committee, was arrested in Tianjin in 1930 and released in 1932. Bo Yibo, the secretary of the Soldier Committee of the Tianjin City Committee and the secretary general of the Military Committee of the Northern Bureau, was arrested in Beiping in 1931 and released in 1936.

The Communists liked to accuse the GMD of being "fascist" for killing revolutionary and "progressive" figures and for having the attitude that "they would rather wrongly kill three thousand people but would not pardon a single (Communist) person." The Nationalists freed Peng Zhen, Liu Ren, and Bo Yibo in the 1930s, however. The release of Bo Yibo and other Communists in Beiping illustrates the effective united-front tactic of the CCUP and the weak GMD rule in North China. These Communists treated the prison guards well with pocket money, played chess with them, and explained to them that the political prisoners were patriotic anti-Japanese Chinese. Above all, under instructions from superiors (particularly Liu Shaoqi) they pretended to be anti-Communist. While these activities helped the Communist prisoners get out, Japanese pressure on the GMD and factional politics among local, Nanjing, and Northeast authorities in North China also played important roles in their release.[15]

In Maoist historiography, Li Lisan and especially the Twenty-Eight Bolsheviks until 1934 were held responsible for all the disastrous operations in so-called White areas. But the Bolsheviks contributed to the CCP effort to maintain a viable organization in Shanghai (and in Beiping–Tianjin), although their activity was overshadowed by the growth of the rural Soviets during 1931–34.[16]

The Twenty-Eight Bolsheviks were influenced by the Comintern charge that one major reason for the Communist failure during 1924–27 was the large number of intellectuals within the Party. The Bolsheviks, therefore, tended to emphasize the proletarian background, not the ability and experience of leading cadres. For example, in 1932 two workers served separately as the secretary of the Beiping City Committee.[17]

In practice, few workers were genuine leading cadres and their activities in Beiping–Tianjin were unremarkable from 1928 to 1934. Even the Beiping Streetcar Riot of 22 October 1929, the most notable example of civil rioting (until the Tiananmen riot of 1976), was not instigated by the Communists.[18] In Tianjin during 1928–37 the GMD had done its best to transform unions into instruments for control of the work force and maintenance of labor–capital cooperation. The main impetus for union organizing thus came not from the CCUP but from the GMD authorities. Former Communists and those who betrayed the CCUP also aided the GMD in their rooting out of Communist activists in the Tianjin labor force.[19]

Also, from 1928 to 1934 the Communists abandoned labor strikes as a main form of struggle in the cities because they were too dangerous. What mattered most during the period for the future Communist strength in Beiping–Tianjin was their united-front activities and the "left-wing cultural movement"—all carried on for political gain by "progressive" students and intellectuals, writers, and artists.

The Communists' emphasis on cultural and student work had emerged at the meeting of the Beijing–Hebei Provincial Committee in December 1928. After that the CCUP became active in encouraging anti-Japanese sentiment; it prompted students and other social groups in Beiping–Tianjin to form "anti-imperialist grand alliance" organizations to attack not only Japanese imperialism but also the GMD authorities, who were charged with appeasing the Japanese. Although these front organizations were later disbanded, they served as a training ground for students and others who later joined the CCP or its Youth League.[20]

In March 1930 the CCP CC in Shanghai established the League of Left-Wing Writers. In response, the northern CCUP established the Northern League of Left-Wing Writers in Beiping and a Tianjin branch. The CCUP also established the Cultural General Alliance in Beiping and Tianjin. Similar to the front organizations in Shanghai, the Beiping–Tianjin cultural organizations helped the Communists' allies obtain revolutionary experience.[21]

Besides participating in the public reburial ceremony for Li Dazhao and in the Anti-Japanese United Army, the left-wing cultural groups were also involved in various activities, such as printing literature, performing plays, and organizing students, other youths, workers, and peasants in northern China. They even contacted "progressive" foreigners, such as Edgar Snow, to help propagate the left-wing cultural movement.[22]

In short, from 1928 to 1934 the (non-Maoist) CCUP was most active on the cultural battlefront with a focus on students and intellectuals. In Beiping–Tianjin the Communists preserved a viable Party organization through student politics and cultural struggle. Far away from the cities during this period, Mao Zedong had the temerity to blame all urban blunders upon Li Lisan and the Twenty-Eight Bolsheviks.

The Zunyi Conference of January 1935 in rural Guizhou during the Long March was a giant step in Mao's quest for supreme power within the CCP. In urban strategy, however, the general resolution of the conference indicated that "the work in White [that is, urban] areas must be established and strengthened [under the leadership of the new Party Central]."[23]

In May 1935 the Party Central sent Chen Yun, the head of the White Areas Work Department, to Shanghai to revive the Party organizations. On 18 October 1935, the CCP Politburo convened a meeting to discuss the work of the Red Army and operation in White areas and among White armies. At this meeting, Peng Dehuai recommended sending trained comrades to work among White troops, and Liu Shaoqi suggested the dispatching of cadres to work in White areas.

During the Wayaobao Conference (17–25 December 1935), the CCP adopted the strategy of the "anti-Japanese national united front." On 29 December the Party Central dispatched Liu Shaoqi to Tianjin to take charge of the Northern Bureau. From March 1936 to February 1938, when he left for Yan'an, Liu reorganized the Bureau and made it the central command for work in White areas. He also strengthened the position of the Beiping–Tianjin CCUP by establishing an anti-Japanese front in the youth and labor movements.[24] His effort was so effective that Liu was glorified by the Party Central in 1945 as "the representative of the correct line in White areas." Accordingly, the Party in North China was regarded as advanced compared with CCUP activities in other enemy-controlled urban areas.[25] Liu's revolutionary activities in White areas complemented Mao's experiences in the countryside.

Even before Liu's arrival in Tianjin in 1936, the CCP's united front with the students had produced positive results. A major student movement occurred on 9

December 1935, which enabled the CCP to bid for the support of patriotic students and to offer them an alternative leadership in the nationalist cause. Another student movement followed on 16 December, beginning in Beiping–Tianjin and later developing into a national salvation movement powerful enough to halt Chiang Kai-shek's appeasement of Japanese aggression and to transform his anti-Communist campaign into a united front against Japan.[26] The most important immediate result of the December Ninth Movement, however, was the creation of a Communist-led youth organization called the Chinese National Liberation Vanguards, a key element in the Chinese youth movement of the time.[27] This organization exemplified the high priority given to expansion and training of student movement leadership.

Realizing the importance of nationalist appeals, the proximity of Beiping–Tianjin to the Japanese invasion in Northeast China, and the large academic and cultural establishments, Liu Shaoqi urged the Communists and the National Vanguards within the CCP-dominated Beiping Student Association and the Tianjin Student Association to support the local GMD 29th Army to deal with the Japanese. The Communist Zhang Kexia (a deputy chief of staff of the 29th Army) worked underground among generals and officers. The students and the National Vanguards tried to influence the soldiers and their commanding officers by involving them in sports and parties and teaching them music. Simultaneously, Liu ordered Peng Zhen and Zhang Youyu (a professor and journalist) to recruit university teachers and high-level GMD members for the North China All-Sectors National Salvation Association.[28]

Further, based on the tactics of the "united front from above and below," Liu Shaoqi and the Communists were involved in the successful anti-Japanese May Twenty-Eighth (1936) Demonstration in Tianjin and the June Thirteenth (1936) Demonstration in Beiping. Both of these demonstrations involved not only students but workers, civilians, and representatives from the industrial and commercial sectors. Liu also rescued a number of Communists from prison; they later made an important contribution to the underground struggle in North China during the 1940s.[29]

From October 1934 to mid-1937, the Beiping–Tianjin CCUP concentrated its activities on students and intellectuals, not on workers. During the period there occurred no significant Communist-instigated labor movement in Beiping–Tianjin.[30] The December Ninth Movement of 1935 indicated the importance of the student movement that revitalized the Communist operations in White areas. By June 1936 there were more than four hundred college and middle school student members within the Beiping CCUP. The students were so vital to the urban Party that it even established a CCP Beiping Student Movement Committee in October 1936. In Tianjin the CCUP also increased its membership at major universities such as Nankai and Beiyang. Using the momentum of the student movement, the CCUP Tianjin City Committee recruited workers in the cotton mills, railway, and telephone service. By late 1936 there were more than four hundred Party members.[31]

In November 1936 the left-wing "Seven Gentlemen" of the Shanghai National Salvation Alliance were arrested by the GMD authorities. The CCUP responded with a four-day class strike at major Beiping–Tianjin universities and gave speeches on Japanese imperialistic activities and the release of patriotic intellectuals. In the same month, the Beiping–Tianjin CCUP dispatched students to salute the military exercise of the GMD 29th Army and launched the student-led Assist-Suiyuan Movement. This effort assisted the anti-Japanese generals, especially Fu Zuoyi,[32] and soldiers who resisted the Japanese invasion in Suiyuan Province.[33]

On 12 December 1936, the Beiping CCUP launched a large demonstration calling for a national anti-Japanese movement. On the same day, the Xi'an Incident occurred. This incident was partially a consequence of the Communist united front with the GMD Northeastern and Northwestern Armies, and of the Communist manipulation of student demonstrations, which demanded the cessation of the GMD-CCP civil war in order to fight the Japanese.[34] The CCUP members, National Vanguards, and youths sent by the Northern Bureau and the Beiping City Committee to work within the Northeastern and Northwestern Armies thus contributed to this Communist united front. It abrogated Chiang Kai-shek's realistic but widely unpopular policy of "first internal pacification, then external resistance."

Before the Xi'an Incident the emerging Maoist approach for operations in the city, under the sponsorship of Liu Shaoqi, aimed to create an "anti-Japanese national united front," which meant "forcing Chiang Kai-shek to fight Japan." After the Xi'an Incident the CCP changed its overall strategy to "uniting with Chiang to fight Japan." And the Xi'an Incident of December 1936 could be seen as an event that not only resulted in the removal of the GMD threat to Communist survival and expansion in rural northern China but also guaranteed continuance of Communist activities in GMD cities.

The Long March period (1934–36) was indeed "a time of transformation from revolutionary idealism to political realism in the general orientation of the CCP."[35] Under the emerging dominance of Mao Zedong, the CCP struggled for survival in the countryside and strengthened its urban activities as a realistic policy in the wake of the December Ninth Movement and the Wayaobao Conference. By mid-1937 students and intellectuals had become the major political force that revitalized the CCUP and the Beiping–Tianjin urban activities. Anti-Japanese nationalism strengthened their united-front strategy, and the Communists worked hard on students, intellectuals, and GMD generals and soldiers. The so-called leading role of the proletariat was just revolutionary rhetoric.

Beiping–Tianjin CCUP, 1937–45

During the wartime period, the "anti-Japanese national united front" made the survival, growth, and eventual triumph of the CCP in China possible.[36] In practice, while Mao Zedong manned the helm at Yan'an, it was Zhou Enlai who skillfully carried out the united front against the GMD in urban China. (Liu Shaoqi operated in the CCP countryside from 1938 to 1949.)

After the Japanese occupation of Beiping–Tianjin in late July of 1937, most of the CCUP members and the National Vanguards retreated to the countryside to help establish anti-Japanese bases and to engage in guerrilla warfare; only a few Communists remained in Beiping–Tianjin. The Northern Bureau also reestablished the Hebei Provincial Committee in the Leased Territories of Tianjin to take charge of the underground operations of the Beiping and Tianjin City Work Committees. In Beiping the Party targeted students, teachers and professors, civilians, peasants, puppet government authorities, and news agencies.[37] In Tianjin the CCUP not only conducted mass work but also allied with the upper-level (Wuhan) GMD members to produce anti-Japanese newspapers and journals.[38]

Also, the Communist 8th Route Army operated in North China and helped establish the Central Hebei, West Beiping, East Hebei, and North Beiping Anti-Japanese Base Areas around Beiping–Tianjin.[39] Since the Japanese rule was strong in the cities and the CCP focused on expansion of power, guerrilla warfare was the main Communist strategy against the Japanese and their puppet armies, and the underground work in Beiping–Tianjin complemented this military strategy.

In "The Guiding Directive Concerning the Local Work in the War of Resistance" (12 August 1937), the CCP CC commanded the CCUP organizations in GMD areas to engage actively in united-front activities and to mobilize the masses. In Japanese-controlled areas the Party organizations had to be absolutely secret and organize legal groups and penetrate legal puppet organizations or armies. Simultaneously the CCUP had to consolidate and expand its clandestine operations.[40]

In July 1938 the East Hebei Party Committee launched an armed revolt against the Japanese. This incident was carried out with the cooperation of GMD members and capitalists. Because this revolt was suppressed by the Japanese, the Hebei Provincial Committee was forced to move to East Hebei. It later became the Hebei–Rehe–Chahar Area Party Committee.

In order to continue the underground work in Beiping–Tianjin, in September 1938 the CCP CC Changjiang Bureau (December 1937–October 1938) established the Beiping–Tianjin–Tangshan Point-Line (Urban Stronghold Line of Communication) Work Committee in Tianjin. In January 1939 the Party Central put the Point-Line Committee under the nominal leadership of the CCP CC Northern Branch Bureau. Until the summer of 1940, the CCP Hebei–Rehe–Chahar Party Committee managed the Point-Line Work Committee. Besides controlling the work in Beiping–Tianjin, this Point-Line Committee was also in charge of Tangshan and work among all the railway lines in North China. Its main function was to penetrate various sectors of society, to expand the influence of the Party through front organizations, to continue transporting young intellectuals, medicine, and other materials to Communist bases, and to assist the guerrilla warfare.[41]

In addition, Party work in Beiping–Tianjin in the period up to 1941 proceeded in accordance with these documents issued by the CCP CC Secretariat in 1940: "Notice on Unfolding Work in Major Cities Behind the Enemy Line" (September 15) and "Directive on the Work in Major Cities Behind the Enemy Line" (October). The first document indicated the importance of recruiting cadres for underground work in the cities, and reaffirmed the policy to lie low for an extended period. The Secretariat also ordered the various central and branch bureaus to establish Urban Work Committees (*Chengshi gongzuo weiyuanhui*).[42] The second document pinpointed Beiping–Tianjin as one major base of underground urban work, and admonished the Party members to separate urban work from the rural work.[43]

In January 1941 an Urban Work Committee was established by the Northern Branch Bureau (soon to become the Shanxi–Chahar–Hebei Branch Bureau), the new supervisory organ over the Beiping–Tianjin–Tangshan Point-Line Committee. Its director, Liu Ren, began managing the underground activities in Beiping–Tianjin. This action was the beginning of the dominance of the Shanxi–Chahar–Hebei Branch Bureau in Beiping.

In August 1941 the Beiping–Tianjin CCUP suffered a major setback when the secretary of the Beiping–Tianjin–Tangshan Point-Line Committee was arrested by the Japanese authorities. But as the CCUP leadership was on a "many heads, single lines" pattern (with no connections among the different work groups or among comrades from different sections of the Party), this arrest did not destroy the whole Beiping–Tianjin CCUP.[44] Nevertheless, the existence of a unified central organ inside Beiping and the arrest of the leading member of this organ prompted the escape of other leading cadres to the base areas.[45]

CCUP members led dangerous lives even when they were not captured or executed by the Japanese. For example, Lou Ping was a Beijing University student and the secretary of the Beiping City Committee in 1937. The Committee had the code name "Elder Sister Ping" and was in charge of the Beiping National Vanguards, whose public title was "Self-Study Society." In order to maintain secrecy, the City Committee communicated with the Railway Committee and other Communist organs within the city through a liaison network with the code name "Younger Sister Lianfan." Nonetheless, the Japanese capture of a National Vanguard member in November 1938 prompted more arrests. Fearful of the possible exposure of his identity, Lou abandoned his work in Beiping and traveled to East Hebei in December 1938.[46]

Zhou Bin was a music student at the Hebei Normal College in Tianjin. In 1937 she led the Tianjin National Vanguards. Being a "new person" in Beiping, she replaced Lou Ping as the secretary of the Beiping City Committee in late 1938. Until the fall of 1941 she and her comrades in Beiping (and Tianjin) continued these tasks: (1) to revive and expand the Party organizations; (2) to develop front organizations (such as choirs, drama clubs, and study groups); (3) to conduct the united-front tactics; (4) to spread anti-Japanese propaganda; (5) to transport manpower to CCP areas; (6) to collect medicine, electrical equipment, and clothes for the base areas. After the Japanese capture of the secretary of the Point-Line Committee in August 1941, however, Zhou had to escape to the foreign settlements in Tianjin. She covered up her real identity for more than two months by working as a part-time music teacher and using a fake residence card. In December 1941 she escaped to the Shanxi–Chahar–Hebei Base Area.[47]

Before the work of the Beiping–Tianjin–Tangshan Point-Line Committee ended in February 1942, the Urban Work Committee of the Shanxi–Chahar–Hebei Branch Bureau had started the strengthening of the CCUP in Beiping–Tianjin. The main purpose of such urban work was to create well-qualified cadres working in concealment inside the city. The committee sought to contact, educate, and ally with "progressive" elements so as to complement the military strategy in the countryside.[48]

Throughout the period 1942–44, the Beiping CCUP focused on these tasks: (1) to recruit students and intellectuals for serving the Shanxi–Chahar–Hebei Branch Bureau and the CCP West Beiping Base Area; (2) to recruit Beiping college and middle school students as CCP members; (3) to establish secret communication lines between Beiping and the Communist base areas. Most of the several hundred urban residents who reached the CCP areas were intellectuals and students.[49] In Tianjin the Commmunists admitted that during the period they were very weak in the labor movement. They mentioned only one CCUP-instigated strike in a Japanese-owned saltworks in April 1944. And the CCUP recruited only four textile workers into the Party. The Communists were more successful among intellectuals and students. The CCUP's major clandestine front organization was the Tianjin All-Sectors Anti-Japanese National Salvation Association. By 1944 there were more than one hundred members. Sixty of them became CCP members and most of them were students and intellectuals.[50] In short, students and intellectuals were the focus of Communist operation in Beiping–Tianjin.

The activities of Wang Ruojun demonstrated the Beiping CCUP's work from 1942 to 1944. In 1937 Wang was a National Vanguard and a graduate of the high school that was affiliated with the Sino-French University in Beiping. In May 1938 she joined the CCP in the Central Hebei Base Area. In late 1941 Liu Ren assigned her to work in Beiping. He stressed that it would be best if she could enter a university there because most students and intellectuals were "progressive" and were potential Party members. Wang could also use the opportunity to acquire knowledge that would be useful for building a new China after liberation. Before leaving for the city, Wang was trained for half a month. During this period she was required to study the works of Mao Zedong and others on the war situation and the methods in urban work. She was not allowed to communicate with other trainees.[51]

With assistance from an aunt who lived in a suburb of Beiping, Wang secured a "good resident identity card" and returned to the city by train. She taught at a Japanese-controlled primary school for six months. In late 1943 she enrolled at Beijing News College and then served as a reporter at the Japanese-controlled China News Agency for two months in the spring of 1944.[52]

Through her social and professional connections, Wang recruited into the CCUP several cousins, several Beijing Normal University students, a Beijing Telecommunications Bureau worker, and a Yanjing Paper Manufacturing Plant worker. She also sent forty "progressive" youths to the base area for training. (Most of the newcomers, or "guests," who arrived and joined the CCP in rural areas were students.) Even Wang's mother volunteered to serve as a "communication person" by taking CCUP members to Communist areas under the pretext of visiting relatives in the countryside. However, early one morning in May 1944 a cousin who worked in the Japanese-controlled New People Society warned Wang that she was being investigated by the authorities. On the same day she was followed by a man with dark glasses. Alarmed, Wang escaped to the Shanxi–Chahar–Hebei Base Area. She avoided arrest and execution but she had planted a number of "revolutionary seeds" within the city.[53]

In the wake of the Japanese spring offensive of 1944, which dealt a severe blow to the GMD troops in Henan, Hunan, and Guangxi, Mao Zedong made a reassessment of the political and military situations in China. In "Our Study and the Current Situation" (April 1944), Mao emphasized the importance of the work in the cities.[54] In the CCP CC Directive on Urban Work (5 June 1944), he further stressed that "the idea of the coordination of the inside and outside is the basic idea of our Party in driving out the enemy from the cities."[55]

At its Enlarged Cadres' Session in September and October of 1944, the Shanxi–Chahar–Hebei Branch Bureau adopted the June Directive of the CCP CC and developed its work in Beiping–Tianjin. (The Shanxi–Chahar–Hebei Urban Work Committee was renamed the Urban Work Department in September.) In the wake of this session, nine local committees in Central Hebei combined to establish the Tianjin Urban Work Committee. They sent four thousand Party members and other reliable workers with appropriate social relations inside the city to Tianjin. Besides, the Northern Bureau, the East Hebei Base Area, and the Bohai Base Area also assigned experienced cadres to launch revolutionary activities in Tianjin.[56] From then on, the underground efforts in Tianjin expanded considerably.

To summarize, the Communist underground movement in Beiping–Tianjin from 1944 to the Japanese surrender was three-pronged: (1) The CCUP did not expose its front organizations; it established a broad relationship with the masses through Party members and so-called progressive elements, who depended on connections with their schoolmates, colleagues, relatives, friends, hometown acquaintances, and other social relations. The CCUP was "embedded in the heart of the enemy" and concealed in the masses. (2) It engaged in propaganda and educational work to develop "positive" and "progressive" elements among the masses. (3) The Party members among the left-wing elements established a concealed CCUP of well-selected cadres.[57]

Throughout the period 1937–45, the Communists still concentrated on work among students and intellectuals. In mid-1944, among the 98 Communists in Beiping, there were 37 students, 25 workers, 3 coolies, 3 puppet policemen, and 30 unidentified ones. Among the 200 "progressives," 110 were students. In August 1945 most of the 200 Party members and the 413 "progressives" (under the leadership of the Shanxi–Chahar–Hebei Branch Bureau) in Beiping were students and intellectuals.[58] In August 1945 there were more than one hundred Communists and one hundred "progressives" in the Tianjin All-Sectors Anti-Japanese National Salvation Association (under the leadership of the Shanxi–Chahar–Hebei Branch Bureau). Most were middle school and university students. There were thirty-three middle schools and universities in the city, and the CCUP was active in more than twenty of them.[59]

During 1937–45 the CCUP controlled and developed Party members and "progressives" among workers (factory, railway, and others) and urban residents in Beiping–Tianjin. But the Communist labor movement in Beiping and particularly Tianjin was insignificant. Likelihood of long-term clandestine activity was decreased by the Japanese suppression, the high degree of workers' mobility (flight to their villages or the countryside from intolerable conditions), and the physical debilitation caused by long work hours and a worsening food supply. Factory workers usually protested in a way that could secure the maximum return while avoiding confrontation with the Japanese authorities. Besides work slowdowns and stealing, workers occasionally took part in sabotage of machinery or acts of arson like burning warehouses. But most worker activity was directed at the short-term goal of survival. They were not interested in Communist propaganda or secret organizing.[60]

While the CCP rural and urban activity helped the Communist cause in (North) China, the internal problems and blunders of the Nationalists also contributed to Communist success. From 1927 to 1937 Chiang Kai-shek was troubled by factional strife, and he never exercised genuine control in North China. The outbreak of the Sino-Japanese War witnessed an unprecedented unity of Chinese youth under the leadership of Chiang Kai-shek. This situation could not last long, however. As Lincoln Li asserts, the political distance between the GMD and the students of the 1930s persisted in the 1940s. The GMD did not trust campus communities, and it regarded student activism as hostile.[61] Widespread corruption among GMD officials and inflation and black marketeering that sapped the economy had further eroded student support for the GMD by 1944. In spite of a loyal following by the Three People's Principles Youth Corps (established in 1938), many students and other urban residents by the end of the war had become apathetic or hostile toward the GMD. This phenomenon would play an important role in the outcome of the CCP-GMD struggle in Beiping–Tianjin during the Civil War period.

Further, the Xi'an Incident and particularly the Japanese invasion of China gave the Communists the opportunity to expand power in the countryside. In the urban arena, Liu Shaoqi, followed by Zhou Enlai, was the Communist spokesperson for the work in White areas. In Beiping–Tianjin, Liu Ren emerged to be the major cadre in the underground struggle in the cities. Above all, the united-front strategy and party-building tremendously strengthened the wartime CCP and made it a major contender for national power in the postwar period. The small Beiping–Tianjin CCUP would continue to make use of the united front and party-building (especially among students and intellectuals) to accumulate strength.

Summary

A general overview of the organizations, membership figures, and levels of activity of the Beijing–Tianjin Communist Party during the period 1921–45 demonstrates that it very often focused upon students and intellectuals. In the 1930s the CCUP also began to realize the importance of political work among the enemy troops to create political strength. However, there had been a general lack of CCP organization and mobilization of the working class in Beiping–Tianjin. Although the Party membership in Tianjin—the economic center of North China—was majority proletarian from 1921 to 1927, the Communists were always subjected to intellectual/student–centered leadership. By utilizing Maoist class labels to view the CCP history in Beiping–Tianjin, one may argue that the "middle bourgeoisie and petite bourgeoisie"—that is, students and intellectuals—had been the genuine leading revolutionary force in the urban arena. Through the mobilization of the student and cultural movements, anti-Japanese nationalism, and exploitation of the GMD's weakness, factionalism, and corruption, the Communists managed to survive and conserve power in the pre-1945 era. By 1945 the Beiping–Tianjin CCUP also had become an advanced revolutionary organization in urban China. Nevertheless, during the wartime period, the CCUP could only play a very subordinate role to the military struggle in the countryside because the Japanese tightly controlled Beijing–Tianjin. However, the small CCUP and its front organizations would continue to use student nationalism and the GMD's problems to further their urban revolution. The CCUP would be indispensable for the coming Communists' multiclass but student-based struggles in Beiping–Tianjin.

Notes

1. See Zhonggong Beijing Shiwei Dangshi Yanjiushi et al., *Beijing dang zuzhi de chuangjian huodong*, pp. 254–59. Furthermore, in January 1920, because of the warlord government's repression, Chen Duxiu had to leave Beijing for Shanghai. Li Dazhao personally rented a carriage and escorted Chen to Tianjin. It was on the way to Tianjin that they discussed the dissemination of Marxism and the establishment of a political party in China. See *BGD*, p. 12.

2. Ibid., pp. 40, 54, 68–69, 89, 93–94.

3. See David Strand, *Rickshaw Beijing*, pp. 143–47, 191.

4. See "Gongrenbu eryuefen gongzuo baogao," in Zhonggong Beijing Shiwei Dangshi Yanjiushi, *Diyici guogong hezuo zai Beijing*, pp. 385–87.

5. *TXGY*, pp. 35–36, 39; *TJ*, p. 295; Gail Hershatter, *The Workers of Tianjin*, p. 219.

6. *TXGY*, p. 64.

7. See Chen Zhili, *Zhongguo gongchandang jianshe shi*, p. 120; Zhu Hanguo, Xie Chungtao, and Fan Tianshun, *Zhongguo gongchandang jiansheshi*, p. 60.

8. Wang Naide, "Tudian geming zhanzheng shiqi Huabei diqu Zhonggong Shun-Zhi Shengwei he Beifangju zuzhi yange genggai," p. 105.

9. See Chen Zhili, *Zhongguo gongchandang jianshe shi*, pp. 142–43.

10. Wang Xiaoting and Wang Wenyi, *Zhandou zai Beida de gongchandang ren*, p. 16; *BGD*, pp. 102–4, 106; *BXG*, p. 86; Xie Zhonghou, Fang Erzhuang, and Liu Gangfan, *Jindai Hebei shiyao*, p. 297.

11. *TXGY*, p. 77.

12. *BGD*, pp. 113, 130; *TJ*, p. 323.

13. *BGD*, pp. 133, 137, 159, 172, 178; *TJ*, pp. 323, 326.

14. After his release from jail, Peng served as the secretary of the Tianjin City Committee and director of the Organization Department of the CCP CC Northern Bureau (1935–37). He was active in the Communist student movement from 1936 to 1937. During the Sino-Japanese War, Peng worked as the secretary of the CCP CC Shanxi–Chahar–Hebei Branch Bureau and later the Director of the CCP CC Organization Department. In 1945 he became a regular member of the Seventh CCP CC and a regular member of the Politburo. In February 1949 Peng was appointed the secretary of the CCP Beiping Municipal Committee.

15. See Xiong Haiji, *Tiandi you zhengqi*, pp. 75–126.

16. See Lawrence R. Sullivan, "Reconstruction and Rectification of the Communist Party in the Shanghai Underground," pp. 78–97. See also Patricia Stranahan, "Strange Bedfellows," p. 30 n. 12 .

17. See Wang Jingshan, " 'Erzhan' shiqi 'zuo' qing cuowu dui Beijing dang de gongzuo de yingxiang," pp. 192–93.

18. See *BGD*, pp. 115–16. There is no mention of Communist leadership in Chang Kai et al., *Zhongguo gongyunshi cidian*, pp. 144–45. See also Strand, *Rickshaw Beijing*, ch. 11.

19. Hershatter, *Workers of Tianjin*, pp. 221–24, 227.

20. Ibid., pp. 211, 222–23; *BGD*, pp. 169, 171–72, 174; *TXGY*, pp. 114–15.

21. Ibid., pp. 225–33; Stranahan, "Strange Bedfellows," p. 29 n. 10.

22. Xie Yinming, "Zhongguo gongchandang," pp. 234–52.

23. Zhang Wentian, *Zhang Wentian xuanji*, pp. 57–58.

24. See Zhao Gengqi and Liang Xiangshan, "Kangzhan qianxi Liu Shaoqi tongzhi zai Ping-Jin gongzuo," pp. 3–15; Chen Shaochou, *Liu Shaoqi zai baiqu*, chaps. 8–12; Zhang Jingru, *Zhongguo gongchandang sixiangshi*, pp. 211–16.

25. In as early as August 1936, the CCP CC praised the work of Liu Shaoqi (alias Hu Fu) in strengthening the Party in North China; see "The Directive Letter of the CCP CC Secretariat to the Northern Bureau and the Hebei Provincial Committee" (5 August 1936), in Zhonggong Beijing Shiwei Dangshi Ziliao Zhengji Weiyuanhui, *Yier jiu yundong*, p. 96. In the same directive, the CCP CC echoed Liu's emphasis on the correct separation and union between overt and covert work; see idem., p. 97.

26. See ibid.; John Israel and Donald W. Klein, *Rebels and Bureaucrats*, introduction; Lincoln Li, *Student Nationalism in China*, pp. 50, 92, 111.

27. This organization was an adjunct to the Communist Youth League (26 January

1925–1 November 1936). Although the GMD agents had infiltrated the National Liberation Vanguards (such as their propaganda department), the Nationalists failed to dominate the whole organization. The Vanguards were outlawed by the GMD in August 1938. The CCP disbanded the organization in November 1938. Some members of the Vanguards later joined the CCP and other Communist youth organizations such as the Northwest Youth National Salvation Association.

28. See Liang Xianghan and Zhao Gengqi, "Zhang Kexia tongzhi tan canjia geming," pp. 30–48; Zhang Youyu, "Wo zai Tianjin congshi mimi gongzuo," pp. 39–68; "Zai Shaoqi tongzhi lingdao xia gongzuo," pp. 14–25.

29. The best-known case was the rescue of sixty-one CCP members (including Bo Yibo) from the Caolanzi Prison. They were branded as traitors by the Gang of Four during the Cultural Revolution. See Xiong Haiji's *Tiandi you zhengi*. See also n. 15.

30. *BGD* and Chang Kai's *Zhongguo gongyunshi cidian* reported nothing important about the labor movement.

31. *TXGY*, pp. 133–37; *TJ*, pp. 341, 343; *BDJ*, pp. 88–89.

32. In 1938 Fu Zuoyi asked Zhou Beifeng, a "red professor," to seek the aid of the CCP in Yan'an to fight the Japanese. The Communists agreed to help and recruited three thousand soldiers for Fu's 35th Army. Zhou Enlai and Mao Zedong also wrote Fu to participate in the "anti-Japanese united front," and prominent Communists such as Nan Hanchen, Zeng Shan, Peng Xuefeng, and Cheng Zihua contacted Fu. The Communists carried on their united front within Fu's army and family until 1949. Zhou Beifeng was also involved in the peace negotiation in 1948–49. See Jiang Shuchen, *Fu Zuoyi zhuanlüe*, pp. 59–60; Yao Longjing, Li Zhenji, and Xu Shiying, *Zhongguo gongchandang tongyi zhanxian shi*, pp. 386–87. Fu's defection to the CCP in 1949 was not accidental.

33. See *BGD*, pp. 209–11; *TXGY*, pp. 140–41; *TJ*, pp. 342–44.

34. See Benjamin Yang, *From Revolution to Politics*, pp. 220–26.

35. Ibid., p. 7.

36. See Shum Kui-Kwong's *The Chinese Communists' Road to Power*.

37. See Zhao Gengqi and Liang Xianghan, " 'Qiqi' Shibiao zhi yijiu sanba nian zai Beiping congshi dang de dixia douzheng," pp. 77–78; *BGD*, p. 225.

38. *TXGY*, p. 152.

39. See Xie Zhonghou, Fang Erzhuang, and Liu Gangfan, *Jindai Hebei shiyao*, pp. 357–61, 396–98.

40. See *ZZWX*, vol. 10, pp. 313–15.

41. Ibid., p. 153; *BXG*, pp. 151–55; *BGD*, pp. 234–35, 240.

42. See Shum, *Chinese Communists' Road to Power*, pp. 180, 284 n. 142; "Zhongguo Gongchandang Jianshe Dacidian" Bianji Weiyuanhui, *Zhongguo gongchandang jianshe dacidian*, p. 961.

43. See *Zhonggong de tewu huodong*, pp. 5–11; Warren Kuo, *Analytical History of the Chinese Communist Party*, vol. IV, pp. 203–9; *BXG*, pp. 157–58.

44. Zhao Gengqi and Liang Xianghan, "Yijiu sanba nian de zhi yijiu siyi nian zai Beiping congshi dang de dixia douzheng de qingkuang," p. 85.

45. See Zhang Dazhong, "Beiping dixia kangri douzheng de huiyi," p. 23.

46. See Zhao and Liang, "Yijiu sanba," pp. 76–81.

47. See ibid., pp. 82–86.

48. See Zhang Dazhong, "Beiping dixia kangri douzheng," p. 24.

49. Ibid., pp. 17–23.

50. See *TXGY*, pp. 163–69; *TJ*, pp. 381–85.

51. See *BDDS*, pp. 321–25.

52. Ibid., pp. 326–31.

53. Ibid., pp. 331–37.

54. *SWMT*, vol. III, p. 171; see n. 9 in the conclusion.

55. See *ZDCZ*, vol. V, pp. 217–24.

56. *TXGY*, p. 172; *TJ*, p. 378.

57. See Zhang Dazhong, "Beiping dixia kangri douzheng," pp. 26–29.

58. *BGD*, pp. 258, 262.

59. Chen Deren, "Riwei tongzhi shiqi Tianjin jishi," p. 56. See also *TJ*, pp. 383–84; *TXGY*, pp. 167–68.

60. See Hershatter, *Workers of Tianjin*, pp. 227–29.

61. Li, *Student Nationalism in China*, pp. 121–22.

2

National and International
Levels of the Civil War

The Chinese Civil War was a political struggle, complicated by the Soviet invasion of Northeast China and the American intervention in North China during
1945–46. Political developments in China influenced the rivalry between the
United States and the Soviet Union in East Asia; the Soviet-American rivalry
also affected the GMD-CCP power struggle in China.[1] Ultimately, however, the
relative strategies and strengths of the CCP and the GMD, not the international
factor, were more responsible for the Communist success in 1949.

The Soviet Union, the United States, and China, 1945–46

By August 1945 the Soviet-American Cold War had emerged and begun to
influence postwar international politics in East Asia. On the Soviet side, their
policy toward China was flexible and aimed at maintaining Soviet influence in
Chinese politics.

On the one hand, Joseph Stalin did not expect the weaker CCP to win the
Civil War, and he asked them to negotiate with the GMD (and vice versa) and
become a partner in the coalition government. The Soviets also signed a Treaty
of Friendship and Alliance with the GMD government on 14 August 1945. This
treaty secured Soviet interests in Mongolia and Manchuria, and it was also an
attempt to lure Chiang Kai-shek away from his pro-American orientation.[2]

On the other hand, before their retreat from Manchuria in May 1946, the
Soviets facilitated the initial CCP effort to establish an organizational and military structure in the region, and frustrated the GMD takeover operations.[3] After

their withdrawal, Stalin also carried out the unilateral policy of building Chinese Communist military strength in Manchuria, because Chiang Kai-shek refused to meet with him to talk about the exclusion of American influence there.[4]

But when CCP forces were winning the war, Stalin suggested to Liu Shaoqi (in July 1948) that they hold the line at the Yangzi River.[5] In the end, Stalin had miscalculated and failed to create the weak GMD-CCP coalition government in China that would best serve the Soviet interests.

On the GMD side, Chiang Kai-shek wanted to secure Soviet neutrality in the Civil War, and he therefore endorsed the treaty with them. In January 1946 a young GMD takeover official, Zhang Shenfu, was murdered by Communist soldiers in Northeast China. This prompted a large-scale anti-Soviet (that is, anti-Communist) student parade in Chongqing on 22 February 1946, while the GMD government was carefully pursuing a policy of negotiations short of appeasement and stressing to their own people the significance of Sino-Soviet friendship.[6] Even after Zhang's murder, Chiang Kai-shek emphasized that the Northeast (the Soviet) issue must be resolved rationally, and he expressed his anger to Chen Lifu about the students' action.[7] Above all, the Soviet withdrawal in May 1946 heralded full-scale war in Manchuria and China, worsened GMD-Soviet relations, and pushed Chiang further toward a pro-American stance.

On the American side, traditional concern for China's territorial integrity and the Soviet threat conditioned American China policy. The additional orthodox view of the CCP as an instrument of Russian expansionism strengthened the pro–Chiang Kai-shek position of the United States government. In order to counterbalance Soviet influence in Manchuria and to check Communist expansion into the territories being surrendered by the Japanese, the United States sent its Marines to help the GMD take over urban North China. Indeed, the "conjunction between American policy in North China and Soviet policy in Manchuria demonstrated the close politicostrategic link between the two regions which the later course of the Civil War amply confirmed. The two powers were partly responsible for the structure of conflict that emerged from the Nationalist takeover of North China and the Communist seizure of a toehold in the Northeast."[8]

In the fall of 1945 the United States significantly helped the GMD in its race with the CCP to take over major cities in Japanese-occupied territories. The occupation of Beiping–Tianjin by American Marines and the airlifting of GMD troops were conspicuous examples of American assistance to Chiang Kai-shek. By the end of 1945 the United States had also turned over to the GMD captured Japanese equipment, and contributed U.S. $500 million to the United Nations Relief and Rehabilitation Administration's China program, the great bulk of which was delivered to GMD areas. In June 1946 the Americans signed a Lend-Lease Credit Agreement with the GMD government, and two months later they concluded another agreement on the sale of war surplus to China at a bargain price.[9]

For those in China who opposed the Civil War, the huge American aid to the GMD seemed to justify the Communist charge that such support served only to stiffen Chiang Kai-shek's determination to fight. The problem of discipline and misconduct among American troops was but an added aggravation.[10] By mid-1946 the Americans had been involved in truck accidents that killed a considerable number of Chinese citizens. According to a left-wing newspaper in Chongqing, more than a thousand Chinese were killed in accidents involving American Jeeps from August 1945 to July 1946. Worst of all, more than three hundred Chinese women reportedly had been raped by Americans in the same period.[11] This kind of negative report had turned some of the population against the Americans. Even *Yishi bao* (Social welfare, a Catholic publication) in Tianjin condemned the American brutality, and compared it with the former Japanese aggression.[12] By the fall of 1946 the American presence was resented by some Chinese, and the resentment was exploited by the Communists.

On the diplomatic front, by the spring of 1946 the Marshall Mission had been undermined by the continuous GMD-CCP conflict. Large-scale fighting occurred in April 1946, and the resolutions of the Political Consultative Conference on a new constitution and a new cabinet system of government remained dreams on paper. Both the GMD and the CCP were dissatisfied with General George C. Marshall, who they felt actually obstructed their quests for victory. In early July, Chiang Kai-shek told him that "it was necessary to deal harshly with the Communists, and later, after two to three months, to adopt a generous attitude."[13] On the other hand, the Communists on 5 and 7 June ordered the Americans to end immediately their support for the GMD in the Chinese Civil War and in "the massacre of people in the Northeast."[14] On 23 June Mao Zedong also declared Communist opposition to the China Aid Act, which provided U.S. military assistance to Chiang. Mao demanded the withdrawal of the American troops in China.[15] Indeed, in mid-1946 both the GMD and the CCP had decided to embark upon a new course of political-military action disregarding Marshall, whose influence had faded.

Moreover, the Americans not only had a bad image among Chinese people and politicians but also suffered casualties in their futile mediation effort in the GMD-CCP conflict. The most serious incident was the Communist ambush of Marines at Anping, a village between Tianjin and Beiping, on 29 July 1946. Three Marines were killed, one died later of wounds, and a dozen others were injured.[16] The Communists claimed that the American Marines and the GMD troops fired upon the units of the 8th Route Army first.[17] Both the Americans and the GMD disputed this account and put the blame on the Communists. A Communist corps leader was captured, and his account concurred with the American and the Nationalist versions.[18] This Anping incident ended with no solution satisfactory to all three sides.[19] It probably heightened the American frustration with its mediation in the Chinese Civil War. By the end of 1946 the American presence and mediation effort had become unpopular and unwelcome in China. Simultaneously, the United States government was dissatisfied and frustrated.[20] The explosive Shen Chong Incident—the alleged rape of a Beijing

University student by two American Marines—would soon send Marshall and the Marines back to the United States.[21]

Strategies in Conflict, 1945–49

Japanese aggression against China had ended in a Pyrrhic victory for the GMD. During its early stage, the Sino-Japanese War elevated Chiang Kai-shek to the national symbol of resistance against Japan. However, by mid-1944 the GMD military and government had been plagued by popular discontent, political opposition, maladministration, and widespread corruption. This negative image of the GMD not only crippled its future political and military battles against the Communists but also neutralized the early heroic anti-Japanese struggles of the GMD troops. Besides, Chiang Kai-shek lost many of his best military units and a large number of irreplaceable loyal officers.

Since the war fatally sapped the strength of the GMD government and undermined Chiang's military power base, the Nationalists should have taken advantage of the Japanese surrender to renew their political mandate. However, the GMD takeover in the fall and winter of 1945 turned out to be the beginning of urban popular disillusionment. The Nationalists failed to use effective strategies to secure and strengthen their urban bases. In autumn 1945, however, according to Chen Lifu, the GMD regime was still strong enough to defeat the CCP. He cited two Nationalist mistakes that set in motion forces that enhanced Communist power. First, the Nationalist tactical errors in 1945 enabled Communist guerrilla forces to seize much of North China, to absorb large numbers of puppet troops, and to extend their control over the countryside. The CCP then began to cut the communication links with GMD cities, thereby making urban inflation worse and separating the cities from their rural hinterlands. Second, Chiang Kai-shek made a political error when he endorsed the Marshall Mission in late 1945. Chiang's decision made relations worse between the United States and the GMD, but certainly no more than if Chiang had refused President Truman's impossible task of mediating in a civil war that had raged for over twenty years. (Chen believed that Chiang Kai-shek should have concentrated on dealing with the Soviet Union.) It also gave the CCP time to consolidate its power in North and Northeast China, infiltrate the GMD government and military with its spies, and sow discord and dissension in GMD cities.[22]

By early 1945 the Second GMD-CCP United Front had collapsed and the relationship was strained to the point of open war. Negotiations failed to produce an agreement on several key issues: the legal status of the CCP areas and local governments; the size of the Communist army to be incorporated into a reorganized national army; and the procedure by which the national government would be democratized. All-out civil war was postponed only because the war against Japan was still the paramount issue. But in the spring of 1945, when the defeat of Japan was imminent, relations between the GMD and the CCP deteriorated rapidly.

Nonetheless, moved by the popular desire for peace and by the Soviet and American factors, the latter particularly, from August 1945 to mid-1946 the GMD, the CCP, and the so-called Third Force discussed "peaceful national reconstruction." According to the CCP, the Nationalists emphasized "national unity [under the GMD's dictatorial leadership] and democratic politics," while the Democratic League—the major "Third Force," which lacked military power and eschewed class-based or mobilizational politics[23]—stressed "democratic unity [under various political parties] and peaceful national reconstruction [without GMD-CCP conflict]."[24]

What was the Communist role in the "peaceful national reconstruction" movement? According to the findings of Odd Westad, the CCP leadership had neither wanted nor planned for civil war. Had it not been for Chiang Kai-shek's repudiation of the agreements of the Political Consultative Conference and his military campaign in Northeast China, Mao Zedong would probably not have allowed Lin Biao to escalate the war in the region.[25] In other words, the CCP was sincere and serious about peaceful national reconstruction.

According to the directive (dated 1 February 1946) of the CCP Central, the Political Consultative Conference made impressive achievements. "From now on China is entering the new stage of peaceful and democratic reconstruction," the directive stated. But in early July 1946, Chairman Mao changed his tone and stressed the importance of achieving peace by military victory. By then the peaceful and democratic reconstruction of China had proved to be impractical.[26]

Mainland Chinese scholars have generally viewed the Communist involvement in the "peaceful national reconstruction" movement as a positive strategy, or "bold attempt." At the time, the CCP understood why the people, the United States, and the Soviet Union wanted peace in China. However, the CCP did not abandon its perception of the dictatorial nature of the GMD. The CCP was not trapped by the illusion of peace and democracy, and it would never surrender its military forces to any coalition government. Armed struggle and peaceful negotiation were simply two complementary methods to force Chiang Kai-shek to form a coalition government. During the negotiations with the GMD, the CCP established new party organizations and upgraded its military forces. It was ready for the Civil War.[27]

In "On Coalition Government" (April 1945), Mao Zedong had stated that the postwar Chinese government should not be dominated by "landlords, feudal elements, fascists, or bourgeois democrats." He demanded the termination of the GMD dictatorship, the establishment of a coalition government, the repeal of all laws and decrees that interfered with basic freedoms, recognition of the legal status of all democratic political parties, acceptance of all anti-Japanese armed forces as part of the national army, and recognition of all popularly elected governments in CCP areas. Above all, Mao suggested a "New Democratic" government for the Chinese people.[28] This document was a shrewd political statement. Mao not only denounced the GMD as dictatorial and "fascist" in nature, but made the CCP appear as a patriotic and freedom-loving political party fighting for the interests of the "people." He said that the Communists were "democratic" and therefore should be given a legal status. The "New Democratic" regime was supposed to be a much better alternative to the Nationalist one. Mao also appealed to other political parties by suggesting a role for them in the coalition "New Democratic" government. His suggestion was a brilliant tactic in the "united front from above and below." In short, all of Mao's demands were the conditions for the negotiation of a settlement with the GMD. In terms of a life-or-death political and military struggle, the GMD would never accept such demands, and the CCP would not expect the GMD to do so. But if these demands were refused, Mao and the CCP could put the blame on the GMD, which did not accede to "popular" desires.

When the war against Japan was over, Mao appeared to be peace-loving because his armies were still in a vulnerable military position and he foresaw many difficulties ahead. Even though there was evidence of CCP interest in good relations with Washington and in gaining power peacefully,[29] the GMD-CCP conflict remained unchanged. While Mao talked peace, he simultaneously ordered the Communists to capture as much land as possible. In "The Situation and Our Policy after the Victory in the War of Resistance Against Japan" (13 August 1945), Mao emphasized that the Communist policy was to give Chiang Kai-shek "tit for tat and to fight for every inch of land." In urban areas, the Communists should educate and propagandize among the masses, and lead the "people" against the civil war, which would be launched by the GMD, not the CCP.[30] Common sense showed, however, that both the GMD and the CCP were preparing for war. The rush to seize land and cities on both sides after the Japanese surrender was an undeclared civil war.

While Mao's document clearly pointed toward a preparation for civil war, the Party's public announcement was another matter. On 25 August 1945, the CCP CC issued a declaration on the current situation. It reiterated the demands that had been raised in Mao's "On Coalition Government," and stressed the themes of "peace, democracy, and unity."[31]

In the immediate postwar period, Chiang Kai-shek was pressured by the United States and liberal groups within China (especially the Democratic League) to invite Mao Zedong to Chongqing to reopen negotiations. Talks between the CCP and the GMD representatives had continued on and off for several years prior to Japan's surrender. While neither the Nationalists nor the Communists were sincere in reaching a common agreement, one point was clear: The GMD lost ground to the Communists in North China during the peace talks in the wartime period. The Japanese surrender complicated the political situation. It was an illusion to think a genuine agreement would materialize in the tense situation when the common enemy was gone. After days of high-level talks, the final communiqué, issued by Chiang and Mao on 10 October 1945, stressed only their agreement on the convocation of a Political Consultative Conference and the importance of peaceful reconstruction. The important issues of the Communist army reorganization and the status of the CCP areas were not solved.[32]

What was the intention of the Communist side in the Chongqing negotiations? On the eve of his departure for Chongqing on 26 August 1945, Mao circulated a notice within the Party. It stressed the necessity of the negotiations and of making concessions to gain the political initiative, to win the sympathy of world public opinion and the "middle-of-the roaders" within China, and to obtain legal status for the CCP. However, the CCP should never forget these principles: "unity, struggle, unity through struggle; to wage struggles with good reason, with advantage, and with restraint; and to make use of contradictions, win over the many, oppose the few, and crush our enemies one by one."[33]

After his return to Yan'an, Mao made a report on the negotiations at a cadres' conference. He saw no quick solution to the problems confronting the country, but advised the Party to brace itself for a hard struggle. Nowhere in the report was Mao optimistic about the possibility of a peaceful settlement. He emphasized a war of self-defense against the Nationalist attack on CCP areas.[34]

The Communist strategy thus focused on territorial and military expansion under the mild slogan of "peace, democracy, and unity" and prevention of civil war in China. This Communist strategy remained intact until mid-1946, when the Communists accused the GMD of launching an all-front civil war.

On 10 January 1946, a truce was declared and the Political Consultative Conference was convened. By the end of the month, the conferees had reached some agreements. A military subcommittee, with General George C. Marshall as an advisor, had begun work on the major problem—army reorganization. On the basis of the relative strength and distribution of forces of both sides at that moment, the subcommittee, under the influence of General Marshall, agreed upon a reduction of the entire Chinese army to fifty government divisions, including ten Communist divisions, at the end of eighteen months.[35]

Hopes that this Conference might at last be the beginning of peace proved unjustified. The greatest obstacle, said a frustrated General Marshall as he left China in January 1947, was the "complete, almost overwhelming suspicion with which the CCP and the GMD regard each other."[36] Besides this basic mutual mistrust, the Conference could not resolve the Communist problem in Northeast China. The GMD-CCP struggle in that area went unchecked, and the Communists continued to expand. Above all, the actual military situation changed faster than the negotiations. Without an effective organ to enforce any truce, the GMD-CCP talks at the Political Consultative Conference and the American mediation were simply a waste of time. Both the GMD and the CCP used the talks as a means to gain political or military advantage. They were two antagonistic political parties engaged in a life-or-death struggle; a third force without a concrete stronger military backbone could never induce them to form a coalition government.

In the end, the peace talks in Chongqing and the Political Consultative Conference benefited the Communists and weakened the Nationalists. Even the CCP itself acknowledged the advantages the talks gave the Party. In "The Past Year's Negotiations and the Prospects" (18 December 1946), Zhou Enlai, then chief Communist negotiator in Chongqing, explained: (1) The status of the CCP was recognized; (2) the status of the conference of the political parties was recognized; (3) the status and size of the PLA were recognized; (4) Chiang Kai-shek had been forced to accept a temporary truce. The CCP needed the truce to consolidate its strength in Northeast and North China, where the CCP areas had never before been so vast.[37] In "Launch a Massive Nationwide Counter-Offensive to Overthrow Chiang Kai-shek" (28 December 1947), Zhou summed up the importance of the peace talks and truce agreements to the CCP: ". . . by peaceful means we meant consolidating the Liberated [CCP] Areas and mobilizing the masses in GMD areas. . . . we lost nothing by this method. During that period our army marched into Northeast China. Wasn't that a victory?"[38]

Because of the peace talks and truce agreements, the CCP gained time to consolidate and expand its territories and armed forces. The CCP also used the peace talks and the truce agreements to demonstrate the peace-loving nature of the CCP and its fight for the political interests of the "people" and of the other minor political parties in the cities.

In the immediate postwar period, the CCP also designed a realistic military strategy that combined with the political strategy of negotiating with the GMD. While Mao Zedong was in Chongqing for negotiations, Liu Shaoqi was acting chairman of the CCP. In an inner-Party directive entitled "Our Present Tasks and the Strategic Deployment of Our Forces" (19 September 1945), Liu explained the general Communist strategy: "Our general strategic policy is to expand in the north while defending ourselves against the enemy in the south. Provided we have the Northeast and Rehe and Chahar Provinces under our control, and provided there is a coordinated struggle by people in the Liberated [CCP] Areas and all the other parts of the country, victory is guaranteed for the Chinese people."[39] (Compare Li Zongren's advice to Chiang Kai-shek in late 1945 on the strategic importance of the North: "War [rages] in South China, [the real Communist] problem [is] in North China.")[40] In other words, the CCP decided to "abandon [temporarily] South China, diminish East China, consolidate North China, seize and develop Northeast China fully." In accordance with this general policy, the 1.2 million Communist troops were reorganized into several field armies and local army corps to consolidate and expand their control in North China and Northeast China.[41] Success in the Battle of Handan in October–November 1945 was a direct result of the Communist strategy to attack the GMD troops moving north. In addition, the defection of the GMD general Gao Shuxun in this battle also indicated Communist political warfare in action.

In December 1945 Mao directed the Party to intensify its work to demoralize enemy forces by political means. In "Policy for Work in the Liberated [CCP] Areas for 1946" (15 December 1945), Mao urged the Communists to organize "uprisings" within the GMD army and spread the "Gao Shuxun Movement."

Mao's hope was that at crucial moments in the fighting, large numbers of GMD troops would follow Gao's example and come over to the Communist side.[42]

Other tactics had been used by the Communists in the military struggle from 1927 on. These included writing "progressive" letters to acquaintances in enemy units, transmitting front-line propaganda with loudspeakers, permitting prisoners-of-war to return to their own lines if they chose to do so, and, above all, direct infiltration of enemy ranks. This last tactic can be found in the secret document entitled "Strategy and Tactics for Work with Friendly Troops," issued by the CCP CC Central Plains Bureau in the winter of 1939. It stressed secrecy, fortitude, and endurance to guarantee the success of their surreptitious mission. The plan was to attack the weakest links in the GMD's political leadership, thereby sabotaging the effectiveness of the whole chain. The objective was to demoralize and destroy the GMD troops.[43]

Furthermore, the CCP before 1945 had also realized the importance of placing soldiers within the enemy ranks in the cities. They sent political and military agents to infiltrate the GMD military ranks, from the headquarters down to the lowest level. These agents performed well in order to get the confidence of their commanding officers. Simultaneously, they observed and analyzed the psychology of individuals, the morale of the troops, the disagreements between man and man, between unit and unit, and between the troops and the masses. They did their work quietly. When their organization had penetrated deeply into the troops, and both the officers and soldiers had good impressions of them, the time was ripe for action. They aroused mistrust between GMD generals so that they would not help each other; created internal dissension within units; fomented hatred between the GMD troops and the masses; and tried to prompt a military coup, so that the troops would defect to the Communist side.[44]

In the fall of 1945, northern China was definitely the main area of Communist activity. Based on the policy to expand in the north, the Party Central sent ten CC members (including Chen Yun, Lin Biao, and Peng Zhen), ten CC alternate members, twenty thousand cadres, and 110,000 troops to operate in Manchuria. The Northeast People's Self-Rule Army (renamed Northeast Democratic United Army in January 1946), consisting of former puppet troops and Japanese advisors under Communist leadership, was a major military threat to the GMD.

In a directive dated 28 December 1945 to the CCP Northeast Bureau, Mao Zedong ordered the Communists in Northeast China not to build bases in the big cities or along the main communication lines, or in regions close to these cities and lines, which might be occupied by the GMD. However, the Party must pay attention to underground work in GMD (urban) areas.[45] This tactic of "abandoning the big roads and occupying the two sides" played a significant role in consolidating the Communists' strength in the countryside and in towns far away from GMD areas—essential conditions for future military triumph.

It must be noted, however, that the Communist base area in the Northeast was different from other CCP territories because it contained medium-size and small cities and secondary railroads. Harbin and other CCP cities functioned as administrative centers and military headquarters, and were used for cadre training and for industrial, commercial, and cultural activity. Further, the power of the Party in the Northeast cities had an important psychological impact on the Communist leaders. It reassured them that their long march to power was nearing completion. In short, the cities played a special role in building the revolutionary base, were vital assets to the ultimate Communist triumph in the region, and provided valuable experiences in the post-"Liberation" city-led national reconstruction.[46]

On the other hand, Chiang Kai-shek also was determined to retake Northeast China in the winter and spring of 1945–46. However, while he sent Chiang Ching-kuo and his best troops to the region, Chiang Kai-shek's personnel arrangements were much weaker than those of the Communists. Chiang failed to dispatch a significant number of important and capable party cadres to the Northeast, although he stressed how important it was to the GMD.[47]

In brief, the Communists returned from the Political Consultative Conference as a party recognized by the GMD. They used the peace talks, truce agreements, and the Gao Shuxun Movement to gain political and military advantages, and to continue their policy of consolidation and expansion in northern China. They were ready for a nonguerrilla warfare as a result of army reorganization during the winter and spring of 1945–46. The outbreak of a large-scale military conflict between the GMD and the CCP in mid-1946 signaled the end of hope for genuine peace and unity. August 1945 to June 1946 was the beginning of, not the lull before, the big storm in Chinese politics.

The GMD offensive in the Communist Central Plains Area in North China in June 1946 was, according to the CCP, the beginning of the Civil War. By mid-1946 the GMD had captured several cities and Communist territories but could not gain the upper hand in the overall military struggle. Worst of all, the GMD failed to knock the Communists out of strategic North China, despite an October–November 1945 campaign to conquer the area. Besides losing the Battle of Handan, the GMD also suffered setbacks along the Beiping–Suiyuan and the Datong–Fenglidu railways.[48]

Mid-1947 was a turning point in the fighting. On the surface, the GMD had won the Civil War. In the second half of 1946, the Nationalists captured 165 cities and towns and 174,000 square kilometers of territory. In March 1947 the GMD seized Yan'an. Chiang Kai-shek told the American ambassador confidently that the Communists could be defeated totally or driven to the hinterland by August or September. In June 1947 the Communists indeed seemed to be retreating when they "lost" 191,000 square kilometers of land that held 18 million people.[49]

The Nationalist victory was an illusion. The attack on the Central Plains Area in mid-1946 did not succeed. Before achieving complete control of the Central Plains, the GMD moved on to attack Yan'an and the Shaanxi–Gansu–Ningxia Border Region in Northwest China. This move proved to be "a vain attempt to settle the Northwest question first, cut off our Party's [CCP's] right arm, drive our Party's Central Committee and the General Headquarters of the People's Liberation Army from the Northwest, then move its troops to attack northern China and so achieve the objectives of defeating our forces one by one."[50] Indeed, the GMD had mistaken the Communist retreat as cowardice and the abandonment of a number of cities (particularly Yan'an) as defeat. The GMD had hoped to finish off the Communists south of the Great Wall in three to six months and then to destroy them in the Northeast. But in May 1947 the GMD had not fulfilled its grand strategy. Instead, its troops were in desperate straits: they were trapped in reconquered areas.[51] The CCP claimed that the Nationalist victories were allowed by strategic Communist retreats. The military strength of the CCP was enhanced because the GMD had to assign many soldiers to garrison duties in reconquered areas, with a corresponding reduction in the actual fighting force.

On the political front the GMD also did not reap any genuine victory. On 4 July 1946, the GMD government announced unilaterally that it would convene the National Assembly on 12 November. This was in open disregard of the Political Consultative Conference resolution that no such assembly should be called before the formation of the coalition government. The CCP and the Democratic League proclaimed a boycott of this "illegal" assembly, and Mao Zedong called for a war of self-defense. In perspective, the GMD political offensive at this time might be justified because of the chain of military victories and the ineffective American mediation. Also, the Communists would never surrender their armed forces to a coalition government—the basic reason for the futility of the GMD-CCP peace talks. However, the GMD's action openly broke the resolution of the Political Consultative Conference and closed the door to peaceful consultation. This act not only showed bad faith to the Chinese people and the foreign observers, but also disregarded the American effort to achieve peace. The Marshall Mission had failed. The United States was disappointed with Chiang Kai-shek and would not underwrite the Chinese Civil War. Furthermore, the GMD's action pushed the left-wing "democratic personalities" (especially in the Democratic League) into the Communist camp.

From mid-1946 to mid-1947, the GMD also suffered a severe blow from the Communists' student-led activities in urban areas. In addition, the continued GMD economic mismanagement aggravated its political and military problems and paved the way for a catastrophic economic crisis (August 1948 through fall 1949), which further alienated the urban population and helped seal the doom of the GMD in urban China.

On the Communist side, by mid-1946 the focus of their work in "Liberated Areas" was consolidation, particularly in North and Northeast China. Consolidation went hand in hand with military defense and conquest. In GMD areas, the CCP continued its political struggle. In his policy for the work in CCP areas for 1946, Mao stressed: ". . . our Party on the one hand persists in its stand for self-government and self-defense in Liberated [CCP] Areas. . . . On the other hand, we support the democratic movement now developing in GMD areas (as marked by the student strike at Kunming) in order to isolate the reactionaries, win numerous allies for ourselves and expand the national democratic united front under our Party's influence."[52]

By mid-1946 the CCUP in urban GMD China had developed its undercover work after operating in the open for a while. Every effort would be made, especially in the youth movement, to emphasize "democracy," to discredit the GMD in the cities, and to use student nationalism to force American troops out of China.

By early 1947 the Communist student-based anti-American movement had succeeded and the Marshall Mission had gone home, and it was crystal clear that all-out civil war was inevitable. The GMD and the CCP represented two opposite extremes of Chinese society. In order for either side to win, it had to secure the sympathy and support of the population, which was mostly indifferent to the ideology of either side.

In July 1947 the GMD government announced the general order of mobilization against the CCP. One month later the GMD Central passed a resolution on "suppression of [Communist] rebellion [first] and national reconstruction [later]." In GMD areas, the authorities were ordered to obtain food supply, recruit soldiers, and engage in security work. In reconquered areas, they had to mobilize the masses to investigate enemy activities and destroy the hidden Communists. In CCP areas, the Nationalists must establish secret action groups to engage in economic and other kinds of sabotage. The GMD also disbanded the Political Consultative Conference and arrested members of the Democratic League. By early 1948, however, all the GMD measures had failed to be effective in combating the Communists. Chiang Kai-shek admitted that the general mobilization had not materialized and that the GMD army had suffered heavy losses. Worse still, before suppressing the CCP, the GMD government unilaterally launched its presidential race from March to May 1948. The election of Li Zongren as Vice President heightened the factional conflict between President Chiang Kai-shek and the Guangxi Clique.[53] In short, from mid-1947 to mid-1948, the GMD authorities were wasting energy in an internal power struggle, and they were ineffective in the war against the CCP. Their harsh treatment of the Democratic League and other "democratic parties" antagonized the intelligentsia and prompted some of them to join the Communist cause.

On the other side, the CCP had to convince people that Chiang Kai-shek and the GMD were doomed and that the CCP best represented their interests. The PLA manifesto of 10 October 1947 formally declared the strategic slogan of "Overthrow Chiang Kai-shek and liberate all China." It also urged: "United workers, peasants, soldiers, intellectuals and businessmen, all oppressed classes, all people's organizations, democratic parties, minority nationalities, overseas Chinese and other patriots form a national united front;

overthrow the dictatorial Chiang Kai-shek's government; and establish a democratic coalition government."[54] This was the PLA's and the CCP's fundamental program.

In "The Present Situation and Our Tasks" (25 December 1947), Mao Zedong echoed this plea. The Party should also develop the "progressive" forces, win over the "middle" (neither pro-GMD nor pro-CCP) forces, and isolate the die-hard forces.[55] In "On Some Important Problems of the Party's Present Policy" (18 January 1948), Mao reaffirmed the broadest united front to include "workers, peasants (including the new rich peasants), small independent craftsmen and traders, middle and small capitalists oppressed and injured by the reactionary forces, the students, teachers, professors and ordinary intellectuals, professionals, enlightened gentry, ordinary government employees, oppressed minority nationalities and overseas Chinese."[56] By then, every Chinese could be a friend of the revolution if he or she was "progressive," "democratic," or "patriotic" without respect to his or her social background and relationships. Mao's expedient tactic of siding with anyone who would help the Party, not his general class designations, turned out to be the Communists' most important (urban) class policy during the Civil War. (In 1940 Mao had already realized the futility of a proletarian revolution in the GMD-controlled urban areas and advocated a proletarian-led [that is, CCP-led] multiclass revolution.)[57] After the expulsion of Communist representatives from the GMD urban areas in early March of 1947, the CCP shifted more attention to underground work in the cities.

By 1948 the GMD was in deep trouble. On the war front, it had lost the momentum of its earlier offensive against the CCP. On the Central Plains the GMD forces were on the defensive after the Communist victories under the leadership of three army groups (Liu Bocheng's and Deng Xiaoping's Shanxi–Hebei–Shandong–Henan Front Army; Chen Yi's and Su Yu's East China Front Army, and Chen Geng's and Xie Fuzhi's Army). The Nationalist cities, Wuhan and Nanjing, were threatened by the Communists. In Northwest China the GMD suffered heavy losses, and Yan'an was recaptured by the Communists in April 1948. The strategically unimportant mountainous Northwest drained 400,000 GMD troops. In the Northeast, Lin Biao had inflicted severe casualties on the crack GMD army and had encircled it in the small triangular area between Shenyang, Changchun, and Jinzhou; 470,000 GMD troops were ultimately slaughtered or captured in Northeast China. In North China the Communist East China Army occupied most of Shandong; and the GMD troops under Fu Zuoyi were defensively confined to the Beiping–Tianjin–Baoding area and Tangshan. The GMD aborted its use of the Bandit-Suppression General Headquarters (North China, Northeast China, Xuzhou [or East China], Central China, and Xi'an [or Northwest China]) to "clear Central China, to strengthen North China, and to recover Northeast China."[58]

From September 1948 to January 1949, the GMD lost well over one million men; the heart of their army was destroyed and what was left could no longer fight. Above all, the loss of Beiping–Tianjin signaled the collapse of GMD North China. Coupled with the earlier fall of Northeast China to the CCP, the GMD regime was doomed.

In early 1949 the Communists regrouped and rested their troops north of the Yangzi River. On the other side, on 8 January, the GMD government requested the American, British, French, and Soviet governments to act as intermediaries in peace negotiations with the CCP. All refused. After his resignation on 21 January 1949, Chiang Kai-shek was succeeded as President by Li Zongren. Li negotiated peace with the CCP while Chiang continued to command the GMD campaigns against the Communists. The peace negotiations broke down in April 1949. Nanjing fell on 23 April, and Shanghai was "liberated" in late May. The GMD government withdrew to Guangzhou and then Southwest China to continue a hopeless resistance effort. It finally escaped to Taiwan. On 1 October 1949, in Beijing, Mao Zedong proclaimed the founding of the People's Republic of China.

Summary

The Soviet-American Cold War and rivalry in China influenced the course of the Chinese Civil War. From the Nationalist standpoint, the United States, rather than the Soviet Union, prevented them from using the military solution to solve the Communist problem in the fall of 1945 and early 1946, when the GMD still had a good chance of winning the Civil War. But since the GMD military was still superior to the Communist troops even in mid-1948, it would be difficult for the GMD to put all the blame for their ultimate defeat on the foreigners. Nonmilitary factors must have played a vital role in the GMD collapse in 1949. It will be shown that the disastrous GMD takeover and its inability to secure its urban bases and the allegiance of the urban populace were major factors in its loss of mainland China.

During 1945–46 the CCP was careful and shrewd in dealing with the GMD, the United States, and the Soviet Union. Because of the miscalculations of Chiang Kai-shek (who thought the United States would unconditionally support his anti-CCP campaign) and of Joseph Stalin (who thought the Soviet Union would benefit from a weak GMD-CCP coalition government) and the impossible mediation of the Marshall Mission, the CCP succeeded in gaining time, land, cities, and prestige. It will be shown that having been helped by the Soviets militarily in Manchuria, the CCP also succeeded in using the student-based "democratic" movement to discredit both the United States and the GMD. The withdrawal of American troops by early 1947 got rid of one strong and hostile foreign element to the Communist revolutionary activities in China. The Communist urban united front and party-building strategies were effective in gaining political advantages in the national and international levels of conflict.

Notes

1. These are the main topics of Odd Arne Westad's *Cold War and Revolution.*
2. See Steven I. Levine, *Anvil of Victory,* pp. 26–33, 41–43, 45–51, 65–68, 72–74, 77–86; Westad, *Cold War and Revolution,* ch. 4.
3. See Westad, *Cold War and Revolution,* ch. 4.
4. See Richard C. Thornton, *China,* pp. 195–96.
5. See Lowell Dittmer, *Sino-Soviet Normalization and Its International Implications,* p. 159.
6. Levine, *Anvil of Victory,* p. 67.
7. Guo Tingyi, *Jindai Zhongguo shigang,* pp. 760–61.
8. See Levine, *Anvil of Victory,* pp. 33–41; Westad, *Cold War and Revolution,* ch. 5.
9. See Suzanne Pepper, *Civil War in China,* p. 53.
10. Ibid. See also Jon W. Huebner, "Chinese Anti-Americanism, 1946–48," p. 117.
11. Cited in Beijing Daxue Lishixi "Beijing daxue xuesheng yundongshi" Bianxiezu, *Beijing daxue xuesheng yundongshi,* p. 197.
12. See its editorial on 15 Sept. 1946.
13. Quoted in Immanuel C. Y. Hsü, *The Rise of Modern China,* p. 628.
14. See the articles "The United States Should Immediately End Its Support of the Chinese Civil War" and "Oppose the American Support in the Massacre of People in the Northeast" in *Jiefang ribao,* Yan'an, 5 and 7 June 1946.
15. See ibid., 23 June 1946.
16. See Henry I. Shaw, Jr., *The U.S. Marines in North China,* pp. 17–18; ZMZS, 7 : 3, pp. 201–6; Jonathan D. Spence, *The Search for Modern China,* pp. 489–90.
17. See *Jiefang ribao,* Yan'an, 26 Nov. 1946.
18. See *ZMZS,* 7 : 3, p. 206.
19. See the editorial on *Huabei ribao,* Beiping, 9 Aug. 1946.
20. Such an attitude was implied in the Statement by President Truman on United States Policy Toward China, 18 Dec. 1946, in United States State Department, *The China White Paper,* pp. 689–94; see also the Chinese translation in *ZMZS,* 7 : 3, pp. 255–62.
21. See ch. 5 for more details on the Shen Chong Incident.
22. See Sidney H. Chang and Ramon H. Myers, *The Storm Clouds Clear over China,* pp. xxi–xxiii, 179–95.
23. See the theme of the powerlessness of the "Third Force" in Roger B. Jeans's *Roads Not Taken.*
24. See Guofang Daxue Dangshi Dangjian Zhenggong Jiaoyanshi, *Zhongguo gongchandang de zhanlüe celüe,* pp. 290–91, 293–94.
25. Westad, *Civil War and Revolution,* p. 170.
26. See Guofang Daxue Dangshi Dangjian Zhenggong Jiaoyanshi, *Zhongguo gongchandang de zhanlüe celüe,* p. 307; Fang Xiao, *Zhonggong dangshi bianyilu,* p. 742.
27. See Fang Xiao, *Zhonggong dangshi bianyilu,* pp. 743–51; Guofang Daxue Dangshi Dangjian Zhenggong Jiaoyanshi, *Zhongguo gongchandang de zhanlüe celüe,* pp. 294–311.
28. See *MZJ,* vol. IX, pp. 183–275.
29. See Dittmer, *Sino-Soviet Normalization and Its International Implications,* p. 157.
30. See *MZX,* vol. IV, pp. 1123–36.
31. *ZZWX,* vol. XIII, pp. 135–36.
32. See *ZMZS,* 7 : 2, pp. 23–102; *ZDCZ,* vol. VI, pp. 11–15.
33. *MZX,* vol. IV, pp. 1152–55.
34. Ibid., pp. 1155–66.
35. See *ZMZS,* 7 : 2, pp. 229–41.

36. George C. Marshall, *Marshall's Mission to China*, vol. II, p. 516.

37. See *ZEX*, vol. I, pp. 252–55.

38. *SWZE*, vol. I, p. 305.

39. *ZZWX*, vol. XIII, pp. 147–48.

40. Tang Degang and Li Zongren, *Li Zongren huiyilu*, p. 558.

41. For a general account of this military reorganization, see Wang Degui et al., *Bayiwu qianhou de Zhongguo zhengju*, pp. 57–58.

42. See *MZX*, vol. IV, pp. 1174–75. See ch. 3 on the "Gao Shuxun Movement."

43. See Zhonghua Minguo Kaiguo Wushinian Wenxian Bianzuan Weiyuanhui and Guoli Zhengzhi Daxue Guoji Guanxi Yanjiu Zhongxin, *Gongfei huoguo shiliao huibian*, vol. III, pp. 170–73; Warren Kuo, *Analytical History of the Chinese Communist Party*, vol. IV, pp. 47–51; Sifa Xingzhengbu Tianchaju, *Gongfei shentou zhanshu zhi yanjiu*, ch. 4.

44. Yang Ruzhou, *Zhonggong qunzhong luxian yanjiu*, p. 141.

45. See *MZX*, vol. IV, pp. 1179–83.

46. Levine, *Anvil of Victory*, p. 12; Yang Guodong, "Jiefang zhanzheng chuqi Dongbei geming genjudi de jianli ji qi lishi tedian," p. 84.

47. See Zhang Guoqing, "Kangzhan shengli hou Meisu Guogong zai Dongbei de juezhu," p. 124; Hsü, *Rise of Modern China*, p. 624.

48. On the Battle of Handan, see ch. 3. On the battles of Shangdang and Suiyuan, see Wang Qingkui, *Zhongguo renmin jiefangjun zhanyiji*, pp. 276–77, 366. See also the Nationalist account of the Communist military attack on its takeover process in North China in *ZMZS*, 5 : 4, pp. 374–80.

49. Hsü, *Rise of Modern China*, p. 630.

50. See "On the Temporary Abandonment of Yan'an and the Defense of the Shaanxi–Gansu–Ningxia Border Region—Two Documents Issued by the CCP CC" (Nov. 1946 and April 1947), *SWMT*, vol. IV, p. 130.

51. See "The Chiang Kai-shek Government is Besieged by the Whole People" (30 May 1947), *MZX*, vol. IV, p. 1226.

52. Ibid., p. 1177.

53. See Wang Gongan and Mao Lei, *Guogong liangdang guanxi tongshi*, pp. 846–49.

54. *SWMT*, vol. IV, pp. 149–50.

55. *MZJ*, vol. X, pp. 111–12.

56. *MZX*, vol. IV, p. 1268.

57. See "On New Democracy" (Jan. 1940) in *MZJ*, vol. VII, pp. 143–202.

58. See Zhang Xianwen, *Zhonghua minguo shigang*, pp. 709–15; *Shijie ribao*, Beiping, 9 Feb. 1948. Shijiazhuang, the strategic city in South Hebei, was captured by the Communists in Nov. 1947; see *Jin-Cha-Ji ribao*, Leibao, 14–21 Nov. 1947.

3

GMD-CCP Organizations and Strategies in North China

North China was critical to the CCP's expansion of power during the period of the Sino-Japanese War. The withdrawal of the GMD from North China (and the coastal areas) into the Southwest created a splendid opportunity for the Communists to fill the political vacuum. It was the Japanese success in battles against the non-Communist forces that left the CCP the only rallying point for anti-Japanese resistance, and thus paved the road to political success for the CCP.[1] The Communist armed struggle against the Japanese also elevated the CCP's patriotic status. In the cities, the CCUP focused on party-building and the united front with the anti-Japanese elements. Above all, carrying out the policy of "70 percent expansion," the Communists were much less engaged in fighting the Japanese than in the process of consolidating and developing their own strength. Having expanded the army, strengthened the Party, and destroyed the GMD-affiliated armed forces in much of rural North China, by 1945 the CCP had become a political force that could challenge the GMD for supreme power.[2]

Nationalist blunders enhanced Communist power. During the early phase of the Civil War, the numerically stronger but factionalized GMD military and political organizations in (North) China and Beiping-Tianjin committed strategic and tactical errors that compromised their chance of securing urban popular support and developing their cities into strong anti-Communist bases. In particular, the disastrous GMD postwar takeover in North China laid the foundation of the Nationalist collapse in the urban areas. Meanwhile, the Communists created commonsense but flexible and effective strategies and tactics that undermined GMD power in urban areas.

GMD Organizations in North China and Beiping–Tianjin

In terms of both political and military power, the GMD looked strong in urban North China, Beiping, and Tianjin.[3] The Nationalist party and youth corps organizations, government officials, military forces, police, special units, security troops, and various kinds of local defense corps permeated the region.

In September 1945 Chiang Kai-shek appointed Li Zongren to be the director of the Beiping Executive Headquarters, which was the highest political-military authority in North China until May 1948. On the surface, this Headquarters could exert authority over Hebei, Shandong, Chahar, Suiyuan, Rehe, Beiping–Tianjin, and Qingdao. In actuality, all the local political and military agencies followed orders from their respective superiors. Li Zongren wielded no power at all over the military forces in North China. Obviously, Chiang did not expect Li to fight the Communists. Li did not even know in advance when the mayor of Beiping was replaced. Li's appointment to the directorship of the Headquarters was either a tactic of Chiang Kai-shek to separate Li from the latter's power base in Southwest China, or it was Chiang's attempt to appease a longtime political rival. Li did not value the post and complained that his Headquarters in Beiping was "an office suspended in midair."[4]

Until December 1947 the real strongman in Beiping–Tianjin was General Sun Lianzhong, who commanded two hundred thousand troops. Ineffectual in fighting the Communists, Sun was transferred to Nanjing in January 1948. Determined to crush the Communist offensive, Chiang Kai-shek in 1947–48 established five Bandit-Suppression General Headquarters throughout China. In December 1947 Fu Zuoyi was appointed as the commander-in-chief of the North China Bandit-Suppression Headquarters.

This Suppression Headquarters had military authority over Hebei, Suiyuan, Rehe, Chahar, and Beiping–Tianjin. (Shanxi was under the nominal authority of the Headquarters, but Yan Xishan was the *de facto* ruler of Shanxi.) In the summer of 1948, it absorbed all the remaining personnel of the Beiping Executive Headquarters. At its zenith, the Bandit Suppression commanded half a million troops.[5] By the time of the Battle of Beiping–Tianjin, however, the PLA already enjoyed superior military strength. Earlier, in mid-1947, Chiang Kai-shek realized the difficulty of suppressing the Communists. He remembered the successful work of the Special Units in the early phase of the Bandit-Suppression Campaign in Jiangxi in the 1930s and decided to establish a Pacification General Corps under the authority of the Defense Ministry. In September 1947 the 1st General Corps of this Special Unit (or the 0760 Corps) started to operate in Beiping–Tianjin.[6] As the GMD already had more than a quarter of a million troops and various kinds of police and security forces in the Beiping–Tianjin area, the necessity of assigning another Special Unit to help fight the Communists demonstrated the growing troubles of the GMD.

In Beiping the GMD Municipal Party Bureau and the Three People's Principles Youth Corps, which was merged with the party in September 1947, were accountable to the authorities in Nanjing. The Party Bureau did not control the municipal government, however, nor could it wield power over all the military forces. On the other hand, the Youth Corps was often in conflict with the party for power and money. Besides, the Youth Corps could not effectively contain or suppress the Communist youth movement in the city. The inherent weaknesses and rivalry between the party and the Youth Corps in Beiping (and China) showed the general disunity and incompetence of the GMD.[7]

Beiping was a special municipality of the Central Government. The structure of the government was as follows: (1) a mayor and a deputy mayor; (2) an administrative council; (3) nine bureaus; (4) a municipal council. Together with the Security Police General Corps and the Transportation Police General Corps, the Police Bureau helped the military, including its military police, in fighting the Communists.

The 5th Supply District Command Headquarters of the United Logistical Affairs General Headquarters was another major GMD military organization in Beiping–Tianjin. The Headquarters was in charge of salaries and supplies for all the military organizations in North China.

The GMD secret-service systems also operated in Beiping–Tianjin. After the Japanese surrender, the Bureau of Statistics and Investigation of the National Military Council (or simply, the Military Statistics) and the Bureau of Statistics and Investigation of the GMD Central Executive Committee (or simply, the Central Statistics) immediately sent agents to take over key Japanese and puppet facilities and to arrest Chinese collaborators.[8] In Beiping–Tianjin, Military Statistics prevailed over Central Statistics in power and prestige; the former also had a special relationship with the 0760 Corps. Although these two intelligence systems were not infiltrated successfully by the Communists, they quarreled between themselves for power and money.

The GMD also controlled all the courts and the district attorney offices as well as the public utilities (especially the railways and the three-thousand-employee telecommunications system) and the 70th Arsenal. Nevertheless, because of internal dissension and the Communist infiltration of its organizations, the GMD became impotent in suppressing the enemy, within and without.

As in Beiping, the GMD Municipal Party Bureau and the Youth Corps in Tianjin were plagued by internal quarrels. In Tianjin it was the struggle for power between the Nanjing Faction and the Local Faction, between the CC (Chen Lifu and Chen Guofu) Clique and the Zhu Jiahua (or the Political Study) Clique. These internecine conflicts hampered the party and the Youth Corps and inhibited cooperation between them.

Tianjin and Beiping were special municipalities of the Nanjing government. They were not accountable to the Hebei provincial government, whose headquarters shifted from Baoding to Beiping in late January 1948. The structure of the Tianjin municipal government was identical with that of Beiping. The municipal police, the Security Police General Corps, and the Transportation Police General Corps assisted the military in maintaining law and order.

Since Tianjin was a strategic and economic center in North China, the GMD stationed many troops there. In the Battle of Beiping–Tianjin, Fu Zuoyi assigned his favorite general, Chen Changjie, to be the defense commander of Tianjin. Chen commanded 130,000 troops. Like his boss, Commander Chen was the *de facto* ruler of the city, because military affairs dominated all else. As in Beiping, the 0760 Corps, Military Statistics, and Central Statistics also operated in Tianjin. With these units and other military, police, and local defense forces at its command, the GMD again appeared to be strong, but actually it was not.

Communist Organizations in North China

During the Civil War period the Communist party and military organizations in the Shanxi–Chahar–Hebei, the Shanxi–Hebei–Shandong–Henan (Jin-Ji-Lu-Yu), and the Shanxi–Suiyuan (Jin–Sui) base areas were important to the Communist activities in the region.

The Shanxi–Chahar–Hebei Base Area was the first Communist "democratic" political regime in the "anti-Japanese national united front." It was regarded by the CCP Central as "the model anti-Japanese base area behind the enemy line and the model region in the united front."[9] It was also the base area that strategically threatened GMD Beiping–Tianjin during the Civil War.

From the winter of 1937 to November 1938, Nie Rongzhen was the representative of the CCP Central in the base area. During March–November 1938, Peng Zhen served as the representative of the CCP CC Northern Bureau, and he assisted Nie in directing Party affairs in the area.

From November 1938 to January 1939, a CCP CC Shanxi–Chahar–Hebei Branch Bureau, which was under the authority of the Northern Bureau, was in charge of Party matters. From January 1939 to January 1941, the Branch Bureau was renamed the CCP CC Northern Branch Bureau. After the departure of the Bureau secretary, Peng Zhen, to Yan'an in 1941, the Northern Branch Bureau was changed back to the Shanxi–Chahar–Hebei Branch Bureau. The Branch Bureau also controlled the Party organizations in West Beiping, North Beiping, East Hebei, and Central Hebei. On 25 August 1945, the Branch Bureau became the CCP Shanxi–Chahar–Hebei Central Bureau. On 9 May 1948, the Central Bureau combined with the CCP Jin-Ji-Lu-Yu Central Bureau to form the CCP CC North China Bureau. Furthermore, when the Liu Shaoqi–led Central Work Committee and later the CCP Central stayed in rural Hebei from May 1947 to March 1949, the Shanxi–Chahar–Hebei Central Bureau, or the North China Bureau, became the key regional Party organization.

The Shanxi–Chahar–Hebei Military Region (November 1937–September 1945) was controlled by the Party bureau. In November 1945 the main forces were organized as the 1st and 2nd Field Armies of the military region. In May

1948 the front armies were merged into the North China Field Army. Together with the Northeast Field Army, the North China Army took part in the Battle of Beiping–Tianjin.

On 20 August 1945, the Communists established the CCP CC Jin-Ji-Lu-Yu Central Bureau and the Jin-Ji-Lu-Yu Military Region. On 9 May 1948, the Jin-Ji-Lu-Yu Party and military structures were reorganized into the North China Bureau and Military Region.

In September 1943 the CCP CC Jin-Sui Branch Bureau was established to direct Party affairs in Shanxi and Suiyuan. When the war with Japan was over, the Communists controlled strategic strongholds in the Jin-Sui border area. Until April 1949 the Communist troops in Jin-Sui were part of the Northwest Field Army. Afterward, the North China Bureau directed the Jin-Sui armies.

Besides, Northwest Shanxi of the Jin-Sui Base Area was important because the Ye Jianying–led Central Rear Committee operated in the region from late 1947 to May 1948, when it reunited with the Party Central in Xibaipo Village, Hebei Province.

In short, the Communist political and military organizations in the Shanxi–Chahar–Hebei, Jin-Ji-Lu-Yu, and Jin-Sui base areas were the political-military capital of the Communists to combat the GMD in North China and Beiping–Tianjin.

Communist Urban Strategies

The pre-1949 Communist movement was more than a "peasant revolution." Even Mao Zedong himself did not deny the pivotal importance of cities in the revolution. While scholars still debate whether Mao's "A Single Spark Can Start a Prairie Fire" (5 January 1930) signaled the "basic formation" of his "revolutionary road or theory of using the countryside to encircle [and capture] the city," they tend to agree that his "The Chinese Revolution and the CCP" (15 December 1939) signified the "final formation" of the "revolutionary theory."[10]

In reality, since the CCP was weak and powerless to take over either the Japanese or the Nationalist urban strongholds, Mao's strategy of using the countryside to encircle the cities remained a theory throughout the wartime period. Paradoxically, the "final formation" of Mao's rural strategy in 1939 was the theoretical beginning of the serious revival of the urban-centered ideology and activity of the CCP.

Indeed, "The Chinese Revolution and the CCP" recognized not the supreme status of the rural areas but the pivotal role of cities in the revolution. Mao wrote: "[S]tressing the work in the rural base areas does not mean abandoning our work in the cities . . . without the work in the cities . . . our own rural base areas would be isolated and the revolution would suffer defeat . . . the final objective of the revolution is the capture of the cities . . . this objective cannot be achieved without adequate work in the cities."[11]

Moreover, according to the CCP historiography, Mao Zedong created the guiding principle of urban work while Liu Shaoqi was his supreme representative in White areas. In fact, except for a brief period of negotiations with the GMD in Chongqing, Mao operated in the rural Red areas during 1928–49. Certainly, Liu Shaoqi was the highest-ranking Communist in Beiping–Tianjin and urban North China during 1936–38. But from 1939 to 1949, at the national level it was Zhou Enlai who was the key Communist in urban struggles. Other Party leaders also contributed to the theory of urban work. In the Beiping–Tianjin area, from 1941 to 1949 it was Liu Ren who played the leading role in underground activities.

According to the memoirs of Mao Qihua, a Communist labor leader, on the second day of the Wayaobao Conference (18 December 1935) Mao Zedong spelled out the guideline for work in White areas. Mao said the Party "must have well-selected cadres working underground, must accumulate strength for a long time and must bide its time (in urban areas)." Mao Zedong made such a statement concerning work in the enemy-controlled areas *after* listening to Mao Qihua's detailed report on such activity, especially in Shanghai.[12]

Three years later, urban work became so important to Mao Zedong that in "The Chinese Revolution and the CCP" (December 1939) he went on to stress that the organizational work in the cities "must have well-selected cadres working underground, must accumulate strength and bide its time there" (*jinbi jinggan, jixu liliang, yidai shiji*). The CCP must also "wage struggles on just grounds, to its advantage, and with restraint."[13] (On 25 May 1939, the CCP CC had already ordered the Party cadres in White areas to carry out seriously the operating guideline of "working underground for a long time, accumulating strength, and biding time" [*changqi maifu, jixu liliang, yidai shiji*].)[14]

In 1940 Mao Zedong continued to talk about the guideline for urban work even though he operated only in rural Northwest China. In "Freely Expand the Anti-Japanese Forces and Resist the Onslaughts of the Anti-Communist Die-Hards" (4 May 1940), "On Policy" (25 December 1940), and "The Directive on the [Underground] Work in Shaanxi" (composed sometime in 1940), Mao reputedly created the so-called Sixteen-Character Guideline for the underground urban work: "well-selected cadres working underground for a long time, accumulating strength, and biding their time" (*jinbi jinggan, changqi maifu, jixu liliang, yidai shiji*).[15]

In perspective, the guiding principle of Communist urban activity was aimed at glorifying Mao Zedong's cardinal theoretical contribution to the work in White areas. This kind of historiography reflects the Mao Zedong–centered CCP history. But it also can be used to argue that Mao understood the importance of restoring the revolution to the cities in 1939–40.

The high status of Liu Shaoqi in the Communist struggle in White areas was established mainly during his tenure as the head of the CCP CC Northern Bureau in 1936–38. Besides his concrete activities in Beiping–Tianjin, Liu's writings in the period also heightened his reputation as an authority on the "correct" way of doing urban work.

In "Eliminate Closed-doorism and Adventurism" and "Guidelines for the Labor Movement in White Areas" (April 1936), Liu Shaoqi expressed the importance of open and underground work, the union of overt and covert activities, and the separation of Party and mass work.[16] Earlier, in March 1936, Liu wrote "A Letter Concerning the Work in White Areas" to the Party Central. In it Liu summarized the "leftist" errors since 1931, and he urged transformation in strategy concerning the work in White areas.[17] Liu was not the first Communist to stress the change in the work in White areas, but his clear-cut focus on the necessity and the nature of the transformation was actually in support of Mao and his new policies since the Zunyi Conference. This could be the reason why Liu ultimately became the spokesman for the Communist work in White areas.

At the Conference of Party Representatives from the White areas in Yan'an (17 May–10 June 1937), Liu Shaoqi was the leading figure in summarizing the urban work for the previous decade. Liu stressed the significance of coordinating overt and covert work, and the proper relationship between the Party and the urban masses.[18] At the conference, Zhang Wentian, "the person with overall responsibility" of the CCP, also discussed the central tasks in Communist urban activities.[19] (In 1936 Zhang was also busy writing about the work in White areas. Because of his identification with the Twenty-Eight Bolsheviks and his work base being the Red areas, not the White areas, Zhang's status was eclipsed by that of Liu Shaoqi.) The White-areas conference also indicated that the CCP had noted and never downplayed the significance of urban activity.

In addition, even local Party personnel spelled out the content of urban work earlier than Mao Zedong. For example, the policy of the CCP Hebei Provincial Committee in Beiping–Tianjin in mid-July 1937 was "to conceal the organization, to accumulate strength, to bide its time and wait for opportunity, to coordinate work from inside and outside" (*yinbi zuzhi, xuji liliang, dengdai shiji, liying waihe*).[20]

Above all, the status of Zhou Enlai in the Communist urban struggle should not be underrated. As early as 1928, Zhou had made a statement that echoed the guiding principle of urban work. At the conference of the Beijing–Hebei Provincial Committee in December, Zhou Enlai, at that time the director of the CCP CC Organization Department, emphasized that the major task in White areas was "to accumulate strength [*jixu liliang*], to await opportunities [*yidai shiji*], to gain support among the masses, to develop struggle, and to be ready for the new high tide in the revolution."[21]

From February to September 1937, Zhou Enlai was the chief Communist negotiator with the GMD government. The "anti-Japanese national united front" was formalized after his six rounds of negotiation with the Nationalists. In December 1937 Zhou served as the Deputy Secretary of the CCP CC Changjiang Bureau and was responsible for the united-front work. From January 1939 to August 1943, Zhou was the Secretary of the CCP CC Southern Bureau and stayed in Chongqing, the GMD wartime capital. Zhou was in charge of the CCP's work in all GMD areas except those in the Northwest (the location of the Shaan–Gan–Ning Base Area). In the Communist united-front work, their well-known policy of "three diligences" (*sanqin*)—"be diligent in studies, careers, and making friends" (in GMD areas)—was attributed to Zhou Enlai during 1941–42. (Under authorization from the Party Central, the Southern Bureau issued the policies of *sanqin* and "three processes" [*sanhua*]—that is, "be professional and socialized, and be legitimate in political activities.") Zhou was at his best when involved in the "united front from above and below" with higher and "progressive" intellectuals, patriotic elements, international friends, and students. From 1939 to 1949 Zhou Enlai, not Liu Shaoqi, was the top Communist cadre in the urban political struggle against the GMD. During the wartime period, Zhou contributed most to the effort in trying to make the Southwest CCUP "a truly and totally underground Party, maintaining ties with the masses."[22] During the Civil War, "Comrade Zhou Enlai was in charge, entrusted by the Party leadership with the underground work of the Party."[23]

In practical work in Tianjin and particularly Beiping, Liu Ren stood out as the Communist most responsible for the growth and consolidation of the Party. Liu was a native of Sichuan Province. In 1945 he was the director of the Urban Work Department and the Enemy Work Department of the Shanxi–Chahar–Hebei Central Bureau. In 1948 he maintained his directorship of the Urban Work Department and also served as the deputy director of the Organization Department of the North China Bureau. (After the establishment of the People's Republic, Liu held a number of important political and military posts in Beijing. He was one of the first victims of the Cultural Revolution. In June 1966 Liu was replaced by Wu De in his most important position—the second secretary of the CCP Beijing Municipal Committee. Liu was arrested by the Red Guards in December 1966. He was shackled for a long time, and died miserably in October 1973 in the prison the Communists had built for the suppression of "counterrevolutionaries." His death was due to his close connection with Liu Shaoqi, Peng Zhen, and Liu Ningyi—all of them had contributed to the Communist achievements in [urban] North China before 1949.)[24]

It was in the fall of 1941 that Liu Ren began to establish secret communication networks from Fuping (location of the Shanxi–Chahar–Hebei Branch Bureau) to Yan'an in the west, to the Taihang Mountains in the south, to Central Hebei to the east, and to West Beiping, North Beiping, and East Hebei to the north. Liu was also responsible for the delivery of the Party's internal documents and journals.[25]

Liu Ren, Yao Yilin, and other leaders were also in charge of training the CCUP members in Beiping–Tianjin. The instruction was based on Mao Zedong's "The Chinese Revolution and the CCP" (1939) and emphasized the anti-Japanese war of resistance. The trainees studied Mao's guiding principle of urban work and learned how to be Communist Party members. Liu also had personal talks with all the trainees to learn their ideological stands, assigned duties to them, and taught them his own revolutionary experiences in the CCUP.[26] Liu wrote a booklet entitled "The Concealment Policy of Urban Work." This handbook described the Party line, the program, the principles, and the methods of urban work. Echoing the teaching of Mao and Liu Shaoqi, this booklet denounced "the leftist adventurism" tendency among young students, and the vacillation and weakness of petit-bourgeois intellectuals.[27]

Most of the trainees in underground work were young students. Liu Ren admonished the Beiping–Tianjin CCUP to select the "progressive" students, especially those whose families had a high social status in the cities, and to visit and study in the base areas. The Party would then develop new members to expand the ranks of the underground in Beiping–Tianjin.[28]

Concealment was the essence of underground work. During their training in the same classroom or meeting place, the trainees were separated individually by cloth curtains so that they could not recognize each other. The purpose was to avoid development of any connections among them as they conducted underground work in the cities.[29]

In order to lessen the danger of disrupting the whole organization because of the arrest of one leader, Liu Ren's Urban Work Committee (or Department) continued the effective tactic of "many heads, single lines." The Party's central organ in Beiping–Tianjin, however, was no longer inside the cities but was located in the Shanxi–Chahar–Hebei Base Area. All lines of operation had to report directly to the Urban Work Committee, and the Committee assigned various unrelated agents to communicate with the Party organs within Beiping and Tianjin. This tactic of "[central] leadership in a separate land [away from the cities]" strengthened the secrecy of underground operations.[30]

Further, the Urban Work Committee required the CCUP members to endure hardship as the poor masses did and to fight for the interests of the masses with reason, with benefit, and with restraint. Members had to conceal their identities, avoid rashness, use appropriate slogans, and employ flexible tactics. These techniques developed the strength of the CCUP during the Sino-Japanese War.[31]

Before the Civil War period started, Liu Ren had sowed the "red seeds" in Beiping–Tianjin (and Tangshan). By August 1945 there were five hundred CCUP members in Beiping–Tianjin–Tangshan under the authority of the Urban Work Department of the Shanxi–Chahar–Hebei Central Bureau; two hundred of them operated in Beiping.[32] Liu Ren fulfilled the task of accumulating strength: "Every agent sent [to Beiping], every person developed [into a Party member], is a time bomb in the heart of the enemy."[33] The Communist urban strategy in Beiping–Tianjin in the period 1945–49 would be indebted to his efforts. All the tactics used in urban underground work had been well developed by Liu Ren and others in the Sino-Japanese War period.

To summarize, the strategy of the CCUP in GMD areas was to have "well-selected cadres working underground for a long time, accumulating strength, and biding their time in the cities." In tactics, the CCUP demanded its members to be "diligent in studies, careers, and making friends," to be "professional and socialized, and legitimate in activities," to coordinate overt work with underground work, to separate legal work from illegal work, and to separate mass organizations from the CCUP. In practice, Liu Ren and the Communists on the urban spot would try hard to materialize the strategy and the tactics in their struggles in North China.

GMD Postwar Takeover

The Japanese surrender in August 1945 was the signal for a fierce GMD-CCP race to seize Japanese-occupied territories. In urban North China, the GMD takeover was challenged initially by the CCP. In Beiping–Tianjin the Communists at first attempted to use only military force to capture the cities; ultimately it was their combined political-military strategy that achieved the conquest.

On the day after the Japanese acceptance of the Potsdam Declaration, Zhu De, the commander-in-chief of the Communist forces, ignored the order of Chiang Kai-shek to remain in position pending further instructions. He instructed his troops to advance on all fronts to accept the surrender of Japanese and puppet armies and regimes. Zhu's action presaged a Communist attack on Beiping–Tianjin, where the GMD had ordered the Japanese and the puppet forces to hold their positions.

On 12 August 1945, the Communists appointed their mayors and garrison commanders for Beiping and Tianjin and set up camp fifteen miles north of Beiping. Inside Beiping the Communists captured some arms, posted notices concerning the takeover by the 8th Route Army, and prompted a few puppet units to revolt against the Japanese authorities. But because of the effective Japanese and pro-GMD puppet security measures, the small CCUP was powerless to incite any armed insurrection to take over the city, which remained practically undisturbed.[34] Besides, the Communist forces in the Shanxi–Chahar–Hebei Base Area were no match for the Beiping-based hundred-thousand–man strong Japanese North China Army that held the major urban centers of Hebei and Shandong together.[35]

The Communist offensive in Tianjin was stronger because the Japanese and puppet troops there were weaker. Following Zhu De's order, the Central Hebei Area Party Committee and Military Region launched an offensive on Tanggu and the suburbs of Tianjin. On 19 August 1945, the Communists occupied the West Station of the city. By 28 August they had encircled the Tianjin urban district. In order to facilitate a forthcoming occupation of Tianjin, the Central Hebei Area Party Committee unified all the underground work. Its Tianjin Work Committee issued notices to encourage fellow Chinese to attack the Japanese and the puppets and help the 8th Route Army to "liberate" the city.[36]

In early September, however, after assessing the political situation of the

GMD takeover (with American, Japanese, and puppet assistance) and of the peace talks in Chongqing, the CCP CC issued a directive to all base areas stressing the policy of "consolidating the occupied cities and towns, and not capturing at the time the unoccupied ones."[37] Accordingly, the Tianjin Work Committee decided that the Communists should "have a long-term plan, prepare strength, patiently wait, and carry out work in the surrounding rural areas." Besides, the Communists should "consolidate their concealed strength inside the city." They should distinguish between the open activities and the underground ones.[38]

After the arrival of American Marines in Tianjin, the Communists had no hope of seizing the city. Because of this and other developments, the Shanxi–Chahar–Hebei Central Bureau issued a "Directive on Our Urgent Work Task under the Situation of the American Troops' Landing in Tanggu" (date unknown). Its policy for the CCUP in Beiping–Tianjin was as follows:

> The Party must be . . . concealed . . . to infiltrate into all possible relationships, groups, schools and newspaper offices, to organize . . . formal and "gray" mass organizations . . . must maintain the long-term new struggle under the coordination effort from within and from without. . . . Based on the actions of the American troops and the degree of consciousness of the masses, the Party step by step must expose the reactionary plot of the American support of the GMD in terms of the American troops' landing action in order to eliminate the illusion toward the United States among the masses.[39]

The CCUP in Beiping and Tianjin followed this general policy and respectively carried out their underground and open activities. They were also eager to get rid of the American troops in China.

On the other side, when Japan surrendered, the GMD was not ready to take over North China, where the CCP controlled most of the countryside. While the GMD troops did not yet control the area, Chiang Kai-shek's government in Chongqing declared Xiong Bin mayor of Beiping and Zhang Tinge mayor of Tianjin. In order to facilitate the takeover and to resist Communist attack, the GMD ordered all Japanese troops to defend their original positions, keep communication lines open, and await the arrival of GMD troops. The Japanese were also asked to recover positions recently taken by any "irregular forces," that is, the Communists.

The GMD used Japanese and puppet troops to maintain law and order in North China because the lack of transportation made it impossible to move GMD troops immediately to the extensive areas under Japanese control. Certainly, the use of Japanese troops and Chinese collaborators for expediency was not easily accepted by the Chinese population, especially those who had suffered so much in Japanese-controlled territories.

The GMD appointed collaborators to help return Nationalist rule to Beiping–Tianjin. In Beiping, Men Zhizhong became the commander-in-chief of the Hebei

Advance Army. Wang Nanpeng and Cui Jianchu became the director and associate director, respectively, of the Beiping Military Police and Municipal Police Joint Office. These temporary Chinese authorities joined hands with the Japanese military forces to await the arrival of GMD "Central" troops; a Security Committee of the city was led by Wang and the Japanese defense commander of Beiping. Because of the security measures, the city interior and the suburbs were free from serious disturbances.

In Tianjin, in order to avoid a Communist takeover of the city, the GMD appointed collaborators Li Zhuoxiong and Du Xunzhi as military and political leaders with orders to use the Japanese to repel Communist attack and to maintain law and order. This arrangement paved the way for the Nationalist occupation of the Beiping–Tianjin area.

By 10 October 1945, the GMD had taken over Beiping–Tianjin with the assistance of Japanese, puppet, and American forces. No sooner, however, had the GMD accepted the Japanese surrender than it was to face a major military setback in North China, which caused the future strategic weakness of the GMD in the Beiping–Tianjin area.

In early October General Sun Lianzhong's troops in Henan attempted to reach Beiping–Tianjin along the Beiping–Wuhan Railway. Between 20 October and 3 November, however, these GMD forces were ambushed and defeated by Communist units in Handan in southern Hebei. Then Gao Shuxun, a non-"Central" deputy commander of the 11th War Zone and commander of the New 8th Army, defected to the Communists. Gao was the first high-level GMD general to surrender to the CCP and his defection was the first major triumph of the Communist soldiers' movement during the Civil War period. The Communists glorified his defection by launching the "Gao Shuxun Movement." Gao's so-called uprising was an important part of the defection of more than a thousand generals and 1.77 million GMD troops to the Communists during the CCP-GMD conflict. These numerical figures represented 22 percent of all the GMD soldiers (8.07 million) that the PLA had succeeded in destroying or absorbing by mid-1950. These massive defections accelerated the GMD collapse. The Nationalist "uprisings" were so important to Communist victory that certain mainland Chinese scholars viewed them as the "Third Battlefront" in the revolution.[40] Besides, the loss of the Battle of Handan demonstrated not only the GMD military weakness but the effect of factionalism within the GMD military and political structure.

After the Battle of Handan, the GMD never again ruled the areas around the northern section of the Beiping–Wuhan Railway. The GMD could not entirely control Hebei, Henan, and Shanxi. The GMD in Hebei had to confine itself to the Beiping–Tianjin–Baoding triangular area. The Communists thus could use the manpower and resources in these provinces to threaten the GMD cities there.[41]

The military-strategic weaknesses of the GMD in Beiping–Tianjin were aggravated by the complex political-military hierarchy in North China in the immediate postwar period: (1) Li Zongren—director of the Beiping Executive Headquarters; (2) Sun Lianzhong—11th War Zone commander; (3) Fu Zuoyi—12th War Zone commander; (4) Xiong Bin—mayor of Beiping (later succeeded by He Siyuan and Liu Yaozhang); (5) Zhang Tinge—mayor of Tianjin (later succeeded by Du Jianshi).

On the surface, the above assignments were appropriate. Li was a veteran military leader from Guangxi and had connections with all GMD factions; he was certainly qualified to administer North China. Sun was born in Hebei and was one of the highest leaders of the Northwestern Army. Xiong Bin of Hubei had also served in the Northwestern Army. At that time, many puppet commanders in North China (such as Men Zhizhong) were also members of that army. The appointment of Sun and Xiong was aimed at controlling these puppet military leaders and thus North China. Zhang Tinge was a former mayor of Tianjin in the pre-1937 period. Fu Zuoyi of Shanxi had distinguished himself in Suiyuan in the wartime period. The appointments were reasonable and should have stabilized and strengthened the GMD rule in North China.[42]

Unfortunately for the GMD, reality differed from expectations. Li Zongren requested Chiang Kai-shek to transfer Li's Guangxi troops to North China to fight the Communists, but Chiang refused. In the postwar period, Chiang attempted to unify military power by breaking up the prewar regional military forces and strengthening his "Central" Army.[43] Chiang's policy naturally aroused the antipathy of non-"Central" military leaders, who charged Chiang with favoritism and with trying to destroy them. The lack of cooperation between the GMD "Central" armies and the local ones even under GMD banners was the basic factor in the military weakness of the GMD, although its troops outnumbered the Communist troops most of the time.

In GMD politics, no guns usually meant no power during the Civil War period. Without his loyal troops in North China, Li Zongren's office in Beiping was indeed "suspended in midair." Sun, Fu, Xiong, and Zhang could ignore Li. There was also no close cooperation among Sun and Fu, Xiong, and Zhang. This chaotic situation continued until Chiang appointed Fu in December 1947 to be the de facto political and military leader of North China. Backed by his own troops, Fu became the strongman in GMD North China. Ironically, the military and political cohesion came too late. Fu, who served Yan Xishan in Shanxi in the 1920s but became one of Chiang's most trusted non-"Central" generals, surrendered to the Communists without a serious fight in Beiping.

Worst of all, the GMD takeover of urban (North) China was a disaster. The Chinese term for "takeover" (jieshou) means nothing more than "to accept" or "to receive." However, as public frustration and anger grew with the unprecedented corruption of the Nationalists, jieshou was replaced by another homophonous term (with different Chinese characters) meaning "to plunder, seize openly, or rob the poor."[44]

Because of widespread corruption among the takeover authorities, the takeover officials were ridiculed and denounced as stressing *youtiao youli* ("have gold bars, have reason"). They were accused of endorsing *sanyang kaitai* ("admiring the Western Ocean [the United States], loving the Eastern Ocean [Japanese women], and demanding the Current Ocean [hard cash]") and desiring *wuzi dengke* (gold bars, automobiles, houses, Japanese women, and actresses [or "face" or money bills]). A popular folk song (provided or encouraged by the CCP) also emerged to express the anger and disillusionment of the people with the GMD. It had these verses: "Thinking about the central government and looking forward to welcoming it back; but when it returns, we suffer much more" (*xiang zhongyang, pan zhongyang, zhongyang lailiao geng zaoyang*).[45]

Adding fuel to the contempt for the GMD was its slowness in disarming and repatriating the Japanese, and its reluctance to punish Chinese collaborators. While the temporary use of Japanese and puppet troops might be necessary, this was not a permanent solution. (The CCP also used Japanese and especially puppet troops, although they attacked the GMD for the same measure.) But at the end of 1945, there were still fully armed Japanese soldiers living off the land. These holdovers, and especially those incorporated into Yan Xishan's army in Shanxi, were an embarrassment to the GMD government and definitely detracted from the image of victory that the government hoped would secure the loyalty of the people. Certainly, the fact that Japanese troops stayed in China until 1949 served as a constant reminder of how weak and vulnerable the GMD was, and helped to disillusion the populace.

As for the puppet troops, about forty thousand of them were under the nominal authority of the Beiping Executive Headquarters. This Nationalist use of the former puppet armies in North China aroused "contempt and anger with regard to such a serious problem" among the residents. The puppet armies could not be decisive in defeating the CCP, but the use of them was a major blow to national discipline and morality.[46] (However, the GMD's disbandment of most of the puppet armies, especially those in the Northeast, weakened its military power but strengthened the Communists, who gladly recruited them.)

Worse still, the GMD was slow to punish Chinese collaborators.[47] A Chongqing newspaper on 5 November 1945 complained that the whole group of collaborators and puppets in the Beiping–Tianjin area had scarcely been touched, although one batch of traitors had been arrested.[48] In response, the GMD government announced a set of regulations for the punishment of collaborators and traitors. These regulations emphasized position and rank but did not take into consideration the crimes against the people committed by collaborators. Above all, Articles Three and Six aroused much criticism among the population. Article Three stipulated that collaborators could appeal for leniency if they could prove they had served the anti-Japanese war or had done something beneficial for the people during their tenure in office. Based on this article, some notorious collaborators claimed that they had served the anti-Japanese resistance in "underground activities." While some collaborators might indeed be GMD "underground workers," others could get off lightly with a bribe. There was not a single impartial court or official body to verify all the accusations and the defendants' claims.[49]

Article Six stipulated that those collaborators who surrendered to the authorities after 10 August 1945 could not appeal for leniency. But critics of this article claimed that no one had to wait until that date to know that Japan was going to lose the war.[50] Collaborators should not be judged simply on the time of their surrender to the GMD.

The GMD government later announced a revised set of regulations for the punishment of collaborators. This sixteen-article paper added more details on matters such as what kind of activities made a person a traitor. This revised set of rules removed the previously embarrassing Articles Three and Six. The damage had been done, however; the general public was cynical about the effectiveness and fairness of the GMD measures to punish collaborators.

While the people did not trust the spirit or the letter of the government regulations about collaborators, they were even more disappointed with the officials who were in charge of indictments and arrests. The Beiping–Tianjin area was the center for major collaborators in North China. Chiang Kai-shek did not assign the task and power of dealing with these collaborators to the local governments of Beiping–Tianjin or even the Beiping Executive Headquarters or the War Zone commanders. Instead, he gave the job to Dai Li's Military Statistics. This bureau's personnel could bully and blackmail the local populace merely by using the term "traitor." Genuine traitors in Beiping–Tianjin were shaken down for money and property by such agents.

The GMD also infuriated the general public by its economic measures at the end of the Sino-Japanese War. During the wartime period, the GMD regime in Southwest China had already been in deep economic and financial trouble. The recovery of the Japanese-occupied territories should have been a blessing in terms of the economy. The relatively low level of physical destruction should have made it possible for industrial production to continue with little interruption, thereby helping to offset the adverse effects of the depression in Southwest China.

However, the GMD's policy created economic stagnation for several months in these areas. The GMD closed all enemy-owned industrial enterprises and banned the movement of raw materials, food, and other commodities from enemy-owned warehouses. A sharp decline in industrial output occurred. For instance, in November 1945 about 90 percent of Tianjin's factories ceased production.[51] Worse still, the initial postwar slump was followed by soaring prices and the rapid growth of black market activities. The GMD was not able to curb the ever-rising prices and thus avert disastrous hyperinflation.

Currency policy was a key factor that would influence the success or failure of the GMD government. In the immediate postwar period, currency policy meant currency reform. In the former Japanese-occupied areas, there were two basic currencies. The Central Reserve Bank (CRB) notes began circulating in the Nanjing–Shanghai area in 1941; the Federal Reserve Bank (FRB) notes, in North China in 1938. The GMD government waited six weeks before fixing the exchange rate of 200 CRB notes to 1 *fabi* ("legal currency" used in GMD China), an exorbitant rate that drastically reduced the savings and cash reserves of the people in Central and South China.[52]

The currency problem in North China was more realistically resolved, but it could not prevent the future collapse of the GMD financial system. Zhang Guowei, the Hebei–Shandong–Chahar–Rehe (that is, North China) special agent of the GMD Finance Ministry, was responsible for the implementation of the currency reform policy in North China. In order to avoid local conflicts between those who used *fabi* (mostly takeover officials and GMD troops) and the general population, Zhang's office in Beiping tentatively fixed the exchange rate at 5 FRB to 1 *fabi*. This was the official rate announced on 21 November 1945; it was comparable to the black market rate, and thus reflected the real value of FRB notes.[53] This exchange rate contributed to the stabilization of commodity prices and maintenance of law and order in Beiping–Tianjin. Unfortunately, the psychological and social effect of the unreasonable 200:1 exchange rate eclipsed the more reasonable currency reform in North China. The GMD had created another major negative image in the minds of the Chinese in the recovered areas. Indeed, while not all officials were corrupt and incompetent, the honest and satisfactory work of some could not make up for the general chaos and disappointment. The public was angry, frustrated, and disillusioned.

Such circumstances provided an opportunity for the Communists to denounce the GMD for failing at the takeover task. The Communists summarized the "gifts" of the GMD takeover officials to the people in the recovered territories: suspension of industrial production, closure of commercial enterprises, unemployment, rising prices, and labor unrest.[54] Unfortunately for the GMD, the Communist propaganda was generally true.

The Communist propaganda machine was still weak in urban areas, however. The GMD had lost much prestige, but there were few demands for a change of government and especially for a Communist mandate to rule China. The most common plea was simply for reform. But the passage of time showed that the GMD could neither reform nor suppress the CCP. In their urban power bases, the Nationalists could not resolve the problems that aroused so much criticism during the takeover period. Indeed, the confusion and incompetence continued uninterrupted, providing the Communists the chance to neutralize the GMD and to wrest urban China from it. When the GMD lost its popular urban support, it was doomed.

To conclude, Nationalist weaknesses and blunders were apparent during the postwar takeover process. The use of Japanese, puppet, and American troops for the takeover process and the defeat in the Battle of Handan indicated the political and military weaknesses of the GMD in urban North China. Further, the GMD antagonized practically every social group in the recovered cities—and in the interior. In the political realm, most of the collaborators were either pardoned or used by the GMD authorities or both. Japanese troops remained and assisted the government; Japanese officers worked as military advisors and subordinates. Many workers were unemployed, and businessmen were ruined by the sharp decline in industrial production and the depression in the hinterland.[55] Entrepreneurs in the interior were also forced into bankruptcy when anticipated revenue did not materialize. Rising prices,[56] and especially the currency exchange policy, reduced the incomes of salaried groups and the middle class. Teachers and students were worried and antagonized by the government's education policy, although in June 1946 the GMD unofficially canceled the examination requirements and recognized the school work, diplomas, and qualifications of teachers and students in the recovered urban areas.[57] The venality of the takeover officials also significantly damaged the economy and the popular image of the GMD. In short, the takeover turned out to be a huge blunder and was an important factor in the GMD's ultimate defeat on mainland China.[58] Above all, the GMD missed an excellent strategy for using the takeover operations—seriously punishing collaborators, controlling inflation, treating teachers and students well, and appointing honest and efficient officials—as a support-building program in urban China.

Notes

1. Lincoln Li, *The Japanese Army in North China*, pp. 231–32.
2. See Warren Kuo, *Analytical History of the Chinese Communist Party*, vol. IV, chaps. 34–37; Qiao Jinou, "Kangri shiqi balujun zai Huabei de kuozhan zuoda," in *Gongdang wenti yanjiu*, part I, pp. 63–70; part II, pp. 86–103; part III, pp. 89–104; part IV, pp. 59–78. On the Communist destruction of the GMD troops in Hebei, see idem, part III, pp. 87–91. On the CCP's "70 percent expansion" policy that strengthened the Party during the wartime period, see Ke Siming, "Lun kangzhan shiqi Zhonggong de 'Qieryi fanzhen,' " pp. 164–79. On the issue of the Communists' being firmly entrenched in North China and ready to wrest power from the GMD, see the field reports in Jack Belden's *China Shakes the World*, and Claire and William Band, *Two Years with the Chinese Communists*.
3. One common saying of the time indicated this situation. "There are three 'manys' in Beiping: many bureaucracies, many soldiers, and many three-wheeled rickshaws" (*Beiping you san duo, jiguan duo, bing duo, sanlun duo*).
4. See Tang Degang and Li Zongren, *Li Zongren huiyilu*, pp. 558–60, 569.
5. See Zhong Wen, "Guanyu Fu Zuoyi de 'Huabei Jiaozong,' " pp. 340–49.
6. See Chen Gongshu, *Ping-Jin diqu suijing kanluan*, preface and ch. 1.
7. See Lloyd E. Eastman, *Seeds of Destruction*, ch. 4; Chiang Kai-shek himself admitted the disunity and impotence of the GMD; see idem, ch. 9.
8. Military Statistics' Student Movement Section and Central Statistics' Information Section also cooperated with the Youth Corps and the Nationalist party branches in fighting the Communist student activities in Tianjin (and Beiping); see *TXGY*, p. 231.
9. "Jin-Cha-Ji Kangri Genjudi" Shiliao Congshu Bianshen Weiyuanhui, *Jin-Cha-Ji kangri genjudu*, vol. I: *Wenxian xuanbian*, p. 3.
10. The debate on the "basic and final formation" of Mao's rural strategy is beyond the scope of this book. See Fang Xiao, *Zhonggong dangshi bianyilu*, pp. 328–33; Wang

Fuxuan, "Nongcun baowei chengshi daolu lilun xingcheng de shijian yu biaozhi zhuyao guandian pingxi," pp. 86–90.

11. *MZJ*, vol. VII, pp. 110–11.

12. *BDS*, pp. 114, 130.

13. Ibid., p. 111.

14. Quoted in ibid., p. 137.

15. These sixteen characters were not printed in the original documents; they were included in the later edited works of Mao Zedong. See *MZX*, vol. II, pp. 756, 765; *SWMT*, vol. II, pp. 435, 442. In "Freely Expand the Anti-Japanese Forces and Resist the On-slaughts of the Anti-Communist Die-Hards," Mao only wrote: *changgi maifu, jixu liliang, yidai shiji*. In "On Policy," Mao wrote *yinbi jinggan* first, and separated these four charac-ters from *changgi maifu, jixu liliang, yidai shiji*. Strictly speaking, there should be a "Twelve-Character Guideline" (*changgi maifu, jixu liliang, yidai shiji*) for underground work. See Li Ping, "Guanyu wo Dang Zhongyang kangri zhanzheng zhong zai Guomindang tongzhiqu gongzuo fangzhen de tifa," pp. 463–64. See also Weng Zhonger, "Guomindang tongzhiqu de aiguo minzhu yundong," p. 81 n. 2.

16. See *LSX*, vol. I, pp. 23–40.

17. *BDJ*, p. 100; *BDS*, p. 130.

18. See *LSX*, vol. I, pp. 55–71; Chen Shaochou, *Liu Shaoqi zai baiqu*, pp. 204–5.

19. See Chen, *Liu Shaoqi*, pp. 206–7.

20. Quoted in *TXGY*, p. 151.

21. See ibid., p. 83.

22. See Nanfangju Dangshi Ziliao Bianji Xiaozu, *Nanfangju dangshi ziliao*, pp. 3, 58–60; *BDS*, pp. 168–69; *ZEX*, vol. I, p. 111.

23. Quoted in Laszlo Ladany, *The Communist Party of China and Marxism*, p. 103 n. 2.

24. Although Zhou Enlai was the key figure in the Communist underground activities in GMD areas during the Civil War, Liu Ren was closer to Liu Shaoqi because of the latter's earlier work experiences in North China and the location of the Central Work Committee in Hebei. For example, on 13 December 1947, at Xibaipo Village, Liu Shaoqi chaired a committee meeting discussing the work in GMD areas. It was Liu Ren who reported to Liu Shaoqi and other participants the condition of the CCUP in Beiping–Tian-jin. See *BDJ*, p. 290. Liu Ningyi was a native of Hebei and operated underground in GMD areas before 1949. He had served as a member of the Organization Department of the Hebei Provincial Committee (1930–32), as secretary of the Tangshan City Committee (1932), as director of the Organization Department of the Beiping City Committee (1933), as secretary-general of the CCP CC Urban Work Department, and as secretary of the CCP CC Professional Workers' Movement Committee (1946). He was arrested by the GMD authorities in 1933 but was released in Nanjing in 1937. During the Civil War period, Liu was active in the employees' and workers' movement in GMD cities, including Beiping–Tianjin.

25. See *Jin-Cha-Ji ribao Bianxiezu, Jin-Cha-Ji ribao dashiji*, p. 79.

26. Zhang Dazhong, "Beiping dianxia kangri douzheng," p. 25.

27. *Mianhuai Liu Ren tongzi*, p. 34.

28. Ibid., p. 35.

29. Ibid.

30. Zhang Dazhong, "Beiping dianxia kangri douzheng," p. 25; see also *BXG*, pp. 159–60.

31. See *BXG*, pp. 160–63.

32. Zhang Dazhong, "Beiping dixia kangri douzheng," p. 29.

33. Quoted in *Mianhuai Liu Ren tongzhi*, p. 9.

34. See Beijingshi Shehui Kexue Yaniuzuo and "Beijing Lishi Jinian" Bianxiezu,

Beijing lishi jinian, pp. 349–50; see also George Moorad, *Lost Peace in China*, pp. 72–73.

35. Moorad, *Lost Peace*, pp. 73–74. There were about 50,000 Japanese troops inside Beiping; see Henry I. Shaw, Jr., *The U.S. Marines in North China*, p. 4.

36. *TXGY*, p. 179. The Tianjin Work Committee was called the Tianjin Liberation Committee in public. These two committees were another example of "two brand names, one set of personnel."

37. See *ZZWX*, vol. XIII, pp. 140–41.

38. *TXGY*, pp. 179–80.

39. Quoted in ibid., pp. 181–82; see also Odd Arne Westad, *Cold War and Revolution*, pp. 107–8. "Gray" mass organizations referred to those that were either under Communist leadership or organized by "progressives" who had links with the CCP. Because they did not represent themselves as revolutionary, it was possible for these neutral organizations to avoid oppression by the GMD authorities.

40. See Zhang Chunying, "Lun jiefang zhanzheng shiqi de disantiao zhanxian," pp. 60–66; Wang Gongan and Mao Lei, *Guogong liangdang guanxi tongshi*, pp. 853–89. The concept of the "Third Battlefront" was inspired by Zhu De's article, "Celebrating the Anniversary of the Uprising of General Gao Shuxun" (30 October 1946). Zhu stressed that these "tidal currents"—the Gao Shuxun Movement (i.e., the "uprisings" of GMD officers and soldiers), the military and civilian resistance against the GMD in CCP areas, and the "people's democratic movement" in GMD areas—were a tripartite balance of forces to defeat the GMD. See *Zhu De xuanji*, pp. 190–92. Note that Zhu used "tidal current," not "battlefront," to describe the significance of the "Gao Shuxun Movement." See ch. 5 for information about the "First Battlefront" and the "Second Battlefront." See also Feng Zhi and Dong Lixiang, "Jiefang zhanzheng shiqi Guomindang jiangling qiyi toucheng shulun," pp. 64, 67; Jiang Shaozhen, "Jiefang zhanzheng shiqi Guomindangjun qiyi shulun," pp. 216–32. Further, during the wartime period, the CCUP already operated among Gao's soldiers; see Ji Ruisan et al., "Kangzhan qijian Gongchandang zai Guo Shuxun bu de gongzuo," pp. 37–54.

41. See Ji, "Kangzhan qijian Gongchandang," pp. 59–60; Wang Yuting, "Huabei zhi shoufu yu xianluo," part II, pp. 122–23.

42. See Wang Yuting, "Hubei," part I, pp. 79–80.

43. See ibid.; Ch'i Hsi-sheng, *Nationalist China at War*, ch. 5.

44. Suzanne Pepper, *Civil War in China*, p. 8, n. 4.

45. Quoted in *TXGY*, p. 181.

46. See Pepper, *Civil War in China*, pp. 15–16, n. 25.

47. The CCUP claimed that it initiated the first strike against the collaborators in GMD cities in the immediate postwar period. On 22 August 1945, three students—two Communist and one "positive"—encouraged fellow schoolmates to take part in "celebrate victory, punish traitor" activities at St. John's University, the strongest Communist base among the schools in Shanghai. Principal Shen Silang, who collaborated with the Japanese during the wartime period, asked the Japanese military police to arrest the three students. This action resulted in an uproar within the academic community. Under pressures from the university administration, professors, students and their parents, and public opinion, Shen was forced to resign in October 1945. He was arrested as a traitor by the GMD authorities in June 1946. It took the GMD nine months to punish Shen. See Shi Weigun, *Zhongguo xuesheng yundongshi*, pp. 9–11.

48. See Pepper, *Civil War in China*, p. 16.

49. Ibid., p. 13.

50. Ibid.

51. Ibid., p. 33.

52. See Immanuel C. Y. Hsü, *The Rise of Modern China*, p. 641.

53. Zhang Guowei, *Fusheng de jingli yu jianzheng*, pp. 76–77; see also Pepper, *Civil War in China*, p. 35.

54. See *Jiefang ribao*, Yan'an, 23 Nov. 1945.

55. There existed no close alliance between the GMD and the capitalists, who did not control or significantly influence the Nanjing GMD regime from 1928 to 1937. The GMD government wanted solely to "emasculate the urban elite politically and to milk the modern sector of the economy." It did not represent any social class; it was essentially an autonomous force based on military power. See Marie-Claire Bergere, *The Golden Age of the Chinese Bourgeoisie*, pp. 272–84; Parks M. Coble, Jr.'s *The Shanghai Capitalists and the Nationalist Government*. See also Patricia Stranahan, "Strange Bedfellows," p. 26 n. 2. The GMD remained a regime based on military power during the Civil War period. And the postwar uncontrolled inflation generally undermined the business interests and prevented the emergence of a politically powerful capitalist class.

56. According to Gu Zhengwen, a Military Statistics agent who operated within the Communist military in North China and returned to serve Dai Li in Beiping in late 1945, a major reason for the rising prices was the Communist tactic of using all kinds of acceptable GMD and puppet currencies to purchase large quantities of food and commodities in Beiping (and in other GMD cities) and bringing them back to the CCP countryside. See *Sing Tao ribao*, San Francisco, 19 Sept. and 31 Oct. 1993. This kind of Communist economic and currency warfare is also discussed in Wang Qiachuan, "Gongfei panluan shiqi de 'huobian douzheng,'" pp. 92–95. Besides, Ji Chaoding, a Columbia Ph.D. in economics and the principal advisor to Kong Xiangxi (the GMD finance minister), was a CCUP member. Most of the GMD financial policies were drafted by Ji. From October 1948 to January 1949, Ji also served as the director of the Economic Department of the North China Bandit-Suppression Headquarters. Nonetheless, the Communist economic and subversive activity should not exonerate the GMD from the responsibility of economic mismanagement.

57. See ch. 5 for information about the GMD education policy and the Communist student movement.

58. See Yin Shubo, " 'Jieshou' dui Guomindang zhengquan shuaibai de yingxiang," pp. 45–48.

4

Beiping–Tianjin: Urban Environments for Political Struggle

In the Civil War period, the GMD looked impressive politically and militarily in Beiping–Tianjin. However, the cities lacked a strong economic infrastructure that might have strengthened and facilitated the GMD rule. The poor quality of the communication systems, public utilities, and general living conditions created popular resentment toward the GMD authorities. Uncontrolled inflation further alienated the urban residents, who wondered whether life would not have been better under the Japanese. This attitude favored the Communists, who characterized the GMD areas as "reactionary" or "dark."[1] Moreover, since the Communists planned to take over the cities, they had to study the urban conditions prevailing at the time and their effect on people's attitudes, and what institutions, groups, and places would have to be seized, neutralized, or occupied. In short, the CCUP had to consider the strategic question of control, use the organizational approach to develop and consolidate strength, and assign appropriate cadres to do urban work. Such political infiltration of Beiping–Tianjin by the Communists coordinated with their later military siege and attack.

Beiping

Beiping occupies a strategic position on the northern edge of the North China Plain and is a nodal point in relation to the Mongolian Plain, the Northeast China Plain, and the Lowlands of the Yellow River and Huai River.

Map 1. **The Beiping–Tianjin–Baoding Area**

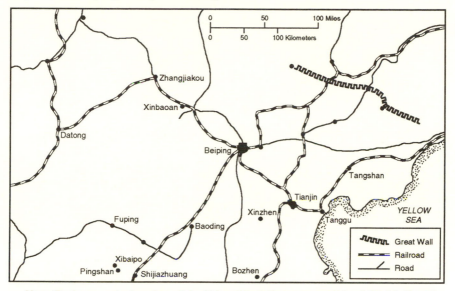

Note: Fuping was the location of the Urban Work Department of the CCP CC Shanxi–Chahar–Hebei Branch Bureau; Bozhen, the location of the Urban Work Department of the CCP Shanxi–Chahar–Hebei Central Bureau (later the CCP CC North China Bureau). Xinzhen was the location of the Urban Work Department of the CCP Central Hebei Area Party Committee.

The total built-up area of Beiping was 61.95 square kilometers. Until 1950, the city was composed of four walled portions: Forbidden City (or Palace City), Imperial City, Inner City (Northern or Manzhou City), and Outer City (Southern or Chinese City). While the walls helped the GMD's defense of the city, they also facilitated the Communist siege of Beiping. This structural phenomenon allowed time for both the Communists and Fu Zuoyi to negotiate peace in late 1948.

In mid-1948 the population of Beiping was 1.72 million. Residential areas in the city were divided into two parts: Northern City (including Western City and Eastern City) and Southern City. Western City was noted for its many aristocratic residences, schools, apartments, and inns. Most students and government employees lived in Western City, as the rent in Eastern City was much higher. The concentration of students and government personnel could be a major reason for the CCUP to establish their main facilities in Western City. Eastern City had big houses and fewer apartments, and its real estate was more highly priced than that of Western City. The colloquial phrase "Eastern Wealth and Western Nobility" referred to the high density of wealthy households in Eastern City and of officials in Western City. It was no surprise that most of the Communist underground facilities such as radio stations, printing shops, and liaison offices existed

Map 2. **Approximate Locations of Major Schools, GMD and CCUP Organizations, and Facilities in Beiping, 1947–49**

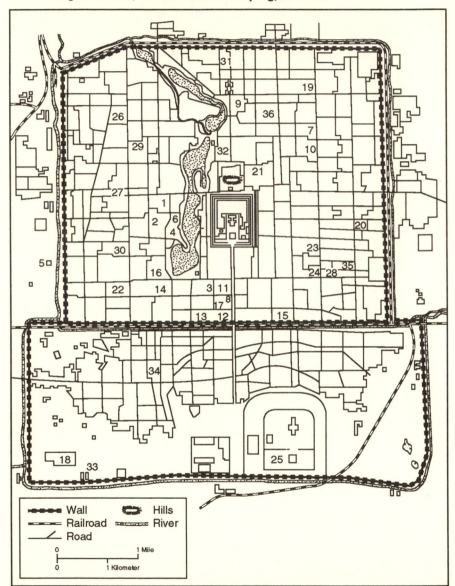

Wall   Hills
Railroad   River
Road

0   1 Mile
0   1 Kilometer

Note: These major schools and facilities are not shown on the map: Qinghua University and Yanjing University in the northwestern suburb of the walled city; the Changxindian Railcars Factory, the Shijingshan Electric Plant, the Shijingshan Iron and Steel Works, the Mentougou Coal Mine, and the Xijiao Airport in the western suburb; the Nanyuan Airport in the southern suburb; the Fengtai Railway Station in the southwestern suburb; and the two separate water supply facilities in the northeastern and eastern suburbs of Beiping.

    1 GMD Beiping Municipal Party Bureau
    2 Beiping Municipal Government
    3 Beiping Municipal Council
    4 Beiping Executive Headquarters
    5 North China Bandit-Suppression General Headquarters,
       December 1947-November 1948
    6 North China Bandit-Suppression General Headquarters,
       December 1948-January 1949
    7 Beiping Garrison Command Post
    8 GMD 5th Supply District Command Headquarters
    9 Beiping Municipal Police Bureau
   10 0760 Corps Headquarters
   11 Beiping Municipal Court and Higher Courts
   12 Beiping Municipal Automatic Water Management Bureau
   13 Northern Hebei Electric Power Company (Beiping Branch)
   14 General Post Office and Cable Service
   15 Beiping Telecommunications Bureau
   16 Central Broadcasting Bureau (Central Radio Station)
   17 Beiping-Tianjin Area Railway Bureau
   18 Central Printing Bureau
   19 70th Arsenal
   20 North China Clothing General Plant
   21 Beijing University (Main Campus)
   22 Beijing Normal College (University)
   23 Beiman Middle School
   24 Temporary Airport at Tongdan
   25 Temporary Airport at Tiantan
   26 Huatong Commercial Firm (1947)
   27 Wenchang Printing Bureau (1948)
   28 Dongtan Printing Production Cooperative (1948)
       (26-28 were the locations of the major Communist
       underground printing facilities.)
   29 Longyun Electric Materials Shop
   30 Jiujiu Photo Shop
       (29 and 30 were the bases of the Communist secret radio
       communication networks.)
31-36 Locations of secret radio stations.
       In 1948 the third station moved from 33 to 34; in late 1948 two more stations
       (35) and (36) emerged.

Sources:

   Beiping Municipal Public Works Bureau. Map of Beiping, November 1946
   Fang Ting, "Nanwang de zhandou suiye," pp. 234-50.
   Mianhuai Liu Ren tongzhi, pp. 111-16
   Zhongguo Renmin Zhengzhi Xieshang Huiyi Quanguo Weiyuanhui Wenshi Ziliao
   Yanjiu Weiyuanhui, *Ping-Jin zhenyi qinliji*, Map 10.
   Ziyuan weiyuanhui dang'an shiliao chubian. Map of Beiping

in Western City, the center of GMD and student power. The CCUP was indeed "embedded in the heart of the enemy" during the Civil War period.

Beiping did not have large slum areas. Poor residents lived in Northern City and Southern City. Dragon Beard Ditch, which lay north of Tiantan (Temple of Heaven), had been the most notoriously filthy place in Beiping. Yet the poorest laboring people—small tradesmen, blacksmiths, barrel-makers, dyers, grass-hat plaiters, sock-makers, sewing women, other handicraftspersons, rickshaw men, and haulers—had to live in this disgusting area in crowded sheds, no better than pigsties. There was no piped water, only dirty well-water. When it rained, the ditch often overflowed and flooded the sheds, and the lanes became muddy swamps. In Maoist class analysis, these semiproletariat, urban coolies, and part of the lumpen proletariat would join or support the revolution. But one shall see that they did nothing significant to threaten the GMD authorities, and the CCUP did not target these supposedly revolutionary elements.

Public transport within and outside the city was backward during the Civil War period. Streetcars first operated in Beiping in 1924. From 1946 to 1948 about eighty trams of the Beiping Street-Car Company served ten lines; the daily volume was between fifty thousand and seventy thousand passengers. On the eve of the Communist takeover, there were fifty-nine trams, and the daily volume of passengers was less than three thousand. All services halted in mid-December 1948, when the electric supply was cut off for fifty hours (15–17 December) because of the CCP-GMD battle at the electric stations outside the city. The Communists resumed the supply after establishing control of the facilities.[2] They wanted to win the goodwill of the besieged Beiping residents.

Public buses first operated in 1935. In 1946 the Beiping municipal government converted one hundred Japanese military trucks into public vehicles and established the Beiping Public Vehicle Management Bureau. In 1947 there were forty-five buses, and the bureau was reorganized as the Beiping Public Vehicle Company in November of that year. Because of mismanagement inside the company and the stealing and selling of parts for profit, only five of the remaining buses could serve two lines just before the Communist takeover.[3]

Because of low pay, poor working conditions, and constant harassment by military and police personnel who refused to pay for tickets, streetcar and public-vehicle workers should have been elements for Communist recruitment.[4] The Communist membership within the Public Vehicle Company staff is unknown. There were fifty-one CCUP members among the streetcar workers in 1947. But only four Communists remained to operate in 1948, and they were involved in several politically insignificant wildcat strikes.[5] In general, the CCUP failed to organize the workers vigorously in the "bureaucratic-capitalist" (that is, GMD-controlled) transportation companies.

Since public transportation was underdeveloped, most residents simply walked. Within the city, however, additional transportation was provided by privately operated two-wheeled or three-wheeled rickshaws. Before the Communist takeover, these vehicles served roughly about 80 percent of the passenger traffic inside Beiping; the average number was twenty thousand.[6] There is no detailed report on the Communist movement among the rickshaw men, but apparently they played an unimportant role in urban struggle.

The Beijing Railway Station was built in 1903. Since then all incoming trains have stopped at the Front Gate, where the station is located. In the late 1940s, the main railway lines were the Beiping–Hankou, Beiping–Suiyuan, Beiping–Chengde lines, and the Beiping–Shenyang line. Nationalist inefficiency and mismanagement plagued the railway system.[7] Because of the strategic importance of railways, the workers were a target of CCUP organizers. In February 1946 there were 172 Communists among the several thousand railway workers. Particularly, the Changxindian Railcars Factory (which had 192 office personnel and 2,306 workers in December 1948) was the Communist stronghold in its railway workers' movement in the Beiping area from late 1944 to late 1948. Although the CCUP organization was severely crippled by the GMD authorities in early 1948, Communist activities continued until their takeover of the factory.[8]

The city's first airport was built in Nanyuan in 1913. Before the Communist takeover, three commercial airlines operated: China Airlines and Central Airlines served Shanghai–Beiping; Euro-Asia Airlines served Guangzhou–Beiping. The GMD also built a military airport at Xijiao (Western Suburb). Before their surrender, the GMD authorities built two temporary airfields in Dongdan and Tiantan, as the other two airports were under Communist artillery attack. The extent of CCUP activities among airport workers is not clear.

Beijing's first water system began operating in 1910. The water supply facility was located in the northeastern suburb, where the Sun River was the main source. Before the Communist takeover, the GMD established another water facility in the eastern suburb. Both systems served 640,000 people—mostly the wealthy in the east and north sections of Beiping, about one-third of the population.[9] The rest of the residents had to put up with dirty well-water. Whether the Communists infiltrated the Beiping Municipal Automatic Water Management Bureau is also unclear.

After the Japanese surrender, the GMD took over all the electrical companies in Beiping, and on 1 March 1946 it established the Northern Hebei Electric Power Company with headquarters in Beiping. In August they started operating the largest electric installation in North China, the Shijingshan Electric Plant (a leftover from the Japanese) in the western suburb of Beiping. There were only 116,000 customers in late 1947, however. More than half of the power supply was used by the GMD political and military elite; factories and civilians received little power.[10]

Electricity was expensive. One unit cost 0.22 Chinese dollar before the war with Japan. In late 1947 it was Ch $4,100; in August 1948, Ch $15,000 per unit![11] These figures demonstrated the seriousness of the GMD inflation in Beiping and other Chinese cities. To complicate matters, certain privileged authorities either refused to pay the bills or stole electricity. Management problems, outdated equipment, low-level technology, and frequent stoppage of electric power in 1947–48 prompted some residents to call the Northern Hebei Electric Power Company the "Darkness Company," and its general manager, the "King of Darkness." The CCUP membership inside this company is unclear, but they convinced many employees to stay put for "liberation" and to help preserve the company records. Communist agents, however, were active in the Shijingshan Electric Plant. There were twelve CCUP members at this plant on the eve of the Communist takeover.[12]

During the Civil War period, the GMD Beiping Postal Administration Management Bureau was also in trouble. In late 1946 the GMD launched a "reform the postal administration" movement in the cities. It soon failed because of mismanagement and rampant inflation. On 14 September 1945, the charge for one character in the cable service was twenty dollars. On 21 July 1948, one character cost Ch $40,000! The urban residents were frustrated with the expensive and fluctuating charges. More important, since the GMD military and political authorities frequently used the postal and especially the cable service, the CCUP targeted the workers in the bureau. In late 1948 there were forty-four Communists.[13]

The inefficiency of the public utilities and their vulnerability to breakdown indicated the incompetence of the GMD authorities. These problems angered the residents because they expected a better life and administration of public services after the Japanese surrender. The Communists would exploit such popular indignation to serve their political interests. The CCUP also understood the strategic importance of the public utilities.

Beiping was mainly a consumer city up to 1949. What little industry it had was poorly equipped and used outdated technology. The quality of the industrial products was low and costs were high. A typical example was the Shijingshan Iron and Steel Works, the largest metallurgical industry in Beiping. Although the GMD newspapers claimed that the factory was the only source of iron production for China, it could not produce any pig iron in 1946–47. When it finally did start production in January 1948, the yield was only twenty tons per day. Before the Communist takeover, the production never exceeded one hundred tons daily. Even the GMD *Huabei ribao* inquired how the small quantity of iron produced by the works could serve the whole of China. And the works never produced a single piece of steel.[14]

Nevertheless, the Shijingshan Iron and Steel Works was a major industrial plant in a strategic location. While there were only 2,348 workers at most in 1948 (36,000 in early 1943), the GMD authorities assigned 1,500 troops to protect the installation and they recruited 530 workers (many technicians and supervisors) to be GMD party members. Based on the working-class ideology and the strategic value of the works, the CCUP had to be active in this plant, although there may have been fewer than twenty agents in late 1948.[15]

During the Civil War period, the United Logistical Affairs General Headquarters of the GMD Ministry of Defense controlled the 70th Arsenal in Beiping. Since it was the largest arsenal in North China and served the GMD armies in the region, the CCUP targeted the workers there. Seven Communists operated in the arsenal in the fall of 1948.[16]

The coal industry of the Beiping area before the Communist takeover was a tragedy. Exploitation, extortion, forced labor, child labor, and high job mortality illustrated the miserable conditions. In the Beiping–Tianjin area, the Mentougou Coal Mine in the western mining district of Beiping was the main source of coal. The Communists established a work committee as early as 1930. There were ninety CCUP members before the Communist takeover. From 1945 to 1949 the underground Communists launched labor struggles against the GMD.[17]

The textile industry in Beijing has had a long history. It started in the Han Dynasty, and has continued until the present. In the late 1940s the GMD Ministry of Military Administration operated an eleven-branch military supplies and clothing industry in North China with less than ten thousand employees, 3,200 spindles, and sixty looms. The industry produced only coarse army blankets and poor-quality serge. In Beiping the CCUP was active in several branches of the industry that employed 4,359 persons. By December 1948 the Party had recruited eleven members in the Qinghe Woolen Mill, a major branch factory. In early 1949 the CCUP membership in the branches was ninety-seven.[18]

Private textile industry in Beiping fared worse. Under the pressures of inflation and high costs, most of the textile factories producing dye, knitwear, wool, and cotton halted production during 1947–48. In terms of the returns on investments, in those days textile production was not as profitable as commerce or speculation. When the Communists occupied Beiping, there were only 5,457 workers in the private textile industry.[19] The Communist activity among them is unclear.

In the Civil War period, the GMD established a number of newspapers in Beiping. The two most important ones were *Huabei ribao*, the GMD official newspaper, and *Pingming ribao* (Fair and bright daily), the voice of the North China Bandit-Suppression Headquarters. The CCUP was most successful in infiltrating the latter.[20]

During the GMD–CCP peace negotiations in the spring of 1946, the Communists set up an official newspaper in Beiping called *Jiefang* (Liberation), which was published every two or three days. After printing thirty-seven issues, the newspaper stopped publication when the GMD authorities suppressed it on 29 May 1946. Nevertheless, the Communists maintained their underground printing facilities in the city to issue propaganda against the GMD.[21]

Obviously, the news media were valuable in the Communist struggle for political-military information and for popular and public opinion. On the other hand, the inability of the GMD to prevent Communist infiltration of its official news organizations, and the toleration of the publication of Communist (and left-wing) newspapers (and journals) in GMD cities (until early 1947) showed Nationalist weaknesses in the mass-media front.

Nevertheless, the GMD-controlled printing facilities had better machinery, but because of mismanagement and inefficiency, the business was poor and many workers were laid off. According to a survey made in February 1949, there were 280 printing houses in Beiping and a total of 2,969 employees in both public and private sectors.[22] While it was important to infiltrate the Nationalist printing facility, the Communists admitted that there was no revolutionary activity within the GMD's Central Printing Bureau in Beiping.[23]

From September 1945 to late 1948, other kinds of light industry also suffered. For the first two years, the arrival of GMD officials and American troops stimulated the consumer market and thus light industry too. For instance, there was an increase in match factories, leather shops, wineries, and cigarette-rolling plants. Flour mills also flourished for a short time. However, after 1947 Beiping light industry declined drastically. The withdrawal of American troops, the influx of cheaper imported goods, and, above all, the emerging hyperinflation significantly lowered the production in light industry. On the eve of the Communist takeover, only twenty-six thousand people worked in light industry in Beiping.[24]

Industry in suburban Beiping also was antiquated. Production of bricks, shoes, and other items depended on outdated equipment and manual labor. The total number of workers in factories and home industries was around ten thousand.[25] The Communist activities among the private light industries in the Beiping area are unknown.

During the Civil War period, twenty-six public and private banking institutions and two foreign banks operated in Beiping. In the last days of the GMD rule in the city, these institutions, especially those of the GMD, were in a chaotic state as a result of the financial collapse and hyperinflation of GMD China. It seems that the CCUP did not exert effort within the banking system. But just before the Communist takeover, the CCUP tried hard to preserve the banking facilities.

Above all, during 1947–48 there were 153,472 students in Beiping, including 18,332 in colleges and universities and 39,524 in secondary schools.[26] The best-known educational institution was, of course, Beijing University (Beida), which has been in the vanguard of democratic and revolutionary movements throughout modern Chinese history. Qinghua University (Qingda) also enjoyed high status in the Chinese revolution. These two universities and Yanjing University (Yanda) were the core of the Communist student movement in the city in the 1940s. The three universities can be regarded as the pillars of the Communist student movement, not only in Beiping but in North China.

About one-third of all the college students in Beiping were enrolled at Beida, Qingda, and Yanda. At Beida, there were 3,420 students in the 1946–47 academic year, 3,535 in 1947–48, and 2,924 in 1948–49. At Qingda, there were 2,300 students in 1946–47. At Yanda, there were 901 students in late 1947.[27]

Further, the headquarters and the faculties of arts, law, and sciences of Beida were located in the Santan district, the central area of Northern City, within Beiping. It was no surprise that the CCUP within these faculties was most active in its struggles against the GMD authorities.[28] The location of Beida in the central district of Beiping, and of Qingda and Yanda in the northwestern suburb of the walled city aptly indicated the internal-external coordination of the Communist student movement.

Uncontrolled inflation had a serious impact upon the students. For example, in April 1947 a Beida student's scholarship was worth Ch $144,000, but food alone for one academic year cost Ch $160,000–170,000. In order to save money, on 5 May 1947, Beida students had to give up eating meat at the school cafeteria. In April 1948 the highest salary for a professor was only Ch $5 million; the lowest one got Ch $3.8 million. As for the nonadministrative staff, their highest pay was Ch $1.5 million; Ch $1.15 million was the lowest. How could the faculty and staff survive well when the cost of two catties of millet per day for one month was Ch $1.4 million?[29] Such miserable living conditions facilitated the CCUP's anti-GMD activities on school campuses. The same situation occurred in Tianjin.

For ideological and political reasons the Chinese Communists tended to paint the worst possible picture of the GMD cities. But when the Communists wanted to capture Beiping peacefully, they shifted to a "bright" picture of widening support and emphasized the cultural richness of Beiping. Of course, few Chinese would dispute the pre-1949 cultural status of the city, although novels such as Lao She's *Rickshaw* (1937) depicted the corruption and injustice of Beijing society. Among the foreigners, John Blofeld's *City of Lingering Splendour* (1989), David Kidd's *Peking Story* (1988), and George N. Kate's *The Years That Were Fat* (1988) are good examples to demonstrate the general appreciation of and nostalgia for a way of life long vanished because of the Communist "liberation." Above all, when the Communists besieged Beiping and encouraged Fu Zuoyi to launch an "uprising," they stressed that his cooperation would contribute tremendously to the Chinese people because it would avert the destruction of a preeminent cultural city.

CCUP Organizations in Beiping

The major component of the CCUP in Beiping was the Five Work Committees under the leadership of the Urban Work Department of the CCP Shanxi–Chahar–Hebei Central Bureau.[30] The Five Work Committees were established one by one in 1945–46. They were under the authority of a Beiping City Work Committee from September 1945 to October 1946. Afterward, the Urban Work Department abolished the City Work Committee and controlled the Committees directly. In August 1946, the Urban Work Department also incorporated the Beiping Work Committee of the CCP Central Hebei Area Party Committee; the latter had focused its work on students and female workers.[31] The director of this Urban Work Department, Liu Ren, was the most important Communist for underground activities in Beiping and, to a certain degree, in Tianjin.

The Five Work Committees of the CCUP reflected an acute understanding of the political-military and socioeconomic conditions of Beiping. The Student Work Committee (*Xuesheng gongzuo weiyuanhui*), from October 1945 to January 1949, was the leader; by early 1948 it had set up a University Work Committee (November 1947), a Middle School Work Committee (June 1947), a Professional Youths Work Committee, and a Middle and Primary School Teachers Committee (July 1947). This Student Committee indicated the Communists' recognition of the paramount importance of Chinese youth and the intelligentsia rather than the industrial workers in urban political struggle. The relatively large student population in Beiping also rendered it necessary to work in the academic community. The Student Committee had the largest number of Party members, many of them from Beida and Qingda.

Two groups of Communists worked among the students. The Northern Group was controlled by the Urban Work Department of the Shanxi–Chahar–Hebei Central Bureau, later the North China Bureau. The Southern Group was under the leadership of the Urban Work Department of the CCP CC Southern Bureau, later under the control of the CCP CC Shanghai Bureau (April 1946–October 1949).[32] The Southern Group Party members originally studied at Southwest Associated University in Kunming and at Yanda in Chengdu during the wartime period. These CCUP members returned with their schools to Beiping in the summer and fall of 1946 and continued to study and "work" at Beida, Qingda, Yanda, and other institutions of higher education. In late 1947 these Communists established the Beiping–Tianjin Student Work Committee. (Because of the Southern Bureau's policy of "changing work site but not party affiliation," the Southern Group members were separated from the Northern Group.) In November 1948 these two groups were united under the leadership of the Urban Work Department of the North China Bureau. The combined Student Work Committee controlled two major Communist front organizations in Beiping: the Northern Group's Democratic Youth League (Minzhu Qingnian Lianmeng or *minlian*, 1947–49) and the Southern Group's Democratic Youth Alliance (Minzhu Qingnian Tongmeng or *minqing*, 1945–49).[33] In short, the Student Work Committee of the CCUP was the most powerful organization for open and secret work in Beiping.

The Worker Work Committee (*Gongren gongzuo weiyuanhui*) (October 1945–November 1947) was considerably less important than the Student Work Committee. Until late 1947, the Worker Committee operated in two ways. In the suburbs it established the Mentougou Area Work Committee (abolished in November 1946) and the Shijingshan Area Work Committee. Within the walled city the Committee was in charge of a number of district work committees. In March 1946 it set up three work groups: Factory, Municipal Administration, and Handicraft.

In late 1947 Liu Ren and others reported to Liu Shaoqi on the CCUP work in Beiping. Liu Shaoqi stressed that the municipal administration workers were the main force. The CCUP must concentrate its activity among the municipal administration workers, especially those in telecommunications systems, so as to coordinate with the future Communist military assault from without. Because of this instruction from Liu Shaoqi, the Worker Work Committee was reorganized as the Municipal Administration Worker Work Committee (*Shizheng gongren gongzuo weiyuanhui*) (December 1947–January 1949). This Committee sent Party members to work in four areas: (1) mail service and telecommunications (telephone service, cable service, broadcasting, and radio stations); (2) streetcars, public buses, and water supply; (3) military factories; (4) clothing factories.[34]

The CCUP realized the strategic importance of railways and established the Railway Worker Work Committee (*Tielu gongren gongzuo weiyuanhui*) (October 1945–January 1949). This Committee included the Beiping City Inner District Railway Work Committee (or the Front Gate Work Committee), the Changxindian Railway Work Committee, the Nankou Railway Work Committee, and the Fengtai–Langfang Section Railway Work Committee outside the walled city. In June 1946 the Urban Work Department of the Shanxi–Chahar–Hebei Central Bureau decided to shift the focus from the outside to the inside and abolished the work committees in Nankou and Changxindian. Railway and especially municipal administration workers, not industrial ones, were the focus of the CCUP operations among urban workers.[35]

The Commoner Work Committee (*Pingmin gongzuo weiyuanhui*) (October 1945–January 1949) concentrated its activities among the lower classes in the city. From November 1946 to December 1947, there were two separate committees: the Inner City District Committee and the Outer City District Committee. In late 1947 the Urban Work Department of the Shanxi–Chahar–Hebei Central Bureau ordered them to merge into a new Commoner Work Committee. The Urban Work Department also discovered that it was better to carry out work according to professions and trades rather than GMD districts (seven inside the city, five outside). New committees were set up to work among ordinary residents and the people employed in these categories: (1) bathhouses; (2) oil and salt shops; (3) the weaving trade; (4) man-powered three-wheeled rickshaws; (5) construction trades; (6) carpet trade; (7) vegetable plantations in the suburbs. Some Communist cadres were assigned to work among teachers, the military, the military and municipal police,[36] and the upper social classes. The Commoner Work Committee was most active among the workers in bathhouses and oil and salt shops.[37]

The Culture Work Committee (*Wenhua gongzuo weiyuanhui*) (June 1946–July 1947) was the last one among the Five Committees to start work in Beiping. In July 1947 it was incorporated into the Student Work Committee. The scope of activities of the Culture Work Committee included: (1) newspaper offices, news agencies, and the United States Information Service; (2) publishing houses and bookstores; (3) literary arts—theatrical groups and personalities; (4) united-front work with certain upper-level "democratic personalities."[38]

These Five Work Committees of the Urban Work Department of the Shanxi–Chahar–Hebei Central Bureau (later the North China Bureau) operated in Beiping, the "heart of the enemy" in North China. The main underground work of the Five Committees (which had no direct contact with each other for security reasons until late 1948) was strengthened by five secret radio stations and complemented by three major Communist secret-service systems in the Beiping–Tianjin area, including one controlled by the Urban Work Department of the same bureau.[39]

By late 1948 the total CCUP membership in Beiping was 3,376. Among these members, students comprised 41.28 percent (1,394); workers, 27.49 percent (928); peasants, 16.17 percent (546); professionals, intellectuals, and others, 15.06 percent (508). The Urban Work Department of the North China Bureau controlled 2,862 Party members (84.77 percent of total CCUP membership) and 5,000 Democratic Youth League and Democratic Youth Alliance members. The Student Work Committee and the Culture Committee controlled 1,470 members (51.36 percent of the membership of the Urban Work Department) and more than 4,000 Democratic Youth League and Democratic Youth Alliance members. The Municipal Administration Committee controlled 308 members (10.76 percent), the Railway Committee 201 members (7.0 percent), the Commoner Committee 497 members (17.36 percent); 386 members (13.52 percent) were under other kinds of organizational control. [40]

In December 1948 the CCUP established the Beiping Liberation Command Headquarters, led by the members of the combined Student Work Committee.[41] In early January 1949 this Headquarters began to cooperate with the CCP CC Beiping City Committee (established on 13 December 1948 and located in Liang Village outside Beiping), the highest Communist organization for the "liberation" work of Beiping.[42]

In summary, as Beiping was mainly a consumer city, and the number of industrial workers was relatively small, the Communist activity among them was limited. In the Communist struggle for the city, the students were far more important as an asset than were Beiping's workers. Beiping was a major center of higher education and the student population was large, and it was imperative for the Communists to win over the intelligentsia and the students. In fact, the Communist student movement was more significant than its labor movement. Even a leading member (Lu Yu) of the Municipal Administration Work Committee admitted that the student movement was more vigorous and dynamic than the labor movement because there were only about seventy thousand industrial workers in Beiping.[43] (There were at least twice as many students in Beiping.) Further, since "bureaucratic capitalism" was much involved in heavy and light industries, the CCUP had to focus its work on the GMD industrial plants, not the private ones, for economic and political reasons. In other words, the CCUP had to target Mao Zedong's category of industrial proletariat—railway, mining, and textile workers—who served in the enterprises related to "bureaucratic capitalism." By early 1948, among the laborers, municipal workers had become the key target for the CCUP to grasp for achieving political-military control.

Tianjin

Tianjin is situated at the northeastern part of the North China Plain. To its east is the Gulf of Bohai and to the north are hills; the southwest parts of the city blend into plains. Tianjin is the strategic gateway not only to Beijing but to all of North China. During the Civil War, Tianjin was more populous than Beiping; in mid-1948 its population was 1.77 million. Above all, Tianjin was the cardinal economic center and the largest port of North China.

A characteristic feature of the economic development of Tianjin was its "treaty port" status before 1949. At the end of the nineteenth century, as a result of the growth of foreign trade, modern industrial enterprises appeared in Tianjin. These light industries were engaged mainly in the processing of raw materials for export, and they met the needs of the city itself and of North China. Until the war with Japan, more than half of the industrial enterprises in Tianjin were in the hands of foreigners. Nevertheless, as a whole, prior to the Communist takeover, Tianjin was mainly a commercial and consumer city, secondarily an industrial one. In 1947 there were 229,833 industrial and handicraft workers, and 283,311 employees in the commercial sector.[44]

Politically speaking, Tianjin was beset by unrest, chaos, and war until 1949. As for the CCP, the city was a major center of open and underground activities from 1912 to 1949. Its proximity to Beijing, its economic importance, and its large proletarian class made Tianjin a unique place in the urban component of the Chinese Communist movement.

Tianjin had been a walled city. The wall was torn down after the antiforeign Boxer Movement of 1900–1901, but its outlines were preserved. The total built-up area of Tianjin at the time of Communist conquest was 61 square kilometers, of which the former foreign concessions (English, French, American, German, Italian, Japanese, Austrian, Belgian, and Russian "leased territories") comprised almost one-fourth. In terms of built-up areas, Tianjin was almost as large as Beiping. The territory of Tianjin formed a triangle, stretched out from the northwest to the southeast down the Hai River. The seat of GMD political and military authorities was located in the former English and French concessions by the Hai River. These areas were the focus of Communist attention.

The regions of the city differed greatly from each other in terms of buildings, roads and streets, public utilities, sanitary conditions, and the like. A dense population, small houses, and narrow, dirty streets distinguished the northeastern suburb along the banks of the Jinzhong River, the region near the Chilong River behind the South Gate of the Old City (before 1901), and the southwestern part

Map 3. Approximate Locations of Major Schools, GMD and CCUP Organizations, and Facilities in Tianjin, 1947–49

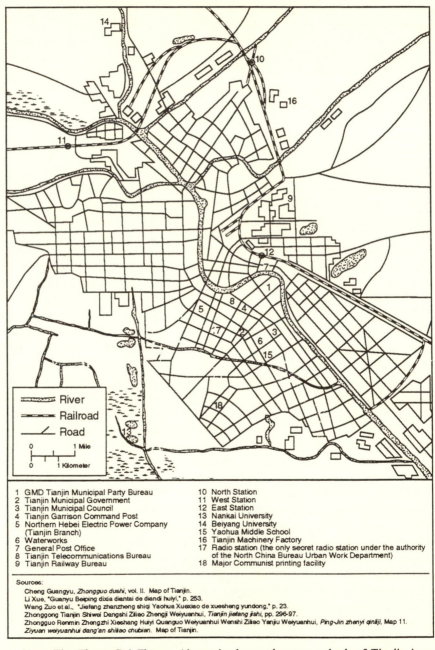

	River
	Railroad
	Road

0   1 Mile

0   1 Kilometer

1 GMD Tianjin Municipal Party Bureau	10 North Station
2 Tianjin Municipal Government	11 West Station
3 Tianjin Municipal Council	12 East Station
4 Tianjin Garrison Command Post	13 Nankai University
5 Northern Hebei Electric Power Company	14 Beiyang University
(Tianjin Branch)	15 Yaohua Middle School
6 Waterworks	16 Tianjin Machinery Factory
7 General Post Office	17 Radio station (the only secret radio station under the authority
8 Tianjin Telecommunications Bureau	of the North China Bureau Urban Work Department)
9 Tianjin Railway Bureau	18 Major Communist printing facility

Sources:

Cheng Guangyu, *Zhongguo dushi*, vol. II. Map of Tianjin.
Li Xue, "Guanyu Beiping dixia diantai de diandi huiyi," p. 253.
Wang Zuo et al., "Jiefang zhanzheng shiqi Yaohua Xuexiao de xuesheng yundong," p. 23.
Zhonggong Tianjin Shiwei Dangshi Ziliao Zhengji Weiyuanhui, *Tianjin jiefang jishi*, pp. 296-97.
Zhongguo Renmin Zhengzhi Xieshang Huiyi Quanguo Weiyuanhui Wenshi Ziliao Yanjiu Weiyuanhui, *Ping-Jin zhanyi qinliji*, Map 11.
Ziyuan weiyuanhui dang'an shiliao chubian. Map of Tianjin.

Note: The Zhang Gui Zhuang Airport in the southeastern suburb of Tianjin is not shown on the map.

of the city near the Nankai pond. There were canals but little drinkable water, and sanitary conditions were terrible. On the other hand, the leased territories were picturesque residential districts with large, comfortable, and beautiful houses, wide streets, good sanitary conditions, and sparse population.

The rivers and waterways in the Tianjin area affected the way the Nationalist defenders built their fortresses and bunkers.[45] In the Tanggu district, in late 1948, the Defense Command Post was on a warship, a logical choice since Tanggu was a seaport and the GMD could escape by sea. However, the location of the GMD command on a warship ready for a fast getaway was a telling metaphor for the lack of Nationalist anchorage in local society and confidence in the war against the Communists.

Before Communist conquest the workers of Tianjin lived in brick, lime, or earthen dwellings in the poor districts. The underclass in the city fared even worse; they lived in huts consisting of a wood frame covered with mud and grass, or in ramshackle lean-tos of reed mats. These miserable huts sometimes were built in graveyards.[46] Tianjin workers and the lumpen proletariat were too deeply sunk in poverty to play a big role in urban political struggle.

As in Beiping, public transport in Tianjin was underdeveloped. From 1946 to 1949 the Tianjin Municipal Public Utilities Bureau operated only two hundred streetcars and buses, serving seventeen lines. In late 1948 the situation grew worse because of the economic conditions; there were only eight lines with twenty-five vehicles. The Communist activities among the public-vehicle workers are unclear. Two-wheeled and three-wheeled rickshaws augmented the public transportation service, but only a few residents could afford these expensive cycles. The CCUP failed to mention anything significant about its work among the rickshaw men.

Being the commercial center and main port of North China, Tianjin boasted a large number of transport coolies, the oldest urban sector of the Tianjin working class. These transport workers were enmeshed in a traditional structure and a set of loyalties that effectively blocked their participation in the making of a class-conscious labor force.[47] Just before the Communist conquest, Tianjin had 227 separate transport guilds, and 3,032 bosses. There were 901 big bosses; 422 were members of the Green Gang (qingbang, a secret society); 301 joined the GMD and the Youth Corps, and 154 had connections with the Military Statistics.[48] As the GMD had close relations with the qingbang and the Red Gang (hongbang, another major secret society among the transport coolies), it practically dominated the transport industry. The CCUP could not mobilize this urban sector of workers.

Tianjin was a center of railway transportation, the main railroad being the Tianjin–Pukou line. There were three stations inside the city: the West, the Central (the North), and the East. Unlike the CCUP in Beiping, the Tianjin CCUP had no specific railway committee to deal with the workers, although railways were of strategic importance.

Tianjin has long been a sea and river port. Before the Communist conquest the important Xingang Harbor was not navigable. Situated in the southeastern part of

Tianjin is the Tanggu district. The Japanese planned to construct a new port there during their occupation, but they could not finish the project. The GMD did not maintain the Japanese installations, and in January 1949 they were demolished by the retreating GMD troops. There was only one Communist operating underground in the Xingang Harbor Engineering Bureau. He did not sabotage the Tanggu port; on the contrary, he helped preserve the remaining installations.[49]

The only airport in Tianjin during the Civil War period was located at Zhang Gui Zhuang, built in 1941 by the Japanese. It is not known whether the Communists infiltrated the airport authority. Water supply service started in 1898. Prior to the Communist conquest the city water pipes served only 40 percent of the residents. About half a million poor workers had to use the bad-smelling well-water or the unpurified water of the rivers, reservoirs, and canals.[50] The CCUP activities against the water supply authority are unclear. As in Beiping, electric power in Tianjin was controlled by the Northern Hebei Electric Power Company, the "Darkness Company." Communist interference with the company is not clear.

Before the Communist conquest, the industry of Tianjin, which had a long history of development, occupied an important place in GMD China. Nevertheless, the importance of industry in the economy of the city in the Civil War period was less than that of foreign and domestic trade. As stated before, Tianjin was more a commercial than an industrial society. The structure of Tianjin's industry was inefficient: Small enterprises dominated the economy; equipment was mostly obsolete; and manufacturing methods were antiquated. After the Japanese surrender, the GMD seized about 270 puppet and Japanese industrial enterprises and put more than seventy major ones under bureaucratic control.[51] In this way the GMD dominated and manipulated the bulk of Tianjin industry.

The cotton industry, which was the main industrial strength of Tianjin, was completely dependent on the United States for necessary raw materials. The shortage of raw materials as well as the flood of American goods disrupted the textile, milling, tobacco, match, and other enterprises. While the CCUP operated in various cotton mills, it failed to launch significant labor struggles against the authorities.

Because of the importance of the cultural front, the Communists were certainly active in the news and printing industry. The CCUP infiltrated particularly *Dagong bao* (controlled by the GMD Political Study Clique), *Yishi bao*, *Xinsheng wanbao* (New life evening news; publisher was a Christian), and *Tianjin ribao* (Tianjin daily).[52] They also maintained secret printing facilities for propaganda use against the GMD authorities.

Heavy industry in Tianjin also suffered during the Civil War. The machine-construction enterprises were not able to do more than repair the GMD military vehicles and could not carry out other production. The electrotechnical plants were engaged only in the assembling of receiving sets with components from the United States. The steel casting and steel rolling plants frequently stood idle. From August 1945 to January 1949, the light and heavy industries of Tianjin were unstable. The year 1947 was the best in industrial production; in late 1948, however, industrial production dropped significantly as a result of the Civil War and inflation. Prior to the Communist conquest, Tianjin industry was at a standstill.

In short, although Tianjin was the second most important industrial city in China, it was very limited in technology and production knowledge. Major machinery was almost exclusively imported from abroad; foreigners controlled technological information. In addition, power equipment was inadequate. Tianjin industry thus could not produce independently. Small enterprises occupied the major part of Tianjin industry. Hand labor predominated, technology was at a low level, and management was backward.[53]

Nevertheless, given the numerous workers in Tianjin who led very difficult lives, one might suppose that the Communists would have developed a powerful political force among them. In reality, industrial workers played virtually only a minor role in the political fate of Tianjin.[54] As in Beiping, the Communist labor movement in Tianjin was insignificant. The student movement was far more important, although the Communist student committee was not the largest organization.

When Tianjin was conquered by the Communists, there were eleven institutions of higher education with 5,500 students and 750 instructors; forty-nine middle schools with 23,822 students and 1,001 teachers; 2,293 primary schools with 288,323 pupils and 6,937 teachers.[55] Nankai and Beiyang were the top universities and thus the center of Communist activities. In January 1947 Nankai, which owned buildings inside and outside the city, had 604 students. There were 1,215 students in 1947–48 and 1,225 students in 1948–49. At Beiyang, there were 1,783 students in 1946–47 and 1,167 in 1947–48.[56] In late 1948 Nankai and Beiyang students comprised about 45 percent of all the college students in the city. Further, since there were more middle school students than college students in Tianjin (the ratio was 5 to 1; in Beiping it was 2 to 1), the CCUP activity among the middle schools in the city was particularly strong. Among the middle schools, Yaohua seemed to be the dominant Communist base.[57]

Rampant inflation had a serious and even fatal impact upon Tianjin's school campuses. For instance, in the fall of 1948, the cost of one catty of millet per day for one month was Ch $6 million. One medical professor at Nankai University earned only Ch $8 million per month. Both he and his wife committed suicide because they could not take care of their six children. Such an incident further damaged the reputation of the GMD and facilitated the CCP's anti-GMD propaganda.[58]

Prior to the Communist conquest there existed thirty-eight public and private banks and six foreign ones. As in Beiping, hyperinflation either ruined or crippled these financial institutions. The CCUP was more interested in taking them over, and had no need for sabotage.

CCUP Organizations in Tianjin

From 1945 up to the summer of 1948, the main part of the CCUP in Tianjin was under the control of the CCP Jizhong (Central Hebei) Area Party Committee. On

28 August 1945, the Party Committee established the CCP Tianjin Work Committee (it was called the Tianjin Liberation Committee in public), which united the underground organizations from other systems. On 1 September 1945, the Work Committee established four branch committees, a Worker Work Committee, and a Student Work Committee, which controlled a Women's Work Committee. The Tianjin Work Committee also established a major youth organization—the Tianjin Democratic Youth Association.[59]

In January 1946 the branch committees were abolished and replaced by four district committees; later on, the six committees were all abolished. Two new committees emerged, the Worker Movement and Student Movement Committees. In April 1946 the Tianjin Work Committee was reorganized as the Tianjin City Committee, which was in charge of four systems: labor movement (in 1947 there were 450 CCUP members in the railways, wharfs, and textile, clothing, and shoe trades), student movement, urban residents (in 1947 there were 777 CCUP members among shop assistants, coolies, hawkers, rickshaw men, small tradesmen, and workers in bathhouses, hotels, and hospitals), and the (upper) united front. Two months later the City Committee was renamed the Tianjin Work Committee. In March 1947 this Committee was abolished; the activities inside Tianjin were then directly controlled by the Urban Work Department of the Jizhong Area Party Committee. In May 1947 the Work Department established a Professional Youth Work Committee under a reorganized Student Work Committee. In late 1947 the Urban Work Department controlled 1,340 Party members in Tianjin.[60]

In January 1948 this Work Department was merged into the Urban Work Department of the Shanxi–Chahar–Hebei Bureau. On 21 May 1948, the Urban Work Department of the North China Bureau was in control of the activities in Tianjin. In November 1948, in accordance with the order from the CCP CC, the North China Bureau established the CCP Tianjin Work Committee and combined all the local underground Party organizations with the Beiping–Tianjin Work Committee (its Student Committee was the key organization) under the authority of the CCP CC Shanghai Bureau. The open title of the Tianjin Work Committee was "Welcome Tianjin's Liberation Action Committee"; its leading cadres came from the former Southern Group CCUP, which had been most active in youth work.[61] This Tianjin Work Committee was composed of the Municipal Administration and Bank Committee, Enterprise Committee, and School Committee. The focuses of Party work were the students, labor, and the united front. [62]

As in Beiping, students and intellectuals played the dominant role in the Communist underground struggle. While their student work committee was not the largest organization in terms of Party membership, it infiltrated Nankai and Beiyang universities, Yaohua Middle School, and others. In the fall of 1946, the Northern and Southern groups (and their Democratic Youth League and Democratic Youth Alliance) of the Beiping Student Work Committee started work among the students and other youths in Tianjin.[63] In November 1948 the Urban

Work Department of the North China Bureau combined the Student Work Committees of Beiping and Tianjin and put the Southern Group members directly under its supervision. It must be emphasized that this merging of the Student Committees gave rise to the formation of the CCP Tianjin Work Committee. By late 1948, this Work Committee controlled 1,030 Party members. The CCUP student committee controlled more than eighty Party members and more than three hundred Democratic Youth Alliance members. On 15 January 1949, the total CCUP membership was 1,564.[64]

In summary, while there were more industrial workers in Tianjin than in Beiping, the Communist influence among them was generally insignificant in the urban struggle against the GMD authorities. Students remained the focus of Communist activity in Tianjin. Further, as in Beiping, the GMD public utilities in Tianjin were inefficient and vulnerable to breakdown. Moreover, although the CCUP's united-front work among the capitalists and other upper-level social elements was quite effective, it failed to convince General Chen Changjie to launch an "uprising." The CCP had to take over the city by force.

Summary

During the Civil War period, the geographical environment and socioeconomics of Beiping–Tianjin influenced the policy and activity of the GMD and the CCUP. The poor economic infrastructure infuriated the urban residents and hampered the building of a strong relationship between the GMD and the local societies. Moreover, although the GMD had an impressive political-military structure with many members and branches, it was factionalized and its power diffused. The CCUP was much smaller and forced to work in secret but gradually accumulated strength and infiltrated some important sectors of the population. The Communist work committees in Beiping–Tianjin also showed their strategic calculation of control and the organizational approach to achieve political-military goals. All available information points to the fact that the Communists did not focus their activities on the proletarian workers, but rather on the large student populations in both Beiping and Tianjin.[65] This focus enabled the Communists, beginning in 1945, to gear up for what turned out to be a decisive struggle "in the heart of the enemy."

Notes

1. For example, the Communists used "local folk music" to smear the GMD rule in Beiping during its last days. "There are many secret-service men, many disorganized soldiers, many armed bandits, many thieves and many sellers of silver dollars [by then no one accepted the GMD paper currency]" (*tewu duo, sanbing youyong duo, qiangfei duo, xiaotou duo, yinyuan fanzi duo*). See *Renmin ribao* (overseas ed.), 4 May 1992.
2. See Yang Hongyun and Zhao Yunqiu, *Beijing jingji shihua*, pp. 131–33; Beijingshi Dang'anguan and Zhongguo Renmin Daxue Danganxi Wenxian Bianzuanxue Jiaoyanshi, *Beijing dianche gongsi dang'an shiliao*, pp. 15–17, 19.

3. See Beijingshi Dang'anguan, *Beijing dianche gongsi*, pp. 8, 567; Yang and Zhao, *Beijing*, p. 133; Hou Renzhi and Jin Tao, *Beijing shihua*, p. 249.

4. See Beijingshi Dang'anguan and Zhonggong Renmin Daxue Danganxi Wenxian Bianzuanxue Jiaoyanshi, *Beijing dianche*, pp. 30–31, 38–40.

5. See ibid., pp. 39–40, 547–54, 567; *BGJC*, p. 461.

6. Yang and Zhao, *Beijing*, p. 133.

7. See ibid., p. 129; Guofangbu Zhande Zhengwuju, *Beipingshi diqu yanjiu*, pp. 22–24.

8. See Changxindian Jiche Cheliang Gongchang Changshi, *Beifang de hongxing*, pp. 315–16, 326–29; Guo Ruokai, "Changxindian jichang jiefang qianhou," pp. 42–43; *BGJC*, p. 442.

9. Yang and Zhao, *Beijing*, pp. 8–9; see also *Beijing zilaishui gongsi*, p. 14.

10. See Zhongguo Renmin Daxue Gongye Jingjixi, *Beijing gongye*, pp. 140–41.

11. See ibid., p. 142; *Xinmin bao*, Beiping, 10 Dec. 1947.

12. See Pan Zhiting's *Fadianchang nei wushi nian*; Shijingshan Fadian Zongchang Shizhi Ban(gongshi), "Yingjie jiefang de riri yeye," p. 36; *BGJC*, p. 463.

13. See *BGJC*, p. 460; Youdianbu Youdianshi Bianjishi, *Zhongguo jindai youdianshi*, pp. 206–10.

14. Yang and Zhao, *Beijing*, pp. 160–61; Zhongguo Renmin Daxue Gongye Jingjixi, *Beijing gongye*, pp. 38–40.

15. See Zhongguo Renmin Daxue Gongye Jingjixi, *Beijing gongye*, pp. 38–39; *BDL*, pp. 278, 280; *BGJC*, pp. 441–42.

16. *BGJC*, pp. 465–66; *BDDS*, p. 877. See also Zhang Jinke and Zhou Wenbin, "Ba shengchan gao tanhuan, rang diren tuantuan zhuan," pp. 869–902.

17. See Beijing Shifan Daxue Lishixi Sannianji, Yanjiuban, *Mentougou meikuang shigao*, pp. 32, 38–49; He Wencheng and Jia Chengzhong, "Guanghui de zhandou licheng," pp. 36–37.

18. See Hu Chia, *Peking*, p. 102; *BDDS*, p. 448; Qinghe Zhinichang Changshi Bianweihui, *Beijing Qinghe Zhinichang wushi nian*, pp. 38–55; Sanwu Lingyi Chang Changshi Bianxie Xiaozu, "Baoji huchang, yingjie jiefang," p. 33; *BGJC*, p. 464.

19. Zhongguo Renmin Daxue Gongye Jingjixi, *Beijing gongye*, pp. 315–16.

20. See Ji Gang, "Wo zai *Pingming ribao* dang jishe," pp. 516–22.

21. See ibid., pp. 207–17, 504–15; Sun Shuhong, " '*Jiefang*,' '*Jiefang ribao*' he Xinhuashe Beiping fenshe wei dengji beian yu Guomindang dangju douzheng shimo," p. 84.

22. Zhongguo Renmin Daxue Gongye Jingjixi, *Beiping gongye*, pp. 392–93.

23. See *BGJC*, pp. 466–67.

24. See Zhongguo Renmin Daxue Gongye Jingjixi, *Beijing gongye*, pp. 445–46.

25. Ibid., p. 519.

26. See Suzanne Pepper, *Civil War in China*, p. 55 n. 22.

27. Xiao Chaoran, *Beijing daxue xiaoshi*, pp. 406–7; Wu Weiling and Li He, *Beijing gaodeng jiaoyu shiliao*, pp. 36, 183.

28. See Xiao Chaoran, *Beijing daxue xiaoshi*, pp. 417–18; *BDDS*, pp. 543–600.

29. Xiao Chaoran, *Beijing daxue xiaoshi*, pp. 431, 433.

30. There was a separate or sixth committee, Police Work Committee (*Jingcha gongzuo weiyuanhui*) (November 1946–November 1947) under the direct control of the Urban Work Department of the Shanxi–Chahar–Hebei Central Bureau; it controlled few Party members and was not established by the original CCP Beiping City Work Committee. See *BGD*, p. 299; "Dangdai Zhongguo" Congshu Bianji Weiyuanhui, *Dangdai Zhongguo de Beijing*, vol. 1, p. 34; *BGJC*, p. 27. This Police Work Committee was not mentioned in *BDDS* or *Mianhuai Liu Ren tongzhi*.

31. See *BGD*, p. 270; *BGJC*, p. 29; Zhao Fan and Ji Yuan, "Zhonggong Jizhong Quwei Beiping Gongzuo Weiyuanhui de jianli ji qi huodong," pp. 32–35. Communist

cadres from other political and military systems also operated underground in Beiping during the Civil War period. See Fang Ting, "Jiefang zhanzheng shiqi Beiping dixiadang de douzheng," p. 320 n. 2. See also Wang Xiaoting and Wang Wenyi, *Zhandou zai Beida de gongchandang ren*, pp. 411–13.

32. The Southern Bureau was renamed the CCP CC Chongqing Bureau from December 1945 to May 1946. In May 1946 it was renamed the CCP CC Nanjing Bureau. From 1946 to 1948 Qian Ying, a leading female member of the Shanghai Bureau, was in charge of the student movement in GMD areas and the Southern Group cadres in Beiping–Tianjin.

33. *BDDS*, pp. 12–14; *BGD*, pp. 265, 274; *BGJC*, p. 39. The Democratic Youth Association (Minzhu Qingnian Xiehui, or *Minxie*) established in Chengdu in 1944 was another important Communist student organization; see Gongqingtuan Beijing Shiwei Qingnian Yundongshi Yanjiushi, *Beijing qingnian yundongshi*, p. 368; Zheng Guang and Lo Chengquan, *Zhongguo qingnian yundong liushi nian*, pp. 306–7. But *minxie* was rarely mentioned in the memoirs of the Beiping–Tianjin CCUP members. Probably it had been regarded as *minqing*. During the Civil War years, other lesser Beiping–Tianjin youth organizations with the title "Minzhu qingnian" in their whole names (e.g., Minzhu Qingnian Jianguo Hui) were also abbreviated as *minqing*. In the fall of 1948, the Urban Work Department of the North China Bureau directed the CCUP to use different titles for the front organizations because the name "*minqing*" had been discovered by the GMD authorities; see Zuo Jian and Qin Ge, "Jiefang zhanzheng shiqi de Tianjin xuesheng yundong," p. 33. As a whole, *minqing* was the most powerful Communist front (youth) organization in Beiping–Tianjin.

34. Zuo and Qin, "Tianjin xuesheng yundong," pp. 274–75, 325–26; *BDDS*, pp. 129–57.

35. See *BGD*, p. 275; *BDDS*, pp. 158–63; *BDZW*, pp. 413–23.

36. Probably the Commoner Work Committee took over the operation of the Police Work Committee.

37. *BGD*, pp. 275, 327; *BDDS*, pp. 172–77; *BGJC*, p. 26; She Diqing et al., "Fan Chiang Fanmei douzheng zhong de xianfeng," pp. 22, 24, 26.

38. *BGD*, pp. 275–76; *BDDS*, pp. 197–206.

39. Two other major intelligence systems were the CCP CC Social Affairs Department and the PLA Enemy Work Department. The former was involved in intelligence work; the latter focused on military information and the instigation of rebellion within the enemy troops. See *BGD*, p. 356.

40. See Dong Shigui and Zhang Yanzhi, *Beiping hetan jishi*, p. 305; Xi Xionghou, "Beiping dangzuzhi gongkai," p. 43.

41. The "person with overall responsibility" (She Diqing) of this organization was a former secretary of the Northern Group's Student Work Committee.

42. At the first meeting of the Beiping City Committee on 17 December 1948, Peng Zhen was declared the Secretary; Ye Jianying the First Deputy Secretary; and Liu Ren a committee member.

43. *BDDS*, p. 129.

44. See table 1 in Gail Hershatter, *The Workers of Tianjin*, p. 45.

45. See Chen Changjie, "Tianjin kangju renmin jiefang zhanzheng de huiyi," pp. 236–38.

46. Hershatter, *Workers of Tianjin*, p. 79.

47. See ibid., ch. 5.

48. See "Tianjin de jiaohang," p. 25.

49. *TJJ*, pp. 316–19

50. See Gu Shutang et al., *Tianjin jingji gaikuang*, p. 13.

51. See Fu Tao and Zhao Zuchang, *Tianjin gongye sanshiwu nian*, p. 13.

52. *TJJ*, pp. 266–67.

53. See Fu and Zhao, *Tianjin gongye*, pp. 18–22.
54. For a sophisticated explanation of this phenomenon, see Hershatter, *Workers of Tianjin*, ch. 8.
55. Dong Kunjing et al., *Tianjin tonglan*, p. 299.
56. Nankai Daxue Xiaoshi Bianxiezu, *Nankai daxue xiaoshi*, p. 334; Beiyang Daxue–Tianjin Daxue Xiaoshi Bianxiezu, *Beiyang daxue*, pp. 344–45.
57. See Wang Zuo et al., "Jiefang zhanzheng shiqi Yaohua Xuexiao de xuesheng yundong," pp. 1–24.
58. See Zhonggong Tianjin Shiwei Dangshi Ziliao Zhengji Weiyuanhui Bangongshi, "Yingjie Tianjin jiefang—Ji Ping-Jin zhanyi zhong de Tianjin dixiadang," p. 683.
59. Tianjinshi Difangzhi Bianxiu Weiyuanhui, *Tianjin jianshi*, p. 118.
60. Ibid., pp. 118–19; *TXGY*, p. 230.
61. See *TJJ*, pp. 196–97, 206–7. The Tianjin Work Committee and the Liberation Action Committee were another example of "two brand names, one set of personnel."
62. See *TJ*, pp. 394, 402, 425–26; *TXGY*, pp. 179, 205, 230, 236, 257–58; Wang Jie, "Huiyi jiefang zhanzheng shiqi dang zai Tianjin gongwei," pp. 217–22; Feng Dongsheng, "Dixiadang," pp. 202–3; Li Zhinan, "Tianjin nanxi," pp. 195–97; Wang Wenhua, "Liming qian de zhandou," pp. 206–7; Zuo and Qin, "Tianjin xuesheng yundong," pp. 13, 32–33, 37. Besides, the Tianjin Work Committee did not absorb the Tianjin underground agents of the Beiping–Tianjin Work Committee (established in Beiping in August 1948) of the CCP Hebei–Rehe–Chahar Area Party Committee. The Party Committee's forty members were transferred to the CCP Beiping Municipal Committee after the "liberation" of the city. See *BGJC*, pp. 29–30.
63. Note that from the standpoint of the Southern Group, all the local Communist (student) committees and front organizations in Beiping–Tianjin were regarded as the Northern Group.
64. See *BGD*, p. 364; Fang Ting, "Beiping dixiadang de douzheng," p. 310; *TXGY*, p. 257; Wu Mu, "Tianjin xueyun," p. 16; Zuo and Qin, "Tianjin xuesheng yundong," p. 33; Tianjinshi Difangzhi Bianxiu Weiyuanhui, *Tianjin jianshi*, p. 119.
65. The following is a representative sample that helps illustrate the central work of the student cadres, the concealed nature of the CCUP among the academic population, the young age of the cadres (in their twenties and thirties), their gender (male and female), and their places of origin (Beijing, Tianjin, and elsewhere) in the late 1940s: (1) *CCUP's Southern Group*: Yuan Yongxi (1917–   )—Beijingese, a CCP member since 1938, "the person with overall responsibility" of the Group from July 1946 to September 1947. Chen Lian (1919–1966)—Yuan's Zhejiangese wife, a CCP member since 1939, a teacher at Beiman Middle School in Beiping from September 1946 to September 1947. Liu Xin (1922–1987)—Sichuanese, a CCP member since 1939, a history student and "the person with overall responsibility" of the Group at Qinghua University in 1946–47. Shi Yu (1921–   )—Hunanese, a CCP member since 1946, secretary of the Group at Beijing University from July–October 1947. Li Zhinan (1920–   )—Jiangxuese, a CCP member since 1938, "the person with overall responsibility" of the Group in the Tianjin student movement in 1946–48, a member of the Tianjin Work Committee in late 1948. Wang Hanbin (1925–   )—Fujianese, a CCP member since 1941, a member of the Group's Student Work Committee and secretary of the University Work Committee in Beiping in 1948. See n. 12 in the introduction. (2) *CCUP's Northern Group*: Xiang Ziming (1921–1990)—Anhuiese, a CCP member since 1938, "the person with overall responsibility" of the Group at Beijing University. Wang Wenhua (1921–   )—Shandongese, a CCP member since 1942, a member of the Tianjin Work Committee in late 1948. Sha Xiaoquan (?–   )—Shandongese, a female CCP member since 1945, an economics student at Beijing University in 1944–46, a Party secretary at Nankai Univer-

sity in 1947–48, a member of the Tianjin student committee in October 1948. Liu Jun-ying (1920–   )—Tianjinese, a female CCP member since 1946, a Beijing University graduate, a member of the Middle School Committee in Beiping in January 1948. Xu Yan (1921–   )—Korean and Beijing resident, a female CCP member since 1941, a medical doctor at the Tongren Hospital in Beiping from April 1946 to May 1948, underground work in Tianjin from November 1948 to January 1949. See Wang Xiaoting and Wang Wenyi, *Zhandou zai Beida de gongchandang ren*, pp. 181, 186, 195, 204–5, 231, 425, 449, 461, 495, 522–23.

5

The Communist Student Movement, 1945–1948

The importance of the youth movement, especially the student movement, in the Communist revolution is undisputed. In "Orientation of Youth Movement" (4 May 1939), Mao Zedong had praised the young people's vanguard role in taking the lead and marching in the forefront of the revolutionary ranks. Young intellectuals and students were an important army against imperialism and feudalism.[1] In "An Address to the Second Anniversary of the Anwu Youth Training Class" (5 October 1939) and in "The Chinese Revolution and the CCP" (1939), Mao went on to stress the vanguard role of the petit-bourgeois intellectuals and students. Without them, "the ranks of the revolution could not develop and the revolution could not triumph."[2]

Students and intellectuals were so important for the CCP that Mao even suggested a way to resolve their weaknesses of inexperience and vacillation: to participate personally in the revolution and the mass struggles.[3] What should the students and intellectuals do for the CCP? In "Orientation of Youth Movement," Mao instructed them to mobilize and organize among the workers and peasants, who made up 90 percent of the population.[4]

It is clear that Mao and the CCP wanted the students and intellectuals to become an important front army to help the workers and peasants develop into the main force of the revolution. In other words, the youth army should lead this main force to fight for the Communist cause. The generally petit-bourgeois students and intellectuals should play a more important role in the revolution in urban and rural China, although in theory the proletariat were the leading force in the revolution. Since students were so important in the revolution, the CCP naturally focused its work on school campuses.

Indeed, Chinese students had been eagerly involved in the revolution since the May Fourth Movement of 1919. Both the GMD and the CCP had tried to capture the mainstream of the Chinese student movement. During the wartime period, however, the GMD and Youth Corps organizations had experienced problems in administration and work-styles, youth activities, and educational practices.[5] Worse still, in the Civil War period, the ruling GMD lost the trust of the student movement, which became antigovernment. The worsening economic situation, the issue of foreign imperialism, and the GMD's inappropriate responses to various student protests galvanized the students and intellectuals into a movement that challenged the authority of the GMD government. The ineffectiveness of the GMD in dealing with the students highlighted the Communists' effectiveness at mobilization. The alienation of the students from the government contributed to the Communist neutralization of the GMD authority in the cities. But it should be noted that not all the students were antigovernment. In fact, few favored the idea of national rule by the CCP. Yet they were dissatisfied with the insensitivity and corruption of the GMD government. Above all, the government's harsh measures were further alienating the students, to the point of driving many of them into the Communist camp.[6]

In short, the student movements of 1945–48 greatly benefited the CCP, and they were the center of the Communists' struggle in Beiping–Tianjin. The successful Communist mobilization of student protests over political, economic, and academic or school-related issues was a powerful weapon that undermined the prestige and authority of the GMD in urban North China.

August 1945–June 1946

In Beiping–Tianjin the Student Work Committees were the most important organs of Communist underground activities. From August 1945 to June 1946, the Communist student movement in Beiping–Tianjin, and in all other urban areas, was based on the struggle for "peace and democracy," and on eliminating the GMD reeducation programs and examinations.

In August 1945 the Beiping–Tianjin CCUP had members in universities, colleges, middle schools, and professional schools. While the CCUP mainly transported personnel and medical and other supplies to the rural bases and did not engage in any significant student movement within Beiping–Tianjin in the wartime period, the surrender of Japan provided a new opportunity to be active among the students in the cities. In the immediate postwar period, with American assistance the GMD was busily airlifting troops and officials to Beiping–Tianjin. After realizing that they could not seize Beiping–Tianjin by external force and internal insurrection similar to the case of the liberation of Paris in 1944, the Tianjin CCUP and the Urban Work Department of the Shanxi–Chahar–Hebei

Central Bureau promptly changed their strategy and focused their operations on the student movement, which was to help launch the anti-GMD democratic movement. In September the Tianjin Work Committee's directive illustrated the main task of the student work. The Party's primary tasks were to win the freedoms of speech, publication, assembly, and association; to establish newspapers and student self-governing associations (*xuesheng zizhihui*, the most important open and legal student organizations in GMD China); to carry out propaganda activities; and to develop the democratic movement. In action, the Beiping–Tianjin CCUP mobilized its underground members in all the schools to establish wall newspaper societies, reading groups, choirs, and food corps, and to publish all kinds of newspapers.[7]

The GMD also realized the importance of winning the allegiance of the youth. One of the GMD takeover organs was the Three People's Principles Youth Corps. Once in Beiping–Tianjin, it started recruiting members from the students and published a journal entitled *Beiping qingnian* (Beiping youth) on 18 September 1945. While the Youth Corps approved the student strikes during the era of antiforeign imperialism (before the end of the war with Japan), it was against student class strikes, demonstrations, and protests in an age of postwar national reconstruction. In short, the youth should, as Chiang Kai-shek had declared in his 18 September public lecture, "get rid of the past bad habit of embellishing the state of being panic-stricken" (that is, get rid of the use of class strikes, demonstrations, and protests).[8] In addition, those youths who really wanted to make China strong should join the Youth Corps.[9] The Youth Corps was determined to unify the ideology, organization, and action of the youth in Beiping–Tianjin.[10] However, the Communist student movement in the area proved that the Youth Corps failed in its task of controlling the students.

In the wake of the Japanese surrender, the public and the CCP demanded the punishment of "educational traitors" and an overhaul of the Japanese and puppet educational systems and policies. However, the GMD government arrested only a few of the "educational traitors" (such as Zhou Zuoren, who served the puppet regime in Beijing).

On 26 September 1945, the GMD Education Ministry announced the examination guidelines for middle school and college students and the formation of temporary reeducation centers in the major cities. "Puppet students" were required to attend courses designed to reacquaint them with the needs of national reconstruction and the GMD ideology. The reorientation courses included the study of the Three People's Principles, the public speeches of Chiang Kai-shek, Chinese history and geography, current events, and military training.[11] Centers for the "puppet college students" were known as Provisional Universities. Similar courses were also made mandatory at the middle and primary school levels. Students who completed the reorientation courses had to take special examinations to continue their schooling. Those who had already graduated from universities, colleges, and middle schools during the Japanese occupation were required to pass a written examination on the Three People's Principles before their diplomas could be recognized by the Education Ministry. Teachers in the recovered territories had to take an examination on academic competence as well as knowledge of and loyalty to the GMD.[12]

From the viewpoint of the GMD, all students in the recovered cities had been corrupted by enemy propaganda; they should be suitably reeducated and their thoughts cleansed before any further education. This attitude was understandable. However, the stigma officially attached to all who were required to participate in the reeducation program antagonized both the teachers and the students. The GMD government viewed them as "puppet teachers and students," although the GMD Education Minister insisted that they were not.

Private schools and universities in occupied China had maintained a great degree of independence from government interference. Therefore, the reeducation program for students of private institutions was less stringent. This inconsistency alienated particularly those students who could not afford to study in any one of the private universities in Beiping–Tianjin.

Although the GMD reorientation program and the compulsory examinations were later modified in Beiping–Tianjin and other urban areas, irritation and resentment had already darkened the reputation of the government.[13] With the coming of victory, people in the recovered areas sensed the difference between themselves and those who had withdrawn to Southwest China. This feeling was intensified by the behavior and attitude of the takeover officials, who were the first to return from the hinterland. They seemed to have a superiority complex, although in their conduct these men of position and influence had not shown themselves to be superior to the local population. These men, a "new nobility," were interested mainly in profiteering. As a Tianjin newspaper observed, the residents at first felt inferior and regretted not having retreated with the GMD government to the interior. But after witnessing the chaos created by the returning officials, people no longer felt the necessity of appearing humble.[14] Nevertheless, these officials had the authority to evaluate local teachers and students, and to influence their academic and professional lives in the reorientation program. Under these circumstances, the intellectuals could not be blamed for speaking out in protest. The government, concluded the editorial of another Tianjin newspaper, should not examine teachers and students, and "had better consider its public functionaries and other things, so far as the psychology of the people in the liberated [GMD] areas is concerned."[15]

The GMD reorientation program and examinations gave the CCUP its first opportunity to denounce the "reactionary" nature of the GMD government. Thus it began the "Anti-Examination Movement" (*Fan zhenshen yundong*) (October 1945–June 1946), the first important Communist student movement in Beiping–Tianjin (and in China) during the Civil War period.

In Beiping the Communist Student Work Committee held the view that the reorientation and examination programs were used to strengthen the Nationalist anti-Communist ideology, and thus to prepare for the civil war. The Communists had to attack this "reactionary" GMD measure.[16] The CCUP decided that it should begin the fight by concentrating on the several thousand college graduates in the city. These graduates were the direct victims of the measure and thus were most enraged and ready to battle for their interests. The Party established an Anti-Examination Party Corps (led by Song Rufen), responsible for the work among the alumni associations—a legal and open form of struggle. Through a delicate work scheme (such as informing the alumni one by one), a Communist engineering graduate of Beida successfully captured the chairmanship of the Beida Alumni Association (composed of the alumni from the colleges of arts, science, law, engineering, medicine, and agriculture). Since the Alumni Association of Beijing Normal University (Shida) was controlled by "progressive" students, the CCUP decided that the focus of the Anti-Examination Movement should be on the combined alumni associations of Beida and Shida.[17] By November 1945 the chairman of the Beida Alumni Association had become the chairman of the Beida–Shida Alumni United Association. In March 1946 the Communists further established the Beiping Special Vocational and Higher Schools Alumni United Association to incorporate the graduates from other colleges and special vocational schools. By then about five thousand college graduates had been organized in this alumni association under a Communist chairman and deputy chairman. Another deputy chairman was a Central Statistics member. Even though members of the GMD and the Youth Corps were inside the Alumni United Association, they could not seize its leadership. The Communists were successful in using this legal alumni association to harass the GMD government.[18]

In Tianjin the Communists used a different tactic to deal with the Anti-Examination Movement. In the fall of 1945 there were two universities and thirty-one middle schools in the city. The Communist influence within Nankai University and Beiyang University was minimal.[19] The strongest Communist base was at the Yaohua Middle School. The CCUP also had some influence at nineteen other middle schools. Unlike Beiping, where the Party made use of the alumni associations to fight the authorities, the Tianjin CCUP manipulated middle school students, who also suffered from the GMD education policy. In early October Yaohua and several other Communist-infiltrated middle schools petitioned the Tianjin Education Bureau to "rescind the examination order." Naturally, there was no response.[20] The attempt of seven middle schools to settle on a concerted action on the examination issue also failed in mid-October.[21]

Back in Beiping, the founding member of the Beida–Shida Alumni United Association was also the chairman of the first Anti-Examination Conference in October. The Conference generally approved the Anti-Examination theme, and exposed the antagonism between the GMD government and the people. After the Conference, the Youth Corps endorsed the GMD education policy openly. Two opposing groups of alumni and students emerged. In this situation, the CCUP decided to convene a second Anti-Examination Conference on the campus of Shida. The majority of the students and alumni at this Conference demanded that the government rescind its order. Certain GMD and Youth Corps members were accused by the Communists of threatening the Conference with their declarations of "Don't be in opposition to the government" and "The government possesses machine guns; antigovernment is futile." GMD army and police units surrounded Shida. Nonetheless, the Conference finally passed a resolution "Against the Examination" and a letter of protest. These were presented to a staff officer of the Beiping Executive Headquarters who had arrived during the Conference. He also told the Conference that the government had just issued a new ordinance canceling the required examination and instead requiring participants in the reorientation programs just to hand in two essays. While this GMD "new method" was still under dispute, the Second Conference concluded peacefully. The government accepted the resolution and the letter of protest. The Communist-instigated Anti-Examination Movement was successful (temporarily).[22]

The failure of the GMD to suppress this movement in the fall of 1945 was a sign of weakness. A telegram from Chiang Kai-shek to Mayor Xiong Bin of Beiping in October demonstrated the GMD awareness of Communist activities among the students.[23] In December the Anti-Examination Movement was under police surveillance.[24] Nonetheless, Xiong and other GMD leaders could not control the student movement. The Communist spark of fire in the youth movement would kindle a fireball that would engulf the GMD in the urban political struggle.

The Anti-Examination Movement in Beiping influenced similar revolutionary actions in other recovered cities.[25] The first aftershock was in Tianjin. After receiving "A Letter to the Young Fellow Students in the Recovered Areas" from the students in Beiping in early November, the Anti-Examination Movement in Tianjin was strengthened. This letter (drafted by the Communist or "progressive" students) denounced the GMD in this way: "We did not hear about the measures to deal with traitors, running dogs, and ruthless officials except the government measure of demanding examinations of the pure and powerless young people. Outsiders could not understand the painful feelings and the irritation among the students. All fellow students must be united to fight the government with reason."[26]

On 19 December 1945, representatives from eighteen Tianjin schools assembled in the Guangdong Middle School (a private institution, whose principal supported the Anti-Examination students) to hold a second Anti-Examination meeting. Unlike the first meeting in October, the second one achieved a common understanding on the theme of Anti-Examination.[27]

A day later, the GMD newspaper in Tianjin published an article entitled "A Talk on Examination in the Midst of the Sound of Anti-Examination." This article claimed that the students in the occupied territories were disappointed and frustrated because they were separated from their mother country. Their social position was low, and they were passive and pessimistic. To advocate the examination was actually to help the future of these students. The examination was an opportunity in a thousand years for the students to express themselves, to have genuine knowledge and patriotic passion. The article admonished the students not to oppose the examination.[28]

The above article could not stop the Anti-Examination Movement. On 22 December students from twenty-two schools attended the third Anti-Examination meeting, and agreed to establish an Anti-Examination Committee of the Tianjin Students. This committee issued a Support-Teacher, Anti-Examination Telegram to other parts of China. (Teachers also had to take certain examinations for their jobs and promotion.) This was, the CCUP claimed, a high tide in the Anti-Examination struggle.[29]

On 26 December the Anti-Examination Committee developed into the Tianjin Student Association, a broader and more united student organization for the Communists to use as a tool to fight the GMD education policy. One CCUP member was on the presidium of this association; another member in the same Yaohua Middle School participated in the activities of the association as the school representative.[30]

On 28 December nineteen representatives of the twenty-thousand-strong Tianjin Student Association petitioned the Tianjin Education Bureau chief in person and demanded the cancellation of the Examination for both teachers and students. The representatives also called for freedoms of speech, assembly, and association. The bureau chief excused himself and promised nothing. The representatives gave him three days to come up with a satisfactory response.[31]

The local GMD in Tianjin tried to dilute the Anti-Examination Movement. On 29 December the Education Bureau announced that the examination could be delayed, and that a student's parents could apply for delay individually. Further, the municipal government would grant scholarships to those who passed the examination with high scores. Simultaneously, all the schools were ordered to take the winter break earlier than usual; no student gatherings were allowed. Confronted with these tactics of the local authority, the Student Association held an emergency meeting and agreed to get even more students to petition on 31 December.[32]

On the last day of 1945, six thousand students marched toward the Education Bureau. They gathered outside the office while the student representatives negotiated with the bureau chief inside. After a futile three-hour conference, the Communist student representative from Yaohua Middle School suggested that the bureau chief talk directly to the students outside. The students got the message, but the door was guarded by the police force. Reluctant to fire upon the students who marched forward and climbed over the wall of the office, the police stood by, and the bureau chief finally allowed the students to enter his office. He was forced to sign a paper acknowledging the legal status of all student self-governing associations. Above all, the bureau chief agreed to cancel the examination temporarily. This was a victory for the student movement in Tianjin.[33]

In historical perspective, while the Communist-infiltrated Yaohua Middle

School played a conspicuous role in the Anti-Examination Movement, one cannot conclude that the movement was totally the product of the Communists. The unpopularity of the GMD education policy invited criticism from society and created support for the students. In this atmosphere, Communist activity flourished among the students. The inability of the GMD to control the Communist student movement in Tianjin once again showed the political weakness of the GMD. An unreasonable educational policy in a transitional period inflicted damage on the GMD itself. While the Communists were not yet strong enough to rule China, the incapacity of the GMD to extinguish sparks of Communist fire in the student movement in Beiping–Tianjin (and other urban areas) would cause major troubles for it in the months to come.

The year 1946 began with a GMD plea for "national unity and political democracy." It stressed the importance of the unity of political and military command and the return of all armies (particularly the Communist ones) to a unified control under the state. Further, it called for sincere cooperation in the forthcoming National Assembly to discuss "the return of power to the people." In short, "national unity and political democracy" was declared the basis of national reconstruction in the postwar period.[34]

While the Communists advocated "peace, democracy, and unity," which concurred with the Nationalist wish, they would certainly not integrate their military forces into the GMD. Nevertheless, under a Marshall-initiated truce, they accepted the establishment of a tripartite Executive Headquarters, consisting of one Nationalist, one Communist, and one American member. Three-party teams were sent into the field to supervise the cease-fire.

On 13 January 1946, Ye Jianying, the Communist representative of the Beiping Military Mediation Executive Headquarters, arrived in the city.[35] Soon the Communist delegation established the Beiping branch of the Xinhuashe (New China News Agency) and the newspaper *Jiefang* to spread Communist views openly in Beiping. This was a legal form of struggle in GMD urban areas. Through their propaganda, these Communist organizations also strengthened the continuous Anti-Examination Movement and the subsequent mass movements in Beiping–Tianjin.[36]

The CCUP was more active in Tianjin in the first month of 1946. After the signing of the truce and the cease-fire in early January, the Communist Tianjin Work Committee directed its Student Committee to organize a city-wide demonstration and parade displaying placards. The Student Committee decided to use the Tianjin Student Association to organize openly a "consolidation for peace" assembly, demonstration, and parade. It proposed: (1) to resist civil war, to achieve democracy and peace, and to call for a successful conclusion of the Political Consultative Conference; (2) to memorialize the martyrs of the "December First (1945) Atrocious Incident" in Kunming,[37] and to protest the crime of killing students by the government; (3) To celebrate the establishment of the Tianjin Student Association.[38]

On 25 January the Tianjin Student Association held the "consolidation for peace" assembly and a parade with slogans like "consolidation for peace and opposition to civil war," "political consultative conference must succeed and cannot fail," "to end one-party [that is, the GMD's] dictatorship and to establish a coalition government," "to release political prisoners," "to end secret-service activities," and "to withdraw the American troops in China."[39]

The Communists claimed that the January Twenty-Fifth Assembly and Parade was an impressive political influence, but admitted that some of the slogans were not yet accepted by the masses. Some could not be understood by the young students, for instance, "to establish a coalition government." Some exposed directly the political nature of the Tianjin Student Association. Those slogans included "Policemen are the public servants of the people, and should not scold or beat the masters" and "Destroy the tool of ruling the people—the *baojia* system [a GMD local household registration and security system]."[40]

The GMD in Tianjin did not let the Communist attack go without response. On 5 January the GMD newspaper *Minguo ribao* (Republican daily) denounced the Tianjin Student Association for launching the Anti-Examination Movement for purposes other than simply fighting for freedom. It implied that the association worked for the Communists.[41] The Communists claimed that in late January the Tianjin school authorities demanded that students join the Youth Corps, or else they would be accused of being Communists.[42] On 30 January the Youth Corps monopolized the appointments of primary and middle school instructors in discipline and training.[43]

February was a month of anti-Communist and anti-Soviet movements. On 8 February the Tianjin authorities dismissed the principal of Guangdong Middle School, who had supported the antigovernment activities of the Tianjin Student Association. Simultaneously, the GMD Education Ministry ordered the Tianjin Education Bureau to dismiss any student who had supported the student movement, and even to close the school that the student attended if necessary. Tianjin Municipal Government also ordered every means to change the "student tide" into an anti-Communist movement.[44] On 10 February a number of "democratic personalities" (such as Li Gongpo) were attacked by the anti-Communists at the Jianchangkou incident in Chongqing. On 20 February the "Hebei Refugees Return to Native Place Petition Group" held an anti-Communist parade and demolished the Communist office of the Beiping Mediation Executive Headquarters.[45]

On 22 February a large-scale anti-Soviet student parade occurred in Chongqing. The GMD claimed that the party and the Youth Corps did not plan the movement in advance. In fact, Chiang Kai-shek was angry with the student movement for diplomatic reasons. Nevertheless, they guided it after the anti-Communist students and other social elements had raised the anti-Soviet and anti-Communist slogans.[46] A similar thirty-thousand-strong student parade took place in Beiping on 26 February. The Communist policy to deal with this GMD-controlled movement was twofold: (1) The CCUP must try hard to discourage the students in their strongholds such as Beida, Qingda, and Yanda from participation. (If the Communist and the "progressive" students participated in the parade, it might be difficult for them to gain support from fellow students for their future anti-GMD activities.) (2) Party, "progressive," and "positive" students in GMD-dominated schools must join the parade if they were coerced to do so, to hide their Communist identity. Their job was to sabotage the parade if possible. Because of inexperience in participating in an anti-Communist parade and late preparation for the parade, the CCUP was on the defensive in Beiping and other cities.[47] This "February Twenty-Second Movement" was the only student movement that the Communists could not infiltrate or control.[48] The movement was not a real threat to the CCUP, however. Above all, it was the first and the last major GMD student and mass movement in the Civil War period. The Nationalists were not interested in launching more large-scale anti-Communist movements, probably because Chiang Kai-shek detested student protests or the GMD and the Youth Corps could not muster enough support for such endeavors.

In Tianjin the GMD Municipal Party Bureau invited the Student Association to lead the anti-Soviet movement. Confronted with this embarrassing situation and the GMD plot to isolate the Communists from others, the CCUP decided to deal with the challenge on individual bases: (1) In those schools where the Party was strong, the underground members should convince the masses to boycott the parade. (2) In the schools where the majority of the masses would join the parade, underground members and "progressive" elements should do the same to avoid exposure and isolation. (3) Party members should not shout anti-Soviet and anti-Communist slogans. Simultaneously, the Tianjin Student Association refused to participate in the parade under the pretext that it was ignorant of what was going on in Northeast China (Russians invaded and occupied Chinese territory).[49]

The anti-Soviet, anti-Communist movement of February 1946 subdued temporarily the Communist-instigated "student tides." But since the Shanxi–Chahar–Hebei Central Bureau had emphasized on 1 February that students and educated youth were the focus of work in Beiping, the CCUP very soon resumed its student activities.[50] On 2 March the GMD government announced "Regulations on Employment of University Graduates in Occupied Territories." These regulations demanded that college graduates in recovered areas take examinations or else they would not get promoted. This was certainly unpopular among the college graduates and students in light of the fact that puppet soldiers could become part of the Nationalist (and Communist) army and Japanese technicians could remain to serve without any examinations.[51] Exploiting this anger and frustration, the Communists, through the Third Conference of the Beida–Shida Alumni United Association, publicly declared refusal to take examinations and issued a public letter urging students in other cities to attack the unfairness and unreasonableness of the GMD examination and employment policies.[52]

However, the GMD would not accede easily to the demands of the Alumni

United Association. On 3 April the authorities raided the Communist offices of the newspaper *Jiefang* and the 8th Route Army in Beiping.[53] They also arrested eight hundred residents during a night raid in the city.[54] On the same day the Education Ministry issued extended rules on examinations of students and graduates in the recovered areas.[55]

In the meantime, in Beiping the Nationalist party bureau and the municipal government also raised the salaries of the middle school teachers and succeeded in discouraging them from launching strikes and causing chaos on campuses. This time the CCUP could not exploit the teachers' economic problem.[56]

In order to continue and expand its struggles against the GMD on the education front, however, the Communist Student Work Committee established a bigger and legal Beiping Special Vocational and Higher Schools Alumni United Association in March 1946. On 21 April the association, under the title of "Beiping National Assembly Representatives' Election Promotion Association," sponsored a public lecture at the Music Hall of Zhongshan Park. The message of the lecture was that the GMD National Assembly was antidemocratic. A disturbance erupted during the meeting, and the Communists claimed Professor Chen Jinkun of Chaoyang University, the speaker, was beaten by the GMD secret-service men. In the wake of this incident, Chen, assisted by the CCUP, traveled to Yan'an. Communist and left-wing scholars and "democratic personalities," including Guo Moruo, Shen Junru, Li Gongpo, and Tian Han, criticized the GMD and upheld the ideals of freedom and human rights.[57]

While the Communist-initiated meeting ended in chaos, the Party insisted that it educated the masses about the "reactionary" GMD rule. Then, to counter the GMD anti-Soviet and anti-Communist movement, the CCUP decided to take a number of "middle" and "progressive" students to visit the Zhangjiakou "Liberated" Area in March, April, and May. This trip was to show the students that the "bright" CCP areas were much better than the "dark" GMD areas. Some students joined the CCP and returned to Beiping for underground activities.[58] The student visits to Zhangjiakou and its Communist North China Associated University were under the surveillance of the GMD Beiping Education Bureau and the Police Bureau, but the authorities did not halt or suppress them.[59]

The Communist Student Work Committee was active in other areas. In March 1946 a spontaneous craze broke out among Beiping students for publishing wall newspapers, which dealt with the contemporary condition. The CCUP organized some of the papers. They emphasized topics such as the government's economic mismanagement.[60]

On 26 May the CCUP struck again at the examination issue. The Beiping Special Vocational and Higher Schools Alumni United Association held a Fourth Conference and demanded an immediate cancellation of all the examinations. Exploiting again the enraged mood of the participants, the Communist leaders of the association organized successfully a three-hundred-man parade and marched to the office of the Beiping Executive Headquarters. On the following day Director Li Zongren of the Executive Headquarters agreed to present their grievances to the Education Ministry. The Communists claimed another victory in the Anti-Examination Movement.[61] The Communists contacted Li not only because he was the nominal political leader of Beiping–Tianjin, but because they knew he disagreed with Chiang Kai-shek and other "centrally" appointed GMD leaders in Beiping. It was a Communist united-front tactic to neutralize the GMD from within and from above. Li was sympathetic to the students and the intellectuals because he wanted to improve his image among them.

The GMD anti-Soviet, anti-Communist movement tried to impede the activities of the Tianjin Student Association. In order to revive the momentum of their student movement, the Communists decided to study the Assist-Student Movement in Shanghai, and develop it into a city-wide "Revere-Teacher, Assist-Student Movement" in Tianjin.[62]

On 26 April 1946, the Student Association held its first Revere-Teacher, Assist-Student meeting. Four days later, a second meeting of nineteen schools established the Tianjin Student Association Revere-Teacher, Assist-Student Committee. From 4 May to 6 May, the committee assigned small groups of students (in all, about two thousand) to collect money on behalf of the teachers. The local authorities did not welcome this movement and tried hard to cut it short. However, the committee did collect Ch $6.4 million for twelve hundred middle school teachers. Each teacher would get Ch $5,000, which could purchase only ten catties of white flour. The Revere-Teacher, Assist-Student Movement in Tianjin was a powerful protest because it exposed the education and economic crises in GMD areas. (The pay raise that the middle school teachers had received from the GMD authorities several weeks earlier was inadequate.) Simultaneously, this movement benefited the teachers and received support and sympathy from the masses. For the youth the movement could be seen as political education. The Communists claimed another victory against the GMD.[63]

While a push for "peace and democracy" was the basic Communist theme from the end of the war up to June 1946, the core of the student movement in Beiping–Tianjin was actually the Anti-Examination Movement. *Peace* and *democracy* were abstract terms; there was no proof that all the students and teachers bought the "peace and democracy" argument. However, they were certainly more concerned with their immediate status and livelihood as determined by the examination. The Communists used shrewdly the unpopular GMD education measures to influence the mood of the students and teachers for political aims. Simultaneously, the harsh GMD attitude toward the people and its corruption in Beiping–Tianjin naturally aroused antipathy among the residents.

Obviously, from August 1945 to June 1946, the GMD was unable to control the mainstream of the student movement in Beiping–Tianjin, but one should not exaggerate the Communist achievement among the youth. Underground Communist members among the college and middle school students were a small minority. During the period there were less than ten CCP members in Yanda, thirty members each in Qingda and Shida, and more than thirty members in Beida.[64] The CCUP membership in Nankai and Beiyang universities and among the middle schools is unclear but could not have been numerous. Besides, in June 1946 more than twenty Communists at Shida had to retreat to CCP areas because their identities were exposed to the GMD authorities.[65] The small Communist underground force grew as time went on, however. More and more "progressive" and "positive" elements were recruited into the Party and became the backbone of a more vigorous youth movement in Beiping–Tianjin.

The Communist efforts among faculty members also developed, and complemented the activities among the students. The Communist successes were products of the "united front from above and below." For the Communists, struggle on the education front was an auspicious beginning in the postwar period.

Furthermore, the CCUP targeted students and intellectuals in its anti-GMD cultural front. In September 1945 the Beiping CCUP established the Lihua Printing Factory within the city; it printed Communist and "progressive" materials. The Student Work Committee established a weekly journal entitled *Renyen* (People's words), which accused the GMD of sabotaging the peace talks. The Communists also established two newspapers for propaganda purposes in Beiping: *Guokuang ribao* (National glory daily) and *Lu Xun wanbao* (Lu Xun evening news). But these papers were too "progressive," and they were forced to close by the GMD. In February–March 1946 the Communists established *Jiefang* and the Xinhuashe Beiping Branch Office. This and seventy-five other newspapers and journals were suppressed by the GMD authorities on 29 May 1946.[66] With their own publications out of action, the Communist Culture Work Committee began to infiltrate the GMD and other civilian news agencies. There were secret Party members in *Yishi bao* and *Pingming ribao*; they also infiltrated the Beiping Branch office of *Dagong bao*, the Branch Office of the Central News Agency, and even the United States Information Agency in Beiping–Tianjin.[67]

In the field of publications, Zhongwai Publications Agency was the major Communist cultural unit in North China. With an external face of being "middle," this agency secretly printed much Communist literature, including the writings of Mao Zedong.[68] The CCUP also operated two bookstores and had a number of movable "libraries" selling Communist and "progressive" literature. They moved from place to place, and the authorities could not suppress them easily.[69]

Theater also was used for propaganda. The largest cultural unit under the control of the CCUP was the Fatherland Theatrical Group. Another important unit was the Second Theatrical Corps under the authority of the GMD Defense Ministry in Nanjing. The Corps defected to the Communists in the fall of 1948. In March 1946 the CCUP established the Beiping City Theatrical Groups United Association. The CCUP used the association to spread influence within university and middle school theatrical groups such as the Beijing University Theatrical Society and the Beiman Middle School Theatrical Society.[70]

In Tianjin the Communists also established a number of newspapers, printed other publications, and opened bookstores. In September 1945 the Tianjin Work Committee published in the suburbs a Party newspaper entitled *Tianjin daobao* (Tianjin guide). After twenty-five issues, the Party decided to end this openly published newspaper and established *Zhongguo xinwen* (Chinese news) underground inside the city. The GMD authorities, however, were able to shut down *Zhongguo xinwen* on 18 April 1946. The CCUP opened Zhishi Bookstore, Dujie Bookstore, and Qiqi Bookstore. They published Communist and "progressive" literature, and helped recruit "progressive" youth.[71]

The Student Committee also published *Qingnian zhiyou* (Friends of youth), later changed to *Tongxue men* (Fellow students), to direct the student movement. The Tianjin Student Association published *Tianjin xuelian* (Tianjin student association). A number of smaller "progressive" publications were started in Tianjin, and the Tianjin Student Association organized the Tianjin Youth Publication Joint Association, which published *Kanglian* (Resistance union).[72]

In accordance with the directive of the Tianjin Work Committee to unify work in the cultural sphere, a number of Communists and "progressive" elements established the Tianjin Cultural Man Association on 7 October 1945. This Association published a monthly (later bimonthly) journal, *Wenlian* (Literary union), which provided stories, political essays, and articles from newspapers in GMD cities and CCP areas. *Wenlian* attacked the GMD takeover process, the insincerity of its acceptance of the 10 October GMD-CCP Agreement, and the misbehavior of the American troops (especially the alleged rape of Chinese women). It praised the positive contributions of the Soviet armies in the war against Japan. After operating on a legal basis for a while, *Wenlian* was suppressed by the GMD authorities, and the Cultural Association turned underground in late June 1946.[73] (The GMD authorities suppressed twenty-one publications on 18 June.) The Cultural Association was another example of the Communist united-front tactic in the city. While the influence of *Wenlian* was not great (a total of sixteen issues with an average circulation of 2,500 monthly), the GMD could not prevent the spread of left-wing views among the educated portion of the population. The GMD suppression of a large number of left-wing publications did not help them monopolize public opinion.

In general, from August 1945 to June 1946, the Beiping–Tianjin GMD authorities did not use excessive force toward the urban protesters.[74] Perhaps it was because the GMD was too busy with the takeover operation. Or the Nationalists thought they could control the situation mainly by moderate means. Nonetheless, they showed their weaknesses by often conceding to the demands and tolerating the activities of the CCUP and the "progressive" students. For example, in December 1945 the GMD authorities arrested six student representatives who were involved in the Anti-Examination Movement. But under popular pressure the authorities released them quickly.[75] The unwillingness or incapacity of the GMD to suppress the Communist student activities paved the way for the emergence of a revolutionary urban situation in the postwar period, although the CCUP had no big chance yet to contribute to the GMD's loss of authority. Nevertheless, the GMD's weakness in North China and its decision to limit efforts to several big cities (particularly Beiping–Tianjin) showed its overall insecure position. Seeds of destruction, not recovery, had already been sown in the first ten months after the Japanese surrender.

Above all, the CCP wanted to conquer urban China after the Japanese surrender. The negative aspects of the weak GMD rule in the cities definitely aided the Communist activities there. The Beiping–Tianjin CCUP in the period exploited the mood and predisposition of the urban residents and scored some points in the political struggle against the GMD, especially in the student movement. By June 1946 students had become the main allies of the Communists in their struggle in Beiping–Tianjin.

June 1946–June 1947

Students and other educated youths remained the core of the Communist democratic movement in Beiping–Tianjin. The return of Beida, Qingda, Nankai, and Yanjing universities to Beiping–Tianjin in the summer and fall of 1946 was very important in the Communist student movement. The cooperation and later union of the Southern Group and the Northern Group CCUP was a powerful force in the student movement.

Besides following Mao Zedong's "Sixteen-Character Guideline," the Southern Group also adopted other tactics before its arrival in Beiping: (1) Communicate and cooperate with the original CCUP in the city. (2) Penetrate deeper into the student movement and unite with the broadest masses; leave the small circle of fellow students at the Southwest Associated University, and establish good relations and cooperation with the broad masses of "middle" and "later progressive" students. (3) Pay attention to the political situation in Beiping and the ideological condition of students; join political and ideological work with activities of entertainment and service; avoid immediate and inappropriate political activity. (4) Utilize fully all kinds of legal organizations; seize the leadership of student self-governing associations, and establish class associations, fellow provincial associations, sports clubs, religious groups, and wall newspapers.[76]

Liu Ren of the Shanxi–Chahar–Hebei Central Bureau ordered its Student Work Committee to communicate with the Southern Group and learn from its experiences in Southwest China.[77] In September 1946 the Student Committee contacted "the person with overall responsibility" (Yuan Yongxi) of the Southern Group. Thus began the cooperation of the North and South in the Communist student movement in Beiping.[78] At an enlarged cadres' meeting on 11 August 1946, the Tianjin City Work Committee also reported on the importance of the Southern Group to the student movement in the city. Members of the Tianjin

Student Committee began to cooperate with the Southern Group and the Northern (Beiping) Group in 1947.[79]

Following the policy of student activity designed by the Southern Group, the Communists and the Democratic Youth League and Alliance members centered on uniting the students and capturing the leadership of the self-governing associations. At Beijing University the CCUP members stressed the equal status of the Beida students at the Southwest Associated University and those at the Provisional University (the reeducation center) in Beiping. This was an appeal to the second group of students to cooperate with the first one.[80] Ke Zaishuo (1924–), a Fujianese and an economics student (1946–48), became the two-time chairman of Beida Self-Governing Association (1947–48). (Later, this Southern Group member served as chairman of the North China Student Association.)[81] At Qingda the Communists emphasized the same theme of equal status among students from the North and the South, and on 26 December 1946 took control of the Student Self-Governing Association.[82] At Yanda the "progressive" students took control of the Student Self-Governing Association in June 1946. In the same month the association turned a farewell party for J. Leighton Stuart, chancellor of Yanda who became the new United States ambassador to China, into a protest against the American support of Chiang Kai-shek in the Chinese Civil War.[83]

In Tianjin the CCUP and its "progressive" allies also controlled the student self-governing associations. At Nankai University, Yang Lu, a Shandongese and an economics student (1946–47), was the chairman of the Student Self-Governing Association.[84] At Beiyang University, under the leadership of Sha Xiaoquan, the CCUP and the "progressives" controlled the Student Self-Governing Association from August 1946 to January 1949. Beiyang was thus the "reddest" university in Tianjin.[85]

Outside the campuses, the Communists also attempted to discredit the GMD government. As the Anti-Examination Movement had already subsided, the Communists turned to the issue of American troops in China. In September 1946 the Beiping Special Vocational and Higher Schools Alumni United Association protested strongly the shooting of a Chinese youth by the American military police.[86]

In Tianjin the CCUP also used the anti-American sentiment to discredit the GMD. But in mid-1946 the CCUP in the city had to face a crisis as a result of the GMD attack on the Communist Central Plains and other "Liberated" Areas. On 5 May 1946, the Tianjin Work Committee had ordered the underground organizations in the city to be on high alert for the outbreak of civil war. The top priority at the time was to keep the organizations intact; all activities could be put on hold. The cadres whose identities had been discovered by the GMD authorities were required to retreat to CCP areas.[87] This measure was caused by the GMD assault on Shengfangzhen in the rural area of Tianjin.[88]

On 7 and 8 July 1946, the Tianjin Work Committee twice ordered the retreat of all exposed Party members and "progressives," even at the risk of temporary cessation of work in the city. By the end of August 150 members and "progressives" had left Tianjin; the majority of them were the backbone of the student movement.[89] This emergency action was a direct result of the GMD crackdown on students. The GMD installed its own principals at the "progressive" schools, such as Yaohua and Guangdong middle schools. Even the chairman of the Tianjin Student Association was arrested, capping a major setback for the Communist student movement.[90]

The struggle between the GMD (and its Three People's Principles Youth Corps) and the CCUP within the schools was so fierce that a newspaper in Beiping argued in August that the schools should not be bases for party struggles.[91] But how could the parties (especially the CCP) abandon their activities among the youth, the center of urban political struggle?

In September 1946 the Communist underground remained strong in the student movement even though most of the members and "progressives" had gone. By this time Nankai University had returned to Tianjin, and other universities and colleges had done the same. Besides, some teachers and students in Beiping were also transferred to Tianjin. A new situation thus emerged in the Communist student activities. There were three groups: Northern Group and its Democratic Youth League; Southern Group and its Democratic Youth Alliance; and Local Group (Urban Work Department of the Central Hebei Base Area replacing the Tianjin Work Committee) and its Democratic Youth Alliance. These three Communist groups redeveloped activities in the respective schools and waited for an occasion that would revitalize their student movement.

One incident in Beiping brought the anti-American sentiment to the boiling point. On Christmas Eve of 1946, two American Marines were accused of assaulting and raping a Beida student, Shen Chong.[92] This incident was reported in several Beiping newspapers on 26 December.[93] No details were given. However, that the case was mentioned at all in GMD Beiping was evidently an accident or due to oversight in censorship or in editorial supervision.[94] Four months after the episode, the Beiping Police Chief stated that the case could have been settled satisfactorily if there had been complete secrecy. The press reports, however, complicated everything, and in consequence it became a national issue.[95]

On 25 December the CCUP at Beida learned about the Shen Chong Incident from an underground Communist (Li Bingquan) who worked as a reporter at *Pingming ribao*. The following day the CCUP female students launched an anti-American protest on campus. On 27 December the History Society at Beida arranged a meeting of representatives of various departments and societies at the university. When the meeting broke up in confusion amid anti-American and progovernment shouts, a Preparatory Committee of Beida Students Protesting the Brutality of American Military Personnel was formed—the nucleus for the forthcoming anti-American demonstration. By then the rape case was blown out of proportion and magnified into an emotional issue of national dignity.[96]

Student activism at Beida was interpreted by the authorities as basically anti-government. Unable to prevent students from organizing for political action, the Nationalists tried to "counter organization with organization"—that is, *agents provocateurs* were mobilized to stage a counterattack. On 29 December, because of interference by GMD agents and right-wing students from off campus, the meeting of the representatives from all the colleges of Beida to further discuss the incident had to be canceled.[97]

By then, however, the CCUP had begun to use the spontaneous reactions on the rape case and considered an anti-American demonstration. Based on support from both the Northern Group and the Southern Group, the CCUP Student Work Committee sent agents to communicate with Qingda and Yanda students. On the morning of 30 December, the CCUP finally decided to participate in a parade using all propaganda materials, including flags made the night before, after learning that Qingda and Yanda had agreed to take part.[98]

At Qingda, the CCUP and its Democratic Youth Alliance at first were cautious about the launching of an anti-American demonstration. First, they did not know the opinion of the masses, and, second, examinations at the university were approaching. Therefore they decided to spread the news of the alleged rape first within the campus. Having received a strong response from the students, the CCUP and the Democratic Youth Alliance in the Qingda Self-Governing Association mobilized other "progressive" students in the association and various departmental societies to deliberate on a demonstration. In order to avoid isolated agitation by Beida in the parade (it would be weak in momentum), the CCUP concluded that Qingda should mobilize other schools to create a large vanguard at the forthcoming demonstration. In response to the heated student meeting on 29 December at Beida, the Qingda CCUP finally discussed the parade issue with student representatives from Yanda.[99]

At Yanjing, the Communist-infiltrated Student Self-Governing Association (most of them were Democratic Youth Alliance members) decided to have class strikes on 28 December to protest the brutality of American troops. (Yanda was a unique place of protest because it was established by American Christian missionaries.) Having learned the news of the student meeting at Beida, the Yanda Student Self-Governing Association decided to join with Qingda students in the forthcoming demonstration.[100]

In the early hours of 30 December, the Qingda and Yanda students resolved to launch the parade and informed Beida of this decision. Afterward the CCUP and Democratic Youth Alliance members went to prepare various materials. After daybreak Qingda and Yanda students marched into Beiping and joined with Beida students.[101]

The GMD authorities were aware of the powder keg created by the Shen Chong Incident. One GMD newspaper on 29 December noted that "public sentiment was aroused to a fury. At the time we were instructed repeatedly by local authorities to be discreet in publicizing the news. Now ... we cannot keep silence. . . . Severe punishment should be meted out to the criminals involved. . . . As a consequence Sino-American friendship will be impaired. . . . The problem whether American troops should be withdrawn from China will affect major policies of both the Chinese and American governments."[102] On the same day, however, another newspaper reported that the director of the GMD Beiping Municipal Party Bureau, Wu Zhuren, "with a view to controlling the current situation . . . and preventing exploitation of the incident by intriguers . . . , advised the local press not to give undue prominence to the affair, . . . so as not to mix it up with politics."[103]

On the afternoon of 30 December, about five thousand students from eight universities and colleges and several thousand more from middle schools and other social sectors paraded on the main streets of Beiping. Their activities were confined largely to shouting anti-American slogans, such as "Get away U.S. Army!" "Go home, GI's!" and "Demonstration against brutalities of American military personnel!"[104] Communist members were in the midst of the parade. They claimed that they directed the demonstration and avoided confrontation with the GMD police and soldiers.[105] The GMD authorities actually wanted to prevent the students from any violence, and the demonstrators could do little more than chant slogans. Also, the Nationalists were not determined to break up the demonstration, although the Central Statistics Bureau was aware of the Communist instigation activities at Beijing, Qinghua, Yanjing, and Nankai universities.[106]

The parade lasted for more than two hours, but there were no incidents involving Americans. In Beiping there were more than six thousand American troops. American vehicles dominated traffic; U.S. troops operated the city's two airports, and they guarded the only rail communications to the sea. A demonstration might have had disastrous consequences. American military personnel were therefore confined to quarters, and other Americans were advised to stay off the streets. Machine guns were mounted on the walls at various Marine barracks. On the following day, however, Americans found it safe to go about their business.[107]

Among intellectuals the bitterness was intense. Thirteen professors of Yanda, including two American members of the faculty, signed a petition demanding the withdrawal of American troops from China. Yanda students petitioned for suspension of accommodations for American teachers and students and their families on the campus and for settlement of the rape case.[108] Hu Shi, chancellor of Beida, expressed sympathy with the students and offered to serve as counsel for the victim, but he also urged settlement through legal channels and tried to persuade the students not to go on strike.[109] Mayor He Siyuan, following the demonstration, said that he would have joined it himself if he were younger. He demanded that the American authorities punish the culprits.[110] Other university professors and social organizations also demanded punishment and the evacuation of American forces.

The furor over the rape case spread to other big cities. In Tianjin, Nankai University was the first school to mobilize against the American troops. On 27

December twenty-four Communists and "progressive" students at the university posted the first protest article on campus. This article stressed that the brutal rape case blemished the Chinese nation.[111] On the following day, a protest letter signed by "a group of middle school female students" was sent to a major newspaper, condemning the rape case and demanding the punishment of the culprits and the withdrawal of American troops.[112] On 30 December a Tianjin Students Protest American Brutality Association was formed. That night the deputy secretary of the CCUP student committee (of the Northern Group) personally asked the Yaohua Middle School underground party's "person with overall responsibility" to mobilize students to demand the withdrawal of American troops. The following day the representatives of the self-governing associations of Nankai and Beiyang universities visited Yaohua and discussed the mobilization of university and middle school students for the "antibrutality" parade. Under the influence of the underground Party and "positive" members, Yaohua representatives decided to participate in the forthcoming demonstration.[113]

Around the same time Mayor Du Jianshi pressured Nankai and Beiyang authorities to urge students to resume classes. The Three People's Principles Youth Corps also organized a Tianjin City Students Righteous Association and published newspaper articles, which emphasized the separation of the rape case from the American national policy (of stationing troops in China) and argued that students should not carry out any anti-American action. But the GMD efforts were of little avail. On New Year's Day of 1947, three thousand college and middle school students launched an anti-American demonstration in the city. On the same day an American military police Jeep coincidentally struck and injured a six-year-old Chinese boy. Under students' pressure, Mayor Du gave his blessing to the students' demands for withdrawal of American troops and for an American apology to the Chinese authorities.[114]

Since Mayor Du endorsed the demands, the student strikes at various schools ended in Tianjin on 3 and 4 January. Furthermore, the students at Nankai and Beiyang universities declared that resuming studies was neither a compromise nor an end to the anti-American movement. They would not be satisfied until all American troops left China.[115]

On 30 January a Beiping–Tianjin Schools Protest American Brutality Association was formed and it united the students in North China. The association made three demands: the adoption of an independent foreign policy by the GMD government; an immediate end to the Civil War; and the establishment of a coalition government.[116] The underground Student Work Committee also used the same association to establish the Beiping City Human Rights Protection Committee, which appealed to students, "progressive" professors, and well-known personalities for sympathy and support.[117]

As for the two American Marines involved in the rape case, one of them (Pierson William) was found guilty at a Navy court-martial (not in Chinese court) in Beiping and sentenced to ten years imprisonment. The two Marines left

China in February 1947, however, and the verdict was overturned by the U.S. naval authorities in Washington, D.C., on 17 June 1947. This legal outcome was a severe political embarrassment to the GMD government.[118]

In historical perspective, the Shen Chong Incident was a major case study in the Chinese student movement during the Civil War. The first issue was the victim herself. The fact that her father was a section chief in the GMD Transportation Ministry and her grandfather (Shen Baozhen) a well-known official in the Qing Dynasty made the matter particularly sensitive and sensational. The GMD seemed to admit that the rape took place but charged that she was a Communist. (In 1950 the CCP in Nanjing openly declared that Shen Chong had been a Communist member.)[119] No matter what, her rape case did develop into a national issue.

Why did this rape case become a *cause célèbre*? One explanation was student elitism. The rape of a coed from Beida, the institution most closely associated with the May Fourth tradition, was not only an insult to the leading national university, but also an insult to China itself. The incident also became a symbol of crumbling hopes for a sovereign and respected China devoid of foreign imperialism. The privileges enjoyed by the Americans in China reminded the students of a hundred years of national humiliation. Chinese nationalism was thus a key element in the anti-American movement. Furthermore, the student protests in this incident associated the Americans with the Chinese Civil War. The United States was supporting the GMD, and some Chinese put the primary blame for failure of negotiations for a coalition government on the American-assisted GMD. Sino-American incidents had been resented but tolerated during World War II, for American aid met the needs of the nation. In the winter of 1946–47, when benefits of the American intrusion were being questioned, long-submerged resentments surfaced with violence.[120]

As for the GMD, the Shen Chong Incident placed it in a most awkward position. If the Nationalists denounced the Americans to appease the populace and to head off what might easily develop into an antigovernment demonstration, they risked trouble with the Americans and possible loss of the support so necessary to them. If they shielded the Americans they would be subject to more violent criticism from the populace. By playing on the prejudices of the populace, their political enemies could use the incident as a wedge for a Communist-led rebellion.[121] It turned out that the GMD authorities had to condemn the American brutality and were obliged to lead the agitation in order to control it.

In late 1946 the GMD authorities regarded the Shen Chong Incident as a legal issue and did not want it to become more serious.[122] In his New Year (1947) address to the Chinese people, Chiang Kai-shek urged the youth to help construct the nation and not to waste their energy in abstract political struggles, because they would be manipulated by treacherous politicians (that is, Communists and left-wingers). In other words, the Chinese youth should not get involved in student movements.[123] In early January the GMD Executive and

Education ministries issued orders forbidding students to participate in parades and demonstrations.[124] Although they had initially shown considerable tolerance toward the demonstrations, the GMD authorities resorted to wholesale arrests in February 1947, because of their inability to control the situation by peaceful means. On 18 February the GMD Beiping authorities carried out a house-to-house investigation. During the process eight thousand soldiers and policemen arrested more than two thousand residents who had no identification papers, owned illegal weapons, or consumed unlawful drugs. Among the arrested were professors, teachers, students, traders, and bookstore owners. Although the authorities later released more than a thousand of them, their actions were still condemned as "totalitarian" repression and violation of human rights.[125] (The GMD was also condemned earlier for the assassinations of Li Gongpu and Wen Yiduo, two important members of the Democratic League, in Kunming in July 1946.)

Refusing to demand withdrawal of all American influence contributed to the Nationalists' image as a client of the United States. This was a serious problem at a time when the United States was being depicted by the Communists as "imperialist leader of the West." The commitment of the GMD to Chinese nationalism was being questioned.[126] The anti-American demonstrations were the first move since the beginning of the anti-Japanese war to unite all organized student activity independent of the GMD government. A Communist-dominated All-China Students Association developed, causing the end of GMD control within the student community.[127]

The CCP welcomed the Shen Chong Incident because it gave it a good reason to demand the complete withdrawal of American troops and the end of American influence. On 1 July 1946, the CCP CC had already decided on launching an anti-American movement. On 7 July the Communist Beiping Urban Work Committee had issued a Directive on Anti-American Work. It stated that according to the current internal and external conditions, the Americans challenged the Chinese people directly. In fighting the American government for the benefit of the Chinese people and the world proletarian class, the Communists must attack the United States and isolate the GMD. The Communists should appeal to the masses and inform them of the "atrocities" of the Americans—the suppression of the Chinese people, the insulting of Chinese women, and the casualties caused by American military vehicles.[128] On 31 December the CCP CC issued a directive that called for the Communist organizing of masses in the big cities to support the Beiping student movement.[129]

The CCP CC directive of 5 January 1947 emphasized the emerging high tide of anti-American feeling. It called for mobilizing students and women to discredit the GMD and the United States.[130] One day later, the CCP CC emphasized the important impact of the anti-American student movement in Beiping–Tianjin, Nanjing, and Shanghai, which gradually was coordinating with the self-defense war in Communist areas. The CCP CC directed all local, central, and branch Party bureaus to use the student movement to expand patriotic ideology and to expose the Nationalist–American cooperation in sabotaging the cease-fire and prolonging the Civil War. The Party should continue to develop "positive" students and to strengthen various student organizations for future struggles.[131] Obviously, the student movement was the core of Communist activity in Beiping–Tianjin and other GMD cities.

On 29 January 1947, the United States announced that it had decided to abandon its role as mediator between the Chinese government and the CCP. American personnel involved in that effort would be withdrawn as rapidly as possible. Although a plan for the continuing reduction of American troops in China had already been announced on 18 December 1946, the Shen Chong Incident might have hastened the abandonment of the mediation. Most of the American troops were gone by the end of 1947.[132] The Communist-instigated "American Troops Quit China Movement," supported by the spontaneous public reaction to American misbehavior, was satisfied.

Communist literature stressed the Party's leadership role in the protests as an expression of the will of the people.[133] According to their accounts of the anti-American movement, the Communists and the Democratic Youth Alliance members were involved in the self-governing associations of Qinghua, Yanjing, Nankai, and Beiyang universities. But involvement did not guarantee the successful use of these student organizations in the anti-American movement. At the time there existed no self-governing association at Beida, and the Communist influence there could not be great. As discussed before, the Communist underground at Beida was at first hesitant about a large-scale demonstration against the Americans. We may conclude, therefore, that the Communists and their allies were just a small minority within the major universities in Beiping–Tianjin. They were, however, determined to undermine the American support of the GMD and were "opportunists" who exploited the anti-American sentiment among some students and intellectuals for their political aims. While most of these students remained unenthusiastic about communism, they appreciated the propaganda and material support of the Communists. The seeming similarity of goals between these two groups made easier the future acceptance of radical leadership in student organizations.

The Communists claimed that half a million people were involved in the anti-American movement in various major cities in China.[134] But this was a small minority in terms of China's population (about 500 million). There was no evidence of massive activity, although the populace in general supported or sympathized with anti-Americanism. The origins of that sentiment were to be found not only in the Communist anti-imperialist ideology and rhetoric, but also in the protests of the non-Communist urban educated elite.[135]

The impact of the Communist propaganda—that there had been more than three thousand Chinese casualties inflicted by American military personnel since September 1945—on the Chinese people was unknown. However, the "Movement Protesting the Brutality of American Military Personnel in China" gave new life to the Communist student movement.[136] The inability of the GMD to control the students presented an opportunity for the CCP to grasp the flag of Chinese nationalism and gradually lead the students. The movement illustrated the significance of student power in Chinese politics, a fact that the CCP would continue to exploit. In "Greet the New High Tide of the Chinese Revolution" (1 February 1947), Mao Zedong praised the student movement in Beiping, which had spread to other big cities, as a new upsurge in the struggle against the GMD.[137] The Antibrutality Movement was so successful that the Beiping Student Work Committee glorified it as a great mass movement as historically important as the May Fourth Movement, the May Thirteenth Movement, and the December Ninth Movement. Furthermore, the anti-American content of the Anti-brutality Movement coordinated with the "peace and democracy" or "anti–Civil War and fight for freedom" slogan of the December First Movement.[138] The GMD equally understood the significance of the Antibrutality Movement and student power but failed to work hard to shift the student community to its side.

Moreover, by early 1947 Zhou Enlai had become the spokesman for the CCUP operation in GMD China. Even before he assumed the directorship of the CCP CC Urban Work Department on 29 April 1947 (he retained the title until 26 September 1948), on 28 February 1947 Zhou had drafted a directive for the CCP CC concerning the tactics for struggles in GMD areas. It stressed that

> the Communists must ... strive to form a broad front ... leading ... the students ... against the United States. ... [They] should first unite the majority of the students to demand that the school authorities help to guarantee their personal safety and release their fellow students, and then unite with the school authorities to demand that the local authorities do the same. If arrests continue, the students should take defensive measures in their schools, such as going out and coming back in groups for mutual protection. And when conditions are ripe, they can take such actions as boycotting classes and demanding the release of their fellow students. At the same time, by linking the students' struggle with the economic struggle and sometimes by switching to the latter, we can mobilize more people to join in and make it easier for the struggle to become legal.[139]

This CCP CC document showed that by early 1947 the students had become the most important elements in the Communist "patriotic and democratic movement." The CCP said the movement "had gradually been able to coordinate with the victory of the self-defense war in Liberated [CCP] Areas."[140] In order to avoid the annihilation of the student movement in GMD areas, Zhou Enlai suggested a temporary defensive tactic in light of the GMD suppression of the students and expulsion of Communist representatives from the GMD cities in February 1947.[141] The student movement thus subsided for a short while. Indeed, in a directive dated 1 March 1947, the CCP CC called for a defensive and legal form of struggle for the "patriotic and democratic movement." Communist students and workers should conceal themselves by consolidating the majority masses within their schools and factories.[142]

On 3 May 1947, the GMD Central News Agency published the CCP's (top-secret) "Resolution on the Program on the Line for Underground Struggle" (passed by the CCP Politburo on 11 March 1947). The Communists stressed the important task of uniting with China's "middle" parties (for example, by sending agents to attend the meetings of the Democratic League) in neutralizing the GMD and winning the support of the population. The CCUP's agitation groups and core organizations should also go to work among the GMD, the Democratic Socialist Party, and the China Youth Party to neutralize their organizations. In labor groups, the CCUP must spread the Party's policy in the "yellow unions" (enemy-controlled unions) and particularly in every communication organ.[143]

In a CCP CC directive on the "patriotic and democratic movement" in GMD areas (5 May 1947), Zhou Enlai gave these instructions:

> . . . [the GMD] are unable to extricate themselves from their . . . crises. . . . They have fabricated[?] a "Program of the CCP on the Line for Underground Struggle." . . . e.g., [We should] protect our Party and the other democratic, progressive forces . . . mobilizing the masses to oppose the United States and Chiang Kai-shek. . . . To mobilize the masses, you [the Communists] should encourage them to put forward slogans which correspond to their urgent demands. . . . In the Party's propaganda work, emphasis should be laid on having non-Party people who hold jobs and have some degree of social standing criticize the current political situation and sharpen discontent through legal publications, newspapers, and public gatherings. . . . As for the Party's relations with democratic bodies, mass organizations, and leading progressives, we should recruit more well-hidden Party members and sympathizers.[144]

Since most workers were not well educated and enjoyed no social standing, Zhou's instructions were actually mainly concerned with the protection of and further work among intellectuals and students. The Communist urban activity would remain in tune with Mao Zedong's "Sixteen-Character Guideline."

In reality, the Communists did resume their activities in April and May 1947, focusing on the issues of economic hardship and the Civil War. This time there was no single precipitating incident. The movement gained strength from the momentum created by the anti-American demonstrations and from economic problems and mismanagement by the Nationalists.

In early 1947 China was in economic trouble, particularly because the GMD could not check rising inflation. In February the GMD government announced an emergency economic program, freezing the cost-of-living index to which wages had been pegged. Ceilings were placed on prices of essential commodities. Yet prices continued to rise, and rice riots broke out in many GMD cities. The whole populace was affected by the unbearable rising cost of living in April and May.[145] In the academic community, some students lacked sufficient food and clothing and even had to abandon studies because they could not afford the school expenses. Professors' salaries were greatly reduced as a result of inflation, and a few of them even committed suicide because of poverty.[146]

At this time the Chinese people saw the Civil War as the major cause of China's economic plight. In this climate a new wave of student demonstrations erupted in May 1947 (in the wake of a number of rice riots in South China in April). These student protests originated in the Nanjing–Shanghai area and spread to other urban centers.[147]

In Beiping–Tianjin the slogan of the student protests was "oppose hunger, oppose Civil War."[148] In February 1947 the CCP CC cabled the Shanxi–Chahar–Hebei Central Bureau to strengthen its leadership over the Party in the Beiping–Tianjin White area and to expand the students' patriotic movement. Accordingly, the Communist Student Committee in Beiping carried out the order of the CCP CC by launching a new wave of protests in the forthcoming May Fourth Memorial Week.[149]

Beida was the center of the Memorial Week. During this period the CCUP paid particular attention to working with professors in various activities. Simultaneously, the Communists used the occasion to communicate with other college and middle school students. They spread the May Fourth spirit in "struggling for sovereignty externally, and exterminating national enemy [GMD implied] internally."[150] Above all, the Communists claimed that they had captured the leadership of the student association of Beida—the College and Department United Association.[151]

In order to ignite the fire of student protests, the Communist Student Committee on 8 and 13 May instigated a middle school protest against the graduation examination system implemented by the GMD Education Ministry. The mayor of Beiping agreed to refer the matter to the Education Ministry.[152] The CCUP scored a minor victory—a warm-up exercise for the coming large-scale movement.

Around the same time there occurred a four-college protest against merging with other universities because of GMD budget cuts for education. Various schools in Beiping also mobilized an antihunger movement because of the economic hardships of both teachers and students caused by the GMD's "emergency economic measure," that is, a new exchange rate between *fabi* and U.S. dollars that devalued the former by three quarters in the previous February.[153] These issues jointly created the largest anti–Civil War protest of the period.

It was at Beida that the CCUP adopted the slogan "antihunger and anti–Civil War" and started an Antihunger Anti–Civil War Action Committee on 16 May. (By then the CCUP and its allies made up one-third of the representatives of the Beida College–Department United Association, a prototype of the self-governing association.) At Qingda the students earlier had called for a three-day strike, to begin on 17 May, protesting the Civil War and the government's lack of concern for the living conditions of teachers and students.[154] Also, the CCUP at Qingda first adopted the slogan "antihunger, antipersecution, and anti–Civil War."

A crisis occurred on 18 May. A group of students doing propaganda work in the center of the city were beaten by men of the 208th Division of the GMD Youth Army.[155] On the same day the government promulgated the Provisional Measures for the Maintenance of Public Order.

In the meantime, in Tianjin the Communists used the anti–Civil War sentiment among college and middle school students to agitate for the formation of an Anti–Civil War Committee at Nankai and Beiyang universities. On the evening of 18 May, the GMD special agents were accused of disrupting a school play at Nankai. The play was a response to the beating of a student by the Beiping authorities. The CCUP realized that the time was now ripe for further actions. Besides launching class strikes at Nankai and Beiyang and other colleges and middle schools, the Communists arranged a fifteen-man petition group to visit the municipal government in protest of the incident at Nankai and the Civil War in general. There was no positive response from the local authorities.[156]

On the afternoon of 19 May, the North China Students Antihunger Anti–Civil War United Association composed of fourteen Beiping–Tianjin schools was formed in Beiping.[157] Many different issues in Beiping–Tianjin were expressed openly in large-scale student parades on 20 May in Beiping and Tianjin. Activists of the Northern Group and the Southern Group coordinated the slogans, parade routes, and lineup of the participating student groups.[158]

In Beiping the slogans were "Soldiers of the War of Resistance against Japan do not fight the Civil War!" "Oppose the Civil War! Oppose hunger!" "Stop conscription of soldiers and collection of food!" "Protest the 'May Eighteenth bloody incident'!" "Down with dictatorship!" "Down with the special agents!" and "Fight for basic human rights and freedoms!"[159] In Tianjin slogans included "Oppose the Civil War, demand peace!" "Oppose hunger, demand rice to eat!" "Oppose dictatorship, demand democracy!" and "Abolish exorbitant taxes and dues!"[160]

Until the parade on 20 May, the Nationalists had also tried various means to seize the leadership of the Beiping–Tianjin students. The Three People's Principles Youth Corps was used specifically to promote GMD policies in schools and to attempt to exert control over the student organizations, particularly the self-governing associations. However, the development of student protests on and off the campuses indicated that the Youth Corps failed to become the leaders of student thought. Many students seemed alienated from the GMD and susceptible to Communist propaganda. (The GMD scholars are generally "silent" on the successful GMD-led student movement, except that of the anti-Soviet and anti-Communist movement of February 1946, during the Civil War period. They tend to agree that most of the student protests in the period were Communist-instigated or Communist-led.)[161]

In Beiping the parade on 20 May should have been carried out peacefully, since the director of the Executive Headquarters, Li Zongren, adopted a policy of nonintervention.[162] However, plainclothesmen of unknown identity attacked the students. Li himself could not control the subsequent clashes between the students and the local authorities. Nonetheless, on 27 May the Executive Headquarters announced that the Provisional Measures for the Maintenance of Public Order would henceforth be fully implemented in Beiping.[163] Li had become strict on the maintenance of public order.

The momentum of the "May Twentieth Movement" in GMD cities was so great that Zhou Enlai, in a CCP CC directive (23 May 1947) to the Shanghai Bureau and Hong Kong Branch Bureau, called for the formation of a "Second Battlefront" (Diertiao zhanxian) in the GMD-controlled areas.[164] Seven days later Mao Zedong discussed the same battlefront. But since then Mao, not Zhou, has been regarded as the ultimate authority on the "Two Battlefronts." In his "Chiang Kai-shek's Government Is Besieged by the Whole People" (30 May 1947), Mao stressed:

> There are now two battlefronts in China. The war between Chiang Kai-shek's invading troops and the PLA constitutes the first front. Now a second front has emerged, that is, the sharp struggle between the great and righteous student movement and the reactionary Chiang Kai-shek government. The slogan of the student movement is "Food, Peace, Freedom" or "Against Hunger, Against Civil War, Against Persecution.". . . Public sympathy is all on the side of the students, Chiang Kai-shek . . . [is] isolated. . . . The student movement is part of the whole people's movement, and is also the organizer of the whole people's movement. The upsurge of the student movement will inevitably promote an upsurge of the whole people's movement.[165]

Here the "Second Battlefront" mainly referred to the anti-Chiang (and anti-American) student movement in the GMD-controlled (urban) areas during the Civil War period. The "Second Battlefront" could also mean: (1) the entire Communist work in White areas; (2) the anti-American, anti-Chiang "people's democratic movement" in GMD areas.[166] The "Second Battlefront" nevertheless was very important to the political struggle of the CCP in urban China. Chiang Kai-shek also admitted, "The influence of this 'student tide' on the loss of the national strength is incalculable."[167] He failed to do anything about it, however.

Realizing that the GMD relied on the Youth Army, the local police, and the military units to maintain law and order, the Communists targeted these groups. On 23 May Zhou Enlai drafted a CCP CC directive for work among the Youth Army and the Nationalist military and police units. It clearly stated: "In order to avoid antagonism developed within the Youth Army students, military police, policemen, and soldiers, and to win their sympathy for the student movement so as to break Chiang Kai-shek's persecution . . . you [all those involved in the student movement] should rapidly work among the Youth Army, military and police units by means of various organizations and positive elements."[168] In accordance with this directive, the Communist Student Committee in Beiping sent agents to communicate with the 208th Division of the Youth Army. After that, no more students were beaten by the Youth Army.[169]

In Tianjin the corresponding parade led by Nankai University students on 20 May ended in a bloody confrontation.[170] The Communists accused the Three People's Principles Youth Corps of directing its Tianjin Students and Patriotic Groups Association to break up the legal parade and to beat up dozens of students. The mayor of Tianjin subsequently agreed to punish the assailants and to release seventeen students arrested by the GMD.[171]

So far the academic community had supported the student movement. On 28 May 585 professors and other personnel from universities and colleges in Beiping–Tianjin announced support for the student protest movement. Their influential statement, initiated by the Democratic League, demanded an immediate end to the Civil War and the formation of a coalition government.[172] Since the student protest movement occurred in GMD cities, not in Communist territories, and nothing indicated that both the GMD and the CCP would cease firing and establish a coalition government, the statement was an attack on the GMD government rather than the CCP.

One day later, 102 professors from Beida and Qingda published an open letter to the students and the government concerning the Anti–Civil War Movement. It praised the sincerity and bravery of the students and expressed sympathy for the "pure" (that is, nonpolitical) movement. The letter acknowledged the danger that existed, however, and advised the students not to get into unnecessary trouble. It also chastised the local authorities for suppressing the student protests. Government should stop repression.[173] This letter was balanced in content, but politically it implied a severe criticism of the GMD, not the CCP.

Riding the tide of a nationwide student protest in May, the Communists also planned an Anti–Civil War Movement Day on 2 June. Their seven-point policy for the day was: (1) Organize the movement on a national level; (2) avoid conflict with the military and police forces; (3) launch class, market, and labor strikes; (4) spread propaganda; (5) deal with the GMD special agents; (6) create chaos; (7) strengthen the blockade of food for the GMD urban areas (the Beiping–Tianjin CCUP would attempt to raise food prices or to increase hardship for the residents, who would blame the GMD for the problems).[174] However, since the GMD authorities were well prepared to suppress the parade,[175] the Communist student activists decided to launch the demonstration on various school campuses, not in the streets outside. This change of tactic was intended to avoid further bloodshed, to consolidate the victories won, and to maintain and expand the organizations. Because of this plan, little activity occurred in the streets on the Anti–Civil War Day. Instead, the students in Beiping–Tianjin organized memorial meetings for soldiers and civilians who died in the Civil War.[176] (In a directive dated 3 June 1947, the CCP CC endorsed this tactic in

Beiping–Tianjin.)[177] On the same day the North China Antihunger Anti–Civil War United Association in Beiping was reorganized into the North China Students Association. The All-China Students Association was later formed secretly on 15 June 1947 in Shanghai. Afterward the Communist student movement could claim a national basis.[178]

For the Communists, the Antihunger Anti–Civil War Movement meant victory in their student activity. This view was reflected in the general summary report of the Beiping Student Work Committee and its report to Liu Ren.[179] While the movement in Beiping–Tianjin had shortcomings, such as the students' erroneously blaming soldiers for the rice shortage, it shook the political foundation of the Nationalist rule. The Communists claimed again that they led the movement. They assessed "correctly" the contemporary situation and the sentiment of the masses. They especially fulfilled the demands of the politically sensitive young students, a vanguard in the Chinese revolution. Zhou Enlai also played a conspicuous role in drafting CCP CC directives that guided the movement and prevented unnecessary setbacks. The Communists combined economic and political struggles successfully. By emphasizing the issues of hunger and the huge GMD budget for military affairs, the Communists convinced many people of the "brutality and reaction" of the government.[180]

Also, the movement showed the effectiveness of the united-front tactic. In Beiping–Tianjin many teachers and professors were sympathetic with the student protests and were willing to accuse the government of suppression and atrocities. While not all "democratic personalities" supported the movement, their attitude and actions reflected the growing alienation of the GMD from academic circles and the populace, and thus aided Communist activities.

As for the GMD, the movement once again showed government incompetence in leading the urban youth. Already discredited in the Shen Chong Incident, the GMD was to suffer an even more serious setback in the student movement. The antidemonstration order of the GMD Beiping–Tianjin Garrison Command Post was generally ignored. The Executive Headquarters was ineffectual in controlling the students.[181] Above all, the amalgamation of the Three People's Principles Youth Corps with the GMD in September 1947 signified the failure of the GMD to capture leadership of Chinese students.

From mid-1946 to mid-1947, the CCUP continued its student/intellectual–centered cultural sphere, although in the news agencies and newspaper offices in Beiping, the total number of Party members remained small (fewer than twenty).[182] Nonetheless, the CCUP planted four members in the staff of *Pingming ribao*. Ji Gang (Northern Group member) was responsible for municipal administrative news; Li Mengbei (Northern Group member), for political and military news; Yang Lu (Northern Group member), for economic news. Li Bingquan (Southern Group member) was the supervisor of the Investigation Section. He had a relative who later became the head of the Liaison Section of the North China Bandit-Suppression Headquarters. Ji and Li Mengbei (and

Yang) did not know that Li Bingquan was a CCUP member.[183] (The Nationalists blacklisted Ji Gang and Li Mengbei in August 1948. But tipped off by another underground Communist, Ji and Li retreated easily to CCP areas.) One may see, however, the obvious advantages of such Communist underground help to the political and military activities of the CCP outside Beiping and Tianjin. In June 1947 the Student Work Committee also used its influence within the Fatherland Theatrical Group and the Second Theatrical Corps to establish the Beiping City Theatrical Workers Association. Its stated mission was to serve the welfare of the members, but the association was actually a Communist organizational and united-front tool to increase activity among the professional and university theatrical groups and to show more "progressive" plays to the public.[184]

The CCUP student committees claimed to have established close connections with certain well-known personalities in the engineering and medical fields in Tianjin. The CCUP also sent agents to work among the Tianjin Industrial Association, Tianjin Banking Association, and Tianjin United Youth Society (a respectable community organization sponsored by social dignitaries). The CCUP even infiltrated the American-dominated Christian Youth Association, the majority of whose members joined the mainstream of the student movement.[185] An underground Party member (whose parents were Christians) at Nankai University pretended to be a Christian and worked within the Tianjin Christian Youth Association. Through the Bible study group, summer camp, choir, and poetry club, she developed "positive" students, some of whom later became Democratic Youth Alliance members.[186] But as a whole, the Communist influence within these organizations was not important in 1947–48.

While most of the left-wing student publications in Beiping–Tianjin were suppressed by the GMD, the Communist Zhongwai Publications Agency continued its secret operation, printing and distributing Communist literature in North China. In June 1947 the Communist Student Committee in Beiping established an important journal entitled *Xinmin ziliao* (News materials), which edited news and commentaries broadcast by radios in Communist areas. Until September 1948 *Xinmin ziliao* made a contribution in spreading the Communist views about the war front, the Communist areas, and the Communist urban work.[187]

To conclude, from mid-1946 to mid-1947, student protesters condemned the Americans and the GMD for brutality, hunger, and Civil War. The Nationalists neglected to respond and to vigorously condemn the Soviets and the Chinese Communists for the same things. By mid-1947 there had indeed emerged a "Second Battlefront" that was a constant annoyance to the GMD. Whether the GMD could overcome it was of utmost importance in maintaining law and order in the cities.

During this period the Beiping–Tianjin CCUP made great progress in student activities, especially in the May Twentieth Movement and in dominating the various student self-governing associations. The success in "student tides" prompted the emergence of the important GMD-Controlled Areas Student

Movement Small Group.[188] The Second Battlefront was thus firmly established to harass the GMD. In other words, the CCP had found a powerful political weapon—the students—to weaken the GMD rule in urban China. The Communists' chances to return to the big cities became better.

During the same period the Beiping–Tianjin GMD military and police authorities began to use excessive force, such as the mass arrests in February 1947 and the injury of students on 20 May 1947. The high-handed GMD actions were due to the earlier failure of moderate means. However, the stern Nationalist warnings to the students often turned out to be rhetorical in nature. There was no close cooperation among the various GMD organizations (for example, between Li Zongren's Beiping Executive Headquarters and the GMD's "Central" and youth armies in the city). Even the repressive GMD measures were not strong or ruthless enough to suppress the Communist-instigated student movement. Worse still, the GMD's policies failed to maintain the confidence of students and intellectuals and actually further alienated them.

Indeed, the Shen Chong Incident and the issue of "antihunger and anti–Civil War" were matters of intense public feeling for the CCP to use to stimulate "student tides" aimed at discrediting both the United States and, above all, the GMD. The CCUP within the academic community scored many points in political struggle.

Most important, the Communist student movement and the emergence of the Second Battlefront in the first half of 1947 in GMD areas shook the Nationalists' urban political foundation and disrupted their military strength. The GMD's overwhelming popularity in the immediate wake of the Japanese surrender had been destroyed. The Nationalist "70 percent politics, 30 percent military" policy obviously could not subdue the Communists. In early 1947, Zhu Anping, a Chinese liberal, criticized the GMD and depicted the Nationalist folly in urban China: the GMD's "tyrannical" style of behavior; the skimpy salaries of civil servants and teachers; the corrupt practices of government officials; the extreme dissatisfaction within business and industrial circles; the violent rise in prices; and the continuation of the Civil War.[189]

June 1947–August 1948

The CCUP in Beiping–Tianjin continued to focus on its student activities. Having avoided heavy losses by not demonstrating in the main streets on 2 June 1947, the Communist underground in Beiping reassessed the situation to find a pretext for more student protests. By the summer of 1947 the economy had become so miserable that many students were in danger of forced vacation in the fall. The Communists decided to launch the "Assist-Student Movement" from July to September. This movement was an example of legal struggle. On the one hand, it aimed at the betterment of the students' conditions; on the other hand, the students' loss of education as a result of the economy exposed the Nationalist incompetence. In order to give the movement legitimacy, the students invited university and college chancellors, middle school principals, GMD municipal leaders, the Beiping Executive Headquarters, and even an American consul to be sponsors of or consultants to the Beiping Municipal Assist-Student Committee. About three thousand students from various schools raised funds to finance organizing among the populace. By mid-September the students had raised Ch $500 million (not big money in those days of severe inflation) to assist fifteen hundred fellow students to continue their education at middle school and college levels. The Assist-Student Movement, the Communists claimed, was a successful democratic effort with a broad united front.[190]

The situation was more complicated in Tianjin. Because of the constant disturbances in rural areas, the GMD was more severe in suppressing Communist activities. In July 1947 the GMD announced a general mobilization order against the Communists. In the same month Tianjin authorities built moats and bunkers to strengthen the defenses of the city. Popular self-defense corps were formed, and the GMD mass media spread the theme of anti-Communism.[191]

While the GMD suppressed the activities of the All-China Student Association, the North China Student Association in Tianjin continued its task of recruiting "progressives" into the Communist camp. In the wake of the May Twentieth Movement, the CCUP expanded its influence among the students in Nankai and Beiyang universities. It also worked among legal organizations such as the Christian Youth Association.[192]

Following the advice of the Beiping Communist Student Committee, the CCUP in Tianjin decided to join with the Christian Youth Association in launching the Assist-Student Movement. As in Beiping, the Communist students encouraged prominent social leaders and even GMD politicians to become members of the Committee. While some of them later gave up their positions and even opposed the movement because of Communist infiltration, the project ended with a collection of Ch $300 million.[193]

The Assist-Student Movement was significant because it was broad-based in terms of participating schools and social elements. An article entitled "On Assisting the Students" in *Dagong bao* summed up the meaning of the movement: "The Assist-Student Movement is a social protest. It protests against those people who love wars and destroy education. The essence of the movement is Antihunger and Anti–Civil War."[194]

The Beiping–Tianjin GMD could do nothing to suppress the movement but it did score a major victory in arresting a number of important Southern Group and Northern Group Communists at Beida, Qingda, and Yanda from September to November 1947.[195] In particular, the arrest of Yuan Yongxi and Chen Lian on 6 September showed not the weakness of the Communist underground but the internal decay of the GMD. (Some children and relatives of high-level GMD members were CCUP cadres or "progressives.") During the three-month period the GMD also arrested three other Communist spies—a GMD lieutenant general

(Yuan Xinqing), a GMD major general (Xie Shiyan), and an acting director of the GMD Beiping Land Administration (Dong Jianping)—based on information from another captured CCUP member (Li Zhengxuan), who was in charge of a clandestine radio station in Beiping.[196]

In prison, Yuan Yongxi and Chen Lian refused to admit that they were Communists. Because of their special status (son-in-law and daughter of Chen Bulei, who served as Chiang Kai-shek's personal secretary) and the lack of concrete evidence, the GMD authorities sent them to Nanjing in late November. Since Yuan and Chen were proved to be members of the Democratic Youth Alliance, but not the CCP, Chiang Kai-shek did not persecute them but kept them in prison. Later, the secretary-general of the GMD Executive Yuan helped release Chen and Yuan, in January and May 1948, respectively. After the suicide of Chen Bulei (for despair over the national situation, according to his last testament) in Nanjing in November 1948, the couple reestablished contact with the CCUP in Shanghai and went to work in Beiping in February 1949. For whatever reasons they became Communists or were sympathetic to the CCP, these traitors to the GMD had a significant impact on the collapse of the GMD.

In October, in order to free the arrested students, the Communists in Beida organized a Beida Human Rights Protection Committee with the participation of professors. This was a response not only to the students in prison but to the GMD suppression of Communists everywhere.[197] (The GMD declared the Democratic League an illegal organization in the same month. Afterward the League operated underground.)[198] In the wake of the Yu Zisan Incident (the death of a Communist student leader at Zhejiang University),[199] the Communist Student Work Committee issued a directive on "fully mobilizing the masses to expose the reactionary nature of the GMD, and to hold limited class strikes."[200] In accordance with this directive, the Communists in the North China Student Association used the slogan of "antipersecution, antislander, anti-illegal arrest." The association and the students launched a demonstration on 6 November at Beida.[201] On the same day the Beiping Executive Headquarters forbade groups of ten or more students to move around school campuses. This tactic to destroy contact among various student organizations was aborted.

In Tianjin the GMD arrested a number of students from September to November 1947. Following the events in Beiping, however, the Nankai University established a Human Rights Protection Committee and held a memorial service for Yu Zisan on 6 November. Beiyang University followed suit with a three-day class strike.[202]

In general, though, arrests in the fall of 1947 were a setback for the Communist Student Committee and its activity was confined to school campuses. It did not launch large-scale demonstrations in the streets.

Understanding the importance of the student self-governing associations, the GMD Education Ministry on 14 December revised its rules. The revisions declared that candidates for the associations must be approved by the school authorities, who had the right to annul the decisions of the associations, and could disband them. Furthermore, the associations could not participate in outside activities. This Nationalist measure clearly aimed at breaking Communist control and use of the associations.[203] Three days later, the GMD authorities emphasized open leadership, not secret struggle, as the proper way of leading the students.[204] An attempt to challenge and change these rules at Tongji University in Shanghai resulted in the so-called "Tongji Bloody Incident" or "January Twenty-Ninth Incident."[205]

In order to oppose the revision of the student self-governing association at Tongji, students everywhere launched demonstrations. On 7 February 1948, the North China Student Association held a Beiping–Tianjin Students Support Tongji Joint Protest Meeting at Beida. Eight schools (Beida, Qingda, Yanda, Beiping Normal College, Sino-French University, Nankai University, Beiyang University, and Hebei Technical College) made a joint oath to reject the revised rules for the self-governing associations. The slogan of this meeting was "Anti-persecution, fight for freedom, support Tongji, rescue the arrested fellow students!" On 28 March the North China Student Association organized a huge bonfire in Beida to welcome the students from Tianjin and established a joint association to defend the rights of student self-governing organizations.[206]

By then it was obvious that North China Student Association was an anti-GMD organization that was Communist-controlled or at least Communist-infiltrated. On 29 March the Beiping Executive Headquarters ordered the suppression of the North China Student Association. Simultaneously, the GMD government declared that the students were "rioters" and the student movement "an open Communist plot." The association responded with a call to "defend the Student Association." Under the pretext of commemorating the seventy-two martyrs of the Yellow Flower Mound (who died on 29 March 1911), Beiping–Tianjin–Tangshan students gathered at Beida's "Democratic Square" and protested the GMD suppression of the association. Five thousand soldiers and policemen were present but did not break up the meeting.[207]

The Communist-instigated "April Storm" began with another Beiping–Tianjin student protest. On 2 April, Beida, Qingda, Yanda, Beiping Normal, Sino-French, Nankai, and Beiyang protested the GMD suppression of the North China Student Association and demanded the repeal of the order. On the following day, the students from these seven universities and colleges started a joint antisuppression, antihunger strike. During the two-week strike, the CCUP spread propaganda through the class-strike committees. Groups of ten students distributed anti-GMD pamphlets in the streets and markets, and posted short articles, cartoons, and folk songs on the street walls. Loudspeakers also spread the propaganda.[208]

A simultaneous demand for an increase in teachers' salaries and more public financial support for education was coupled with the movement to protect the North China Student Association. From February up to early April, students, faculty, and staff members at Beiping–Tianjin schools organized strikes demanding larger salaries and more support for education. On 6 April these movements launched the "six strikes" (teaching strike, job strike, research strike, medical attention strike, labor strike, class strike).[209]

On 7 April the GMD Beiping Garrison Command Post demanded the arrest of twelve Beida students accused of instigating labor and class strikes. Because of protest from both the students and the faculty members, the Garrison Command Post abandoned the arrest effort. These twelve students later retreated to CCP areas. The Communists claimed a victory in the "Twelve People Incident."[210]

The Communists created an "April Ninth Bloody Incident" in the aftermath of the beating of students by the GMD. On that day a number of unidentified people attacked Beiping Normal College, beat up some students, and arrested eight of them. On the following day the CCUP organized a six-thousand-man demonstration in front of the Beiping Executive Headquarters. The protesters posted these slogans on walls: "Antipersecution," "Antihunger," "Demand life in front of the mouth of the gun," "Constitution in Nanjing, arrest in Beiping," "Convocation of National Assembly in Nanjing, killing of students in Beiping," "Return life to the people," and "Teachers and students belong to the same family." The authorities finally agreed to send the eight arrested students to the hospital and not to arrest the twelve Beida students.[211]

On 10 April the GMD authorities called the striking students "bandits," and on 11 April they organized a "Beiping Municipal Students and Popular Masses Purge Communists Meeting" at Tiananmen Square. Afterward, the "Anti–Class-Strike Purge Communists Committee" led a parade shouting, "Down with the Communists!" "Down with the North China Student Association!" and "Anti-antihunger!" ("antihunger" was a Communist slogan). The parade stopped at Beida and demolished windows and furniture. The Communists called it the "April Eleventh Incident."[212]

In Tianjin the focus of the Communist student protest was on antipersecution and anti–special agents. On 4 April fifteen hundred students assembled at Beiyang University and raised a "democratic flag" (a gift from Beida students). The following day, the Communists claimed, some Nankai students were beaten up by GMD student agents. On 11 April there was an antipersecution meeting at Nankai with the slogan "Special agents get out of the school!"[213]

Based on the tactic of "struggling with reason, advantage, and restraint," the CCUP ordered the students to resume study on 14 April. In order to continue the united-front tactic, the Communists organized a grand "Beida People" meeting at the "Democratic Square," celebrating the union of students, faculty, and staff members. The GMD did not intervene. The April Storm was over, and the CCUP recruited a number of new Party, Democratic Youth Alliance, and Democratic Youth League members. The total strength of the CCUP at Beida at that time was almost eight hundred.[214]

The undeniable economic plight in North China was an important factor in the rise of the Communist student movement. One GMD measure that aggravated the economic problem in North China was the restrictions on transportation of food from the south to the north (in order hopefully to secure the GMD's political and economic power base in the south).[215] However, hunger itself could not guarantee an organized political movement against the GMD. Because of Communist activities the antihunger issue became linked to the antipersecution issue.

Maria Yen, a "progressive" Beida student in the late 1940s, linked the issues of hunger, the CCUP's activities, and the GMD's persecution (and incompetence) together in these words:

> During the spring and summer of [1947 and] 1948 the food situation got worse, and unrest among the people of Peking [Beijing] grew. Political demonstrations and strikes became our [students'] most familiar textbooks. Each demonstration made more followers for our leaders [CCUP members or their "progressive" allies]. Some students became sympathizers when they saw how stupid and brutal the [GMD] government's measures were against such protests. Others who had gone along mostly for the excitement discovered that official snoopers had put them down on the black list as suspected Communists. Once that label had been pinned on them, what else could they do except follow along behind their leaders?[216]

While the GMD understood clearly the CCUP's role behind the student movement, it could not shift the allegiance of the North China Student Association and the various student self-governing associations to its side. Trying to suppress their activities was a highly unpopular measure that alienated the academic community. The defeat of the GMD on this political front was very damaging to its rule in urban North China.[217]

The Communists carried out the struggle successfully with "reason, advantage, and restraint." The April Storm helped form a broad united front within the academic community and exposed the "reactionary" nature of the GMD in its economic and educational policies. In the wake of the April Storm, the student community in Beiping–Tianjin changed its attitudes. More and more students wanted to abandon study to continue the struggle against the GMD. This leftist mentality was welcomed by the Communists. On 15 June 1948, the Urban Work Department of the North China Bureau issued a report on "The Attitude of the Students in Beiping after the April Movement." It indicated there were two groups: (1) those who failed to see the future clearly, and thought it was better to wait for "liberation" or go to CCP areas at the neglect of urban work; (2) those who hoped to go on with large-scale struggle but were impatient with detailed penetration work. The Urban Work Department demanded that the CCUP in Beiping (and Tianjin) consolidate and expand student power through work among professors and "middle" masses and that it be patient, "with reason, advantage, and restraint," because the time was not ripe for "liberation."[218]

In May and June 1948 the Communists launched a protest against American support of Japan—the last anti-Chiang, anti-American national movement.[219] In May 1947 the American government revealed its intention to rebuild the Japanese and German economies as a result of the emerging Cold War so as to build strong anti-Communist blocs in Europe and Asia. The apprehension that American-supported Japanese troops might be used to fight Communism in China was at the heart of CCP opposition to America's new Japan policy. Oddly enough, the growth of the anti-American sentiment came out of the articles in *Dagong bao*, a newspaper controlled by the Political Study Clique of the GMD.[220] (Note that by then the CCP no longer stressed the issue of anti–Civil War, for it was involved in the war.)

The American publication on 19 May 1948 of the "fact-finding report" of a committee under Percy Johnston and William Draper precipitated an uproar in China against the United States government. The report revealed a massive economic rehabilitation of Japan as part of an overall policy of containing communism, and this U.S. occupation policy in Japan immediately caused widespread comment in the Chinese press. On Chinese campuses, slogans against hunger and oppression gave way to new ones protesting U.S. policy toward Japan.

The Communists would not miss any chance to discredit the United States and the GMD. On 30 April 1948, the CCP CC suggested a major theme for the coming May First Labor Day Celebration: "The national working class and the people unite together to resist the intervention of the American imperialists in China's internal affairs, and their infringement on the Chinese sovereignty, and to resist the American imperialists' assistance in the restoration of the Japanese aggressive forces!"[221] (The CCP neglected the "no war" clause of the Japanese Constitution of 1947.) The CCP believed that the movement against the American support of Japan had a popular basis, and thus it should be emphasized.

On 4 May representatives from 120 Shanghai universities and middle schools gathered on the "Democratic Square" of Jiaotong University campus and established the Shanghai Students Association to Oppose the American Support of Japan and to Relieve the National Crisis. On 30 May twelve universities and middle schools in Beiping–Tianjin established a similar association.

On 4 June the American ambassador, J. Leighton Stuart, warned the students that the anti-American movement might have grave consequences at a time when the United States was preparing a large-scale aid program for the Chinese government. He further declared: "I defy anyone to produce a single shred of evidence that any part of Japanese military power is being restored or that there is any intention on the part of the U.S. other than to assure that it will never rise again."[222] This statement, however, failed to placate the anti-American sentiment of the students. On 5 June a massive parade in Shanghai was broken up by the local authorities. The Beiping–Tianjin CCUP decided to launch a demonstration on 9 June to support the movement in Shanghai and those elsewhere.[223]

The Communists claimed that they directed the demonstrations on 9 June.

The CCUP members in the Student Self-Governing Association of Beida led the parade in Beiping; other important Party members were on the second line. Democratic Youth Alliance and Democratic Youth League members assisted in pasting up posters, in distributing pamphlets, and in giving street lectures. The parade went through the police blockade successfully and joined forces with groups from Qingda and Yanda. This time the slogans of the parade were "Oppose U.S. support of Japan!" "Stop the second Lugouqiao Incident [of 7 July 1937, which precipitated the anti-Japanese war]!" and "Long live the independence of the Chinese nation!"[224]

In Tianjin the Communists focused their movement against the United States at Nankai and Beiyang. On 11 June they used the tactics of "surprise attack" and "exploit the enemy's unpreparedness" to distribute pamphlets and post wall cartoons and slogans to denounce the American support of Japan.[225]

The CCP praised the movement, saying it exposed the "treachery" of "American imperialism" and the "traitorous" actions of the GMD. It also said the movement had reached a high level of consciousness, organizational efficiency, degree of bravery and wit, and perseverance.[226] The Communists scored another political gain, since the government's nonintervention in Japan's rehabilitation and its measures against protests only alienated the students further and forced many who would not otherwise have done so to turn to the Communists. The GMD was again impotent in controlling the student movement, although it warned against the involvement of Communist "professional students."[227]

Troubles came one after another for the GMD. By mid-1948 it had begun retreating from Northeast China. Large numbers of refugee students escaped to the Beiping–Tianjin area. On 3 July the Beiping Municipal Council passed a resolution to assist the Northeast students in Beiping. It aimed to train them as ordinary soldiers. In protest, these Northeast students petitioned the Council to rescind the resolution that drafted them into the GMD army. They damaged the office of the Council and surrounded the residence of the speaker of the Council. The GMD authorities claimed that the Northeast students were "rioters" and had threatened the life of the speaker. GMD troops and police fired upon the crowd. Seventeen students and residents were killed; twenty-four were severely hurt; and more than one hundred suffered lesser injuries in this "July Fifth Bloody Incident."[228]

According to Zhang Yuhe, the GMD official who was responsible for making minutes of the Beiping Municipal Party, Government, Army, and Corps (Youth Corps and the 19th Military Police Regiment) Cadres' Joint Conference (a "B-Grade Conference"),[229] the local faction-ridden GMD failed to design any effective method to suppress the student movement. And the Beiping Garrison commander, fearful of any grave consequence on his career, actually warned against bloodshed against the students. In 1947–48 the major item of discussion at the conference was the issue of how to deal with the student movement. The incompetence of the GMD authorities was exposed when they had to discuss every student demonstration after it had taken place on the street. Further, Zhang claimed that he did not see any workers joining the student demostrations. While the Central Statistics usually knew in advance the dates of the student demonstrations, the Nationalists failed to disperse the demonstrators. Besides using soldiers, police, and military police, the GMD also ordered every shopkeeper to provide one employee (at first free service, later given some pocket money) to help with the task of blocking the main entrance of the school and preventing the students from demonstrating. If the students left the campus, the GMD units were supposed to stop them somewhere and prevent them from joining the demonstrators from other schools. Nonetheless, in reality the Nationalists could not easily halt the demonstrations. A deputy chief of staff of the Executive Headquarters, influenced by the students' reasoning, did not even block the students' way but instead led them to the location of the Headquarters for petition. Last of all, the July Fifth Bloody Incident occurred when the deputy police chief of Beiping, under order from the Garrison commander to disperse the demonstrators, could not prevent the soldiers of the 208th Division from firing at the Northeast students. Zhang remarked that a policeman simply could not command the soldiers.[230]

The CCUP did not know about the demonstration in advance, and they themselves would not invoke the wrath of the 208th Division. The Communists believed that the student movement in Beiping–Tianjin might have been totally suppressed by the GMD authorities if the CCUP had not supported the Northeast students. However, if the CCUP had organized parades, the students might have suffered another bloody day. The Communist Student Work Committee decided to organize a parade for 9 July. The slogans would be "Severely punish the murderers!" "Guarantee no such incident will happen again!" "Oppose persecuting the people!" "Demand life!" and "Oppose murder!"[231]

On 9 July the Communists organized a demonstration outside the residence of the director of the Executive Headquarters, Li Zongren, who agreed to release the Northeast students who had been arrested in Beiping on 5 July. Though the police and soldiers were tense and hostile, there was no bloodshed, and the parade returned to the "Democratic Square" of Beida, where the Northeast and North China Students formed the Protest July Fifth Bloody Incident Association. The Communist students also cooperated with the Northeast students in compiling a booklet entitled "Oppose Persecuting the People, Demand Life," which reported their version of the July Fifth Bloody Incident and the 9 July parade. Obviously, the Communists had formed a united front with the Northeast students.[232]

In Tianjin there were protests at Nankai, Beiyang, and other colleges from 6 July to 9 July against the bloody incident in Beiping. The students denounced the brutality of the GMD authorities, and, like their fellow students in Beiping, they collected money to support the Northeast students.[233]

In mid-July 1948 the GMD authorities in Tianjin entered Beiyang University (the "reddest" university) and searched for an underground radio station. They failed to locate it. Students from Beiyang, Nankai, and other schools protested against this "illegal" act.[234]

In the meantime, the CCP CC Urban Work Department issued "Views on the Beiping–Tianjin Student Movement" (11 July). This document emphasized the importance of preserving and consolidating bases in order to coordinate with the "liberation" and administration of Beiping. It opposed reckless adventurism and impatience that would damage the school and factory bases.[235] In its "Views on the Beiping–Tianjin Work" (13 July), the North China Bureau Urban Work Department also pinpointed the tasks of the student movement: winning the support of the majority of students, especially the "middle" students; developing new cadres among students; dispatching students to work in the areas; carrying out united-front work within all walks of life; sustaining appropriate struggles, and preparing for the final victory.[236]

In perspective, the bloody incident in July gave the Communists occasion to expose the brutality and oppression of the GMD regime and to demonstrate the organizational strength of the Beiping–Tianjin CCUP. The student movement had reached a critical period: It was under the firm influence, if not control, of the Communists. The GMD needed strong determination to suppress it once and for all.

In the same month the GMD held the Guling Conference at Lushan. It decided to arrest Communist students in middle schools, colleges, and universities during the summer vacation. The timing was good because most of the students, but not the Communist "professional students," would leave the school campuses, and there would be no classes to go on strike. This executive order for student arrests was issued on 31 July to all local GMD authorities.[237]

In early August the GMD in Beiping held the Party–Government–Army Joint Conference (an "A-Grade Conference") and prepared for the dragnet.[238] In the meantime, GMD newspapers proclaimed that the government must "destroy the Second Battlefront" and must carry out "life-or-death struggle" with Communist students.[239] On 11 August *Huabei ribao* demanded the "return of the 'leased school territory' [i.e., those campuses dominated by CCUP activists]" and "the use of the knife to cut [off the problem of 'professional students']."[240] On 17 August the GMD Executive Yuan in Nanjing issued an edict on "exterminating [Communist] spies and stabilizing the rear [the cities]." On 18 August a Central News Agency release entitled "Irrefutable Proof of Communist Spies Instigating Innocent Students to Create Student Unrest" was carried by virtually every Chinese-language paper in Shanghai. The statement declared that every instance of "student troubles" had been organized and led by Communist agents. The following day the government announced that special criminal tribunals would deal with "political offenders."[241] In Beiping the GMD authorities on 19 August published a list of 250 people to be arrested or summoned; 71 were Beida students. Later, there appeared two more lists, totaling 463 people, including 247 Beida students.[242] In response, the Beiping CCUP secretly assisted most of the students ("progressives," Party, Democratic Youth Alliance, and Democratic Youth League members) to escape to CCP areas. By the end of September about one hundred people had been arrested by the authorities in Beiping.[243] At the same time students still protested on various campuses with slogans including "Protesting the GMD illegal arrest!" "Protect human rights!" "Protect democracy!" and "Oppose persecution!"

In Tianjin, newspapers on 15 August published the statistics on the "student tides" in the previous one and a half years and their instigation by Communist agents.[244] On 17 August the mayor held the Party–Government–Army Joint Conference (a "B-Grade Conference") and announced the decision of the Beiping authorities to arrest Communist students. The Tianjin authorities decided to arrest the students during the night of 19 August. (Around 6 P.M. Fu Dongju warned the Nankai CCUP about the forthcoming arrests. Although her information did not help all the Nankai Communists and "progressives" to escape, the GMD authorities arrested only seven students during the campus raid that started at 4 A.M. the following morning.)[245]

On 20 August the Tianjin authorities published the names of "professional students." By 21 August only forty-six of the 164 students on the black list in Tianjin had been arrested. (Twenty-three were Nankai students; at least seven were Beiyang students.) Left-wing professors (such as Wu Daren of Nankai University) protected some of the fugitive students.[246] By the end of the month more than two hundred students had fled to CCP areas.[247]

In the end, the GMD "August Nineteenth or Twentieth Great Arrest" (a Communist term) failed to break up the Communist student strength in Beiping–Tianjin, as most of the exposed CCUP, Democratic Youth Alliance, and Democratic Youth League members had escaped safely to CCP areas. Such a failure indicated that the GMD effort to suppress Communist students was doomed. The inability of the GMD to control this core of the Communist Second Battlefront signaled political bankruptcy in the cities. In other words, the August Nineteenth or August Twentieth Great Arrest may have been the beginning of the end of the GMD political control in urban China.

In perspective, from 1945 to the August Nineteenth or Twentieth Great Arrest, the GMD strategy to deal with the Communist student movement was a dismal failure. According to the Communist analysis, the GMD acted in a perfunctory way in the Anti-Examination Movement. In the end, the GMD canceled the examinations. During the December First Movement, the authorities were repressive at the beginning and conciliatory in the end. They "appeased" the students and did not suppress other radical student protests. The GMD also failed to use the February Twenty-Second Movement to dominate the Chinese student movement. During the period, the GMD believed that it could control the students; therefore, it resorted to "soft tactics and manipulation as the main tactic, repression as the auxiliary tactic." The GMD also tolerated the Antibrutality Movement because the Nationalists were winning on the battlefront.[248]

The May Twentieth Movement was the beginning of the GMD use of "repression as the main tactic, soft tactics as the auxiliary method." Various "bloody incidents" emerged. In the wake of the PLA offensive in 1948, the GMD intensified its crackdown on students. Special criminal courts were established and the August Nineteenth Great Arrest occurred. Political degradation, military setback, and economic distress prompted the harsh GMD measures. It had to destroy the Second Battlefront.[249]

The GMD authorities adopted two methods to fight the Communist student movement. The *defensive method* included: (1) party education training; (2) military training and installation of special agents at schools; (3) use of party personnel and Youth Corps to win over the "middle" schools; (4) careful selection of principals and winning teachers over. The *repressive method* included: (1) Use of "propaganda against propaganda, organization against organization, action against action." (In Beiping the authorities censored news about the Shen Chong Incident; during the Antibrutality Movement, the GMD established the Beiping University Students Righteous Association to fight the Communist-infiltrated Beiping Schools Protest American Brutality Association. "Action against action" referred to the use of military and police forces, special agents, party members, and Youth Corps students to deal with the Communist, "progressive," and "positive" students and masses.) (2) Use of harsh tactics. (3) Use of contradictions, crushing enemies one by one. (For example, school authorities asked parents to apply pressure on their children.) (4) Legalizing repression by enacting national security laws and establishing special criminal courts.[250] The methods, however, failed to destroy the Communist student movement.

On the other hand, by August 1948 the CCUP demonstrated its effective urban strategy. "Being diligent in studies, in careers, and in making friends," and "being professional, socialized, and legitimate in political activities," the CCUP members in general scored successes in the "united front from below and from above." While they focused on students, intellectuals, and teachers, the CCUP did not neglect the small but important group of top GMD military and political leaders. Since Li Zongren had a disagreement with Chiang Kai-shek, the Communists petitioned Li to release the students after they were arrested by the GMD. Since Chiang was the primary target in the Chinese revolution, the CCP gave concessions even to Chiang's close allies. Although Fu Zuoyi was a major military and political leader and was Chiang's trusted lieutenant, Fu belonged to the local (Chahar and Suiyuan) power group, a possible source of friction between him and Chiang. Therefore the Beiping CCUP opposed the slogan "Fu Zuoyi be executed" used in the 9 July demonstration in 1948.[251] The CCUP also cooperated temporarily with the 208th Division of the Youth Army.

The Communists realized the importance of winning over the "middle" forces and developing the left-wing ("progressive" or "positive") forces. The slogans "U.S. Army get out!" and "Oppose the American support of Japan!" could be accepted by many nationalistic Chinese. Slogans like "Declare war on hunger!" "Declare war on those who create hunger!" and "Oppose the reactionary civil war policy!" would be accepted by everyone who needed to eat, survive, and live in peace. The CCUP also recruited left-wing elements, especially students. The Antibrutality Movement in Beiping (and Tianjin) illustrated the Communist tactic of patiently instigating the "middle" forces to join in demonstrations. In every instance, the CCUP tried hard to wage struggles "on just grounds, to the Party's interest, and with restraint."[252]

Furthermore, the Communist student committees showed their skills in recruiting "progressive" or "positive" elements into the "external" (*waiwei*, that is, "front") organizations of the CCP. The recruiting process in GMD cities, however, was difficult, delicate, and dangerous. During 1945–46 the Northern Group and the Southern Group seldom recruited members because of the "new" postwar situation, the Nationalist strength on school campuses, and the gradual return of the universities from the Southwest to Beiping–Tianjin in mid-1946. The Antibrutality Movement and the May Twentieth Movement, however, created favorable conditions for recruiting "progressive" and "positive" students. The CCUP intensified the process in 1948.[253]

The Communists adopted three ways to observe and develop candidates. First, CCUP members befriended the targeted students through the same class, the same dormitory, the same student organization, or the sharing of similar interests or hobbies. The Communists and the students gradually became bosom friends. The former then introduced "progressive" literature and ultimately Marxist-Leninist and CCP pamphlets to the latter. Simultaneously, the Communists investigated the students' ideological transformations and their family backgrounds. Second and more important, CCUP cadres evaluated the performance of the candidates in the student movement and other struggles. Those who behaved well and were reliable politically would be allowed to join the front organizations. Further acceptable performance would qualify them to become Communist members. Third, since it was extremely difficult to investigate the family backgrounds and the social relationships of the students in GMD areas, the CCUP members very often had to depend on their own judgment and the students' speech and behavior with relatives. However, for those candidates who had complicated social relationships (for example, children of GMD officials), the CCUP members would report the cases to their superiors for further investigation.[254]

After the candidates became Party members, they were required to work with one to three fellow Communists. They received further education and engaged in "self-criticism." They studied the teachings of Marxism-Leninism and the program, policy, and guidelines of the CCP. They paid attention to the changing political situation and the directives from the Party Central. They learned how to be good Communists: Obey orders unconditionally, keep the Party's secrets, and be highly disciplined. They must understand the viewpoints of the masses, and the strategy and tactics in political struggles. Lastly, they must possess the "revolutionary character," that is, when arrested by the enemy, they should not betray the Party or expose its secrets.[255]

In 1947–48, CCUP members also traveled to CCP areas for further training. As done during the wartime period, Liu Ren and other Communist leaders carried out a policy of concealment in dealing with the urban cadres. Since most of them would return to Beiping–Tianjin for new assignments, the cadres usually studied the required readings alone and talked to their leaders in "rooms" separated by white cloth. During the interviews, the cadres were required to cover their heads with white towels and their mouths with white masks to conceal their identity. This work-style and method of training corresponded with the clandestine nature of the CCUP.[256]

In perspective, while in the end some Communists did betray the Party, the inability of the GMD authorities to demolish the CCUP on Beiping–Tianjin campuses illustrated the relative success of the Communists' underground work. It was actually less dangerous for the Communists to operate under GMD rule than under Japanese rule in the cities. The CCUP dared not launch any significant student movement in occupied Beiping–Tianjin. While the CCUP feared the GMD soldiers (such as the 208th Division), it seemed that they had much less respect for the regular GMD policemen. While the CCUP agents or their student allies had cooperated with the 208th Division and tried not to provoke it, the Communists rarely mentioned their united-front work among the policemen in Beiping–Tianjin. Perhaps it was not that important to operate among the "weak" GMD police, which could explain why the Communists did not elaborate on the activities of their Police Work Committee.[257]

In order to develop solid cadres and to conceal its organizations in the cities, the Party also carried out well-conceived measures. In every organization a branch bureau was formed with three or more members. There might be two or more parallel branch bureaus within the same unit. There was no horizontal relationship between the parallel bureaus, however, and no bureau meeting. Party members were on the single-contact system. Certain members belonged to no bureau at all and depended exclusively on single contact. To separate the legal from the illegal, the open from the concealed, the CCUP carried out a three-line organization. The first line's Party members were the leaders of the legal organizations (particularly the student self-governing associations); their number was limited. The second line were the majority members; they worked among the semiopen organizations (such as the wall newspaper clubs and the study clubs) and the masses. The third line was the concealed core (the CCUP and its front organizations), composed of very few members; they worked among the "middle" forces but were above the first and second lines of the Party organization.[258]

In the period under discussion, the CCUP's Culture Committee in Beiping was merged into the Student Work Committee. In the spring of 1947 the Lihua Printing Factory was shut down by the GMD authorities. In September 1947

Zhongwai Publications Agency was finally suppressed because it published Communist and left-wing books and journals. Communists learned the importance of operating in secret in the publishing industry.[259]

In the fall of 1947 the leading member of the Culture Committee reported to Liu Ren, who gave him instructions: (1) Conceal well-selected cadres and perform the primary task of investigation and study. Any information that can be expressed openly should be published; material that cannot be published legally must be handed over to the organization. Important military and political information must be reported immediately to the Urban Work Department through the underground radio stations. (2) Unite reporters and editors in the news sector in Beiping. Win over the majority but do not concentrate on developing them into Party members. (Many GMD and Youth Corps members worked within the agencies.) (3) Communist reporters should not appear in the student movement. They should conserve power and work underground. (4) In writing articles, reporters should use the terms "Communist troops," "Communist Party," and "Communist side." If refusing to use the term "Communist bandit" would expose one's identity, then follow the writing style of the GMD Central News Agency.[260]

Although the GMD controlled the news sector, the CCUP tried hard to infiltrate it. There were only twenty CCUP members among various agencies in Beiping. Nevertheless, the CCP also emphasized the importance of forming temporary allies within the enemy's camp. One example occurred in early 1948 when a Communist working at *Pingming ribao* was arrested. Because he worked with the publisher of the newspaper, who was a protégé of Fu Zuoyi, the Communist was released. This event showed also the conflict between the Chiang Kai-shek faction and the Fu Zuoyi faction.[261]

In Tianjin the CCUP established the Tianjin Reporters Association in March 1948. It started work in *Xinsheng wanbao* and spread to other newspapers including the GMD *Minguo ribao*. The number of Communist members within the Association is unclear. However, they propagandized about the "war of liberation" and provided information to the CCP.[262]

In general, the Communist cultural work in Beiping–Tianjin was focused primarily on the news media and on publications. The former were more significant because of the availability of vital military and political information for the Communists on the war front.

From mid-1947 to August 1948, the GMD showed signs of impending collapse. Economic distress was accompanied by military disasters. On the political front, the Nationalist defensive and repressive methods failed to suppress the Communist student movement. The Youth Corps' activities, the capture of the leading cadres of the Communist Southern Group, the harsh and soft tactics (such as the arrest followed by the release of student protesters), and the "appeasing" action of the GMD authorities (such as the abandonment by the Beiping Garrison Command of the effort to arrest the twelve CCUP or "progressive" students) were useless in containing the "student tides." The GMD leaders were demoralized by student pressures, and their acknowledgment of the Communist role in the student movement further exposed the weakness of the authorities in dealing with youth, the most important component of the Second Battlefront. Indeed, the CCUP continued to succeed in taking advantage of the student (not labor) protests and strikes (the labor ones happened largely because of "objective" forces such as inflation). The CCP was simply "good at using youth," and the GMD was unable to learn from its pre-1945 failures how to use party organization, efficiency, administrative style, tactics, educational policies, and students' fighting skills in combating the Communists on campus.[263] With the loss of the support and allegiance of a significant number of students and academic leaders, and with the growing alienation of the populace due to economic hardship, the Nationalists lost authority. By August 1948 the Communists' urban activity had become a significant political front that could coordinate with their rural military struggle.

Notes

1. *MZJ*, vol. VI, p. 330.
2. See ibid., pp. 81, 117–18.
3. See ibid., pp. 81, 118.
4. Ibid., p. 331.
5. See Hu Kuo-tai, "The Struggle Between the Kuomintang and the Chinese Communist Party on Campus during the War of Resistance," pp. 319–23. See also Wang Gongan and Mao Lei, *Guogong liangdang guanxishi*, pp. 733–35.
6. See Suzanne Pepper, *Civil War in China*, p. 43.
7. Zuo Jian and Qin Ge, "Jiefang zhanzheng shiqi de Tianjin xuesheng yundong," p. 3; see also Wu Mu, "Tianjin xueyun de jiguo wenti," p. 13; Gongqingtuan Beijing Shiwei Qingnian Yundongshi Yanjiushi, *Beijing qingnian yundongshi*, p. 360.
8. *Beiping qingnian*, Beiping, no. 4, p. 1.
9. See "Another Letter to the Youth in Beiping from the Beiping Sub-Branch Corps, Ping-Jin Branch Corps, Sanmin Zhuyi Youth Corps," in ibid., p. 4.
10. Ibid., no. 2, p. 3.
11. See *Yishi bao*, Tianjin, 27 Sept. 1945.
12. Pepper, *Civil War in China*, p. 57; see also Lincoln Li, *Student Nationalism in China*, p. 43.
13. Lucian W. Pye, who served as an intelligence and Chinese-language officer in the U.S. Marines in Beiping and Tianjin from September 1945 to April 1946, observed the dramatic shift in the attitudes of college students in Beiping–Tianjin. He became "aware of the students' concerns very early on because at almost a weekly rate . . . [the Marines were] . . . getting visits of delegations of students asking . . . whether the Kuomintang [Guomindang] would recognize their academic work, and therefore give them jobs once they graduated. These were young students who had done their high school and college work . . . during Japanese occupation. They were of course aware that many of their fellow students had gone out to West China and that these students were now coming back and would want to get the best jobs that the government had to offer. . . . Most were in the science fields or trained in various technical skills but they were quite worried as to the political implications of their having studied under the Japanese occupation . . . the Marines were in no position to give them an answer. . . . It

became clear that even by early 1946 the Kuomintang was simply not able to make up its mind on this delicate issue. The students were becoming more and more frantic and in this environment the communist[s] were very active." Above all, Pye thinks that "the basis for the core communist strength came out of the student movement and it was certainly not from the industrial workers." Letter to the author, 6 March 1992.

14. Pepper, *Civil War in China*, p. 36 n. 100.

15. Ibid., p. 40.

16. See Song Rufen, Shen Bo, and Xu Wei, "Diyici daji—Huiyi Beiping dixiadang xuewei lingdao de fan zhenshen yundong," p. 34.

17. After the Japanese surrender, the GMD took over this enemy- and puppet-controlled university and converted it into Beiping Normal College in July 1946. It was renamed Beiping Normal University in November 1946.

18. Song, Shen, and Xu, "Diyici daji," pp. 35–36; Shi Weiqun, *Zhongguo xuesheng yundongshi*, pp. 15–16.

19. Nankai University in the occupied Tianjin was different from the one that retreated with the government to the interior. Nankai, Beijing, and Qinghua universities formed the Southwest Associated University. They returned to Beiping–Tianjin in the summer of 1946. The returned Beiyang University started classes in October 1946. During the wartime period the Tianjin CCUP was active in middle schools, not in Nankai and Beiyang; see Wu Mu, "Tianjin xueyun," pp. 14–15.

20. *TXGY*, p. 187.

21. See Zuo and Qin, "Tianjin xuesheng yundong," p. 4.

22. See Song, Shen, and Xu, "Diyici daji," pp. 39–40; *JSBX*, pp. 16–18, 27–29; Shi Weiqun, *Zhongguo xuesheng yundongshi*, p. 17.

23. *ZMZS*, 5: 3, p. 302.

24. See the report of the Beiping Police Bureau to the mayor and deputy mayor dated 3 December 1946, and its secret surveillance order of 10 December, in *JSBX*, pp. 22–26.

25. The Anti-Examination Movement also spread to Shanghai. Since the Communist-led Student Association of six universities appeared in Shanghai in early November, the Beijing University–Beijing Normal University Alumni Association in October could be regarded as the first Communist tool of the Anti-Examination Student Movement.

26. Quoted in Gongqingtuan Zhongyang Qingyunshi Yanjiushi, *Zhongguo qingnian yundongshi*, pp. 230–31.

27. See Zuo and Qin, "Tianjin xuesheng yundong," p. 5.

28. *Minguo ribao*, Tianjin, 20 Dec. 1945.

29. See Zuo and Qin, "Tianjin xuesheng yundong," p. 5.

30. See Wang Zuo et al., "Yaohua Xuexiao de xuesheng yundong," p. 5.

31. Zuo and Qin, "Tianjin xuesheng yundong," p. 6.

32. Ibid.

33. Ibid., pp. 6–7; Wang Zuo et al., "Yaohua Xuexiao," pp. 5–6; Shi Weiqun, *Zhongguo xuesheng yundongshi*, p. 18.

34. See Chiang Kai-shek's New Year Address to the Military Forces and People of the Country, *Zhonghua minguo guomin zhengfu gongbao*, 3 Jan. 1946.

35. According to the GMD, Ye also served as the head of the Communist Northern "Non-Military Struggle Headquarters," which was in charge of North and Northeast China. On the other hand, Zhou Enlai was the leader of the Non-Military Struggle Headquarters, which was based in Nanjing and Shanghai and was responsible for the work in East, Central, and South China, including Hong Kong. See Zhu Wenlin, "Dalu zhong guojia anquan fangju jiqi chengxiao zhi yanjiu," p. 7.

36. See She Diqing and Yang Bozhen, "Diertian zhanxian shang de xianfeng," pp. 19–20.

37. For a brief introduction to the December First Movement, see Pepper, *Civil War in China*, pp. 44–52. For a Nationalist account of the Communist involvement in this movement, see Wang Gan, *Qingyun gongzuo gailun*, pp. 102–4.

38. Zuo and Qin, "Tianjin xuesheng yundong," pp. 7–8.

39. Ibid., p. 8.

40. *TXGY*, p. 191. For a left-wing account of the assembly, parade, and slogans, see *Minzhu zhoukan*, Beiping, no. 3 (Jan. 1946), pp. 15–16.

41. See *Minguo ribao*, Tianjin (5 Jan. 1946).

42. See *Tianjin xuelian*, vol. 2, 27 Jan. 1946; cited in *Renmin ribao* (overseas ed.), 19 Dec. 1991. *Tianjin xuelian* was controlled by "positive" students and Communists.

43. See *Dagong bao*, Tianjin, 30 Jan. 1946.

44. See Zuo and Qin, "Tianjin xuesheng yundong," p. 9.

45. See *BGD*, p. 282.

46. See *ZMZS* 7: 1, pp. 313–70; the GMD Central Executive Committee's Directive Telegram on the Student Activities Pertaining to the Issue of Northeast China to the Authorities of Every Province and City, in idem, pp. 637–38; see also n. 7 in ch. 2 and Odd Arne Westad, *Cold War and Revolution*, p. 156.

47. See Gongqingtuan Zhongyang Qingyunshi Yanjiushi, *Zhongguo qingnian yundongshi*, p. 233.

48. See Wang Gan, *Qingyun gongzuo gailun*, pp. 123–33.

49. *TXGY*, p. 193.

50. *BGD*, p. 281.

51. *Jiefang bao*, Beiping, 2 April 1946.

52. Song, Shen, and Xu, "Diyici daji," p. 42.

53. For a Communist account of the April Third Incident, see Zhao Yongtian, "Yijiu siliu nian Beiping 'Sisan' Shijian shimo," pp. 395–407.

54. See *Renmin ribao* (overseas ed.), 19 Dec. 1991.

55. See *Shijie ribao*, Beiping, 3 April 1946; see also Song, Shen, and Xu, "Diyici daji," p. 42.

56. See part 6 of the memoirs of Wu Zhuren, the secretary of the GMD party bureau in Beiping (March 1946–November 1948), in Wu Zhuren, "Wu Zhuren huiyilu," *Zhongwei zazhi* 3 (1993): 137.

57. For a Communist account of this incident, see Shen Bo et al., "Zhongshan Gongyuan Yin Letang Shijian de qianqian houhou," pp. 833–49; see also *BXG*, pp. 191–94.

58. See Cheng Bi et al., "Nanwang de saiwai zhixing," pp. 435–43; *BXG*, pp. 182–83; *BGD*, p. 286.

59. See *JSBX*, pp. 34–39. This university, established in July 1939 and renamed the North China University in 1948, was eager to recruit students and teachers from the former Japanese-controlled areas. The Communists certainly did not call or look down on them as "puppet students or teachers." Some graduates of this university became CCUP members in Beiping–Tianjin.

60. *BXG*, p. 181.

61. See Song, Shen, and Xu, "Diyici daji," pp. 43–44; Gongqingtuan Beijing Shiwei Qingnian Yundongshi Yanjiushi, *Beijing qingnian yundongshi*, p. 358.

62. For a brief account of the Assist-Student Movement in Shanghai from January to March 1946, see *Shanghai xuesheng yundongshi*, pp. 36–40.

63. See Zuo and Qin, "Tianjin xuesheng yundong," pp. 11–12.

64. See *BDDS*, pp. 51–52, 342–43, 545, 681–82.

65. Ibid., p. 52.

66. See *BGD*, pp. 272, 276; Zhang Wenson and Zhang Quinji, "Beiping wenwei," pp. 198–200.

67. Zhang and Zhang, "Beiping wenwei," p. 163.

68. See Wu Peishen and He Jiadong, "Beiping Zhongwai Chubanshe douzheng jishi," pp. 207–17.

69. Zhang and Zhang, "Beiping wenwei," p. 201.

70. *BDDS*, pp. 201–2; see also *BGD*, p. 285, and Shi Mei, "Yanju Erdui he Zuguo Jutuan," pp. 218–33.

71. *TXGY*, pp. 182–84.

72. Ibid., p. 184.

73. See Wang Xixian, "Huiyi Tianjin Wenhuaren Lianhehui," pp. 98–115.

74. On 1 December 1945, the GMD authorities did kill a music teacher and three students, and injured scores of anti–Civil War and anti-American demonstrators in Kunming. This incident could be regarded as a case of GMD's excessive use of force. Since the GMD was held responsible for the casualties, it was exploited by the Communist propaganda machine. Besides, students, not laborers, prompted the GMD's negative image. See also n. 37; Lincoln Li, *Student Nationalism in China*, pp. 124–29.

75. *BDDS*, p. 342.

76. Yuan Qinghua Daxue Dixiadang Bufen Dangyuan, "Zai dizhan chengshi kaibi 'xiao jiefangqu,' " p. 349.

77. From the outbreak of the Sino-Japanese War to 1939, in GMD-controlled Southwest China the CCP recruited intellectuals and student youths to Yan'an. Because of the increased GMD pressure on such a Communist measure, in mid-1940 the CCP Central shifted the focus of student work to that of "long-term clandestine development, accumulation of power, and winning of popular opinion" on school campuses. CCUP members in the Southwest were ordered to pay attention to school work and discipline; befriend teachers; recruit "progressives"; organize and take part in student associations, fellow provincial or native-place associations, youth clubs, choirs, and athletic teams; enter prestigious colleges or universities, and find employment in educational, industrial, and administrative organizations after graduation. Under the leadership of the CCP CC Southern Bureau, the CCUP members carried out these tactics to confuse the GMD authorities and to establish work on campuses. Because of the policy of "three diligences," many members became honorable students. For example, from 1940 onward the CCUP controlled the student association of the Central University and had more than two hundred members among the student association, drama clubs, choirs, art clubs, and wall newspaper clubs at the Southwest Associated University. The CCUP also helped improve the welfare of students. The chairman of the self-governing association of the Associated University and of the Kunming City Student Association was a Communist who first became popular among fellow students by serving as the head of the university's Food Corps. See Wang Gongan and Mao Lei, *Guogong liangdang guanxishi*, pp. 730–33.

78. *Mianhuai Liu Ren tongzhi*, p. 53. Before the arrival of Yuan Yongxi in Beiping, the Southern Group had established a Party cell in Yanjing University in June 1946. Yanjing was the first university that returned to its Beiping campus. At this stage there was only personal connection between the Northern Group and the Southern Group leaders.

79. See Nankai Daxue Xiaoshi Bianxiezu, *Nankai daxue xiaoshi*, pp. 358–60.

80. See Beijing Daxue Lishixi "Beijing daxue xuesheng yundongshi" Bianxiezu, *Beijing daxue xuesheng yundongshi*, pp. 192–95.

81. Wang Xiaoting and Wang Wenyi, *Zhandou zai Beida de gongchandang ren*, p. 331.

82. Yuan Qinghua Daxue Dixiadang Bufen Dangyuan, " 'Xiao jiefangqu,' " pp. 81–86.

83. See Yuan Yanjing Daxue Dixiadang Bufen Dangyuan, "Weiminghu pan de fengyun—Ji jiefang zhanzheng shiqi Beiping Yanjing daxue dixiadang de douzheng," pp. 682, 685.

84. See Nankai Daxue Xiaoshi Bianxiezu, *Nankai daxue xiaoshi*, p. 360f; Wang Xiaoting and Wang Wenyi, *Zhandou zai Beida de gongchandang ren*, pp. 454–55.

85. See Beiyang Daxue–Tianjin Daxue Xiaoshi Bianxiezu, *Beiyang daxue–Tianjin daxue xiaoshi*, p. 424.

86. See *Jiefang ribao*, Yan'an, 9 Sept. 1946.

87. *TXGY*, p. 202.

88. See *Jin-Cha-Ji ribao*, Leibao, 2 Aug. 1946.

89. *TXGY*, pp. 202–3.

90. Ibid., p. 202.

91. *Shijie ribao*, Beiping, 11 Aug. 1946.

92. For an introduction to the Shen Chong Incident and its aftermath, see Pepper, *Civil War in China*, pp. 54–58.

93. See *Yishi bao*, *Shijie ribao*, and *Xinmin bao*, 26 Dec. 1946.

94. The GMD authorities had frequently closed Communist or left-wing newspaper agencies and journal offices; for instance, in early June 1946, the GMD suppressed seventy-seven newspapers and journals in Beiping. See *Huashang bao*, Hong Kong, 3 June 1946.

95. See *Beiping ribao*, Beiping, 8 April 1947.

96. See Beijing Daxue Lishixi, *Beijing daxue xuesheng yundongshi*, pp. 198–99; Wang Xiaoting and Wang Wenyi, *Zhandou zai Beida de gongchandang ren*, p. 614. For a Communist account of this protest movement, see Zhonggong Beijing Shiwei Dangshi Yanjiushi's *Kangyi meijun zhuhua baoxing yundong ziliao huibian*. See also Li, *Student Nationalism in China*, pp. 132–33.

97. Li, *Student Nationalism*, p. 133.

98. See Xiao Song, Ma Ju, and Song Bai, "Feiteng de Shatan—Jiefang zhanzheng shiqi Beijing daxue dixiadang lingdao Wen, Li, Fa xueyuan xuesheng minzhu yundong de huiyi," p. 549.

99. See Yuan Qinghua Daxue Dixiadang Bufen Dangyuan, " 'Xiao jiefangqu,' " pp. 86–87.

100. See Yuan Yanjing Daxue Dixiadang Bufen Dangyuan, "Yanjing dixiadang," p. 685.

101. Yuan Qinghua Daxue Dixiadang Bufen Dangyuan, " 'Xiao jiefangqu,' " pp. 87–88.

102. *Beiping xinbao*, Beiping, 29 Dec. 1946.

103. *Beiping ribao*, Beiping, 29 Dec. 1946.

104. For an account of the demonstration, see *Pingming ribao*, *Jishi bao*, *Jingshi ribao*, and *Shijie ribao*, Beiping, 31 Dec. 1946.

105. See Xiao, Ma, and Song, "Feiteng de Shatan," p. 552; Beijing Daxue Lishixi, *Beijing daxue xuesheng yundongshi*, p. 202.

106. *JSBX*, p. 82; see also Li, *Student Nationalism in China*, p. 134.

107. One account in *Pingming ribao*, Beiping, 31 Dec. 1946, reported that a group of students shouted, "We demand that the government reclaim Dalian [from the Russians]!"

108. *Jingshi ribao*, Beiping, 31 Dec. 1946.

109. See *Xinmin bao*, Beiping, 31 Dec. 1946 and 7 Jan. 1947.

110. Ibid., 1 Jan. 1947.

111. See Zuo and Qin, "Tianjin xuesheng yundong," p. 14.

112. *Dagong bao*, Tianjin, 28 Dec. 1946.

113. Wang Zuo et al., "Yaohua Xuexiao," p. 10.

114. *TXGY*, pp. 209–10; Zuo and Qin, "Tianjin xuesheng yundong," p. 15; Nankai Daxue Xiaoshi Bianxiezu, *Nankai daxue xiaoshi*, p. 361.

115. Nankai Daxue Xiaoshi Bianxiezu, *Nankai daxue xiaoshi*, p. 210.

116. Ibid. A National Protest American Brutality Association was established in Shanghai on 8 March 1947.

117. *BGD*, p. 306.

118. See Li, *Student Nationalism in China*, p. 134. Lucian Pye was one of the American officers involved in the investigation of the Shen Chong Incident. He went to Beida to try to get Shen Chong to testify. But he could only deal with an "action committee" composed of very aggressive students who demanded that the Marines leave China. The girl would not appear in court and the students would not cooperate in any way. "What had happened was that a Marine sergeant [William] and his other friends had come out of a bar and suddenly he was surrounded by an angry crowd who were shouting at him. He didn't understand what was happening. The MPs had to protect him and get him back to the barracks. The next day we found out in the newspapers that he was accused of committing rape. We never found out where the rape was supposed to have taken place. We never found out anything about the details of it . . . what was significant about this was that by this time the student movement had pretty well swung to the side of the Communists." Letter to the author, 6 March 1992. According to the summary report (dated 21 February 1947) of the Beiping Police Bureau, the evidences at the crime scene and the testimonies of the victim and the witnesses apparently indicated that a rape had occurred. See *JSBX*, pp. 89–92. The GMD authorities did not deny the rape case.

119. See Wang Gan, *Qingyun*, p. 86.

120. See Jesse G. Lutz, "The Chinese Student Movement," pp. 97–99; Jon W. Huebner, "Chinese Anti-Americanism 1946–48," pp. 119–21.

121. See Thurton Griggs, *Americans in China*, p. 8.

122. See *JSBX*, p. 92; Zhonggong Beijing Shiwei Dangshi Yanjiushi, *Kangyi meijun zhuhua baoxing yundong ziliao huibian*, pp. 485, 487–89.

123. See Zhonggong Beijing Shiwei Dangshi Yanjiushi, *Kangyi meijun zhuhua baoxing yundong ziliao huibian*, pp. 479–80.

124. See ibid., pp. 481–83.

125. See ibid., pp. 509–12; *JSBX*, pp. 95–97.

126. See Lutz, "The Chinese Student Movement," pp. 101–2.

127. Pepper, *Civil War in China*, p. 58. The Communists established the All-China Students Protesting the Brutality of American Military Personnel United General Association in Shanghai on 8 March 1947; this Association paved the way for the formation of the All-China Students Association.

128. See Wang Gan, *Qingyun*, p. 84; Wu Han, "Zhonggong de xueyun gongzuo," pp. 15–16.

129. See *ZZQY*, pp. 636–37.

130. Ibid., pp. 641–42.

131. Ibid., pp. 643–44.

132. A contingent of American Marines stationed in Qingdao with a Military Advisory Group in Nanjing; see Harry I. Shaw, Jr., *The U.S. Marines in North China*, pp. 23–24.

133. See She and Yang, "Beiping xuewei," p. 22; Hua Binqing, *Wuerling yundongshi*, ch. 1.

134. See Hua, *Wuerling yundongshi*, ch. 1.

135. See Huebner, "Chinese Anti-Americanism."

136. See the summary report of the Beiping Student Committee on the Antibrutality Movement in *JSBX*, pp. 69–74; *Jiefang ribao*, Yan'an, 10 Jan. 1947.

137. *MZX*, vol. IV, p. 1212.

138. See the summary report of the Beiping Student Work Committee on the Antibrutality Movement in *JSBX*, pp. 69–74; see also Sha Jiansun, "Lun Kangbao Yundong," p. 418.

139. *SWZE*, vol. I, pp. 300–2.

140. Quoted from the CCP CC directive (6 January 1947) on strengthening the organizations and leadership of the student movement in GMD areas in *ZZWX*, vol. XIII, p. 570.

141. For the Communist response to the GMD expulsion of its representatives, see *Jiefang ribao*, Yan'an, 3 March 1947.

142. *ZZQY*, pp. 650–51.

143. See *Zhonggong de tewu huodong*, pp. 107–9; Dou Aizhi, *Zhongguo minzhu dangpai shi*, pp. 135–36.

144. *SWZE*, vol. I, pp. 302–3; *ZEX*, vol. I, pp. 270–71.

145. See *Dagong bao*, Tianjin, 20 April 1947; "A General Summary of the April Economic Storm," in *Guangming bao xunkan*, Hong Kong, vol. 18 (14 May 1947); *Shijie ribao*, Beiping, 6 May 1947.

146. Government employees also had a miserable livelihood; see the editorial in *Shijie ribao*, Beiping, 2 March 1947.

147. See Shao Pengwen and Hao Yingda, *Zhongguo xuesheng yundong jianshi*, pp. 268–72.

148. For a Communist or left-wing view of the Antihunger Anti–Civil War Movement in Beiping–Tianjin, see Chen Lei, *Xiang paokou yao fan chi*, pp. 67–88.

149. Li Kun, "Yijiu siqi nian Beiping diqu de Fan Jie Fan Neizhan Yundong," pp. 429–30.

150. Ibid., p. 430.

151. See Beijing Daxue Lishixi, *Beijing daxue xuesheng yundongshi*, p. 207.

152. See Li Kun, "Beiping Fan Jie Fan Neizhan," pp. 430–31.

153. Ibid.

154. See Beijing Daxue Lishixi, *Beijing daxue xuesheng yundongshi*, p. 210. For a summary report of the Beiping Student Committee on the Antihunger Anti–Civil War Movement, see *JSBX*, pp. 157–63. Earlier, on 12 and 13 May, the CCUP's students at the Central University in Nanjing launched the "Eat All [of the Government's Food Subsidy] Movement" to protest the rising prices, the government's refusal to increase the food subsidy to students, and the theme of hunger. The GMD authorities later raised the food allowances but they did not satisfy the students. See Shi Weiqun, *Zhongguo xuesheng yundongshi*, pp. 122–24. See also n. 77. The Eat All Movement could be regarded as a prelude to the Antihunger Anti–Civil War Movement.

155. See *JSBX*, pp. 157–63.

156. See Zuo and Qin, "Tianjin xuesheng yundong," pp. 18–19.

157. For the general program and slogans of this United Association, see *Kuai bao*, vol. 2 (1947) of Yanjing University.

158. Li Kun, "Beiping Fan Jie Fan Neizhan," p. 434.

159. See Beijing Daxue Lishixi, *Beijing daxue xuesheng yundongshi*, pp. 212–15; Su Cheng, "Beiping fan jie fan neizhan dayouxing jishi," pp. 25–28.

160. *TXGY*, p. 219.

161. For instance, see Wang Gan, *Qingyun*, ch. 1.

162. In his memoir, Li Zongren claimed that he once stopped a planned massacre of students by Ma Hansan, the major agent of the Military Statistics in Beiping. See Tang and Li, *Li Zongren huiyilu*, pp. 567–69. Li tried to create an image of being anti–Military Statistics and prostudents. But in 1948 Ma helped Li to become vice-president of the Republic of China. Nonetheless, for a while the "moderate" Li was popular with certain American politicians, who disliked the "dictatorial" Chiang Kai-shek and wanted Li to become the new Chinese leader. This Li–Chiang rift benefited the CCUP operation in Beiping.

163. See Pepper, *Civil War in China*, pp. 62–63.

164. See *ZZQY*, p. 653.

165. *MZJ*, vol. X, pp. 63–64; *SWMT*, vol. IV, pp. 135–36; *MZX*, vol. IV, p. 1225. *SWMT* and *MZX* deleted "and is also the organizer of the whole people's movement."

166. See Zhongguo Renmin Jiefangjun Nanjing Zhengzhi Xiaoyuan Lishi Xuexi, *Zhongguo xiandaishi zhengminglu*, pp. 619–26; Weng Zhonger, "Guomindang tongzhiqu de aiguo minzhu yundong," pp. 75–91. See also n. 40 in ch. 3.

167. See Chiang's talk on the policy for dealing with the "student tide" in *Yishi bao*, Tianjin, 10 June 1947.

168. Quoted in Zhonggong Beijing Shiwei Dangshi Yanjiushi, Wu Jialin, and Xie Yinming, *Fan jie fan neizhan yundong ziliao huibian*, p. 8. See also the CCP CC directive dated 6 June 1947 in *Wu erling yundong ziliao*, vol. I, pp. 24–25.

169. Li Kun, "Beiping Fan Jie Fan Neizhan," p. 437.

170. On the same day more than one hundred protesting students were injured by the GMD soldiers and policemen in Nanjing. The Communists called the event "May Twentieth Great Bloody Incident."

171. See Zuo and Qin, "Tianjin xuesheng yundong," pp. 19–20; Zhu Zhuying, "Wo he Wu Daren laoshi de jiaowang," p. 253.

172. Pepper, *Civil War in China*, p. 97; *BDJ*, p. 283.

173. See Zhonggong Beijing Shiwei Dangshi Yanjiushi, Wu Jialin, and Xie Yinming, *Fan jie fan neizhan yundong ziliao huibian*, pp. 366–68.

174. See *Shijie ribao*, Beiping, 28 May 1947.

175. See the plan of the Beiping Garrison Command to suppress the student demonstration on 2 June, in *JSBX*, pp. 222–24.

176. See She and Yang, "Diertian zhanxian shang de xianfeng," pp. 23–24; *TXGY*, pp. 218–19; Li Kun, "Beiping Fan Jie Fan Neizhan," p. 439.

177. See Li Kun, "Beiping Fan Jie Fan Neizhan," p. 439.

178. See Pepper, *Civil War in China*, p. 70, n. 39.

179. See *JSBX*, pp. 157–63, 189–91.

180. See Liu Xiao, "Yijiu siqu nian 'Fan jie, fan neizhan, fan pohai' yundong de yixie huigu," pp. 30–33. For a Communist general survey of the May Twentieth Movement, see Hua Binqing's *Wuerling yundongshi*. For a Communist view of the Antihunger Anti–Civil War Movement, see Zhonggong Beijing Shiwei Dangshi Yanjiushi, *Fan jie fan neizhan yundong ziliao huibian*.

181. See Zhonggong Beijing Shiwei Dangshi Yanjiushi, Wu Jialin, and Xie Yinming, *Fan jie tan neizhan yungdong ziliao hubian*, pp. 583–85.

182. See Zhang and Zhang, "Beiping wenwei," pp. 162–64.

183. See Ji Gang, "Wo zai *Pingming ribao* dang jizhe," pp. 516–18.

184. See *BGD*, pp. 318–19.

185. *TJ*, pp. 434–35; see also Chen Xiuping, *Chenfulu*, ch. 5.

186. Sha Xiaoquan and Liu Yan, "Jiefang qianxi Nankai Daxue de tongzhan gongzuo," pp. 248–49.

187. See Lu Yuanchi, "Bianyin *Xinmin ziliao* de qianqian houhou," pp. 504–15.

188. Qian Ying of the CCP CC Shanghai Bureau led this Small Group, which held irregular meetings and focused its work on the exchange of information concerning the student movements in various GMD areas. Yuan Yongxi was one of the Group members. See *BGD*, p. 319. It is unclear when this Group ended its function. Probably it happened in April 1948 when a Communist traitor tried to help the GMD authorities arrest Qian Ying and other senior members of the Shanghai Bureau. Qian left Shanghai for Hong Kong and continued to lead the student work in the Southwest, Hunan, and Hubei. This could be the reason why in May the CCP CC asked the Shanghai Bureau to put its Beiping–Tianjin student organizations under the leadership of the Urban Work Department of the North China Bureau. The transfer was completed in November 1948. See Zhonggong Shanghai Shiwei Dangshi Ziliao Zhengji Weiyuanhui, *Jiefang zhanzheng shiqi de Zhonggong Zhongyang Shanghaiju*, pp. 333, 349.

189. See Pepper, *Civil War in China*, p. 132. See also Wong Young-tsu, "The Fate of Liberalism in Revolutionary China," pp. 457–90.

190. Xiao, Ma, and Song, "Feiteng de Shatan," pp. 564–67; see also Ding Li, "Yijiu shiqi nian shuqi Beiping de zhuxue yundong," pp. 331–40.

191. For instance, see the editorial of *Huabei ribao*, Beiping, 14 July 1947.

192. *TXGY*, pp. 225–26.

193. Zuo and Qin, "Tianjin xuesheng yundong," pp. 22–24.

194. *Dagong bao*, Tianjin, 8 Sept. 1947.

195. *BGD*, p. 322.

196. See *Huasheng bao*, Hong Kong, 29 Sept. 1947; Yuan Xinqing, *Zai Chianglao zhong*, pp. 195–201. These arrests were the GMD's most glorious anti-Communist activities in more than a decade. Unfortunately for the GMD, they failed to sustain the efforts in capturing more CCUP members from within and without in Beiping–Tianjin and elsewhere. In fact, the Communist underground had penetrated into the GMD's highest political and military authorities. Two such prominent Communist underground agents were Liu Fei and Xiong Xianghui. Liu was a GMD lieutenant general and a deputy defense minister in charge of war plans. Xiong was a Qinghua University student and joined the CCUP in 1936. Until 1949 he had served as a personal secretary of General Hu Zongnan, the "GMD's Northwestern King" whose primary duty was to exterminate the Communists in Northwest China. CCUP's activities in "the heart of the enemy" significantly contributed to the GMD collapse in urban and rural China.

197. See Beijing Daxue Lishixi, *Beijing daxue xuesheng yundongshi*, p. 226.

198. According to a report of the GMD Central Secretariat, the CCP used the Democratic League as a united-front tool to contact other parties in antigovernment activities. In Beiping–Tianjin and other cities, the Democratic League was active in the student movement and controlled some student self-governing associations. It also organized academic communities, theatrical groups, bookstores, and newspaper agencies to coordinate with Communist activities. See *ZMZS*, vol. 4, pp. 1, 40, 48. The Communists also stressed their infiltration of the Democratic League and close cooperation with its left-wing members. See Zhao Xihua, *Minmeng shihua*, pp. 437–50.

199. Yu was the chairman of the Zhejiang University Student Self-Governing Association. The GMD claimed that he committed suicide in jail on 29 October 1947; however, the CCP charged that he was murdered.

200. Quoted in Shao and Hao, *Zhongguo xuesheng*, p. 286.

201. Ibid.; see also Beijing Daxue Lishixi, *Beijing daxue xuesheng yundongshi*, p. 227.

202. Zuo and Qin, "Tianjin xuesheng yundong," p. 25.

203. *TXGY*, p. 232; Zuo and Qin, "Tianjin xuesheng yundong," p. 25.

204. See the editorial entitled "How to Lead the Frustrated and Undecided Youth Students of Today," in *Shijie ribao*, Beiping, 17 Dec. 1947.

205. On 29 January 1948, the Shanghai GMD soldiers and policemen injured seventy-three students and arrested more than two hundred protesters. Under pressure from the academic and other communities, the GMD authorities had released almost all the protesters by mid-1948. The leading CCUP members at Tongji and other universities in Shanghai succeeded in retreating to CCP areas and the GMD was once again condemned for its "fascist" action.

206. Beijing Daxue Lishixi, *Beijing daxue xuesheng yundongshi*, pp. 228–30.

207. *TXGY*, p. 234; *BGD*, p. 331.

208. Beijing Daxue Lishixi, *Beijing daxue xuesheng yundongshi*, pp. 231–32; Xiao, Ma, and Song, "Feiteng de Shatan," p. 572.

209. Beijing Daxue Lishixi, *Beijing daxue xuesheng yundongshi*, p. 232.

210. Ibid., pp. 234–35; Xiao, Ma, and Song, "Feiteng de Shatan," pp. 574–75; *BGD*, p. 333.

211. *BGD*, p. 333; Xiao, Ma, and Song, "Feiteng de Shatan," pp. 574–75.

212. Xiao, Ma, and Song, "Feiteng de Shatan," pp. 574–75; *BGD*, p. 334. See also Maria Yen, *The Umbrella Garden*, pp. 7–8.

213. Zuo and Qin, "Tianjin xuesheng yundong," pp. 28–29.

214. Xiao, Ma, and Song, "Feiteng de Shatan," p. 576.

215. See *Xinmin bao*, Beiping, 28 Dec. 1947.

216. See Yen, *Umbrella Garden*, p. 7.

217. In April the GMD authorities demolished the CCUP headquarters in Chongqing. Because of this success, the GMD went on to arrest a large number of Communist cadres and students in eastern Sichuan. However, it was an isolated incident and failed to destroy the political power of the CCUP and its student movement in GMD areas.

218. Xiao, Ma, and Song, "Feiteng de Shatan," p. 577.

219. See *BDS*, ch. 20.

220. Pepper, *Civil War in China*, pp. 72–73.

221. *ZDCZ*, vol. VI, p. 415.

222. Quoted in Pepper, *Civil War in China*, pp. 75–76.

223. Xiao, Ma, and Song, "Feiteng de Shatan," pp. 578–79.

224. Beijing Daxue Lishixi, *Beijing daxue xuesheng yundong*, p. 245; Xiao, Ma, and Song, "Feiteng de Shatan," pp. 579–81.

225. *TXGY*, p. 242.

226. Xiao, Ma, and Song, "Feiteng de Shatan," pp. 581–82; see also the editorial entitled "The New High Tide of the Patriotic Movement" (18 June 1948), Xinhua News Agency in *ZDCZ*, vol. VI, pp. 440–43.

227. See *Huabei ribao*, Beiping, 9–10 June and 18 June 1948. "Professional students" referred to the Communist, Democratic Youth Alliance, Democratic Youth League, and other left-wing students. The GMD authorities regarded them as disruptive and subversive elements endangering national security. In April 1948 the GMD established special criminal tribunals to deal with these political enemies.

228. Ibid., 6 July 1948; *BGD*, p. 339. For a Nationalist account of the incident, see the report of the Beiping Police Bureau in *JSBX*, pp. 468–73.

229. This joint conference dealt with military and political affairs in Beiping and was called the "B-Grade Conference." The Beiping Executive Headquarters also held such a conference. Since the Headquarters managed military and political matters on a much larger scale in North China, its conference was called the "A-Grade Conference."

230. See Zhang Yuhe, "Wo suo zhidao de Beiping 'Yiji huibao,' " pp. 52–70.

231. She and Yang, "Diertian zhanxian shang de xianfeng," pp. 25–26; Xiao, Ma, and Song, "Feiteng de Shatan," p. 585.

232. Xian, Ma, and Song, "Feiteng de Shatan," pp. 585–86; *BGD*, p. 340. See also Yen, *Umbrella Garden*, p. 10.

233. *TXGY*, pp. 245–46.

234. Ibid., p. 246.

235. *BGD*, pp. 340–41.

236. Ibid., p. 341.

237. Zuo and Qin, "Tianjin xuesheng yundong," p. 30; Xiao, Ma, and Song, "Feiteng de Shatan," p. 587.

238. This "A-Grade Conference" was initially organized by the Beiping Executive Headquarters, later maintained by the North China Bandit-Suppression General Headquarters. While Li Zongren and Fu Zuoyi were the leaders, they could not command full support from all the different Party (and Youth Corps), government, and military authorities. The joint conference was mainly a consultative meeting for sharing vital information among different GMD organizations, not an effective anti-Communist organ. See also n. 229.

239. *BDS*, p. 309.

240. *JSBX*, p. 511.

241. Ibid.; *Zhonghua minguo zhongtongfu gongbao*, 20 Aug. 1948; Beiyang Daxue–Tianjin Daxue Xiaoshi Bianxiezu, *Beiyang daxue-Tianjin daxue xiaoshi*, p. 427.

242. Xiao, Ma, and Song, "Feiteng de Shatan," p. 589.

243. Pepper, *Civil War in China*, p. 77.

244. See *Minguo ribao*, Tianjin, 15 Aug. 1948.

245. See Nankai Daxue Xiaoshi Bianxiezu, *Nankai daxue xiaoshi*, pp. 370–71.

246. Zhu Zhuying, "Wo he Wu Daren," p. 255; Nankai Daxue Xiaoshi Bianxiezu, *Nankai daxue xiaoshi*, p. 371; Beiyang Daxue–Tianjin Daxue Xiaoshi Bianxiezu, *Beiyang daxue–Tianjin daxue xiaoshi*, pp. 427–28.

247. *TXGY*, pp. 246–49; Zuo and Qin, "Tianjin xuesheng yundong," pp. 30–32.

248. Liu Jie, "Shixi 1945–1949 nian Guomindang dui xuesheng yundong de celüe," pp. 19–20.

249. Ibid., p. 21.

250. Ibid., pp. 22–23.

251. Fang Ting, "Jiefang zhanzheng shiqi Beiping dixiadang de douzheng," pp. 317–18.

252. Ibid., p. 316.

253. See *BDDS*, p. 367.

254. Ibid., pp. 368–69.

255. Ibid., pp. 370–72.

256. Ibid., pp. 374–75.

257. See nn. 30 and 36 in ch. 4. There was a derogatory saying about the GMD policemen: "No way [to maintain livelihood], work as a policeman" (*mei banfa, dang jingcha*). On the other hand, the Chinese people generally feared the policemen and the public security men in post-"liberation" China.

258. See Yuan Qinghua Daxue Dixiadang Bufen Dangyuan, "Zai dizhan chengshi kaibi 'xiao jiefangqu,' " pp. 377–92.

259. Zhang and Zhang, "Beiping wenwei," pp. 205–6; *BGD*, p. 272.

260. Cited in Ji Gang, "*Pingming ribao* jizhe," pp. 520–23; see also Zhang and Zhang, "Beiping wenwei," pp. 202–3.

261. Zhang and Zhang, "Beiping wenwei," p. 206; Ji Gang, "*Pingming ribao* jizhe," p. 516.

262. *TJ*, p. 434.

263. See n. 5.

6

Communist Labor and Other Activities, 1945–1948

In terms of classical Marxist theory, the labor movement should have been the most important activity of the Communists in China. The "New Democratic" character of the Chinese revolution was defined as "an anti-imperialist and anti-feudal revolution under the leadership of the proletariat, with the workers and peasants forming the main body and with other broad social strata taking part."[1] In reality, it was the students, not the workers, who were the core of the Communist movement in urban areas during the Civil War period.

By the end of the World War II, the CCP was able to resume activities among urban labor. However, although Mao Zedong glorified the revolutionary role of the proletariat, and the CCP claimed to be a working-class party, the Party did not advocate proletarian class struggle and revolution, the central concerns of Communism. In "On Coalition Government" (24 April 1945), Mao asserted: "In the struggle . . . especially for the recovery of the big cities and important lines of communications, the Chinese working class *will* [emphasis added] play a very great role."[2] In practice, in Beiping–Tianjin the Communist labor movement was subordinate to the student movement, and the working class did not play a "very great role" in the ultimate capture of the cities. Since the CCP did not advocate a proletarian armed uprising inside the cities, it downplayed the theme of class struggle. In fact, the CCUP paid much more attention to united-front work among government and business sectors in Beiping–Tianjin. Experienced urban GMD bureaucrats, functionaries, and businessmen were definitely essential (at least temporarily) for the CCP in the post-"Liberation" and "New Democratic" China.

Furthermore, the CCP also paid serious attention to the telecommunications networks because they were the Communist "lifelines" in GMD areas, and "the ears, eyes, and messengers" of the various command headquarters. Through the secret radio stations, the local Party organs could receive promptly directives from above while the Party Central was able to analyze quickly the GMD activities and the various reflections of the public mood and the international opinion in GMD areas. During the Civil War period, the CCP Central, the Southern Bureau, the Nanjing Bureau, and the Shanghai Bureau maintained close contact through their radio stations.[3] Inside Beiping and Tianjin, the secret Communist radio stations communicated constantly with the rural headquarters, which contacted the Party Central and other Party bureaus through their wireless service. The struggle on the telecommunications front was both important and dangerous because the GMD authorities tried hard to destroy all the Communist radio stations in the cities.

August 1945–June 1946

After the Japanese surrender, the strategy of the labor movement in Beiping–Tianjin was revealed in the Party directive entitled "The Current Situation in Tianjin and the Work Policy," issued by the Tianjin Work Committee on 5 September 1945. It indicated that in the aftermath of their defeat, the Japanese and the puppet Chinese sold their commodities, closed shops, and paid their accounts. Therefore, commodity prices dropped sharply, many small and medium-sized shops collapsed, and factories ceased production. A great number of industrial workers and coolies were unemployed, and their livelihood was precarious. In the labor movement, the Communists should organize the industrial workers to demand livelihood allowance and financial assistance. The Communists should also form various kinds of open or semiopen mass organizations, such as labor unions and transport guilds, and should fully utilize legal and open channels. Any excuses that the GMD might make for suppressing the labor movement were to be ignored.[4]

Inside Beiping the GMD Municipal Party Bureau established the Beiping General Labor Union and held its first meeting in early February 1946. (The GMD also established the Beiping Labor Assistance Office.) This union participated in the anti-Soviet, anti-Communist February Twenty-Second Movement.[5] The union thus became the prime "yellow union" for the Communists to attack. However, the Communist influence in the labor movement within Beiping from August 1945 to June 1946 was insignificant because the Communist Worker Work Committee failed to mention anything of importance in the period.[6]

The GMD authorities administered examinations (concerning the GMD ideology) to workers and employees who served in Japanese and puppet factories and enterprises. The Worker Committee did not struggle against the examination, however. While some telecommunications workers in Beiping–Tianjin had taken part in the strike for better pay in February 1946,[7] there was no proof that the CCUP was involved. The CCUP could claim some achievements only in the suburbs of Beiping and in the railway worker movement.

The mining district in Mentougou was close to the West Beiping "Liberated" Area, and early on the Communists started revolutionary activities there. The CCUP claimed it developed about four hundred "positive" elements, and was responsible for the three strikes from September 1945 to the spring of 1946 over the issues of wages and family coal allowances. Ultimately, the mining authorities agreed to raise the wages. These strikes were the first large-scale organized labor activities in postwar Beiping. In March 1946 there were ninety Party members in Mentougou. But from April to June two underground Party cells were destroyed and nine members were arrested by the GMD authorities.[8]

The Communists also had some supporters in the labor unions in the Shijingshan area. The main reasons for the electrical workers' support were the low wages, the frustration with the GMD takeover process, and the disgust with the high pay of the senior managers and engineers whose technological skills were not that sophisticated. The CCUP organized social groups, such as choirs and Beijing opera groups. However, they did nothing significant to damage the GMD strength there except encourage some laborers to slow down their work.[9]

The Changxindian area was another Communist "stronghold" because of its railway worker movement. As early as 1936 the CCP Northern Bureau assigned underground organizations to infiltrate various railway systems. After the end of the war, the CCP established the Railway Work Committee to revive underground activities in the Beiping area. In October 1945 the Communists among the railway staff and workers in Changxindian published pamphlets telling of the "reactionary" history of the Changxindian Branch Union of the (underground GMD) Beiping–Wuhan Railway Labor Union (for example, how the underground GMD union members cooperated with the Japanese and the puppet authorities). The Communist underground in the Fengtai Railway Station also organized self-governing associations to spread the Communist influence. As was the case in Shijingshan, the workers were unhappy with the GMD takeover officials. The CCUP encouraged some workers to sabotage the machines or to slow down their work.[10]

In May 1946 a worker at the Fengtai Railway Station was wounded by a Nationalist Air Force officer. The Communists exploited this incident into a seven-day railway worker strike. Fengtai was a strategic point, as it served as the connecting station for the Beiping–Liaoning, Beiping–Suiyuan, and Beiping–Wuhan railway lines. To avoid any disruption of military transportation on these lines, the GMD authorities—the Beiping GMD Air Force Command Post and the Beiping–Tianjin Area Railway Bureau—finally acceded to the demands of the strikers.[11]

While the railway strike in Fengtai might indeed have been Communist-led, the GMD's failure to cope with or counter the organization of the railway workers in Beiping–Tianjin was a major factor in the outcome of the incident. In the immediate wake of the Japanese surrender, the GMD underground in the Beiping–Wuhan railway system emerged to take over the southern and northern sections of the line. Later the GMD assigned Shi Zhiren, an official of the Transportation Ministry, as special commissioner to supervise the line. Shi ordered the underground GMD Beiping–Wuhan Railway Labor Union (under the authority of the Social Affairs Ministry, a rival government agency) not to operate in the open. Because of the suspension of the union members' activities to help the advancing GMD troops protect the whole Beiping–Hankou line, the Communists seized a strategic county where a railway station was located in southern Hebei. After that the Beiping–Hankou Railway was separated into two sections. Shi also asked the GMD labor union not to mention Communist sabotage of the railway communications, perhaps to cover up Nationalist incompetence. The leaders of the labor union reported Shi's activities to Chen Lifu, head of the GMD Organization Ministry, and Gu Zhenggang, head of the Social Affairs Ministry. Their response was that the labor union should not worry about Shi and should proceed to work as usual. In early 1946 the Organization Ministry and especially the Social Affairs Ministry did organize nineteen branch labor unions on the Beiping–Hankou Railway, and they cooperated with the local GMD railway bureaus. Nevertheless, factional struggles and disorder in management indicated the inability of the GMD to control not only the railway systems but also other areas.[12]

In Tianjin the Communists raised demands for better and back pay, restoration of work, and improvement of social welfare for the labor force. In late August 1945 the CCUP members led two hundred workers in surrounding the management bureau of the East Railway Station. They forced the bureau to pay back three months' wages to the workers. Afterward, the Communists established the Railway Staff and Worker Association, a "progressive" labor union. In February 1946 the Association presented its demands—higher wages and protection of human rights—on behalf of the workers to the railway management bureau, and the GMD authority accepted them. This was accomplished during the visit of the Tripartite Military Mediation Group to the bureau.[13] It was an intentional Communist scheme to act at the best time, and to win support and sympathy from the media and the American representative, too. The Nationalists were more willing to make concessions on such an occasion.

The GMD's own railway labor union in Tianjin (the Tianjin–Pukou Area Railway Labor Union) was inefficient as an anti-Communist organ in light of the general disorder in North China. It did not report any significant anti-Communist activities.[14]

Industry in Tianjin was in shambles after the Japanese surrender. Almost all major factories were pillaged by the GMD takeover officials, soldiers, vagabonds, Japanese, and puppet Chinese. Local security and police forces could not control the destruction and it took the arrival of the GMD "Central" armies to restore order. The former underground GMD labor union did emerge, assisted by a Nationalist representative from Chongqing, to form the Tianjin All-Trades Associated Labor Union. Its factory-protection worker corps could prevent pillage in only a few big factories.[15] The GMD takeover process caused factory output to deteriorate "from many into a few, a few into bad, from bad into none." Many workers became unemployed. According to the statistics of the Tianjin Social Affairs Bureau, there were 580,000 laborers in Tianjin, and 229,000 of them were out of work in 1945.[16]

In January 1946 the Tianjin Work Committee issued two directives for workers and coolies. They emphasized that economic struggle should be the main purpose of the labor movement. Communists should be involved in legal struggles according to the needs, demands, and living conditions of workers. Communists must help the struggle grow into a big one, and move from economics gradually to politics, "with reason, benefit, and restraint." Depending on the degree of consciousness and organization of the masses, the Party members should decide when to organize labor unions and self-governing associations and when to demand fewer work hours.[17]

The Communists were able to develop the labor movement in Tianjin because the GMD failed to monopolize all trade unions. Although the GMD controlled the Tianjin General Labor Union, it could not easily control unions in private industrial enterprises, especially in the privately operated iron factories.[18] Nevertheless, the hostility between capital and labor, especially in GMD-related enterprises, created a favorable atmosphere for Communist activity.

According to the Communists, they caused two major labor incidents in Tianjin in the spring of 1946. In January the Communist-infiltrated labor union in the East Asia Woolen Company forced the management to give flour and cloth to the workers. In a bloody incident in early May, the workers and some unidentified assailants in the Communist-infiltrated labor unions of the Fourth and Fifth cotton mills of the China Textiles Corporation (Tianjin Branch Office) forced the GMD authorities to pay indemnities for the workers injured in the confrontation and to withdraw the military and police forces.[19] During the same period the Beiping Commoner Work Committee helped the workers in the oil and salt shops to obtain gains such as an extra two months' pay. Its overall performance was insignificant, however.[20] The CCUP also boasted that it established the Tianjin Hotels Employee and Worker Association in April 1946. This feat influenced unions to sprout in other service industries, including bathhouse and restaurant businesses.[21]

Regardless of the strength of the Communist underground in the labor movement in Tianjin, it was the economic situation, not Communist activity, that prompted most industrial strikes and incidents. The Tianjin Social Affairs Bureau estimated that there were more than seventy incidents in December 1945 and fifty-three major strikes with 150,000 participants from January to April 1946.[22]

To conclude, the labor movement in postwar Tianjin flourished. Economic struggle, devoid of significant anti-GMD political content, was the thrust of Communist labor activities in Beiping–Tianjin. Relatively speaking, the student movement was much more effective in conveying the political messages of the CCUP in these cities. Nonetheless, the Nationalist weakness in the Beiping–Tianjin labor movement was fertile soil for the CCP's seeds of revolution.

During the period, the CCUP certainly stressed the united-front work among government officials and businessmen. Because of the generally middle- and upper-class backgrounds of the middle school and college students in Tianjin and Beiping, however, the student, not the worker, committees of the CCUP played the major role in carrying out the united-front activities. For example, Wu Mu, a leading cadre of the CCUP among the middle schools, came from a wealthy family that milled flour in Tianjin. (Consider the importance of flour in the livelihood of the urban residents.) His ninth uncle was a good friend of Du Jianshi (who became the mayor in October 1946) and Shi Zizhou (a municipal councillor). Wu's maternal grandfather was a sworn brother of Shi. Li Hanyuan (the police chief) was a student of Wu's maternal grandfather in the past. And the adopted daughter of Wu's mother was a daughter of the Tianjin mayor in 1945. Such social connections as those of Wu Mu facilitated the CCUP's united-front work among the GMD officials.[23]

Furthermore, in Tianjin, Zhou Shutao was a prominent capitalist. The CCUP thus regarded him as a prime united-front target who would "stabilize the mood" of other upper-level capitalists before the Communist takeover. While it was only in late 1948 that the CCUP seriously worked on Zhou, the Communists had recruited a family member in the early 1940s. Zhou Jiliang, a nephew of Zhou Shutao, had joined the Beiping CCUP (as a student) in 1942–43. He would be used to influence his uncle on the eve of "liberation."[24]

June 1946–June 1947

On 26 June 1946, the Communists launched a war against the GMD on all fronts in North China. Simultaneously, the CCUP and its allies in Beiping–Tianjin continued to work underground to aid the military struggle. During this period, China's economic situation continued to deteriorate. Wholesale and retail price indices continued to rise, and the GMD government financed its deficit mainly by printing more *fabi*. In June 1946 the official foreign exchange rate was 2,020 Chinese dollars for one U.S. dollar. This was 101 times more than the rate in the immediate wake of the Japanese surrender.[25]

The Communist labor movement in Beiping and Tianjin continued to lag behind the student movement. In Beiping workers might have supported and even joined the demonstrations in the Shen Chong Incident and the Antihunger Anti–Civil War Movement, but their influence was minimal.

Other than encouraging workers not to work hard and telling them about the victories of the 8th Route Army and the good life in CCP areas, the CCUP at the Changxindian Railcars Factory did not challenge the authorities.[26] The Communist "strongholds" in the industrial plants in suburban Beiping did not create any serious incidents to disrupt the Nationalist industrial production. The poor condition of government-run industry in Beiping was due to inept management and inefficiency, not Communist sabotage. In fact, by April 1946 the GMD had controlled the areas in Shijingshan and Mentougou and had suppressed the labor movement there. Accordingly, the Communist Worker Committee exerted more effort inside the city.[27]

The Communists could at most boast a modest beginning in certain industries within Beiping. For instance, they had fourteen members within the three-thousand-employee GMD telecommunications system. They had to develop their strength under very difficult conditions, for the system was firmly controlled by the GMD, the Youth Corps, Military Statistics, and Central Statistics.[28] In the Beiping 70th Arsenal, there were four to six members under the Communist Worker Committee.[29] In the 4,300-man GMD military supplies and clothing industry in Beiping, there were only three CCUP members.[30] Nonetheless, the CCUP claimed that it organized and led a two-thousand-man strike in late April 1947 to protest the physical abuse of a worker at a clothing factory. The management apologized for the incident and raised wages.[31] As a whole, however, Communist organizations among the industrial enterprises in Beiping were too weak to launch any significant disturbances.

In January 1947 the GMD reorganized the Beiping Municipal General Labor Union. In March it arbitrated only two cases with 96 workers involved; in April, an unknown number of cases with 1,200 workers involved; in May, one case with 96 workers involved. In Tianjin the GMD authorities dealt with fourteen labor disputes with 1,827 workers involved in January, ten cases with 2,048 workers in February, ten cases with 417 workers in March, ten cases with 65 workers in May, and ten cases with 2,191 workers in June.[32] These statistics demonstrate the feeble activities of the workers in the labor movement in Beiping–Tianjin. (There were about 229,000 industrial and handicraft workers in 1947.)

The major purpose of the Beiping Municipal General Labor Union was to fight the Communists. In the wake of the GMD military setback in Northeast China in May 1947, the Communists instructed the underground students and workers in the city to launch class strikes, labor strikes, and market strikes.[33] In response to this threat, the General Labor Union organized the Beiping Municipal Workers Purge Communists Committee. On 11 May (Beida incident), on 2 June (Xizhimen incident), and on 10 June (Xidan incident), the labor corps of this Committee fought the students (not the workers) in the antigovernment demonstrations.[34] The Communists apparently did not have a large following among the industrial workers then. It was the same situation among the handicraft workers, coolies, and other nonindustrial workers.[35]

While the Beiping CCUP claimed success in helping the bathhouse workers to keep their jobs and to establish a labor union in mid-May, the actual Communist involvement is unclear. There were 120 Party members among the oil and salt shop assistants during the first half of 1947; however, the CCUP also admitted the organizational weakness of their nine separate Party branch bureaus.[36]

Comparatively speaking, because of its strategic economic status in North China, Tianjin was a better place for the Communists to develop their labor movement. In the period discussed, the Communists boasted of leading an important strike in the Fourth and Fifth cotton mills in May 1946.[37] In the same month the GMD Municipal Party Bureau in Tianjin sent agents into various major industrial enterprises to coordinate labor, that is, to terminate any Communist-instigated labor disputes. On 16 June the Tianjin authorities dissolved the labor organizations in the Fourth and Fifth cotton mills, arrested the leaders and sixty other workers. The Communists would have suffered more if they had not been warned by a sympathetic, low-ranking GMD officer.[38] In June workers in the Second Cotton Mill also struck. A worker was killed in an industrial accident, and the strikers refused to resume work until management promised to provide a large funeral, with a good-quality coffin, and payments to his family.[39] There was no evidence that the CCUP was involved in this strike. From 22 June to 24 June, the workers in the Hai Ho Engineering Bureau agitated for higher wages. The workers' representatives were arrested by the authorities, and the CCUP probably did not participate in this labor unrest.[40]

On 5 September 1946, the workers in the Tianjin Railway Bureau petitioned on behalf of those laid off in Beiping. The Communists were involved and claimed a victory because the GMD authorities agreed to pay three months' wages for laid-off workers if they resumed work within three months. In early December workers in factories controlled by the GMD Natural Resources Committee also struck for a cost-of-living wage increase. The strike, however, was broken by the GMD military and police authorities. The CCUP probably was not involved in this strike.[41]

During the period, Communist activity among urban residents in Tianjin was insignificant because by late August 1946 more than one hundred CCUP members had retreated to CCP areas as a result of Nationalist suppression.[42] In late 1946, under the pretext of "beautifying the face of the city," the Tianjin authorities attempted to stop the hawkers from operating. A wave of petitions from the hawkers appeared, demanding that authorities rescind their orders.[43] Communist instigation, if any, was insignificant. Ultimately, the GMD did not carry out the order to clear the city of the hawkers, but encouraged protests and petitions instead.

Some labor protests reflected traditional native-place divisions in the workplace, exacerbated by economic competition. For instance, the slowdown at the Fourth Cotton Mill in January 1947 was a protest against the hiring of workers from Shanxi. It is not clear whether the CCUP members in this factory participated in this protest or the attack on the office of the municipal GMD Party Bureau in March 1947.[44]

During the Antihunger Anti–Civil War Movement in May, three CCUP members at the Tianjin Machinery Factory of the GMD National Resources Committee helped the protesting workers collect unpaid wages from management. But there was no evidence that the workers were aware of the Communist instigation and involvement.[45]

Also, the Communists could not control the transport workers, who were enmeshed in a traditional structure and a set of loyalties that effectively blocked their participation in a class-conscious labor force.[46]

As a whole, from mid-1946 to mid-1947, strikes and protests occurred in Beiping–Tianjin mainly because of the rising cost of living. It cannot be determined exactly how many of these activities were a conscious part of the Communist labor movement. It does seem likely, however, that organized militancy even at its height in Tianjin factories (in 1947–48) involved many workers who were casual participants rather than politically conscious activists. Preoccupied with daily survival, workers were often oblivious to larger issues and events. Furthermore, many workers who may have heard of, or even joined, protests in their own factories, were unaware of the role of the CCUP.[47] We may conclude, then, that protests and strikes were almost exclusively economic, not political, in character. There occurred no union of economic and political struggles, unless one wishes to suppose that the fight for a better livelihood was itself a political act against Chiang Kai-shek.

In the labor movement, the Communists failed to make any significant political gains in what remained an almost exclusively economic struggle. Therefore, the labor movement contributed little to the Nationalist loss of authority. Fortunately for the Communists, the economy in urban GMD China continued to deteriorate, further undermining Nationalist authority and prestige.

During the period, the CCP was busily discrediting the American presence in China. Business and industrial interests were also involved in the growing anti-American climate at this time. On 4 November 1946, the United States and the GMD government signed a Treaty of Friendship, Commerce, and Navigation.[48] The Americans received so many commercial privileges that the Communists condemned the agreement as treasonable.[49] They referred sarcastically to "American products" (*meihuo*) as "American disaster" (*meihuo*).[50] Chinese businessmen complained about unfair competition from American products, which dominated the Chinese market. While there were domestic causes for the disruption of Chinese business and industry, Americans still reaped much profit. A "Buy Chinese Movement" was launched by Chinese businessmen with official approval from the GMD toward the end of 1946.[51] The sincerity of the GMD's endorsement of the movement was not the issue. The Communist involvement, if any, in this movement must have been politically unnecessary and insignificant.

In addition, it was the CCUP's student committees, not its worker committees, that played the key role in educating the poor workers and peasants and their children in Beiping–Tianjin. For example, in mid-1946 the Qingda CCUP members organized a free night school for the children. More important, in mid-1947 the Qingda CCUP established a large number of "Understanding Chinese Characters Classes" in the suburbs of Beiping. The courtyard or the area under the big tree was the classroom. The Communists and other "progressive" students printed their textbooks. While the contents of the texts could not be too "red," words such as *revolution* and *production forces* were often found in them.[52]

June 1947–August 1948

During this period the Communist labor movement in Beiping–Tianjin was based on the guidelines expounded in Zhou Enlai's 5 May 1947 directive for struggle in GMD areas.[53] There were three other Party documents that illustrated the labor work in Beiping–Tianjin and other GMD cities.

In a document dated 13 July 1947, the North China Bureau Urban Work Department indicated that the current tasks of labor work were: fighting for job security; opposing the closure of factories and their relocation in the south; strengthening cooperation between workers and staff members; carrying out united-front work among national bourgeoisie; developing new labor cadres; and encouraging skilled workers and management personnel to serve in CCP areas.[54]

Another directive, issued by the Shanxi–Hebei–Shandong–Henan Central Bureau in late 1947, outlined the Communist labor duties: (1) The primary task of the Party is to control big cities; the labor movement is an important part of the urban work. (2) The workers should make economic and political demands under legitimate conditions. (3) The Party should recruit highly skilled workers to unite with ordinary workers. (4) The Communists must neutralize the "yellow unions." (5) When the PLA approaches a city, the CCUP should organize strikes to coordinate with the military assault. (6) The Party should educate the workers and raise their political consciousness.[55]

In late 1947 the leaders of the Beiping Worker Committee reported to the CCP Central Work Committee in Hebei. The Central Work Committee gave these instructions: (1) The CCUP should organize the masses and spread economic and political struggles in terms of immediate interests and demands of residents and laborers. The CCUP should also engage in investigation and study in order to understand the political, economic, and military situations. (2) The CCUP should unite the scattered, single-contact cadres. "Too scattered might be good for concealment but it is without power." (3) In Beiping the CCUP must put its major energy to work on administrative workers, particularly those in telecommunications systems including cable and radio. In accordance with this directive, the Beiping Worker Committee was reorganized into the Municipal Administration Work Committee in the winter of 1947. At this time there were only about seventy Party members.[56]

The CCUP was most active in the three-thousand-employee Beiping Tele-communications Bureau, a major GMD organization. In late 1947 there were twenty-two Communists working underground in the bureau. In December 1947 the CCUP organized a singing group to socialize with the bureau workers. Through the welfare committees, mutual aid associations, study clubs, and approved wall newspapers, the CCUP recruited "progressive" elements to spread Communist ideology.[57]

In April 1948 the CCUP organized an economic struggle. Because of rising inflation, the workers of the Telecommunications Bureau were angry about the salary readjustment proposed by the GMD Transportation Ministry. It cut their "rice stipends," the extra monthly allowance calculated according to the prevailing price of rice. The Municipal Administration Work Committee, under the guidance of Liu Ren, began pushing for reasonable treatment of the workers. On 28 April the CCUP helped establish the hundred-member "Fight for Reasonable Treatment Conference," and a Communist became the chairman. The CCUP also asked the GMD Labor Union to petition the bureau on behalf of the workers. Through a series of negotiations, the bureau agreed to adjust the rice stipends for some of the workers. Although the CCUP failed to win all the demands for all the workers, it decided to end the movement. The Party recruited twenty new members, and the effort was deemed a successful struggle of an open and legal kind.[58]

The CCUP also attempted to reform the GMD Labor Union in the Telecommunications Bureau. Through efforts among the workers who had been involved in the rice-stipends movement, Party members and "progressives" dominated the 161 small sections of the labor union and accordingly also controlled the executive committee. This was another Communist victory.[59]

The Communist penetration of the GMD Telecommunications Bureau was of course a significant achievement of the Beiping Municipal Administration Work Committee, and a threat to the GMD Telecommunications network in the city.

The railways and the telecommunications system were closely related. In March 1948, however, the Communist Railway Committee suffered a major setback. One of its members was arrested. Twenty-eight Party members were later arrested, and the Committee was disbanded temporarily. The surviving leaders escaped to CCP areas.[60] Because of this GMD crackdown, the CCUP members at the Changxindian Railcars Factory had to leave, and their underground work was suspended.[61]

According to a high-level GMD official in Beiping, this Communist setback and resulting paranoia prompted the assassination of seven people inside a Beiping residence in late March. The Communists were worried that the wealthy master of the household, a CCP agent, would betray their organization to the GMD authorities in the city.[62]

Nonetheless, on 3 April the Communist Commoner Committee organized a strike in the Telephone Office, Beiping Telecommunications Section of the Beiping–Tianjin Railway Bureau. On that day a young female employee of the Telephone Office was allegedly insulted by the section police. Believing the incident afforded a chance to mobilize the masses, the two CCUP members working in the section (one was the head of the Telephone Office) launched a strike protesting the treatment of the female employee. Because of complicated internal dissension among various GMD and local organs within the bureau and the threat of a prolonged strike, the Police Affairs Section of the bureau agreed to punish the guilty parties and to express regret to the Telephone Office. This victory heightened the consciousness of the workers in the bureau.[63]

Soon after this strike, the leading member of the Communist Commoner Work Committee was arrested. However, because of the incompetence of the GMD authorities and the corruption of lower-level officers (corporal and lieutenant), he was released on a bond three weeks later. He then escaped to CCP areas.[64]

In the Beiping 70th Arsenal, the CCUP developed under the leadership of the Municipal Administration Work Committee. The primary task of the CCUP in the arsenal was to block the enemy's manufacture of weapons, to cultivate "progressives," and to unite the masses. There were Communists working in the arsenal office and the secretariat. In December 1947 the arsenal workers were furious with the high price index because they could not afford to prepare for the coming Chinese New Year. After analyzing the general mood of workers, the CCUP decided to launch a strike for better treatment. Even though the arsenal officially banned any strike, the CCUP, through the workers and some supervisors, launched two general strikes in two months. This effort ended in pay raises and the recruitment of a number of "progressive" workers. The Communists also claimed to have disrupted the arsenal by making faulty hand grenades, sabotaging furnaces, and slowing production. Also, the CCUP in the arsenal escaped exposure because the Military Statistics did not act on information that it deemed to be inaccurate.[65]

The CCUP also disrupted the GMD's production of other military supplies and clothing. For instance, in the sewing section the clothes were not made according to the prescribed sizes. In the packaging section products were loosely packed. The sabotage was aimed at creating conflict between soldiers on the battlefront and the officers responsible for the supplies. The CCUP members also mailed letters to the GMD officers stationed at the factories. These letters warned against repressing workers and advised the officers to shift to the "people's side." Information gathered about the quality, quantity, and type of clothes ordered and the production deadlines helped the Communists discover GMD troop numbers, locations, and movements.[66]

On 12 March 1948, eight hundred workers at more than twenty newspapers struck for better treatment. Management accepted their demands, although the CCUP involvement in the strike is unclear. In July 1948 the laborers at the Shijingshan Iron and Steel Works also successfully struck for back pay, flour, and coal. Again, CCUP participation is unclear.[67]

As a whole, the Communist Municipal Administration and Commoner Work Committees failed to instigate major labor incidents. Besides the strikes mentioned above, there were several minor labor disputes in the bathhouses, and in the Central Printing Bureau in August and November 1947.[68] In September a labor strike involved 418 workers; in October there was another with ninety-five workers.[69] Communist activities were negligible among workers in city services (streetcars, public buses, water supply system, and postal service), and among the people in the weaving, building, tilers', and carpenters' trades and in other lower-level professions.

Although the Communist labor movement in Beiping from mid-1947 to mid-1948 did disturb the Nationalists on various fronts, it remained minor compared with the student movement. While there were some strikes, there was no concrete proof these were politically motivated. And the GMD had no need to use excessive force to suppress the workers. They played a minimal role in furthering the Nationalist loss of authority.

It was the same situation in Tianjin. In April 1947 the Communist Central Hebei Area Urban Work Department issued "An Assessment of the Situation in Tianjin and an Opinion on the Current Work Among the Eight Sub-Districts":

> We must distinguish between the policy and strategy on the . . . bureaucratic capital and national capital in the labor movement work. In the national bourgeois factories, the labor–capital cooperation can be the content of the propaganda. The concrete application of it must be based on the condition that the capital side improves the living condition of the workers, and then we advocate labor–capital cooperation and appropriate increase in production. . . . We must stress unity with the progressive elements and the leaders of the masses in order to prevent the factory side from using feudal districts [these referred to the geographical districts that the workers came from—Au.] to neutralize and paralyze the workers.[70]

In short, labor–capital cooperation was the Communist theme in the "national bourgeois" factories. And labor–capital struggle in the bureaucratic enterprises was implied in the document.

In 1947 the CCUP labor front had 450 members in sixty branch Party bureaus in Tianjin, scattered among cotton and woolen mills, railroads, wharfs, clothing manufacturers, and shoe factories. In order to stymie the GMD, there were no direct connections among the branch bureaus. The CCUP took various forms: food groups, cooperatives, theatrical groups, martial arts corps, sworn brotherhood and sisterhood. The Communist Urban Residents Work Committee also had 777 members in thirty-nine branch bureaus, dispersed among the poor, rickshaw men, handicraftsmen, dockers, freight haulers, shop assistants, and coolies.[71]

The GMD authorities were naturally concerned about the threat of an organized Communist movement with a working-class base in Tianjin. As they began to lose ground outside Tianjin, GMD repression within the city tightened, as did surveillance of large workplaces. In June 1947 martial law was declared in Tianjin, and a curfew was imposed. Although the restrictions were partially lifted later, the municipal government reimposed martial law intermittently to the end of 1948.[72]

For three days in November 1947, one thousand freight haulers and coolies struck for better pay. Their demands finally were accepted by the guild leaders. The Communist involvement in this strike was unclear.[73] On 9 December 1947, postal workers were angry with a pay cut and carried out a hunger strike for one day. Communists probably were not involved.[74]

On 24 February 1948, fifteen hundred streetcar workers struck against the arrest of some colleagues who had disobeyed the GMD curfew. In order to restore normal streetcar service, the municipal public utilities and police chiefs released the workers and agreed to resolve the problem of streetcar employees who operated during the curfew.[75] From 3 December 1947 up to February 1948, a total of eighty-three Communists were arrested and charged with planning strikes. Among those detained were workers on railroads and docks, factory laborers, freight haulers, and coolies.[76] The arrests were a setback for the CCUP.

Throughout 1948 the local authorities tightened their supervision of large factories. Government patrols were stationed in the factories; soldiers searched workers on the shop floor and on the way to work; workers were required to carry identity cards. Foremen were instructed to report union activities to the authorities, particularly if there was a suspicion that they were connected to the 8th Route Army.[77] Although the GMD repression was stiff, the Communists were active. For instance, in the labor unions, they established the Tianjin Municipal Hotels Trade Staff and Workers Association and launched a protest in June 1947. In August 1948 there was also a Communist-instigated protest over the killing of two workers at the Tianjin Blankets and Clothing Factory.[78]

There were more labor disputes in Tianjin than in Beiping. In July 1947 the GMD authorities arbitrated fourteen labor incidents in Tianjin with 656 workers involved. In August there were eight strikes with 136 workers involved. There were eleven strikes in September with 550 workers involved. A bloody confrontation involving 36 workers occurred in October at the GMD Sixth Cotton Mill in October; there were five casualties. In the same month there were nine more labor disputes with 639 people involved. In November 810 workers were involved in eleven strikes. There were nine disputes in December. In May 1948 the workers at the Xingang Harbor Engineering Bureau struck for better pay. The police arrested twenty-nine who were charged with conspiring with Communist agents.[79] In June there were labor disputes over treatment of workers at the Tianjin Telecommunications Bureau, the Tianjin Streetcar Corporation, and the Tianjin–Pukou Railway Bureau.[80]

Nevertheless, the Communist labor movement in Tianjin never became a real threat to the GMD. The fragmentation of the Tianjin working class based on varying experiences made the development of any united anti-GMD activity unlikely. Even when the workers struck, it was mainly for economic reasons. Perhaps only the Communists cared about the political implication of such struggles.

Moreover, in Tianjin the Communist united-front work among GMD officials and businessmen had a special achievement in mid-1948. From 1946 to 1949 a key Communist organization that dealt with trade and the purchase of war supplies in Beiping–Tianjin was the Yongmao Corporation. Its Party and political matters were controlled by the Central Hebei Area Party Bureau and the Central Hebei Administrative Office, while the commercial ones were led by the North China People's Government (established in September 1948). In June 1948 Lin Xingru, a Communist employee, was ordered to strike a deal—exchanging the cotton in CCP areas with the GMD war supplies—with the general manager of the Tianjin branch of the GMD China Textiles Corporation. Yang Yizhou was the general manager and also the speaker of the Tianjin Municipal Council.[81]

At the time, the GMD was losing on the battlefront and American cotton was in short supply. The Nationalists were worried about the possibility of strikes by a large number of unemployed textile workers. Therefore, Yang Yizhou wanted to purchase the cotton produced in CCP areas. The Communists saw this as an opportunity to test the feasibility of such an unusual deal. Lin Xingru was the cadre selected to fulfill the task.[82]

In order to better understand the situation and the underground operation in Tianjin, the leading cadres at Yongmao Corporation contacted the Urban Work Department of the North China Bureau for detailed information. After much practice and carefully reading the street maps of Tianjin and Beiping, Lin Xingru dressed up and behaved as a Beiping–Tianjin merchant. Assisted by a "communication person," Lin arrived in Tianjin with a fake identity card.[83]

Lin's main contact person in Tianjin was Liu Yiwen, the left-wing director of the local charity hospital and the principal of Buyu Middle School. Liu's husband was a Communist. Because they were friends, Liu could invite Yang Yizhou to her home to discuss the deal with Lin. After two rounds of negotiation, Yang decided to get approval from Fu Zuoyi in Beiping because Commander Chen Changjie of Tianjin would not permit any war supplies to go to the Communists. However, since Fu did not want to express any opinion on the matter because of the "Central" surveillance on his activities, Yang returned to Tianjin and expressed to Lin his regrets on the abortive deal. Yang also asked Lin to inform his superiors of his (Yang's) sincerity.

Although the trade was aborted, the Communists believed that they had acquired good experience in dealing with the upper-level GMD officials and had gathered useful information about Tianjin.[84] (After "liberation," Yang served as the deputy mayor of Tianjin for some time. His appointment was a Communist united-front tactic to convince the former upper-level GMD officials and "bureaucratic capitalists" to stay and help build a new China. In addition, the Yongmao Corporation and the Central Hebei Party Bureau did not know in advance that the Beiping Student Committee was in contact with Yang.)[85]

This unique episode in mid-1948 demonstrated not only the Communist united-front work with the upper-level GMD personnel but also the internal trouble and vacillating attitude of certain Nationalists in Beiping–Tianjin. Their morale was breaking down, and this benefited Communist underground work.

The Communist secret radio stations also performed well in this period. For example, in August 1946 the CCUP established a preliminary station inside Beiping. The station was located inside a temple. It only collected daily messages from the rural headquarters; it did not transmit any information. By late 1948, however, there were three secret radio stations. Cui Yueli, a leading cadre of the Beiping Student Committee, was responsible for cooperating with the telecommunications personnel.[86]

The Longyun Electric Materials Shop was a Communist telecommunications base in Beiping. Cui recommended a local ally, who had wide and good social connections, to be the manager of the shop. The leading cadre of the radio stations (Li Xue) was the "shareholder" and another cadre (Zhao Zhenmin) was an "employee." Jiujiu Photo Shop was another Communist base. Li Xue was the manager, while the radio station "communication person" (Zhang Bin) served as the accountant. Another communication person (Wu Kuande) lived in the shop as a security guard. In the daytime Wu sold cigarettes and candy as a hawker in the street. The student committee's communication person often came to collect messages under the pretext of buying cigarettes and candy.[87]

The CCUP made appropriate "family" arrangements for covering up the identities of the radio station personnel. Zhao Zhenmin was a "nephew" of an affluent old woman. Fang Ting and Ai Shan were "cousins" because Fang's mother was Ai's "aunt." Wang Zhaoxiang and Wang Junshi were "husband" and "wife." These "families" lived in large homes. Li Xue, who lived with his father, traveled on a motorcycle. The GMD military and police regarded him as a wealthy youngster; they did not bother him.[88]

In order to avoid the GMD authorities, who used electronic equipment installed on army Jeeps that moved around the city to detect illegal wireless frequencies, the CCUP employed various ways to fight the Nationalists. The frequencies of the transmissions and the codes were altered often. The station personnel also moved several times. The Communists stored their equipment on the wall or inside the closet. The antennas were camouflaged. Although the GMD authorities demolished a secret radio station belonging to the Southern Group, the Northern Group did not lose any.[89]

To summarize, the inability of the GMD authorities to destroy all the Communist radio stations within Beiping and Tianjin was certainly unfavorable for their rule in the cities. On the other side, through appropriate procedures and methods of operation, the CCUP's urban telecommunications networks succeeded to a great extent in keeping constant contact with the rural superiors and facilitating the urban struggles. The Communists enjoyed a special kind of power on the airwaves in GMD cities.

Notes

1. See Mao's summing up of Party history in April 1945, in *MZX*, vol. III, p. 972.
2. *MZJ*, vol. IX, p. 252. As mentioned before, in 1940 Mao had abandoned the hope of a proletarian revolution in China.
3. See Zheng Deyong and Zhu Yang, *Zhongguo gemingshi changbian*, vol. II, pp. 220–22.
4. *TXGY*, pp. 194–95.
5. See Ma Chaojun, *Zhongguo laogong yundong shi*, vol. VII, pp. 1578, 1587–89.
6. See Lu Yu, "Zuzhu qilai liliang da, liying waihe ying jiefang—Huiyi Beiping dixiadang gongwei he shizheng gongwei lingdao de douzheng," pp. 93–95.
7. See Chang Kai et al., *Zhongguo gongyunshi cidian*, p. 190.
8. Ibid., pp. 94–95; see also Beijing Shifan Daxue Lishixi Sannianji, Yanjiuban, *Mentougou meikuang shigao*, pp. 42–45; Xue Shixiao, *Zhongguo meikuang gongren yundong shi*, p. 653; He Wencheng and Jia Chengzhong, "Guanghui de zhandou licheng," pp. 36–39; *BXG*, pp. 197–98; *BGD*, p. 289.
9. Lu Yu, "Beiping gongwei," p. 95; Pan Zhiting, *Fadianchang nei wushi nian*, pp. 93–97.
10. See Ye Keming, "Pubumie de geming huozhong—Huiyi Beiping dixiadang tiewei lingdao de douzheng," pp. 158–60; see also Changxindian Jiche Cheliang Gongchang Changshi, *Beifang de hongxing*, pp. 319–24.
11. See Yan Zhao, "Xu Yeping Shiqing," pp. 164–71. Xu was the worker who got hurt in the incident.
12. See Ma Chaojun, *Zhongguo laogong*, vol. VII, pp. 1569–71.
13. *TXGY*, p. 195.
14. See Ma Chaojun, *Zhongguo laogong*, vol. VII, pp. 1571–72.
15. Ibid., pp. 1574–78.
16. Cited in *TXGY*, pp. 196–97.
17. Ibid., p. 197.
18. See Ma Chaojun, *Zhongguo laogong*, vol. VII, pp. 1611–64.
19. See *TXGY*, pp. 198–200; *TJ*, p. 407.
20. *BGD*, p. 289.
21. Chang Kai et al., *Zhongguo gongyunshi*, p. 193.
22. *TXGY*, p. 199.
23. Wu Mu, "Tianjin xueyun de jiguo wenti," p. 13.
24. Wang Wenhua, "Huiyi peihe jiefang Tianjin de dixia douzheng," pp. 5–6.
25. See Chang Kia-ngau, *The Inflationary Spiral*, p. 305.
26. See Changxindian Jiche Cheliang Gongchang Changshi, *Beifang de hongxing*, pp. 323–24.
27. See Lu Yu, "Beiping gongwei," p. 95.
28. See Yuan Beiping Dianxinju Bufen Dixia Dangyuan, "Jiefang qian Beiping dianxin gongren de douzheng," p. 138.
29. See Zhang Jinke and Zhou Wenbin, "Ba shengchan gao tanhuan, rang diren tuantuan zhuan—Beiping qishi binggongchang dixiadang douzheng huiyi," p. 875.
30. Meng Zhiyuan, "Qianzhu diren junxu houqin de bozi—Beiping junxu beifu xitong dixiadang douzheng jishi," p. 448.
31. *BGD*, p. 130.
32. See Yujiro Kimura, *A Chronology of the History of the Chinese Labor Movement*, pp. 423–28.
33. See n. 174 in ch. 5.
34. See Ma Chaojun, *Zhongguo laogong*, vol. VII, pp. 1673–78.

35. See Zhao Fan, Peng Siming, and Xu Ping, "Ranqi laodong renmin douzheng de huoyan—Huiyi Beiping dixiadang pingwei lingdao de douzheng," pp. 173–74.

36. *BXG*, pp. 209–10.

37. See Li Yuanchun, "Mianfang sichang chengli chise gonghui qianhou," pp. 60–61.

38. Ibid., p. 61; *TXGY*, p. 201.

39. Gail Hershatter, *The Workers of Tianjin*, p. 235.

40. *TJ*, pp. 407–8.

41. *TXGY*, p. 213; *TJ*, pp. 430–31; Zhu Qihua and Liu Yongze, *Tianjin quanshu*, p. 34.

42. Wang Jie, "Huiyi jiefang zhanzheng shiqi dang zai Tianjin gongwei he shimin xitong de chengshi gongzuo," p. 218.

43. *TXGY*, pp. 213–14.

44. See Hershatter, *Workers of Tianjin*, p. 236.

45. Zhu Baoshan et al., "Jiefang zhanzheng shiqi dang lingdao Tianjin Jiqichang de douzheng," pp. 228–29.

46. See Hershatter, *Workers of Tianjin*, ch. 5.

47. Ibid., p. 237.

48. See *Zhongguo xiandaishi ziliao xuanbian*, vol. V, pp. 657–83.

49. See *Jiefang ribao*, Yan'an, 26 Nov. 1946.

50. See Ling Yaolun et al., *Zhongguo jindai jingjishi*, p. 418.

51. See Suzanne Pepper, *Civil War in China*, p. 53.

52. See *BDDS*, pp. 427–30.

53. See n. 144 in ch. 5.

54. See *Dagong bao*, Tianjin, 8 Sept. 1947.

55. See the article entitled "A Critique of the Communist Labor Movement," in *Gongren ribao*, Tianjin, 8 Aug. 1948.

56. Lu Yu, "Beiping gongwei," pp. 131–32.

57. Yuan Beiping Dianxinju Bufen Dixia Dangyuan, "Jiefang qian Beiping dianxin gongren de douzheng," pp. 138–40.

58. Ibid., pp. 142–45; Lu, "Beiping gongwei," p. 134; Chang Kai et al., *Zhongguo gongyunshi*, p. 206.

59. Yuan Beiping Dianxinju Bufen Dixia Dangyuan, "Beiping dianxin gongren," pp. 146–47; *BGD*, p. 339.

60. Ye Keming, "Beiping tiewei," p. 161; *BGD*, p. 330.

61. See n. 8 in ch. 4.

62. See Lao Zhuang, *Gudu mengnan ji*, p. 8, chaps. 6–8.

63. Zhang Changshan and Wang Yikun, "Liming qian de zhandou," pp. 464–69. See also Chang Kai et al., *Zhongguo gongyunshi*, p. 206.

64. Fu Shijun, "Yingjiu Zhao Fan tongzhi," pp. 191–95.

65. Zhang Jinke and Zhou Wenbin, "Beiping qishi binggongchang," pp. 881–90; *BGD*, pp. 327–28.

66. Meng Zhiyuan, "Beiping junxu beifu," pp. 451–53; *BGD*, pp. 328–29.

67. *BGD*, pp. 330, 341.

68. Wang Zonghua, Li Fuhai, and Wang Ruxian, " 'Dong Sheng Ping' bu pingjing," pp. 186–87; *BGD*, p. 325.

69. Kimura, *Chinese Labor Movement*, pp. 430–31.

70. Quoted in *TXGY*, pp. 229–30.

71. Ibid., p. 230.

72. See *Yishi bao*, Tianjin, 1, 2, 3, 11, 15, 17, 21 June 1947; 24 Nov. and 19 Dec. 1948.

73. Chang Kai et al., *Zhongguo gongyunshi*, pp. 203–4.

74. See *TXGY*, p. 213; *TJ*, pp. 430–31; Zhu Qihua and Liu Yongze, *Tianjin quanshu*, p. 34.

75. *TJ*, p. 432.
76. *Dagong bao*, Tianjin, 18 Feb. 1948; see also *TXGY*, p. 223.
77. Hershatter, *Workers of Tianjin*, pp. 236–37.
78. *TXGY*, pp. 237–38.
79. *TJ*, p. 433.
80. Kimura, *Chinese Labor Movement*, pp. 428–36.
81. See Lin Xingru, "Chuang Tianjinwei zuo teshu de maoyi tanpan," p. 211.
82. Ibid., p. 212.
83. Ibid., pp. 213–14.
84. Ibid., pp. 214–20.
85. See Wang Wenhua, "Huiyi peihe jiefang Tianjin de dixia douzheng," p. 9.
86. *BDDS*, pp. 255–57.
87. Ibid., p. 257.
88. Ibid., p. 260.
89. Ibid., pp. 260–62; see also n. 196 in ch. 5.

7

Final Struggle: August 1948 to January 1949

By the fall of 1948, the GMD was losing the war against the CCP. Since the general order in July 1947 to suppress the Communists, the economy in GMD areas had also deteriorated. Because of the huge deficit, inflation increased and prices rose. Industry and commerce stagnated, and the urban residents endured harsh economic stress. The GMD economy was on the verge of collapse. The introduction of the Gold Yuan on 19 August 1948 aggravated the inflationary trend and paved the way to final bankruptcy in GMD areas. The political costs of GMD economic mismanagement were enormous. It not only eroded the fighting spirit of the underpaid GMD soldiers but also alienated the urban populace beyond redemption. The loss of authority by GMD authorities in Beiping–Tianjin facilitated the CCP's urban revolution.

Communist Urban Strategy and Tactics

From August 1948 to January 1949, the Communist armed forces attacked the GMD on all fronts. After the three decisive campaigns of Liaoxi–Shenyang, Huai-Hai, and Beiping–Tianjin, Mao Zedong was confident that the CCP would win sooner than he had earlier anticipated. In July 1946 he had predicted that it would take five years to overthrow the GMD regime. Now that seemed far too cautious a forecast.

In September 1948 the CCP CC held a conference in Xibaipo Village, Pingshan County, Hebei Province. The circular issued at this September meeting stated:

The Party's work in GMD areas has been crowned with tremendous success . . . *we must . . . strengthen the administration of cities and industry and shift the center of gravity of our Party work step by step from the rural areas to the cities* [emphasis added]. The task of seizing political power throughout the country demands that our Party should quickly and systematically train large numbers of cadres to administer military, political, economic, Party, cultural, and educational affairs. . . . In preparing cadres . . . pay attention to enrolling cadres from the big cities controlled by the GMD. In the big cities . . . there are many workers and intellectuals who can take part in our work and who have, generally speaking, a higher cultural level than the workers and peasants in the old Liberated [CCP] Areas. We should make use of large numbers of working personnel from the GMD's economic, financial, cultural and educational institutions. . . .[1]

Mao assessed the urban work in GMD areas, and thus pointed out the significance of the cities in the overall Communist political strategy. This emphasis on urban work demanded the formation of the broadest united front in GMD areas.

The Urban Work Department of the North China Bureau transmitted the spirit of the September meeting to the Beiping–Tianjin CCUP. The "liberation" of GMD cities was carried out by the PLA. The CCUP did not need to coordinate armed struggles with the PLA. The primary tasks of the CCUP were to preserve the base, to develop the Party organizations, to protect schools and factories, to carry out the united-front work through social relations with the students, to prevent professors and experts from retreating with the GMD to the south, and to dispatch cadres to CCP areas.[2]

August 1948 saw the last Nationalist effort to crush the Communist student movement. On the surface, it seemed to work in the cities. In a CCP CC directive entitled "Cool-Headedness and Flexible Tactics—Requirements of the Struggle in Areas Under the Chiang Regime" (22 August 1948), drafted by Zhou Enlai and revised by Mao Zedong, the Communists urged the CCUP to avoid rashness:

[O]n our present work in GMD areas . . . we should *resolutely follow the tactic of evacuation and concealment, accumulating strength and biding our time . . . it is out of the question to promote unsupported armed uprisings of workers and other inhabitants in GMD cities* [emphasis added]. . . . To do so would be to risk alienating the minority vanguard forces from the masses and incurring heavy losses and even temporary defeats. In particular, before the approach of the PLA and the final collapse of the enemy, it would be most unwise to expend too soon the strength of revolutionary leadership that has been accumulated in the cities over the years . . . the enemy has sounded the final alarm. All cities under Chiang's rule . . . should be evacuated in an orderly fashion. . . . Party members . . . who have been discovered or are being watched by enemy agents should find a way of leaving their present posts and withdrawing to the Liberated [CCP] Areas. . . . Those who have not yet been discovered and are not being watched by enemy agents should continue to lie low; they should resume activities step by step, only after the wave of informing on people has passed, so as to accumulate fresh strength while biding their time. The tactic against the massive informing is to carry on legal struggles. . . . This means appealing to school authorities for protection, opposing indictments for special criminal offenses, fighting for justice in the special criminal courts, organizing rescue efforts by the public.[3]

Because of the inability of the GMD authorities to destroy the CCUP, the policy of "evacuating and working underground, accumulating strength and biding time" (*shusan yinbi, jixu liliang, yidai shiji*) seemed to have worked, and the Communist Student Committees and other organizations in Beiping–Tianjin were prepared to launch new struggles for "liberation."[4]

Liu Ren also outlined the basic principles for the student effort in Beiping–Tianjin. In the summer of 1948, the Urban Work Department of the North China Bureau organized a training class for the important CCUP cadres in North China. Liu Ren summarized the directive of the North China Bureau for the student movement. He indicated that armed struggle was of major importance to the Chinese revolution. The "liberation" of cities depended more on the PLA than on the urban masses, especially the student masses. The general task of the students was to continue the anti-American and anti-Chiang movement to complement the PLA assault and to prepare for "liberating" and managing the cities. In order to facilitate the future takeover and administration of the cities, the CCUP must engage in united-front work of investigation and study. Second, the CCUP must mobilize students to go to CCP areas for training. Third, the Party must send students to the rear of GMD areas (primarily their hometowns) to lead the masses in resisting the requisition of food and manpower. Above all, from then on there should be no more large-scale popular struggles.[5] While the Beiping–Tianjin CCUP sent 2,700 students, "progressives," skilled workers, and technicians to CCP areas for training (two thousand from Beiping, seven hundred from Tianjin),[6] it continued its struggles within the cities. The CCUP also escorted well-known left-wing personalities (including the family members of Wen Yido in Tianjin) to Communist areas.

Certainly, the CCP's main thrust to "liberate" the GMD cities would be military, and the Communists would not launch armed uprisings within Beiping–Tianjin. It implied that the CCUP and its urban allies were not strong enough to rise up against the authorities. It did not mean that the Communist urban activities were insignificant, however. On the contrary, their action was indispensable in facilitating the capture of Beiping–Tianjin and initiating the post-"liberation" tasks.

Intellectuals, Students, Workers, Residents, GMD Personnel, and Capitalists

By the autumn of 1948 the GMD had alienated the academic community. In Beiping a group of college professors were asked how they felt about the political change as a result of the Communist military advances. A former GMD member, long noted as one of China's outstanding liberal thinkers, spoke anonymously on the issue:

> [W]e intellectuals have gone through three phases in our thinking. At first, most of us supported the government, recognizing its many faults, but hoping it would reform. Then we became increasingly discouraged with reform prospects, but saw no feasible alternative. Though the present government, we felt, was bad, what might take its place would be even worse. During this second phase, intellectuals were uncertain and bewildered. Then came the present, third phase. We have become so completely convinced of the hopelessness of the existing government that we feel the sooner it is removed the better. Since the Chinese Communists are obviously the only force capable of making this change, we are now willing to support them as the lesser of two evils. We ourselves prefer a middle course, but this is no longer possible.[7]

While this anti-GMD liberal could not represent the whole Chinese intelligentsia, his views certainly illustrated the unpopularity of the GMD regime among intellectuals.[8]

The student movement in Beiping was relatively calm in September and October 1948. Local newspapers did not record any large-scale student parades and demonstrations. Many students went "home" (that is, to CCP areas).[9] Nonetheless, protests occurred among the primary and secondary school teachers in Beiping and a vigorous student movement developed in Tianjin. These protests, caused by the miserable economic conditions and a severe food shortage, were the last ones in Beiping–Tianjin before the Communist conquest.

The economy of China had already become desperate in the summer of 1948. On 1 July 1948, the headline in *Beiping ribao* read: "Balance the commodity prices [by the government] until what time? Inflation continues until what day?" (*ping ping ping ping dao he shi, zhang zhang zhang zhang dao na tian?*).[10] By October the economy was hopeless. The GMD financial and economic emergency measures (announced in August) had practically collapsed. The Gold Yuan had depreciated so much that it was another worthless piece of paper. Everywhere urban residents engaged daily in a scramble to buy basic commodities. Many factories and shops were closed, and thousands of workers and shop assistants were unemployed. Because of wage depreciation government and academic employees could not maintain even the subsistence level of life. Some professors had to sell personal belongings for survival. And in late October eighty-two Beida professors issued a manifesto demanding a doubling of salary and threatening a three-day strike if it was not forthcoming.[11]

At this critical period of the collapse of the gold yuan and the economy, the CCUP raised the "Antihunger, Fight-for-Warmth-and-Fullness-of-Food Movement." The Beiping teachers launched a "general request for leave" and the CCUP instigated the last student protest in Tianjin before the Communist takeover.

On 19 October 1948, teachers in 234 public primary schools in Beiping decided to request a four-day leave in order to purchase flour. They also petitioned the GMD authorities for flour, higher wages, increased living allowances, coal, and cloth. The leave lasted until 24 October. From 1 November to 7 November, the primary school teachers were joined by teachers in seventeen secondary schools. The GMD authorities finally accepted the basic demands of the teachers. The Communists' involvement was minimal, and they admitted that the CCUP was weak among the tightly controlled primary and secondary schools.[12] However, the protests among the secondary and primary schools demonstrated the unpopularity of the GMD even within its own academic community.

In early October there was a severe food shortage at various schools in Tianjin. On 10 October fifteen universities and colleges petitioned the municipal government to: (1) maintain the regular two bags of flour for three live-on-campus students and deliver the September supply immediately; (2) distribute and sell confiscated food to the schools; (3) distribute the lower-quality flour to the schools for emergency; (4) solve the problem of no oil or salt.[13] Three days later there was another petition. From 25 October to early November, faculty members and students at Nankai and other colleges launched "hunger labor strikes" by cessation of classes.[14]

At this period the Communist labor movement finally took a role in the Antihunger, Fight-for-Warmth-and-Fullness-of-Food Movement. In October the Communist Municipal Administration Committee acted upon the call for an antihunger discussion raised by a "positive" worker at the Beiping Telecommunications Bureau. Since the GMD had declared an emergency measure that legalized killing any worker on strike, the Committee decided that the workers should fight in other ways. If the demands were rejected, the workers would engage in "hunger labor strikes," in which they claimed they were too hungry to work. These strikes would demonstrate the workers' economic plight and also would win the sympathy of the suffering populace. Simultaneously, it would not be in conflict with the emergency measure on labor strikes. On the surface it would be an economic struggle, but it was actually a political one (from the Communist standpoint). The crippling of the telecommunications in Beiping would certainly create grave political consequences in China.[15]

The Communists claimed that they operated the strike from the second line; "positive" elements dominated the open leadership. The hunger labor strike started at midnight on 27 October after the authorities failed to respond satisfactorily to the demands for financial assistance, flour, coal, and a reasonable wage. The hunger labor strike was aimed at commercial service, not the telecommunications involving military and political messages, news, weather broadcasts, and funding for disaster relief. The services that were stopped would not give the authorities any pretext for harsh suppression.[16]

In order to spread political influence, the CCUP organized press conferences and cabled information about the strike to other telecommunications bureaus.

The left-wing *Xinmin bao* from 23 October to 28 October printed daily headlines and news about the hunger labor strike.[17] Under pressure, the GMD authorities at the Beiping Telecommunications Bureau agreed to 80 percent of the financial assistance (a grant of 240, not 300, Gold Yuan) that the workers demanded. The CCUP encouraged the workers to accept this partial settlement and other compromises, and to resume work after a nineteen-hour hunger labor strike. The work stoppage ended with the popular (left-wing) song, "Unity is Power."[18]

The hunger labor strike of the Beiping Telecommunications Bureau was supposed to be a victory of the Urban Work Department of the North China Bureau, Liu Ren, and the Beiping Municipal Administration Committee. It was a combination of legal and illegal struggle, of political and economic struggle, and was based on the principle of struggle "with reason, advantage and restraint." The three-thousand-worker strike paralyzed the GMD telecommunications system in Beiping and achieved the CCP's political goal. The Party also recruited more than sixty new members.[19]

In Tianjin the Telecommunications Bureau echoed the hunger labor strike in Beiping. The workers at the Tianjin Telecommunications Bureau had on 23 October demanded that the municipal government give flour and distribute basic daily necessities to every worker; the government refused to accept the demands. The 27 October strike in Beiping precipitated a similar one in Tianjin on 29 October. The Tianjin telecommunications workers presented the same demands that the Beiping workers had raised. There were two leadership groups. If the first group were arrested, the second one would continue to direct the strike.[20]

The GMD Tianjin Garrison Command Post responded to the hunger labor strike by arresting more than thirty workers' representatives. The Garrison commander, Chen Changjie, accused the Communist Urban Work Department of instigating the strike and threatened to suppress it and to administer the bureau militarily.[21] However, the bureau authorities finally made concessions similar to those in the Beiping strike. The arrested workers were released, and work was fully resumed on 4 November.[22] As in Beiping, the Tianjin authorities did not carry out the emergency measure of killing strikers. They also failed to intimidate them.

During the October of hunger labor strikes, staffers and workers at the Customs Service, as well as the drivers and ticket operators of streetcars and public vehicles in Tianjin, struck for flour and coal.[23] The GMD attempted to quell the strikes with military threat. As in the strike of the Telecommunications Bureau, however, the authorities finally acceded to the demands of the workers.[24]

By November the GMD authorities in Beiping–Tianjin were in deep military, political, and economic trouble. Since the establishment of the North China Bandit-Suppression Headquarters in December 1947, the GMD had not been able to exterminate or even to weaken the Communists in the area. Most of the time the GMD had actually been on the defensive. By June 1948 Baoding was an isolated Nationalist city. The Communists captured a strategic town and controlled the southern and western rural areas of Tianjin. Simultaneously, the deteriorating military situation in Northeast China aggravated the Nationalist political and military burden in the Beiping–Tianjin area. In July Fu Zuoyi expressed his views to a military leader from Nanjing thus: "The Northeast and the North are closely related. Without the Northeast, the North has difficulty existing by itself. Even though now the Northeast has increased our trouble [for example, tens of thousands of refugees and soldiers flocked to Beiping–Tianjin—Au.], we have no complaint. We only hope that they can get hold of the Northeast, correct their 'unreasonable style' [for instance, to use their local currency in North China to purchase gold, U.S. dollars, and materials in Beiping–Tianjin—Au.], stabilize the situation there, and give North China no more troubles in military affairs. If there is any problem in the Northeast, the North will definitely be forced to fall."[25] Fu's predictions turned out to be accurate. The GMD lost Northeast China only three months after Fu's words, and Beiping–Tianjin (and thus North China) fell in less than three months. Fu, however, did not foresee the rapid advance of Lin Biao's army into North China, which upset the military balance in the region.

In June and July 1948, the GMD authorities in Beiping–Tianjin were troubled internally. Li Zongren was elected vice-president of the Republic of China (after a hard fight with several other GMD leaders) on 30 April 1948. He stayed in Nanjing and did not care about his powerless directorship of the Executive Headquarters in Beiping, which officially ended on 30 June 1948. On 25 June, the Police Bureau chief and the councillors quarreled about police matters on the floor of the Beiping Municipal Council. On 2 July Ma Hansan, chief of the Civil Affairs Bureau and a prominent Military Statistics official, was arrested and later executed on corruption charges. In June 1948 the Garrison commander (a general of Chiang Kai-shek's "Central" armies) in Tianjin was replaced by Chen Changjie, a longtime subordinate of Fu Zuoyi. Two months later, Chiang Kai-shek replaced the Beiping Garrison commander because the latter was in conflict with Fu Zuoyi over the control of troops. These events illustrated the incompetence and internal dissension among political and military GMD authorities in Beiping–Tianjin.

The military situation in North China in August 1948 was not yet desperate for the GMD. During this time, Fu's "personal" army won a major battle in East Hebei, the most brilliant one in the two-year campaign against the Communists.[26] However, the deterioration of the GMD military positions in Northeast China and the Central Plains sealed the fate of North China.

In October the fall of Northeast China and Shandong put Fu Zuoyi in a very difficult situation. He had to defend North China without support from the North and the South. The West was already a Communist stronghold, and on the east was the sea. In late October, Fu, by order of Chiang Kai-shek, attempted to score a miracle by capturing Shijiazhuang and Xibaipo, where the CCP CC was stationed. However, an underground Communist (Li Bingquan) working as supervisor of Investigation in *Pingming ribao* in Beiping unexpectedly heard about Fu's plans from a GMD brigadier general, a Military Statistics captain, and a military police captain. Because of the information from this CCUP member, the Communist Central Military Affairs Committee repulsed the Nationalist "surprise" assault.[27] According to the memoirs of a high-ranking Military Statistics agent, who operated in Beiping–Tianjin, in November 1947 Fu Zuoyi also attempted to capture Mao Zedong in the suburbs of Shijiazhuang. Mao had left, however. How Mao knew about the assault is unknown. Perhaps the information came from Fu's daughter (Fu Dongju) or his staff.[28]

In the wake of the disastrous Northeast Campaign in early November, Fu flew to Nanjing to gather support for his defense of North China. Chiang Kai-shek and other GMD leaders, however, were busily engaged in preparation for the coming Battle of Xuzhou-Bengbu (or Battle of Huai-Hai) and had no extra resources. Nevertheless, Chiang made three promises to Fu: (1) Fu would receive American military aid directly. (2) Fu would be in charge of all party, government, military, and economic affairs, including the authority over the Central Bank in North China. (3) A naval task force would be established to support the Tanggu area.[29] Assessing the entire situation in North China, Fu had three choices: (1) To abandon Hebei, Rehe, and Chahar, and move all the troops to the Northwest, also move troops in Suiyuan westward to join the GMD forces (under Hu Zongnan) in Ningxia and Gansu. (2) To abandon Beiping, Baoding, Rehe, and Chahar, and move all the troops to Tianjin and Tanggu, fight the Communist armed forces there, reestablish GMD bases in Hebei, Beiping–Tianjin–Baoding, Rehe, Chahar, and Suiyuan; retreat by sea to join the Battle of Xu-Beng if defeated. (3) To lead all of his own troops back to Chahar and Suiyuan and let others take charge of the "Central" armies in Beiping. Fu finally decided to keep his troops in Suiyuan and to move all other troops to the Beiping–Tianjin area to fight the Communists.[30]

While Fu Zuoyi made up his mind about the strategy to fight the Communists in North China, the CCP was also preparing for a final showdown. After seizing the last GMD stronghold in Shenyang on 2 November, Mao Zedong was confident that the CCP would win the Civil War: "The military situation in China has reached a new turning point and the balance of forces between the two sides in the war has undergone a fundamental change. The PLA, long superior in quality, has now become superior in numbers as well. This is a sign that the victory of the Chinese revolution and the realization of peace in China are at hand."[31]

In order to facilitate the PLA conquest of Beiping–Tianjin, the North China Bureau Urban Work Department decided to unify the leadership of the CCUP in the cities. In early November the secretary of the Communist Student Committee traveled to Bozhen, the location of the Urban Work Department. Liu Ren discussed the current situation and stressed that the CCUP must try to achieve a peaceful liberation of Beiping and Tianjin, because negotiations with Fu Zuoyi might succeed. Secret preliminary contact had been made between the Communists and Fu's subordinates. The CCUP, however, must also prepare for a military conquest in case negotiations failed. But even if the military solution was adopted, the task of the CCUP in Beiping was not to create armed uprisings, but to organize the masses to protect factories and schools, to preserve various documents, materials, and properties, and to guide the entering PLA units. Upon his arrival in Beiping, the secretary of the Student Committee immediately met the leading cadres of other committees; this was the first time that they were together. Horizontal connections between the committees were established, and a headquarters for the "liberation" of the city was set up. Northern Group and Southern Group were united.[32] In Tianjin, under the order of the Urban Work Department, various groups also were united into a new Tianjin Work Committee.[33]

It was obvious to the urban residents of Beiping–Tianjin that crisis loomed in North China. The utter failure of the financial emergency measures and the huge deficit in the fall and winter of 1948–49 rendered any economic recovery impossible. The accompanying military disasters also signaled forthcoming political downfall. Nonetheless, the GMD in North China still sounded optimistic about the overall situation. On 6 November 1948, the *Huabei ribao* published an editorial entitled "The Future of North China Is Absolutely Bright."[34] On 12 November, on the occasion of Dr. Sun Yatsen's birthday, Fu Zuoyi made a speech entitled "Message to the People of North China":

> . . . everyone in North China feels a serious threat . . . our military reverses in the Northeast were due to our own shortcomings . . . we have suffered military setbacks and political failures but these were all the result of our own deterioration and incompetence, which enabled the Communists to make some temporary gains. Corruption and decadence inevitably spell failures, even without Communist attacks. . . . I regard the immediate future of North China not as a *wei-chi* [*weiji*], or a crisis. It is rather a *chuan-chi* [*zhuanji*], or a turn for the better . . . we must spare no efforts in implementing the total war plan. . . . Communist spies and agents should be thoroughly rooted out. . . . Rumor-mongers and Red subversive elements should be eliminated. . . . The fighting strength of the Government forces should be further augmented and the fighting morale bolstered. . . . The Government's economic policies should be in line with the people's interests. . . . The Government should stamp out corruption and graft. . . . Despotism and hatred among cliques and individuals should be discarded. . . . The people's strength should be united. . . . I have no property to protect. Neither am I fighting to maintain my official position or my personal profit. I have no personal comfort to speak of. Everything I am doing is self-sacrifice. But I am very firm and I have never been lax in performing my duties. This firmness and resolution is based on my confidence in the revolutionary principles, my understanding of the times, and my quest for an ideal. Out of my sincerity to serve the country and the people, I am willing to sacrifice myself.[35]

Fu's speech was high-sounding (and ironic when he later defected to the CCP) and summarized negative aspects of the GMD rule, which the Communists exploited.

The GMD authorities in Beiping–Tianjin were in a crisis in November 1948. On 6 November the GMD 19th Military Police Regiment prohibited all military units from establishing offices, communications, liaison agencies, and warehouses in the rear areas in the south. This unprecedented measure was to halt the "southern march [escape] fever" among the troops and the population. Most Beiping–Tianjin residents were pessimistic about the Nationalists' ability to stop the forthcoming Communist attack. On 15 November the acting commander of the Beiping Garrison even asked the municipal police to control the behavior and activities of the nondisciplined soldiers. At midnight on 22 November, a general curfew began in North China. In Tianjin the wounded Nationalist soldiers from Northeast China openly made anti–Civil War (that is, anti-GMD) speeches and were not bothered by the local authorities. Some Communists or "fellow travelers" also dressed as wounded soldiers to spread antiwar propaganda.[36]

In late November Lin Biao's army arrived in North China and joined Nie Rongzhen's North China forces to form a pincer movement against Beiping–Tianjin. This unexpected development upset Fu Zuoyi's plan to concentrate his troops on Beiping–Tianjin. They were still scattered along the Zhangjiakou–Beiping–Tianjin–Tangshan "long-snake formation" (defensive line).

The Communists laid siege to Beiping–Tianjin in December 1948. In early December the Communists ambushed the GMD evacuation of Zhangjiakou, the strategic center of Chahar. Fu's 11th Army inside the city was destroyed. On the way to aid the 11th Army, the 35th Army (Fu's "trump card" troops) as well as the 105th, 106th, and a part of the 16th Army Corps were also exterminated by the Communists at Xinbaoan. Fu then had only one division in Beiping and some troops in Suiyuan and Tianjin. His own military command was gone, and he could not count on the obedience of the other soldiers in Beiping. Fu's grand plan to consolidate his troops in Beiping–Tianjin collapsed. The Communist capture of Zhangjiakou and Xinbaoan broke Fu Zuoyi's Zhangjiakou–Beiping–Tianjin–Tangshan line of defense and effectively blocked Fu's troops from escaping westward. He could only sit still in Beiping and wait.[37] Meanwhile, the CCP mobilized at least 2.6 million people in rural northern China (especially in Hebei) to support logistically the PLA activities.[38] The CCP also ordered the control of the Yellow River by boat around Jinan in Shandong to prevent the GMD armies from escaping to Qingdao. The GMD troops could still retreat by sea in Tanggu, however. The PLA thus decided to encircle Beiping but not to attack it yet; they concentrated on destroying the enemy in Tianjin and Tanggu first. There were about 130,000 GMD soldiers in Tianjin and its environs and fifty thousand in Tanggu. Since Tanggu was full of rivers and lowlands and the GMD headquarters were on a warship, the Communists decided to attack Tianjin first.[39]

On the Communist side, the victories at Zhangjiakou and Xinbaoan signaled the beginning of the Battle of Beiping–Tianjin. After that, the superior Communist forces moved to encircle Beiping and Tianjin and cut communication lines.

It was in this grave military situation that the Beiping CCUP carried out the most successful move of its "united-front tactic from above," resulting in the peaceful conquest of the city. In this "Beiping pattern," the Urban Work Department under the leadership of Liu Ren played a significant historical role. The CCUP also developed personal and social relations to the highest degree in Beiping.

Liu Ren ordered the Student Committee to represent the Communists in negotiating with Fu Zuoyi. Besides using Fu Dongju to persuade her father, the Communists also recruited two other women to work among Fu Zuoyi's colleagues and friends. One was Zeng Changning, who belonged to the CCUP at Nankai University. Her father, Zeng Yanji, was a school friend, a past colleague, and a sworn brother of Fu Zuoyi.[40] Another female was Liu Hangsheng, a Democratic Youth League member at Yaohua Middle School in Tianjin. Her father was Liu Houtong, Fu Zuoyi's teacher and senior political advisor and the chief staff officer of the North China Bandit-Suppression General Headquarters.[41] Both Zeng Yanyi and Liu Houtong ("an old man of peace") had influence on Fu Zuoyi's final decision to surrender to the Communists.[42]

Other figures who played a role in Fu's surrender and in transmitting information on Fu and the North China Bandit-Suppression Headquarters to the Communists included Deng Baoshan, one of the deputy commanders-in-chief of the Headquarters. He was not a Communist but was a close friend of Fu and had connections with the CCP. Wang Kejun, Fu's left-wing personal secretary and director of the Political Work Department,[43] also influenced Fu. Fu's English teacher, Yang Ziming, was assigned by the Communists to work for Fu. The CCUP also used Du Renzhi (a Communist and the chairman of the Political Science Department of North China College) to influence his younger brother Du Jingzhi (director of Military Hospital Department of the Headquarters). Other Nationalist generals and officers, such as Chi Fengcheng, were sympathetic to the Communists in the Headquarters. In short, the North China Bandit-Suppression Headquarters was infiltrated by Communists, and Fu Zuoyi was aware of the situation.[44]

Communist agents also existed among the various army corps and divisions in Beiping. The most prominent case was the 92nd Army, a crack branch of the GMD "Central" Army. Before Fu's surrender the commander of this army and another divisional commander had already cooperated with the Communists and planned to revolt when the battle started. Further, the captain of one of the three "Central" armored units in Beiping also promised to capture one city gate for the PLA. Indeed, if Fu was determined to fight, his chance of winning was slim.[45]

Among the intellectuals there were also Communists and fellow travelers who participated in the peace talks concerning Beiping. Besides Du Renzhi, Zhang Dongsun was another well-known figure. Others involved in the peace negotiations included the chief of the Investigation Section (Li Bingquan) of *Pingming ribao*, and a section chief of the Bandit-Suppression Headquarters.[46]

As the Communists and Fu Zuoyi were secretly working on a peaceful solution to take Beiping,[47] a number of prominent local GMD and social leaders were engaged in an open drive for peace. They had the secret endorsement of Fu Zuoyi. The leaders of this peace movement were He Siyuan, the former mayor of Beiping, and Xu Huidong, the speaker of the Beiping Municipal Council.[48] In the fall of 1948 they established the North China People's Peace Promotion Association, which consisted of councilors from Beiping–Tianjin, Hebei, Shanxi, Chahar, Rehe, and Suiyuan, representatives of various mass organizations, and other well-known local personalities. The association requested the Communists and the Nationalists to resume their peace talks and the Bandit-Suppression Headquarters to settle peacefully the issue of North China.[49]

While the GMD authorities in Beiping–Tianjin were involved in preparation for both peace and war, the CCUP continued the "united front from above and below" through its activities among students, labor, urban residents, and others.

By November 1948 the Communist student movement in Beiping–Tianjin had already made an important contribution to the "war of liberation." In "The Student Movement in GMD Areas—A Letter to Chairman Mao" (14 October 1948), Luo Mai (his real name was Li Weihan; from 1948 to 1964 Li was the head of the Central United-Front Work Department, which replaced the Central Urban Work Department on 26 September 1948) wrote:

> During the two years of the Civil War [1946–48], the students, in the first place the college students, in the GMD-controlled areas have been engaged in brave struggles in defending the fatherland and in the movement for winning democracy and freedom. *Politically speaking, the students have severely undermined the rule of Chiang Kai-shek and the Americans* [emphasis added], and they have supported the "war of liberation," and created a vanguard for the revolutionary popular movements in enemy areas. . . . The sustained nature of the movement, the connections to the masses, the flexibility of tactics, have all surpassed efforts of any other period in the history of the student movement.[50]

From November 1948 to January 1949, the youth in Beiping–Tianjin continued to struggle and to prepare for the arrival of the PLA. By then the GMD's loss of authority was so severe that the students' open hostility to the Nationalists was manifested on the walls and buildings outside the campus, where they scratched Chiang Kai-shek's name in chalk within the outline of a turtle—an extremely derogatory symbol for the cuckold in China.[51] In Beiping the united Communist underground headquarters was busily involved in the new student activities. Communist students were especially active at Beida, Qingda, and Yanda.

In these three major universities, CCUP members carried out the following tasks: (1) They explained the current situation, the CCP's policies, and the conditions of CCP areas. (2) They worked among teachers and students to establish confidence in "liberation." They dispersed doubts among a minority of people, and persuaded certain "wait-and-see" professors to stay. (3) They collected detailed information about school properties and assets, especially expensive equipment and library books. They protected these assets and properties and prevented the enemy from destroying or removing them. (4) They mapped the terrain and roads around the schools. (5) They conducted surveillance on GMD members and former personnel of the Three People's Principles Youth Corps. Indirectly they warned some not to make trouble. (6) They collected information about some people with "reactionary" ideas. (7) They strengthened the patrolling and protection of schools. (8) They saved enough food for three months, and ensured the safety of the water and the electrical systems. (9) They objected to the GMD plan to relocate schools in the south.[52]

At Beijing University—the so-called Liberated Area within Beiping during the Civil War period—the Communist underground carried out these primary tasks. Meanwhile, the GMD stationed troops around the school campus. In late November 1948, the GMD decided to move the major schools out of Beiping–Tianjin. The Beida CCUP immediately mobilized students to convince the professors to stay behind. On 11 November the Communists also published two articles against the southern relocation of universities in the last issue of the *Beida–Qingda Academic Journal*. The Beida Faculty Senate finally decided not to move southward.[53] About the same time, the Nanjing government sent airplanes to the city to pick up those professors and scholars who wanted to go south. The last flight was on 7 January 1949. Some professors planned to escape, but because of the surveillance of left-wing students and even their children, they could not. Beiping fell into the hands of the Communists two weeks later. The thirty-six professors and their families who boarded those two military planes to Nanjing on 7 January were the fortunate ones.[54] (Hu Shi, chancellor of Beida, was on the last flight. Mei Yiqi, chancellor of Qingda, took the last commercial plane to Shanghai on 21 December 1948. Lu Zhiwei, chancellor of Yanda, stayed behind. He Lian, chancellor of Nankai University, flew to Beiping and also took the last commercial plane on 21 December. Zhang Hanying, chancellor of Beiyang University, was in Nanjing in late 1948; he missed the "liberation" of Tianjin. Certainly, some other professors or scholars decided to stay and serve in the new China. According to Sidney Shapiro, an American lawyer who had settled in Beiping in 1948, on the eve of "liberation" groups of Chinese literati began dropping by his steam-heated three-storey house on the campus of the College of Chinese Studies in Beiping [in those days, most Chinese (teachers) could not afford to buy coal to burn in their stoves]. They came "for tea"; actually they discussed how they would coordinate with the impending Communist takeover.)[55]

The CCUP controlled the Beida printing facility. Party members printed the CCP's urban policies, notices to the masses, policies on intellectuals, and news about the CCP areas. They distributed the papers to professors and students.[56]

The underground workers protected Beida, investigated the assets and properties of the university, patrolled the campus, investigated various private and government institutions and enterprises; and through social contacts, they encouraged GMD officers to revolt. In addition, the Party sent some students to investigate the defense structure and artillery installations of the GMD armed forces. For instance, Yue Daiyun, a Democratic Youth League member, prepared maps of the sites of the Imperial Palace and the legation quarters so that the Communist artillery would not accidentally damage them.[57] In short, the eight hundred members in the Party, Democratic Youth League, and Democratic Youth Alliance controlled the situation at Beida, the largest group of the Beiping CCUP. Beida was also one of the four Communist command posts inside the city to direct student and other affairs.[58]

At Qinghua University, the so-called Liberated Area outside Beiping, the Communist underground carried out similar tasks. The only difference was that Qingda was liberated earlier, on 15 December 1948. On 13 December the PLA reached the vicinity of Qingda in the western part of Beiping municipality. Obeying the directive of the united Student Committee to contact the PLA when it approached, the CCUP members met the PLA vanguard and presented maps of the area and the streets and roads of Beiping. Two days later the PLA entered Qingda.[59]

At Yanjing University, the CCUP was engaged in the same preparation for the arrival of the Communist troops. Located near Qingda, the Yanda campus received PLA soldiers on 15 December 1948.[60] The following day Chancellor Lu informed the foreign professors that they were "liberated." On 17 December the university community assembled to listen to an address arranged by PLA political cadres. The theme of the talk was a glowing picture of the future of Yanda under new masters.[61]

In Tianjin the CCUP was also active in protecting schools and preparing for the coming of the PLA. At Nankai University, on 10 and 11 December 1948 the CCUP successfully convinced the Academic Senate and the Faculty Senate not to move the school southward. Using newspapers, discussion sessions, and visiting professors, the CCUP explained the reasons for not relocating the university in the south. The CCUP also established a security committee for the protection of Nankai. On 15 December the Student Self-Governing Association voted to suspend classes; it collected the library books and various kinds of equipment and organized inspector corps to watch over them. The GMD authorities in the meantime garrisoned the campus. The CCUP organized the "Protect-University Committee" to protest. On 22 December forty-four Nankai professors demanded the protection of cultural enterprises in Beiping–Tianjin and appealed to the authorities not to use schools as fortresses and factories as targets of artillery attack. Four days later the GMD troops evacuated the campus.[62]

At Beiyang University, the situation was similar. On 5 December a student meeting decided against moving southward. Afterward the CCUP used the Student Self-Governing Association to form the "Adapt to Circumstances Committee" to transport important materials into the city. Twenty-five professors also signed a petition for safeguarding the life and property of the 4 million people in Beiping–Tianjin and for respecting the Chinese culture (of Beijing) and protecting schools.[63] While some of these professors might be Communist allies, their plea targeted not only the GMD but also the CCP. It indicated the anxieties of those who stayed in Beiping–Tianjin.

The CCUP in the schools and other organizations in Tianjin also collected information beneficial for the military assault and for the coming takeover and administration process. In late September 1947 one CCUP member, who supervised construction of city fortifications, drafted a map of the entire city defense system and presented it to the Communist Urban Work Department.[64] More important, around October 1948 another CCUP member, who worked in the Architecture Section of the GMD Public Works Bureau, stole a general map (inadvertently left behind by the engineer who sat opposite to him) that detailed the defenses of Tianjin. Before returning it, the Party member spent two nights copying the map, which was vital to the Communist armies surrounding the city.[65] Further, the GMD commissioner of Tanggu stayed with the family of Zeng Changning for a while in Tianjin. Zeng found the commissioner's map and recorded the details of Tanggu's defenses.[66] All in all, the Communists claimed that they acquired 6,460 pieces of important information about Tianjin.[67]

The CCUP was equally energetic in protecting factories and other installations and enterprises in Beiping–Tianjin. In Beiping the Municipal Administration Committee organized workers to protect factories and enterprises from destruction by the GMD during its escape. Workers' inspection corps were formed. Party members and other sympathetic elements collected information on the industrial plants, on the activities of the GMD and the former Youth Corps, and on the GMD troops near the factories, fortresses, and bunkers.[68]

For instance, in the 70th Arsenal, the CCUP organized Protect-Factory Units to watch over various units and to prevent the moving of the arsenal to the south. Later the CCUP established worker inspector corps (about 120 members) to prepare for the PLA assault on the city. In early January 1949 the CCUP at the arsenal got the employee name list and sent letters of warning and advice to those who were not "sound" (correct) in their ideological attitudes. Probably because of these letters and the Communist-controlled inspector corps, the arsenal was not damaged during the enemy retreat, and the takeover process was quite smooth.[69]

In October 1948 the GMD authorities planned to move the personnel and the equipment of the Beiping Military Supplies and Clothing Industry to the south. The CCUP put forward the slogan "Men are not separated from machines, machines are not separated from men" and urged workers to boycott the southern move. In late December the CCUP also organized a secret 270-member worker inspector corps. Simultaneously, the Party organized the Employee and Worker Friendship Association to win support from the staff and lower- and middle-level officers. To facilitate the Communist capture of Beiping, the Municipal Administration Committee ordered the Party at the Supplies and Clothing Industry to use the workers and some of the garrison soldiers to open the Chaoyangmen (one of the main city gates) to let the PLA in. Later events made such preparation unnecessary. Furthermore, the Supplies and Clothing Industry itself was undisturbed because of the cooperation, willing or unwilling, of the officers in charge of the various units.[70]

In the Beiping Telecommunications Bureau, the CCUP carried out the same "Protect-Factory Struggle." In late 1948 the Municipal Administration Committee united the eight Party branches within the bureau. The Committee ordered Party members to use every excuse to live in the bureau and communicate with the masses. They posted Communist documents on walls and mobilized employees to join the protect-factory movement. Open slogans included "Machines are the rice bowls of workers" and "Where there are telecommunications workers, there is telecommunications equipment." In the fire brigade of the bureau, the CCUP organized a secret Worker Protect-Factory Corps. Party members warned the "negative" elements not to damage any equipment in the bureau and used money and good clothes to win over the noncooperative GMD military police at the bureau. They also collected information on the leading personnel of the bureau and the installations.[71]

The CCUP also scored successes in the Beiping–Tianjin Area Railway Bureau. The best example was the "liberation" of the Beiping Railway Station. In December 1948 the CCUP sent a Democratic Youth League member to talk with the newly appointed head of the station. The head was told that he had been chosen as the scapegoat in the forthcoming liberation of the city. The only way out for him was to organize employees to protect the installations and equipment from damage and to deliver them to the PLA as a contribution to Beiping and the people. The head of the station agreed to do so and ordered the Transportation, Freight, and Accounting sections to do the same. In addition, at Fengtai and Changxindian, the Communists' "protect-factory corps" saved the equipment from destruction by the GMD. The CCUP also organized the Employee and Worker Friendship Association to complement the work of protecting the railways. Finally, even Shi Zhiren, the director of the Railway Bureau, decided to shift to the Communist side. (Shi later became the deputy head of the Ministry of Railroads of the People's Republic of China.)[72]

Furthermore, twenty CCUP members performed well within the GMD law courts, although these were the less strategic areas of Communist operation. Particularly, Zheng Mengping, a graduate in linguistics from Yanjing University (1946) and female member of the Beiping Student Committee, played a key role in encouraging Wu Yuheng, a member of the Democratic League and the director of the Beiping Municipal Court, to assist the CCUP. Zheng's father and Wu came from the same county and were distant relatives. It was Wu who recommended Zheng Mengping to serve as an interpreter at the municipal court. Wu also arranged several secret meetings between Cui Yueli of the Student Committee and Liu Houtong (Fu Zuoyi's teacher) inside his residence on the compound of the court building. Above all, when the home of She Diqing (secretary of the

Student Committee) was discovered by the GMD secret service in the fall of 1948, Zheng Mengping requested that Wu let She stay in his residence. Wu agreed to help. Before the "liberation," at the Beiping airport Wu convinced Deng Zhexi, director of the Hebei Higher Court, to abandon his plan to escape to the south. Before the PLA entered the city, Wu and Zheng helped maintain the records and properties of the courts. The two led all the remaining personnel of the higher and municipal courts and the district attorney offices to welcome the Communist soldiers who were marching into Beiping. These elements were among the first groups of GMD government functionaries to greet the PLA openly.[73]

Communist underground work in student and labor activities in Beiping went quite smoothly except for a setback among ordinary residents. In late 1948 a Party member of the Commoner Committee, working in an oil and salt store, exposed his identity and was arrested by the GMD authorities. He betrayed other comrades, causing the arrest of another 108 members. Fortunately for the Communists, they were released soon, when Beiping was peacefully "liberated."[74]

In Tianjin the Communist Work Committee was also involved in the protection of factories and other facilities. At the Tianjin Machinery Factory, the CCUP sabotaged the manufacture of land mines and established "protect-factory corps."[75] In addition, the workers resisted the GMD attempt to dismantle the Tianjin Second Steel Mill. Workers and their families occupied the Tianjin Paper Manufacturing Plant and withstood the (weak) attack of the GMD Garrison Command Post. Also the GMD Electric Bureau agreed to guarantee a supply of continuous electricity. The director of the Telecommunications Bureau also provided continuous service and even revealed the GMD wireless frequency so that the PLA could hear the communication of the Tianjin Garrison Command Post with the Bandit-Suppression General Headquarters in Beiping, and with the Nanjing government. The CCUP protected most of the streetcars of the Tianjin Streetcar Company. The general manager of the Tianjin Municipal Enterprises Corporation guaranteed the water supply, and workers also protected the machinery. Furthermore, the Communists organized a seven-hundred-member inspector corps to protect the radio stations, railways, railway stations, and granaries. They even warned the secret society members (Green Gang and Red Gang) not to disturb schools and factories.[76]

The underground-Communist-controlled Tianjin Reporters Association established Meeting Emergency Committees to record the personnel and property of *Minguo ribao* and *Yishi bao*. The CCUP members also investigated *Dagong bao* and *Xinsheng wanbao*. These underground activities facilitated the future Communist control of the Tianjin news media.[77] The CCUP also claimed that it conducted united-front work within the Tianjin Industrial Association, Tianjin Banking Association, Tianjin United Youth Society, and, above all, the city government.[78]

An important example was its influence upon the director of the Tianjin Social Affairs Bureau. Prompted by his Communist daughter, the director defected to the CCP in December 1948. He appointed two CCUP members to serve in the bureau, preserved its records, provided maps of Tianjin factories and lists of wealthy residents to the CCUP, and assigned government Jeeps with special permits to the Communists. These vehicles could enter the compound of the Tianjin Garrison Command Post.[79] (Incidentally, Fu Zuoyi's daughter, Fu Dongju, was engaged to be married to Zhou Fucheng, who served as the special reporter of *Pingming ribao* in Tianjin. The relationship allowed Zhou to acquire GMD military information because he could attend meetings of the Tianjin Garrison Command Post.)[80]

In the united-front work among the Tianjin capitalists, the CCUP used Zhou Jiliang to contact his uncle Zhou Shutao. Through the arrangement of Zhou Jiliang's elder brother, Zhou Weizeng, who owned a trading company, a leading cadre (Wang Wenhua) of the Tianjin Work Committee met Zhou Shutao. Wang requested Zhou Shutao to "stabilize the mood" of other industrialists and bankers in Tianjin. Zhou agreed to help and succeeded in convincing another prominent industrialist, Li Zhuchen, to pacify other capitalists and to spread the Communists' urban policy of "developing production, promoting economic prosperity, giving consideration to both public and private interests, and benefiting both labor and capital."[81] In other words, Tianjin capitalists' properties would be protected and they should feel at ease staying behind in the city to serve the new China. The PLA promised to spare the key factories. (The Seventh Cotton Mill was the only major casualty during the Battle of Tianjin.) Li also tried to convince the defense commander, the mayor, and the police bureau chief of Tianjin to surrender. Although Li's efforts were abortive, they weakened the willpower of the upper-level GMD personalities because of their willingness to negotiate peace with the Communists. In addition, Yang Yizhou, the general manager of the China Textiles Corporation, also cooperated with the CCUP.[82]

In short, the Communist work in Beiping–Tianjin in late 1948 and early 1949 carried out successfully the 13 December directive of the North China Bureau concerning the "liberation" and administration of Beiping–Tianjin. This directive had ordered the CCUP "to complement the PLA assault and to take over and administer these big cities." The central task, then, was "to coordinate the organized mass power within the cities with the PLA power from without, and to use all effective means to achieve a complete takeover and administration of the cities."[83]

Tianjin was supposed to be well defended. On 23 November the Tianjin Garrison Command Post declared martial law and prohibited strikes, demonstrations, and petitions. A People's Self-Defense Corps of thirty thousand members was formed to support the military and police forces. In early December businesses ran as usual, and residents still enjoyed movies and restaurants. Perhaps this peaceful life-style was prompted by optimistic GMD news, or by an apolitical attitude as a result of longtime Japanese occupation. By mid-December, however, the situation had changed. The streets were deserted at night.[84] Sporadic fighting between the GMD and the Communist troops occurred on 20 December and from 5 January to 8 January. Occasionally, the underground Communists fired signals to help the PLA artillery locate targets.[85] Many soldiers became demoralized, and their harsh behavior toward civilians prompted the inhabitants to close their businesses and remain indoors.[86] Worse still, on 25 December 1948, the GMD authorities burned down thirteen villages in the suburbs of Tianjin under the pretext of strengthening their defense structures against the PLA. During the chaos some GMD soldiers engaged in pillaging. It was no surprise that among the 38,000 who lost their homes, some were very eager to help the oncoming Communist troops.[87]

The final assault began on 14 January after the GMD authorities refused to lay down their weapons. It took the Communists just twenty-nine hours to conquer the city. The defense commander, two army commanders, and the mayor were all captured by the PLA. The mayor's wife was a Communist agent, and he was arrested outside the door of his "secret" lodging.[88] Tanggu was conquered two days later, when the GMD troops escaped southward by sea.

The topography of Tianjin also conditioned the GMD-CCP struggle. The Communists realized the defensive advantage of the geographical features of Tianjin and Tanggu (rivers, waterways, and marshes), and devised appropriate plans to overcome them. They skipped Tanggu and concentrated on capturing Tianjin first. As the central district of Tianjin was long from south to north (12.5 kilometers) and shorter from east to west (less than 5 kilometers), the PLA focused its military assault on the west side of Tianjin, with a faked offensive from the south-north direction to divert the GMD troops from the real Communist target. (On 14 January 1949, Jiao Dengyun, a CCUP member and a worker at the GMD electric service, succeeded in cutting off the electric supply to the western defense perimeter. It was during the period of darkness that the PLA broke the GMD defense and rushed into the urban district from the west. In military terms, Jiao's action might have been the only important activity of the Communist labor movement in Tianjin during the entire Civil War period.)[89] The GMD was indeed fooled, and assigned the strongest units to defend the northern part of the city. Because of a strategy based on the geographical situation and vital information about the enemy's military condition, the PLA and the CCUP occupied strongly fortified Tianjin.[90]

In retrospect, the main reason for the GMD defeat in Tianjin was not simply the numerically stronger PLA. The defeat was caused by the Nationalists' loss of will to defend and resupply forces in the north and by the work of Communist agents. Also, because of the previous Nationalist blunders, economic mismanagement, and misbehavior, few local residents had any strong desire or reason to assist the GMD armies. The loss of Tianjin and Tanggu sealed the fate of Beiping and its more than two hundred thousand GMD troops. On the day that Tianjin fell (15 January), *Pingming ribao* suggested a "partial peace" for Beiping. (Peace for Beiping would be partial because the rest of GMD North China was still at war.) Since his newspaper proposed peace and Beiping was encircled, the surrender of Fu Zuoyi was a matter of time.

The situation in Beiping was unique. In fact, the situation in Beiping (and Tianjin) had been unusual since 1900–1901 (the Boxer movement). Despite all the wars fought in North China since that time, no battles had been fought inside these cities until the Communist attack on Tianjin in 1948–49. Perhaps this situation was due to the foreigners in these cities with their legations and leased territories. Such foreign presence ironically had saved the lives and properties of Beiping–Tianjin residents for almost half a century. Certainly, many (wealthy Chinese) residents and foreigners were very anxious or fearful of the situation. On their lips were the questions, "Are you going or staying?" "When are you leaving?" There was, however, a casual life-style in Beiping during the Communist siege (13 December 1948–23 January 1949).[91]

Beiping was a consumer city. The food supply in the winter of 1948–49 could last for a few months, but there were not enough vegetables, which came from other cities and the suburbs. Since the PLA had agreed not to attack the city aggressively, the GMD authorities allowed several city gates to be open for residents to go in and out. The PLA occupied the Shijingshan Electric Plant on 17 December 1948, and they continued to supply the city. The Communists also did not disturb the water supply. Telephone service was not cut off. By these tactics the Communists aimed at assuring the local people that they would be willing to preserve rather than destroy the city. The GMD postal service was limited to the city, but the broadcasting service continued. Schools were on winter vacation, and the municipal government organizations still operated.[92]

The Gold Yuan was unpopular, as it had already greatly depreciated. Residents mainly used silver dollars and copper coins minted in the early years of the Chinese Republic. Soft currency was no longer welcome, and hard coins won the day. Commodity prices did not fluctuate much during the siege, and even pawnshops remained open. The regular markets and temple bazaars still operated. Popular restaurants were crowded with customers. Most of the newspapers were available. There was even less crime than usual.[93] In short, the life of Beiping residents in the winter of 1948–49 was a surprise to those who expected a tense siege situation. The generally relaxed situation helped make residents easily and even happily accept Fu Zuoyi's surrender to the Communists. It was simply a change of city administration such as Beijing had experienced several times since 1912.

In January 1949 the fall of Tianjin and Tanggu accelerated the fall of Beiping. However, the confusion and antagonisms within the GMD ranks also contributed to the loss of the city. Li Zongren, the vice-president and former director of the Beiping Executive Headquarters in Nanjing, suggested peace talks with the CCP. Chiang Kai-shek temporarily stepped down from power, and Li's peace initiative seemed to gain momentum.

In Beiping the North China People's Peace Promotion Association continued to agitate for peace. Well-known scholars, artists, and social dignitaries also urged Fu Zuoyi to "care about the whole situation and to follow the will of the people" (that is, to carry out the "peaceful liberation" of the city).[94] Meanwhile, Fu Zuoyi was secretly engaged in negotiations with the Communists. Fu was the supreme commander, but he could not effectively control the "Central" GMD troops. Besides, Military Statistics and other party organs were accountable to their respective superiors. In short, the GMD authorities in Beiping were paralyzed in mounting a united and determined fight.

When Fu Zuoyi was secretly negotiating with the CCP in December 1948 and January 1949, the Nanjing government and Rear Admiral Oscar C. Badger, commander of U.S. naval forces in the western Pacific, urged him to evacuate his troops southward.[95] Fu declined because he was afraid of losing control over his "personal" armies. (Chiang Kai-shek might have put Fu's troops under "Central" control.) On 17 January 1949, gunshots erupted within Beiping. A small part of the "Central" armies was involved in this skirmish, which was suppressed by Fu's troops. It was rumored that in order to stir up trouble against their sworn enemies, the students, the "Central" armies fired the shots.[96] During the month of January, the PLA also allowed GMD generals and officers who refused to get involved in the "peaceful liberation" to leave the city by plane without attack from the Communist artillery. This was a show of goodwill to Fu Zuoyi. (A Communist air force corps, not informed about the peace negotiations between the PLA and Fu Zuoyi, fired at the GMD transport planes. While the corps personnel failed to shoot down any planes, they were reprimanded by the PLA superiors.)[97] On 21 January 1949, Fu Zuoyi sent his representatives secretly to sign an agreement with the Communists. One day later the peace agreement between Fu and the Communists was publicly announced. Beiping fell into Communist hands.[98]

The "peaceful liberation" of Beiping was brought about by various factors. Militarily, the defeat of the GMD troops in the Northeast and the North isolated Fu Zuoyi and his troops in Beiping; isolation was the basic factor in his defection. The internal decay of the GMD and the propeace public opinion also influenced the outcome of the Battle of Beiping–Tianjin. Without doubt, economic misery and the financial collapse of the GMD government further aggravated the deteriorating military-political situation. However, the constant harassment and effective infiltration of the GMD authorities by Communist and left-wing students and others demonstrated the Nationalist incompetence in mobilizing popular support and securing their bases. The GMD leaders simply lacked urban power and lost the will to defend the cities. All these factors prompted Fu to calculate the likely outcome of choosing to fight. Without the CCUP action, Beiping might not have fallen so peacefully. At the end, Fu was "a hero who understood the times" and readily "fell prey to" the CCUP's politics of personal connection. Fu was definitely a traitor to the GMD. However, his surrender significantly served the political interests of the CCP. Mao Zedong personally met Fu and his associate Deng Baoshan in Xibaipo on 22 February 1949. In a Party meeting, Mao also recommended giving Fu "a few more catties of pork" (that is, a better livelihood), since Fu had accomplished what Lin Biao could not: keeping Beiping intact and incorporating peacefully 240,000 GMD soldiers into the PLA.[99] The conclusion of the Battle of Beiping–Tianjin sealed the GMD's loss of North China. The subsequent Communist control of Northeast and North China was the prelude to the forthcoming collapse of the GMD regime in the South.

Immediate Aftermath of the Communist Takeover

Students played the vanguard role in welcoming the Communists into Tianjin and Beiping. On the afternoon of 15 January 1949, Nankai University students were the first residents to organize propaganda teams on trucks and cry out the slogans of "Long Live the PLA!" "Long Live the CCP!" and "Long Live Mao Zedong!" The student activists also posted on the walls the notices of the Communist Beiping–Tianjin Frontline Command Post, the Tianjin Defense Command Post, and the Tianjin Area Military Control Committee.[100]

The personnel of the GMD General Post Office, the Tianjin Branch Office of the Northern Hebei Electric Power Company, and the Tianjin Branch of the Central News Agency had not evacuated. These offices were taken over smoothly. The Tianjin radio station resumed service on 15 January. The Communist Tianjin Branch Office of the New China News Agency started service on 16 January, and the *Tianjin ribao* (Tianjin daily) published its first issue on the following day.[101] Above all, the CCUP members emerged to coordinate the new task of administering the city with the PLA authorities.

In the Beiping area, Qinghua University students welcomed the "liberation" on 15 December 1948. When the PLA soldiers entered Beiping on 31 January 1949, Beijing University faculty and students greeted the Communist troops at the city gate. On the same day, the Beiping City Military Control Committee took over the GMD Beiping office of the Central News Agency, *Huabei ribao*, and the Beiping radio station. The CCP never forgot the importance of controlling the mass media. Above all, on 4–5 February 1949, more than three thousand CCUP members attended a meeting on the Beida campus. Nie Rongzhen praised the achievements of the underground. Liu Ren, the director of the Urban Work Department of the North China Bureau, also appeared to greet his comrades.[102] The former underground agents and their allies would be important in administering the city.

Last but not least, Chairman Mao and the CCP Central directly controlled the takeover of Beiping–Tianjin because it was the focus of attention of the whole country. Mao declared that the Communists must not follow the example of Li Zicheng (the Ming bandit leader who occupied, pillaged, and then left Beijing in early 1644). The CCP must administer the cities well because they would signify the smooth transformation of the Party's central work from the countryside to the urban areas. The takeover of Beiping and Tianjin represented the beginning of the building of a new world.[103]

Summary

From August 1948 to January 1949, the Beiping–Tianjin GMD was totally out-maneuvered by the Communists. The military defeats in Northeast and North China demoralized the Nationalist forces in Tianjin and especially Beiping. Large-scale Communist "student tides" that might arouse severe Nationalist suppression were no longer necessary because of the forthcoming Communist military triumph. Even the GMD authorities had lost the will to carry out the law of killing strikers. Although the telecommunications (not the factory) workers finally launched a politically effective "hunger labor strike" because of the worsening economic conditions, this did not prompt the GMD to use excessive force. Instead, the GMD authorities acceded to the workers' demands. By then, the activities of students and intellectuals had so weakened the GMD that its "August Nineteenth or Twentieth Great Arrest" had only underscored the GMD's loss of power in urban North China.

In historical perspective, the abortive "August Nineteenth or Twentieth Great Arrest" and the disastrous Gold Yuan financial reform measure made this specific date—"19 or 20 August 1948"—the probable beginning of the Nationalists' irreparable and tremendous loss of popular support in Beiping–Tianjin and other cities. On the other side, the Beiping–Tianjin CCUP managed power well, and it contributed significantly to the military seizure of Tianjin and the peaceful conquest of Beiping. The Communists' dream of returning to the cities was realized. Their urban strategy was successful.

Notes

1. *SWMT*, vol. IV, pp. 271, 273–74.
2. Xiao Song, Ma Ju, and Song Bo, "Feiteng de Shatan—Jiefang zhanzheng shiqi Beijing daxue dixiadang lingdao Wen, Li, Fa xueyuan xuesheng minzhu yundong de huiyi," pp. 597–98; She Diqing and Yang Bozhen, "Diertiao zhanxian shang de xianfeng—Huiyi Beiping dixiadang xuewei lingdao de xuesheng yundong," pp. 26–27.
3. *SWZE*, vol. I, pp. 347–49.
4. See Zhonggong Zhongyang Dangxiao Lilunbu, *Zhongguo gongchandang jianshe chuanshu 1921–1991*, vol. VI, p. 79. This could be regarded as another "Twelve-Character Guideline." It seemed that Zhou Enlai did not personally create the wording. Nevertheless, he was most responsible for the guideline although it was rarely found in Mao Zedong–centered historical accounts.
5. See Zuo Jian and Qin Ge, "Jiefang zhanzheng shiqi de Tianjin xuesheng yundong," pp. 33–34; emphasis added.
6. She and Yang, "Beiping xuewei," p. 27; Zuo and Qin, "Tianjin xuesheng yundong," pp. 34–35.

7. Quoted in Derk Bodde, *Peking Diary*, pp. 23–24.

8. David Kidd, who taught at Qingda in the late 1940s, concurred with the view on the alienation of the intelligentsia from the GMD: "The Communists were popular primarily among [Beiping's] students and intellectuals, most of whom came from places other than [Beiping] . . . not that . . . they brought about the revolution. That came about because of the demoralized, underpaid, and double-crossed Nationalist Army which simply lost its will to fight." Letter to the author, 17 Aug. 1989. See also Wong Young-tsu, "The Fate of Liberalism in Revolutionary China," pp. 479–81, 485–87.

9. See also Maria Yen, *The Umbrella Garden*, p. 10.

10. See *Beiping ribao*, Beiping, 1 July 1948.

11. See *Xinmin bao*, Beiping, 25 Oct. 1948.

12. Chang Kai et al., *Zhongguo gongyunshi cidian*, p. 207; *BGD*, pp. 232–33.

13. See *Dagong bao*, Tianjin, 10 Oct. 1948.

14. See *Huashang bao*, Hong Kong, 2 Nov. 1948.

15. See Yuan Beiping Dianxianju Bufen Dixia Dangyuan, "Jiefang qian Beiping dianxin gongren de douzheng," pp. 148–49.

16. Ibid., pp. 149–52.

17. See the issues from 23 Oct. to 28 Oct.

18. Yuan Beiping Dianxianju Bufen Dixia Dangyuan, "Beiping dianxin gongren," pp. 152–53.

19. Ibid., p. 153. See also *Xinmin bao*, Beiping, 30 Oct. 1948.

20. See Chen Dianming, "Huiyi wo zai Tianjin dianxinju de dixia gongzuo," p. 16; *TXGY*, pp. 254–55.

21. See *Dagong bao*, Tianjin, 2 Nov. 1948.

22. *TXGY*, p. 255.

23. See *Huashang bao*, Hong Kong, 25 and 29 Oct. 1948; *Dagong bao*, Tianjin, 29 Oct. 1948.

24. *TXGY*, p. 254.

25. Quoted in Wang Yuting, "Huabei zhi shoufu yu xianluo," 39: 2, p. 66.

26. See ibid., 39: 1, p. 123.

27. See Zheng Weishan, *Cong Huabei dao Xibei*, pp. 187–98, 213–16; *Mianhuai Liu Ren tongzhi*, pp. 12–13.

28. See Chen Gongshu, *Ping-Jin diqu suijing kanluan*, pp. 152–53.

29. See Du Jianshi, "Cong jieshou Tianjin dao kuatai," p. 55.

30. See Wang Yuting, "Huabei," 39: 2, p. 68.

31. *MZX*, vol. IV, p. 1360.

32. See She and Yang, "Beiping xuewei," p. 27; Yuan Qinghua Daxue Dixiadang Bufen Dangyuan, "Zai dizhan chengshi kaibi 'xiao jiefangqu'" p. 419; see nn. 33, 41, 42 in ch. 4.

33. See nn. 60, 61 in ch. 4.

34. *Huabei ribao*, Beiping, 6 Nov. 1948; see also n. 2 in the introduction.

35. Quoted in *China Magazine* (New York) XIX: 1, pp. 17–21. See also *Xinmin bao*, Beiping, 13 Nov. 1948; *The Peiping Chronicle*, Beiping, 13 Nov. 1948; *Yishi bao*, Tianjin, 13 Nov. 1948.

36. Yu Heng, *Fenghuo shiwu nian*, p. 167.

37. Wang Yuting, "Huabei," 39: 2, pp. 70–71; Zheng Weishan, *Cong Huabei dao Xibei*, pp. 227–33.

38. See Zhonggong Hebei Shengwei Dangshi Yanjiushi, Zhonggong Liaoning Shengwei Dangshi Yanjiushi, Zhonggong Beijing Shiwei Dangshi Yanjiushi, Zhonggong Tianjin Shiwei Dangshi Ziliao Zhengji Weiyuanhui, and Zhonggong Niemenggu Zizhiquwei Dangshi Yanjiushi, *Yiqie weiliao qianxian*.

39. *TXGY*, p. 264; see also p. 71 in this book

40. See Zeng Changning, "Huiyi jiefang qian wozuo fuqin Zeng Yanji de gongzuo," pp. 272–81.

41. See Liu Hangsheng, "Jiefang qian wozuo fuqin Liu Houtong gongzuo de pianduan," pp. 282–83.

42. Wang Su, "Jiefang qian zuo Zeng Yanji, Liu Houtong gongzuo de pianduan huiyi," pp. 284–85. See also Zheng Weishan, *Cong Huabei dao Xibei*, pp. 246–47, 256, 258–59, 261–62.

43. In June 1948 the News Department and the Civil Affairs Department of the North China Bandit-Suppression Headquarters was combined into the Political Work Department. Fu Zuoyi refused to accept Chiang Kai-shek's candidates for the new post. (From the standpoint of Fu, Chiang's appointee inside the Bandit-Suppression Headquarters would carry out surveillance on Fu's activities.) Fu appointed Wang Kejun director. Chiang did not respond to Fu's assignment. See Wang Kejun, "Beiping heping jiefang huiyilu," p. 277. This episode demonstrated the personnel conflict between Fu Zuoyi and the Nanjing government, which was welcomed by the CCP.

44. Ibid., pp. 252–53, 266–67; Shi Ren, "Fu Zuoyi Beiping xianggong jilue," in *Shijie ribao*, Los Angeles, 29 Jan. 1992. See also p. 18 n. 32 in this book. Besides, Communists infiltrated Chiang Kai-shek's military headquarters. There was an element of truth in Mao Zedong's talk to some GMD defectors in 1950 that "we [the Communists] knew every detail about your [GMD's] governmental and military units at all levels, due to the dedication of many selfless comrades." Quoted in Eric Chou, *Mao Tse-tung*, pp. 173–74.

45. See Xue Chengye, Li Jieren, and Ji Hong, "Cedong Guomindang jiushier jun quyi de zhuiji," pp. 821–32. See also Zheng Weishan, *Cong Huabei dao Xibei*, pp. 253–54.

46. Zheng Weishan, *Cong Huabei dao Xibei*, pp. 247, 256, 259, 264.

47. See the memoirs of the participants in the peace negotiations in Zhongguo Renmin Zhengzhi Xieshang Huiyi Quanguo Weiyuanhui Wenshi Ziliao Yanjiu Weiyuanhui, *Fu Zuoyi Shengping*, pp. 263–339.

48. In mid-January the GMD secret service used three time bombs to demolish He's residence. He was hurt and his younger daughter killed. During his mayorship (October 1946–June 1948), he was sympathetic to the "Antihunger, Antipersecution, and Anti–Civil War" student movements; and he supported Li Zongren's vice-presidential race. His peace movement and frequent contact with the CCUP members further antagonized the Nanjing authorities. See Guo Liangyu, "He Siyuan gongguan beizha qianhou," pp. 66–68. See also He Siyuan, "Wo canjia heping jiefang Beiping de huodong," pp. 73–87. This assassination, which was intended to intimidate He and other "progressive" Nationalists, failed miserably; above all, it demonstrated the desperation and folly of GMD authorities.

49. See Xu Zhaolin, "Ji jiefang qian Ping-Jin diqu de fengyun renwu Xu Huidong," pp. 234–37; see also Wang Qiaoping, "Beiping jiefang qianxi 'Huabei Renmin Heping Cujinhui' daibiao chucheng tanpan de jingguo," pp. 21–33.

50. Quoted in Sha Jiansun, "Lun quanguo jiefang zhanzheng shiqi de xuesheng yundong," pp. 1–2.

51. Allyn and Adele Rickett, *Prisoners of Liberation*, p. 10.

52. Yuan Qinghua Daxue Dixiadang Bufen Dangyuan," 'Xiao jiefangqu,' " pp. 419–20.

53. Xiao, Ma, and Song, "Feiteng de Shatan," pp. 596–97. See also Beijing Daxue Lishixi "Beijing daxue xuesheng yundongshi" Bianxiezu, *Beijing daxue xuesheng yundongshi*, pp. 257–58; Zhonggong Beijing Shiwei Dangshi Ziliao Zhengji Weiyuanhui Bangongshi, "Wei jiefang wenhua gudu fendou de Beiping dixiadang," p. 678.

54. See Qian Siliang, "Nanwang de wangshi," pp. 8–10.

55. Sidney Shapiro, *An American in China*, p. 36.

56. Beijing Daxue Lishixi, *Beijing daxue xuesheng yundongshi*, p. 258.

57. Yue Daiyun and Carolyn Wakeman, *To the Storm*, p. 20. See also how the students formed self-defense platoons to stand guard every night in Yen, *Umbrella Garden*, p. 15.

58. Xiao, Ma, and Song, "Feiteng de Shatan," p. 598; Beijing Daxue Lishixi, *Beijing daxue xuesheng yundongshi*, p. 259.

59. Yuan Qinghua Daxue Dixiadang Bufen Dangyuan, " 'Xiao jiefangqu,' " pp. 420–21.

60. Zhu Meiduan, "Yanyuan jiefangshi de riji," pp. 223–24.

61. See the diary of Grace Boynton in ibid., pp. 220–21.

62. Zuo and Qin, "Tianjin xuesheng yundong," pp. 37–38; *TXGY*, pp. 261–63.

63. *TXGY*, p. 263; Zuo and Qin, "Tianjin xuesheng yundong," pp. 37–38. Communists also asked Fu Zuoyi to respect Chinese culture; see p. 65 in this book.

64. See Mai Xuankun, "Wo xiang dang xian chengfang tu," pp. 298–304.

65. Zhang Kecheng, " 'Dao' tu," pp. 305–6; Wang Wenhua, "Huiyi peihe jiefang Tianjin de dixia douzheng," pp. 214–15.

66. Zeng Changning, "Fuqin gongzuo," pp. 280–81.

67. *TXGY*, p. 263.

68. Lu Yu, "Huiyi Beiping dixiadang gongwei he shizheng gongwei lingdao de douzheng," p. 135.

69. See Zhang Jinke and Zhou Wenbin, "Ba shengchan gao tanhuan, rang diren tuantuan zhuan—Beiping qishi binggongchang dixiadang douzheng huiyi," pp. 898–901.

70. *BGD*, p. 348; Meng Zhiyuan, "Beiping junxu beifu xitong dixiadang douzheng jishi," pp. 460–61; Sanwu Lingyi Chang Changshi Bianxie Xiaozu, "Baoji huchang, yingjie jiefang," pp. 33–34.

71. Yuan Beiping Dianxinju Bufen Dixia Dangyuan, "Beiping dianxin gongren," pp. 154–56. See also Lang Guanying, "Dianxin changtong," *Beijing ribao* (Beijing daily), Beijing, 1 Jan. 1979.

72. Yuan Ping-Jin Qu Tieluju Dixiadang Bufen Dangyuan, "Zhandou zai Tieluju neibu de dixia jianbing," pp. 863–64; Zhonggong Beijing Shiwei Dangshi Ziliao Zhengji Weiyuanhui Bangongshi, "Wei jiefang wenhua gudu fendou de Beiping dixiadang," pp. 674–75. See also Jin Shixuan and Xu Wenshu, *Zhongguo tielu fazhan shi*, p. 576.

73. See Zheng Mengping, "Wei jieguan jiu Beiping fayuan zuo zhunbei," pp. 148–54.

74. Zhao Fan, Peng Siming, Xu Ping, "Ranqi laodong renmin douzheng de huoyan—Huiyi Beiping dixiadang pingwei lingdao de douzheng," p. 177.

75. Zhu Baoshan et al., "Jiefang zhanzheng shiqi dan lingdao Tianjin Jiqichang de douzheng," pp. 231–35.

76. *TXGY*, pp. 260–61; Wang Wenhua, "Tianjin dixia douzheng," pp. 207–10.

77. Duan Zhenkun et al., "Huiyi 'Jixie,' " pp. 268–71.

78. Li Zhinan, "Tianjin nanxi dixiadang de zuzhi yu huodong," pp. 198–201.

79. See Wu Menghua, "Wo ren Tianjinshi Shehui Juchang sannian," pp. 90–91.

80. See pp. xvi–xvii in this book.

81. This was actually Mao Zedong's policy; see his "On the Policy Concerning Industry and Commerce" (27 Feb. 1948) in *SWMT*, vol. IV, p. 203. In order to create the broadest united front in the urban areas, Mao only stressed the destruction of "bureaucratic capitalism." "National capitalists" would play a useful role in the "New Democratic" China. See also Zhang Wanlu, "Mao Zedong guanyu Zhongguo zichan jieji de lilun yu shijian," pp. 114–18.

82. Wang Wenhua, "Tianjin dixia douzheng," pp. 6–9; Zhonggong Tianjin Shiwei Dangshi Ziliao Zhengji Weiyuanhui Bangongshi, "Yingjie Tianjin jiefang," p. 687. See also p. 151 in this book.

83. See *BHJQ*, pp. 19–20.

84. See Hong Ze, "Tianjin baoweizhan jianwen," part 1 of four in *Shijie ribao*, Los Angeles, 19 July 1991.

85. Hong Ze, "Tianjin baoweizhan," part 2 of four in ibid., 20 July 1991.

86. *TXGY*, pp. 267–68. See also p. xvi in this book.

87. See Yang Guang, "Guomindang jundui huoshao Jinjiao shisan cun zuixing," pp. 64–66.

88. Hong Ke, "Tianjin baoweizhan," part 2 of four in *Shijie ribao*, Los Angeles, 20 July 1991.

89. See Cheng Shi, "Jinjia yao diandengfang bianqian," p. 116.

90. *TXGY*, pp. 264–67.

91. See Yu Heng, *Fenghuo shiwu nian*, p. 164; Zheng Weishan, *Cong Huabei dao Xibei*, pp. 239–40; Allyn and Adele Rickett, *Prisoners of Liberation*, p. 8.

92. See Chen Gongshu, *Ping-Jin diqu suijing kanluan*, pp. 342–43.

93. Ibid., pp. 344–45.

94. *BGD*, pp. 359–60.

95. In June 1948 Admiral Badger, Ambassador Stuart, and Roger Lapham, head of the Economic Cooperation Administration mission, conducted an assessment of Fu's armies. The "spirit, loyalty, and high morale of Fu's troops" convinced Badger, Stuart, and Lapham so much that they put in a request for U.S. arms and ammunition to supply Fu's armies in an effort to defend North China and "ultimately to open up a relief corridor to beleaguered Nationalist forces in Manchuria." The Joint Chiefs of Staff approved the request. The shipment of 1,210 tons of supplies arrived in Tianjin from Japan on 29 November; however, most of the arms on board were useless because they lacked necessary parts. Fu Zuoyi was unhappy with the defective equipment. See Richard C. Thornton, *China*, pp. 211–12. Furthermore, Chiang Kai-shek ordered Huang Renlin to transport 550 tons of good-quality American arms and ammunition to Beiping from Shanghai in mid-January 1949. The Communists seized the war supplies after Fu's surrender. See Wang Renlin, *Wang Renlin huiyilu*, pp. 172–73. The belated effort of the American government to build a defense of North China failed. Their weapons also indirectly supported the Communist war effort.

96. See Jiang Shuchen, *Fu Zuoyi zhuanlüe*, pp. 221–26; Yen, *Umbrella Garden*, pp. 14–15.

97. See Han Mingyang, "Jieshou Beiping Nanyuan Jichang," p. 11.

98. For a survey of the peace talks and the peaceful Communist takeover of Beiping, see *BHJQ*.

99. See Shi Ren, "Fu Zuoyi," in *Shijie ribao*, Los Angeles, 29 Jan. 1992.

100. See the first page of *Renmin ribao*, Pingshan, dated 21 Jan. 1949, in Zhonggong Hebei Shengwei Dangshi Yanjiushi et al., *Yiqie weiliao qianxian*, p. 174.

101. Ibid.

102. *BDL*, p. 344; *BGD*, p. 364.

103. See Bo Yibo, *Ruogan zhongda juece yu shijian de huiyi*, pp. 5–11.

Conclusion

The triumph of Chinese Communism was a thirty-year political and military struggle. Having suffered a severe debacle in the enemy-controlled urban areas in the 1920s, the Chinese Communist Party, under the leadership of Mao Zedong, Liu Shaoqi, Zhou Enlai, Zhu De, and others, gradually expanded its strength in the countryside. Although the Communists continued to concentrate on developing power in rural areas during the Sino-Japanese War, they did not neglect urban activities. The Communist operations in the Guomindang-controlled cities were crucial for the ultimate success of the CCP, because of the emergence of an urban shield for the rural Communist buildup. The CCP's strategy of the Second GMD-CCP United Front combined a "peasant revolution" with an urban anti-imperialist approach. The neutralization of the Nationalist power in GMD areas by this strategy was the precondition for the Communist rural revolution.[1] By the Civil War period, the CCP adopted and carried out the strategy of using its military strength in the countryside to help it return as ruler and administrator to the cities. And this strategy was significantly complemented by the political "Second Battlefront" within GMD-occupied territories.

The ultimate and unwavering objective of Chairman Mao and the CCP was to control the cities. China is an agricultural country but it also has four thousand years of urban experience. While there is a close interdependence of city and countryside, cities have been the focus of political conflict and conquest since the first Chinese dynasty (Qin) in the third century B.C. Chinese cities are primarily seats of power and control, and the ruling elites in traditional and contemporary China have been urban-based. The urban elites manage, defend, and nurture the rural base, which sustains them and all cities. It was thus in keeping with Chinese political tradition for the CCP to conquer the cities and become the urban-based elite controlling the rural population, although the negative perception of the foreign-dominated "treaty ports" and the Communists' isolation from the cities for twenty-two years (1927–49) had left them with an antiurban legacy.[2]

The Communists regarded the pre-1949 cities as citadels of imperialism, "bureaucratic capitalism," and "reactionary feudalism" hampering China's progress, but this did not mean that they wanted to abandon the cities. There can be no question concerning the importance they attached to returning to Beiping and Tianjin. Although Mao Zedong's antiurbanism and his populist hostility toward bureaucratic elitism were well known,[3] he had no intention of abandoning Beijing and choosing a rural site as the national capital. Ruijin, the capital of the Jiangxi Soviet, and Yan'an, the wartime capital of the CCP, were at best temporary small-town headquarters. As early as August 1944, Mao explained to Qin Bangxian (Bo Gu), the head of *Jiefang ribao* (Liberation daily), that the countryside was a temporary base; it could not be the main foundation of the whole Chinese "New Democratic" society. Without the cities there would not be the greater transformation of China.[4] While it was his strategy to encircle the cities with the CCP rural areas and finally take over, this strategy was adopted by necessity, not by choice. The strategy was developed only after a series of attempts by the Communists to control the cities. The mission of the CCP was to conquer the GMD cities from the countryside because the urban proletariat alone could not accomplish it from within.

It is true that it was the Communist peasant armies that expelled the Nationalists from the mainland, and that urban work was intended to support armed struggle. Nonetheless, the Communist urban organizations and united-front activities played an indispensable role in weakening Nationalist strength, and sabotaging the latter's supply lines, organizations, and popular support. Ideologically, of course, the Communists believed that before a mature communist society could develop in the distant future, China had to develop "productive forces" to an advanced stage, and only urban-based and urban-led modernization and industrialization could achieve such a plan. The Communist urban strategy was, thus, ultimately pivotal in conquering and modernizing China.

Certainly, both the urban and rural activities were part of a single political movement and were important to the CCP in achieving national power. According to the Mao Zedong–centered paradigm of CCP history, however, rural strategy prevailed over urban strategy. Based on the Communists'—particularly Mao Zedong's—assertions and on a review of the history, I argue that from 1939 to 1949, the CCP actually targeted the cities while sustaining and expanding its power in the countryside. The urban side of the CCP's struggle was always important, and it reasserted its dominance over the rural aspect theoretically and practically during the last phase of the Civil War.

The years 1939–49 were an important decade in Chinese communism. In 1939 Mao Zedong's "The Chinese Revolution and the CCP" signified the "final formation" of the rural strategy and simultaneously the theoretical beginning of the revival of the urban-centered ideology and activity of the CCP. This year was also the beginning of Zhou Enlai's decade-long practical urban political struggle against the GMD.

On 15 September 1940, the CCP Secretariat further stated that although the retreat to the countryside had been correct in the past, it was time for the Communists to work their way back to the cities, which constituted their most important objective. In order to accomplish this task, the Secretariat ordered the various local Party bureaus to establish Urban Work Committees.[5]

The CCP Central continued to stress the significance of urban activity. During an interview with Bo Yibo in the spring of 1943,[6] Mao Zedong claimed that in the Chinese revolution there existed two "front armies": the Soviet Areas (the CCP countryside), and the so-called White areas (the enemy-controlled cities).[7] (Note that the CCP had not controlled the entire countryside.) Mao implied that rural work and urban work were equally important.

By the spring of 1944, fascism was on the defensive in Europe, and American troops were racking up successes against the Japanese in the Pacific War. In China, the GMD, hamstrung by ineffective troops, failed to fend off the last major Japanese offensive. In this context, the CCP began to pay more attention to the capture of cities and to its urban strategy.[8] In "Our Study and the Current Situation" (12 April 1944), Mao Zedong stressed that whatever the circumstances, the CCP must pay attention to the big cities, increase lines of communication, and raise the effort in urban areas to the same level as in the base areas.[9] This line of thought was reaffirmed in the CCP CC directive on Urban Work (5 June 1944) and in "The Resolution Concerning Certain Historical Questions," adopted by the Seventh Plenum of the Sixth CCP CC on 20 April 1945.[10]

Furthermore, in "On Coalition Government" (24 April 1945), Mao emphasized the importance of China's industrialization and the modernization of its agriculture for the establishment of the "New Democratic" state. China must "build up powerful national industries and many large modern cities." There would have to be "a long process of transformation of rural into urban inhabitants."[11] In other words, urban work, not rural work, would be the central task in the New Democratic state.

In "Introducing *The Communist*" (4 October 1939), Mao Zedong also wrote about the well-known "three magic weapons" of the CCP—the united front, armed struggle, and party-building.[12] (Mao first mentioned the "three magic weapons" during the opening school ceremony at the North China University on 7 July 1939.) These three ingredients of Communist success were found in its rural strategy. The Communists had no armies in GMD cities, but they carried out an effective united-front policy to neutralize the enemy and to consolidate and expand the CCP.[13]

As a result of Mao Zedong's wartime policy of "70 percent expansion, 20 percent dealing with the GMD, and 10 percent resisting Japan,"[14] the CCP by the end of the war had occupied much of China's countryside. The GMD-CCP conflict would be decided mainly by the struggle for the cities from 1945 to 1949.

On 11 August 1945, the CCP CC issued a directive concerning the Party's task after the Japanese surrender. It directed all local Communist organizations to strengthen urban work and to learn rapidly the financial and economic methods needed to administer cities.[15] Although the Communists' initial attempt to capture as many cities as possible was thwarted by the GMD, the CCP was undaunted in its goal of conquering urban China. Indeed, in a CC directive dated 1 February 1946, Liu Shaoqi had already stressed the equal importance of the work in both the CCP-controlled and the GMD-controlled areas.[16] Demonstrating the growing importance of cities to the CCP were the capture of Harbin in April 1946, the temporary occupation of Kalgan until 11 October 1946 (reoccupied on 24 December 1948), the establishment of the CCP CC Urban Work Department on 29 April 1947 (renamed the CCP CC United-Front Work Department on 26 September 1948), and the launching of the student-based "Second Battlefront" in GMD urban areas (as distinct from the military struggle of the "First Battlefront" in rural areas).[17] Harbin and Kalgan also afforded the Communists considerable experience in urban administration.[18]

By early 1948 the political-military situation had begun to favor the return of Communists to the city. In the "Directive on Paying Attention to the Summary Report of the Urban Work Experience" (25 February 1948), the CCP CC demanded that the Party's attention should not be focused on warfare and rural work, but on urban work.[19]

In early June, 1948, the Party Central distributed a directive composed by the CCP CC Northeast Bureau to other bureaus. This directive emphasized that "every revolutionary soldier, local Party, and administrative personnel, and the people in the Liberated [CCP] Areas, should view the city as the indispensable power in achieving the final victory of the people's revolutionary war."[20]

By the fall of 1948 the CCP had launched a general offensive against the GMD. The Communist-instigated student movement had also undermined the GMD urban rule. And a significant number of towns and lesser cities had fallen to the Communists.[21]

At the urban work conference of the CCP CC Northeast Bureau in late August of 1948, Zhang Wentian, who was in charge of the urban work in the region, stressed that "the city represents a higher productive force, industry, technology, science, and culture. The city represents the most progressive working class. Therefore, the city must be and is qualified to lead the countryside. If society abandons urban industry and the urban working class, society cannot progress and socialism cannot be fulfilled."[22]

At the enlarged meeting of the CCP Politburo in September 1948, Mao Zedong for the first time spoke of shifting the center of gravity of Party work from rural areas to the cities. (During the Seventh Plenum of the Sixth CCP CC [May 1944–April 1945], Mao mentioned shifting of Party work to the Japanese-controlled cities after Japan's defeat.)[23] Confident that the CCP could wipe out the GMD in five years, Mao stressed the importance of strengthening urban administration and industry by pouring in large numbers of economic, financial, cultural, and educational personnel. And the CCP must do its utmost to overcome "the phenomena of indiscipline and anarchy, localism and guerrillaism" that resulted from the long sojourn in the countryside. In other words, the CCP must prepare itself to return to the cities as ruler and administrator, assisted by people with a higher cultural level than the workers and peasants in CCP areas.[24] Capture of the strategic GMD cities in North and Northeast China, such as Jinan (24 September 1948), Changchun (19 October 1948), Shenyang (2 November 1948), Kalgan, Xuzhou (November 1948), Bengbu (January 1949) and, above all, Tianjin (15 January 1949) and Beiping (31 January 1949), accelerated the Communist agenda and prompted the official shift of the center of Party work to the city. In other words, by then the Communist focus on rural revolution had faded. In February 1949 a CCP CC Military Commission document indicated the change of the twenty-year pattern of "first the rural areas, then the cities" to that of "first the cities, then the rural areas."[25] One month later, the CCP announced its urban-centered policy and moved its headquarters to Beiping.[26]

While the significance of CCP rural activity is undisputed throughout the entire Civil War period, by 1949 the Communists had shifted their emphasis to urban areas. CCP rhetoric and action, and the fact that the war reached an *urban conclusion* back the validity of this emphasis. The Communist movement in China was a revolution that began in the cities, spread to the countryside, and returned to the cities. The CCP-led "peasant revolution" played the role of defeating the GMD militarily and carrying the Communists back to their main arenas of politics and revolution—the urban areas. Cities and the urban strategy for seizing political power were, therefore, central to Chinese Communist and Marxist-Leninist ideologies. And it was during the Civil War period that the CCP gradually reasserted its dominant urban effort in the revolution.

This study argues that the urban areas in China—represented by Beiping and Tianjin—played crucial roles in helping to bring the CCP to national power. This interpretation complements more conventional views that locate the origins of the Chinese Communist takeover of power in the rural areas. To accomplish their urban objectives, Communists operated among the students, intellectuals, GMD personnel and soldiers, workers, women, "positive" and "progressive" figures, "patriotic elements," and "democratic personalities" (including the left-wing members of the Democratic League and other "democratic parties"); and they exploited the GMD's enormous corruption, incompetence, economic mismanagement, and internal factionalism. Ultimately, the CCP managed to fill the political vacuum in the cities, even though the number of Communist underground cadres and supporters (especially students) was exceptionally small.

The Communist urban strategy in Beiping–Tianjin in the Civil War period was mainly an underground struggle. In these cities, the CCP developed underground Party organizations during the period of the Sino-Japanese War. The end of the war helped Communists from the southwest and elsewhere to return to these urban areas and temporarily allowed the Party to work openly and legally in light of the GMD takeover of Beiping–Tianjin. However, the outbreak of full-scale Civil War in mid-1946 made underground political work, along with open and legal forms of struggle, an absolute necessity.

During the Civil War period, the CCP was strategically stronger than the GMD in North China. Nevertheless, the CCP Central did not permit the underground Party in Beiping–Tianjin to engage the enemy aggressively. The struggle in the cities was *political*, and the occupation of Beiping and Tianjin had to be accomplished ultimately by armed struggle. Accordingly, the CCUP's struggle in GMD cities did not go beyond class and labor strikes, parades, and demonstrations. A CCP CC directive issued in the wake of the Antihunger Anti–Civil War Movement of Beiping (the May Twentieth Movement) stressed that the general guideline for the student movement (that is, the whole urban work) was to do mass work, to conserve power, to consolidate the bases, and to wait for the final battle. Errors of "blind adventurism" would result if the CCUP's work in Beiping–Tianjin were to go beyond the upper limit.[27] Zhou Enlai and Liu Ren in the fall of 1948 also warned against armed struggles inside the GMD-controlled urban areas. Following this line, the Beiping–Tianjin CCUP did not repeat previous "leftist" errors in the cities. It achieved significant political scores in complementing the military struggle, and its losses in Beiping–Tianjin were relatively small.

During the Civil War period, the Beiping–Tianjin CCUP followed Zhou Enlai's instruction and tried hard to operate as "a truly and totally underground Party, maintaining ties with the masses." The GMD had difficulty dealing with the CCP's policies of "changing work site but not party affiliation" and "many heads, single lines." The different native-place and socioeconomic backgrounds of Party members and other activists also made it very difficult for the GMD authorities to combat these concealed enemies inside the cities. While the GMD captured important underground Communists such as Yuan Yongxi and Chen Lian and temporarily drove many of them out the cities in the fall of 1948, the Nationalists never decimated the entire Beiping–Tianjin CCUP. The Communists were much more effective in fighting the underground war.

In order to complement urban work with rural work, the Communist underground Party headquarters were located in the CCP countryside, not inside the cities. In Beiping the five Work Committees were under the direct control of the Urban Work Department of the CCP Shanxi–Chahar–Hebei Central Bureau (later North China Bureau). In Tianjin the Work Committee was initially under the authority of the Central Hebei Area Party Committee. These organizational measures guaranteed that efforts in the cities would complement the armed struggles in the countryside.

The Beiping–Tianjin CCUP built and consolidated its power by recruiting new converts and mobilizing students and other social forces. While the CCUP could not control all students, faculty, workers, and others, it influenced many of them to move in the desired direction. Therefore, the small, elitist, and conspiratorial CCUP "in the heart of the enemy" was effective in weakening the power of the GMD and undermining its political legitimacy.

Liu Shaoqi, Zhou Enlai, and other Party leaders contributed to the theory and practice of the urban political struggle. Liu was important during the 1930s; Zhou was the key leader in the Civil War period; and Liu Ren was the leading cadre in the Beiping–Tianjin urban struggle during the Civil War period. The career of Liu Ren in North China also demonstrated the importance of local revolutionary cadres in Communist urban activity. Nonetheless, the development of the CCUP in Beiping–Tianjin was generally based on Mao Zedong's guiding principle: "well-selected cadres working underground for a long time must accumulate strength and bide their time in the cities." Under this guiding principle, the CCUP separated carefully the concealed Party organizations from the open ones. In all movements the Communists tried hard to carry out struggles with "reason, advantage, and restraint." In particular, they could claim much success in launching the political struggle in their student movement. Indeed, the CCUP's student cadres and their allies were so successful in harassing the GMD government that it regarded school campuses as "the second leased territory" (*dier zujie*)—that is, the GMD could not rule effectively on campus. This phenomenon demonstrated the GMD incompetence in controlling the students. Chiang Kai-shek once remarked that the crux of the Nationalists' defeat on mainland China was their failure in school education.[28]

Communist and left-wing students, of course, lacked the power to actually topple the GMD regime on their own, and the "liberation" of Beiping–Tianjin was brought about basically by military factors. Nevertheless, the hostile academic community became a political threat to the GMD authorities in Beiping–Tianjin because it succeeded in condemning the Nationalists in terms of corruption, inefficiency, economic mismanagement, civil war, the Shen Chong Incident, brutality, hunger, anti-American nationalism, and anti-Japanese militarism. Student propaganda discredited the GMD authorities, and student pressures prompted the demoralization of GMD leaders and forces. On the other side, the Nationalists' use of the police and military forces to deal with the "student tides" was ineffective and unpopular, and it unveiled the nondemocratic nature of the government, as well as its weaknesses and failures.

The Communist labor movement was much less impressive. The "hunger labor strike" of the telecommunications workers of Beiping (and Tianjin to a lesser degree) dealt a blow to the GMD politically, but telecommunications workers were not the industrial proletariat. Even though militancy was an important activity of Tianjin workers in the 1940s, class protest played virtually no role in the political life of the city. In fact, during the Civil War period the Maoist class analysis ("big bourgeoisie, middle bourgeoisie, petite bourgeoisie, semiproletariat, and proletariat") and class struggle were generally unimportant and submerged under the urban struggle, which was based on the broadest united front. Almost every Chinese could be a friend of the CCP. Mao Zedong appealed to the "national bourgeoisie" by including them in the "people's democratic dictatorship" and by promising that the CCP would not "abolish capitalism in general." Hence, the Party did not emphasize the seizure of property from capitalist and middle classes in the cities and making it available to the nonpropertied classes. In other words, the Communist success in the urban areas was not dependent on a promise to transfer wealth from one class to another. Above all, the students, not the (industrial) workers, were the core of the Communist political front in the cities. There were no armed insurrections by workers.

In the pre-1949 years, the central task of the CCP in the labor movement was not to launch violent insurrections, but to use the workers and the labor unions to facilitate the Communist activity in GMD cities. How would the workers help recover the cities during the Civil War? "The Resolution on the Current Task of the Chinese Labor Movement," adopted by the Sixth All-China Labor Congress (August 1948), provided the answer. Workers in GMD cities were urged to ally with "progressive" factory owners and persuade them to stay in their businesses. In the case of factory owners who had cooperated with the Nationalists, the Communists organized workers to struggle against them. Workers should prevent factory owners and the GMD from destroying machinery when they fled. Workers should, within reasonable boundaries, disrupt the Nationalist military transportation and the manufacture of firearms. In short, the workers in GMD urban areas should communicate well with the masses, expand their power, and facilitate the takeover of cities by the PLA.[29] Indeed, the CCP was generally "intent on liberating the cities from without and on promoting a united front based on labor–capital harmony and muted labor militancy."[30] The CCP restricted its struggle to the GMD-linked "bureaucratic capital" and projected a "passive and supportive role for urban labor, that of maintaining production and protecting industrial properties."[31] Proletarian class struggle was just the rhetorical self-justifying ideology of the CCP, and it played a minimal role in the overall Communist urban strategy, although economic mismanagement and financial collapse were major reasons for the Nationalist downfall in urban China. The Chinese Communist urban political revolution in Beiping–Tianjin was only partially Marxist-Leninist.

Indeed, as Samuel P. Huntington observes, the true revolutionary class in the cities is not the lumpen proletariat or the industrial workers but the middle-class intelligentsia: "The city is the center of opposition within the country; the middle class is the focus of opposition within the city; the intelligentsia is the most active oppositional group within the middle class; and the students are the most coherent and effective revolutionaries within the intelligentsia."[32]

The Communists scored successes in the "united front from below and above." Their Work Committees in Beiping–Tianjin operated among students, workers, middle and primary school teachers, ordinary residents, and "positive" and "progressive" elements. They did not neglect the small but important group of top GMD military and political leaders or the intellectuals. For instance, influence on General Fu Zuoyi was exerted by his daughter, his teacher, his sworn brother, his friend, and his colleague. Communist work among the distinguished Beiping–Tianjin professors was another notable example.

The fall of Beiping was brought about through a combination of GMD military weakness, the Communist siege of the city, and the threat of a forthcoming massive military assault from outside. But one should not underestimate the achievement of the CCP's open and underground work in weakening the GMD and paving the way for the conquest. Although Tianjin was taken by force, the CCP's open work among the population and its secret internal and external organizations inside the city coordinated the military attack from without. While the Battle of Beiping–Tianjin was completed by the PLA and supported logistically by the people in the CCP countryside, the work of the Student Committee and other CCUP members significantly contributed to the emergence of the "Beiping pattern"—the key political method in concluding the so-called war of liberation and arguably the most important example of the "Third Battlefront." Indeed, the Nationalist "uprisings" were a significant part of the "Second Battlefront."

The Communists' military and political strength contributed to their ultimate triumph. But without the blunders committed by the GMD, the outcome of the revolution might have been entirely different. Because of internal disunity and power struggles, the Nationalists failed to deal with social protest, especially the "student tides" and the CCUP.

Indeed, the Nationalists were unable to develop policies that would maintain the confidence and support of the social elements, especially the students and intellectuals, in urban areas; they were intransigent and inclined to rely on force. The GMD's loss of authority and prestige ensued. All the CCP wanted to accomplish before 1949 was to enhance power. So actually it did not matter whether the Communist student and labor movements were for political or economic purposes; the two were inextricably interconnected. All these movements aimed at furthering the GMD's loss of authority and for that the CCP sided with anyone, championed any cause, and did any deed. After the defeat in war that destroyed the deterrent effect of the Nationalist forces in Beiping–Tianjin, the GMD leaders lost their will to fight. A dual sovereignty (GMD and CCP) emerged within Beiping–Tianjin just before the Communist takeover. The CCUP and its allies preserved records and protected properties, schools, factories, shops, and public utilities. It would play a key role in the forthcoming "liberation" and administration of cities.

Furthermore, more disastrous than war weariness and military mistakes was the Nationalist financial and economic mismanagement that jeopardized the livelihood of millions of urban Chinese. While one may argue that the CCP changed from a strategy of military conquest to peaceful takeover because of the rapid deterioration in the economy in late 1948, economic mismanagement alone could not topple the GMD regime. While the opportunities available to any anti-GMD elements increased as the urban economy deteriorated, the CCUP was the major organization that exploited the economic issues to its political advantage. Besides missing the chance of gaining urban support by improving the economy, the GMD also failed to treat the students and teachers well and failed to use the punishment of collaborators as a support-building program. The GMD takeover officials' misbehavior and corruption also seriously damaged the party. The many Nationalist mistakes alienated the urban population. With most of the countryside already in Communist hands, the loss of public confidence in urban China spelled the end of GMD rule.

This study testifies that the student/intellectual–based Chinese Communist Underground Party, armed with the effective organizational approach and united-front tactic, successfully executed its urban strategy in Beiping–Tianjin. However, the political, military, and economic blunders committed by the exhausted GMD after the war with Japan created the required conditions that made possible the Communist success and the GMD collapse.

Last but not least, besides the factors of moderate revolution, state breakdown, discontent, civil war, anti-American and anti-Japanese nationalism, and mass mobilization, *intelligence war* should be remembered as an important element in the CCP urban victory. The Communist secret radio stations and the information collected by the CCUP (student and youth) members through various channels (especially within the GMD hierarchy) were vital to the "war of liberation."

All in all, in the period 1919–49 as a whole, the cities seemed to play a role subordinate to that of the rural areas. But by the Civil War period (1945–49), the cities (the "Second Battlefront") had gradually replaced the countryside (the "First Battlefront") as the arena of political and military struggle. By mid-1946 the GMD was no longer able to monopolize Soviet-American support. By mid-1947 the CCP had succeeded in getting rid of the American presence in China, and the GMD-CCP conflict had focused on the fight for the urban areas. Although Communist urban activity was not the decisive factor, the CCUP's urban political activity in Beiping–Tianjin did play a crucial role in "making urban revolution" amid GMD blunders. In terms of the *urban conclusion* of the revolution in 1949, the armed struggles of the peasant soldiers were only a means to an end. Cities and the urban strategy for seizing political-military power were ultimately pivotal in the Chinese Communist movement.

Notes

1. This is the thesis of Tetsuya Kataoka's *Resistance and Revolution in China*.
2. For a discussion of China's urban and antiurban past, see Rhoads Murphey, *The Fading of the Maoist Vision*, ch. 2.

3. See Maurice Meisner, *Marxism, Maoism and Utopianism*, pp. 98–117.

4. See Mao's letter to Qin in *Mao Zedong shuxin xuanji*, p. 239; Shum Kui-Kwong, *The Chinese Communists' Road to Power*, p. 230.

5. See n. 42 in ch. 1.

6. At the time Bo was a committee member of the CCP CC Taihang Branch Bureau (September 1942–October 1943) in northern China.

7. *BDS*, p. 2; Chen Shaochou, *Liu Shaoqi zai baiqu*, p. 2.

8. Zhou Ruijing, "Shilun 1944 nian 4 yue zhi 1949 nian 3 yue Zhonggong gongzuo zhongxin de zhubu zhuanyi," pp. 38–39.

9. *SWMT*, vol. III, p. 171.

10. See *ZZWX*, vol. XII, pp. 494–95; *MZX*, vol. III, p. 977. See also Shum, *Chinese Communists' Road to Power*, p. 230.

11. *SWMT*, vol. III, pp. 250, 254.

12. See *MZJ*, vol. VII, pp. 68–70, 72, 78; see also vol. X, p. 305.

13. Ibid., vol. VII, p. 78.

14. See Ke Siming, "Lun kangzhan shiqi Zhonggong de 'Qieryi fanzhen,' " pp. 164–79.

15. *ZZWX*, vol. XIII, p. 124.

16. See ibid., p. 321.

17. On the student-led "Second Battlefront," see Shi Weiqun's *Zhongguo xuesheng yundongshi 1945–1949*.

18. See Suzanne Pepper, *Civil War in China*, ch. 8.

19. See *ZZWX*, vol. XIV, pp. 52–53.

20. See "The Party Central's Approved and Transferred Directive of the Northeast Bureau Concerning the Protection of the Recovered Cities" (10 June 1948), quoted in Wang Binglin and Wu Xuguang, "Lun cong nongcun dao chengshi de weida zhanlüe zhuanbian," p. 18.

21. By mid-1948 the CCP already controlled 586 cities, which included municipal units down to the size of county towns; see Pepper, *Civil War in China*, p. 332.

22. Zhang Wentian, *Zhang Wentian xuanji*, p. 389.

23. See *MZX*, vol. III, p. 977.

24. See n. 1 in ch. 7.

25. *SWMT*, vol. IV, p. 337.

26. See pp. xvii–xviii in this book.

27. See Fang Ting, "Jiefang zhanzheng shiqi Beiping dixiadang de douzheng," p. 307.

28. See Wu Han, "Zhonggong de xueyun gongzuo," pp. 12, 17.

29. Zhonghua Quanguo Zonggonghui Zhongguo Gongren Yundongshi Yanjiushi, *Zhongguo gonghui lici daibiao dahui wenxian*, vol. I, pp. 460–62.

30. S. Bernard Thomas, *Labor and the Chinese Revolution*, p. 261.

31. Ibid., p. 264.

32. Samuel P. Huntington, *Political Order in Changing Societies*, p. 290.

Bibliography

See page xi for a list of abbreviations used in the Bibliography.

Armstrong, J. D. *Revolutionary Diplomacy: Chinese Foreign Policy and the United Front Doctrine*. Berkeley and Los Angeles: University of California Press, 1977.

Bai Ding. "Guomindang bengkui qian de yici jingji dalueduo—Ji Beipingshi zhixing Chiang Kai-shek 'Caizheng jingji chufenling' " (One great economic pillage before the collapse of the Guomindang—Reminiscing the execution of Chiang Kai-shek's "Financial and economic executive order" in Beiping), *WZXB* 7 (1983): 241–51.

Band, Claire, and William Band. *Two Years with the Chinese Communists*. New Haven: Yale University Press, 1948.

Bao Jiaoming and He Ciqian. *Tianjin*. Shanghai: Xinzhishi chubanshe, 1958.

Bao Zunpeng. *Zhongguo gongchandang qingnian yundong shilun* (A historical discussion of the CCP's youth movement). Nanjing: Bati shuju, 1947.

———. *Zhongguo qingnian yundong shi* (A history of the Chinese youth movement). Taibei: Zhengzhong shuju, 1974.

Barnett, A. Doak. *China on the Eve of Communist Takeover*. New York: Praeger, 1963.

Beijing Daxue Lishixi "Beijing daxue xuesheng yundongshi" Bianxiezu, comp. *Beijing daxue xuesheng yundongshi* (A history of the Beijing University student movement). Beijing: Beijing chubanshe, 1979.

Beijing fengwuzhi (A record of the scenes and things in Beijing). Beijing: Beijing luyou chubanshe, 1984.

Beijing Gongdianju Dangshijuzhi Bangongshi. "Jiefang qianxi Beiping dianli fengongshi de huchang douzheng" (The protect-factory struggle of the Beiping Electric Branch Company prior to the liberation), *Beijing dangshi yanjiu* (Research on Beijing party history) 6 (1989): 39–41.

Beijing ribao (Beijing daily). Beijing, 1950–.

Beijing Shifan Daxue Lishixi Sannianji, Yanjiuban, comp. *Mentougou meikuang shigao* (A draft history of the Mentougou Coal Mine). Beijing: Renmin chubanshe, 1958.

Beijing zilaishui gongsi dang'an shiliao (Archival and historical materials on the Beijing Automatic Water Company). Beijing: Yanshan chubanshe, 1986.

Beijingshi Dang'anguan, comp. *Beiping heping jiefang qianhou* (Prior to and after the peaceful liberation of Beiping). Beijing: Beijing chubanshe, 1988.

———. *Jiefang zhanzheng shiqi Beiping xuesheng yundong* (The Beiping student movement during the period of the war of liberation). Beijing: Guangming ribao chubanshe, 1991.

Beijingshi Dang'anguan and Zhongguo Renmin Daxue Danganxi Wenxian Bianzuanxue Jiaoyanshi, comps. *Beijing dianche gongsi dang'an shiliao (1921–1949)* (Archival and historical materials on the Beijing Streetcars Company [1921–1949]). Beijing: Yanshan chubanshe, 1988.

Beijingshi Shehui Kexue Yanjiuzuo and "Beijing Lishi Jinian" Bianxiezu, comps. *Beijing lishi jinian* (A chronology of Beijing history). Beijing: Beijing chubanshe, 1984.

Beiping Municipal Public Works Bureau. Map of Beiping, November 1946; available at the Map Room, Library of Congress.

Beiping qingnian (Beiping youth). Beiping, 1945–?

Beiping ribao (Beiping daily). Beiping, 1945–49.

Beiping shibao (Beiping current news). Beiping, 1945–49.

Beiping xinbao (Beiping news). Beiping, 1945–49.

Beiyang Daxue–Tianjin Daxue Xiaoshi Bianxiezu. *Beiyang daxue–Tianjin daxue xiaoshi, (diyijuan), 1895.10–1949.1* (School history of Beiyang University–Tianjin University [vol. I], October 1895–January 1949). Tianjin: Tianjin daxue chubanshe, 1990.

Belden, Jack. *China Shakes the World.* New York: Monthly Review Press, 1970.

Bergere, Marie-Claire. *The Golden Age of the Chinese Bourgeoisie 1911–1937.* Trans. Janet Lloyd. Cambridge: Cambridge University Press, 1989.

Blofeld, John. *City of Lingering Splendour: A Frank Account of Old Peking's Exotic Pleasures.* Boston: Shambhala, 1989.

Bo Yibo. *Ruogan zhongda juece yu shijian de huiyi* (Reminiscing certain major decisions and events). Vol. I. Beijing: Zhonggong zhongyang dangxiao chubanshe, 1991.

Bodde, Derk. *Peking Diary: A Year of Revolution.* New York: Henry Schuman, 1950.

Botjer, George F. *A Short History of Nationalist China, 1919–1949.* New York: G. P. Putnam's, 1979.

Boynton, Grace. "Diary," in Yanda Wenshi Ziliao Bianweihui, *Yanda wenshi ziliao* (q.v.), vol. III, pp. 220–21.

Buck, David D. *Urban Change in China: Politics and Development in Tsinan, Shantung.* Madison: University of Wisconsin Press, 1978.

Cai Huilin and Sun Weihou, eds. *Guangrong de jueze* (The glorious choice). 2 vols. Beijing: Zhongguo renmin jiefangjun guofang daxue chubanshe, 1987.

Chang, Gordon H. *Friends and Enemies: The United States, China, and the Soviet Union, 1948–1972.* Stanford: Stanford University Press, 1990.

Chang Kai et al., eds. *Zhongguo gongyunshi cidian* (A dictionary of the Chinese labor movement). Beijing: Laodong renmin chubanshe, 1990.

Chang Kia-ngau. *The Inflationary Spiral: The Experience of China, 1939–1950.* Cambridge, Mass.: The Technology Press of M.I.T., 1958.

Chang, Sidney H., and Ramon H. Myers, eds. and comps. *The Storm Clouds Clear over China: The Memoirs of Ch'en Li-fu, 1900–1993.* Stanford: Hoover Institution Press, 1994.

Changxindian Jiche Cheliang Gongchang Changshi, comp. *Beifang de hongxing— Changxindian jiche cheliang gongchang liushi nian* (The northern red star—Sixty years of the Changxindian Railcars Factory). Beijing: Zuojia chubanshe, 1960.

Chassin, Lionel M. *The Communist Conquest of China: A History of the Civil War, 1945–1949.* Trans. Timothy Osato and Louis Gelas. Cambridge, Mass.: Harvard University Press, 1965.

Chen Changjie. "Tianjin kangu renmin jiefang zhanzheng de huiyi" (Reminiscing Tianjin's resistance of the people's war of liberation), *TLZ*, pp. 236–50.

Chen Deren. "Riwei tongzhi shiqi Tianjin jishi" (A chronology of events in Tianjin during the period of the Japanese and the puppet rule), *Tianjin shizhi* (A historical account of Tianjin) 3 (1987): 32, 46–56.

———. "Tianjin zhanyi qianhou de Zhongfang Qichang" (The 7th Cotton Mill of the China Textiles prior to and after the Tianjin Campaign), *Tianjin shizhi* 4 (1987): 46, 59–60.

Chen Dianming. "Huiyi wo zai Tianjin dianxinju de dixia gongzuo" (Reminiscing my underground work in the Tianjin Telecommunications Bureau), *TWZX* 26 (1984): 13–18.

Chen Gongshu. *Ping-Jin diqu suijing kanluan* (The pacification and suppression of rebellion in the Beiping-Tianjin area). Taibei: Zhuanji wenxue chubanshe, 1988.

Chen Lei. *Xiang paokou yao fan chi* (Begging food from the mouth of cannons). Shanghai: Zhongguo xuesheng lianhehui, 1947.

Chen Shaochou. *Liu Shaoqi zai baiqu* (Liu Shaoqi in White areas). Beijing: Zhonggong dangshi chubanshe, 1992.

Chen Shaochou, Teng Wenzao, and Lin Jianbo, eds. *Baiqu douzheng jishi* (A factual account of the struggle in White areas). Beijing: Beijing shifan xueyuan chubanshe, 1990.

Chen Ta. "Basic Problems of the Chinese Working Classes," *American Journal of Sociology* 53 (1947): 184–91.

Chen Xiuping. *Chenfulu—Zhongguo qingyun yu jiduxiao nannu qingnian hui* (A record of swimming with the tide—The Chinese youth movement and the YMCA/YWCA). Shanghai: Tongji daxue chubanshe, 1989.

Chen Yun. *Chen Yun wenxuan (1926–1949)* (Selected works of Chen Yun [1926–1949]). Beijing: Renmin chubanshe, 1984.

Chen Yung-fa. *Making Revolution: The Communist Revolution in Eastern and Central China, 1937–1945.* Berkeley and Los Angeles: University of California Press, 1986.

Chen Zhili, ed. *Zhongguo gongchandang jianshe shi* (A history of CCP building). Shanghai: Renmin chubanshe, 1991.

Cheng Bi et al. "Nanwang de saiwai zhixing—Yijiu siliu nian chun Beiping daxuesheng canguan Zhangjiakou jiefangqu huiyi" (The unforgettable travel outside the border—Beiping university students' visit of the Zhangjiakou Liberated Area in the spring of 1946), *BDDS*, pp. 435–43.

Cheng Guangyu. *Zhongguo dushi* (Chinese cities). 2 vols. Taibei: Zhonghua wenhua chuban shiye weiyuanhui, 1955.

Cheng Shi. "Jinjia yao diandengfang bianqian" (The transformations of the electric room of the Jinjia coal pit), in Zhongguo Renmin Zhengzhi Xieshang Huiyi Tianjinshi Hebeiqu Weiyuanhui Wenshi Gongzuo Weiyuanhui, comp. *Tianjin hebei wenshi* (Culture and history in the north of the river in Tianjin) 1 (1987): 112–17.

Ch'i Hsi-sheng. *Nationalist China at War: Military Defeats and Political Collapse, 1937–45.* Ann Arbor: University of Michigan Press, 1982.

China Handbook Editorial Board. *China Handbook, 1950.* New York: Rockport, 1950.

China Magazine. New York, 1948.

Chiu Hungdah with Leng Shao-chuan, eds. *China: Seventy Years After the 1911 Hsin-hai Revolution.* Charlottesville: University Press of Virginia, 1984.

Chiu, S. M., ed. *Chinese Communist Revolutionary Strategy, 1945–1949.* Princeton: Center for International Studies, 1961.

Chongpo liming qian de heian (Pass through the darkness before daybreak). Beijing: Beijing chubanshe, 1961.

Chou, Eric. *Mao Tse-tung: The Man and the Myth.* London: Cassell, 1982.

Coble, Parks M., Jr. *Facing Japan: Chinese Politics and Japanese Imperialism, 1931–1937.* Cambridge, Mass.: Harvard University Press, 1991.

———. *The Shanghai Capitalists and the Nationalist Government, 1927–1937.* Cambridge, Mass.: Harvard University Press, 1980.

Dagong bao (The impartial). Tianjin, 1945–49.

Dai Xugong and Tan Kesheng, eds. *Zhongguo xiandaishi yanjiu gailan* (An overview of the research on modern Chinese history). Wuchang: Huazhong shifan daxue chubanshe, 1990.

"Dangdai Zhongguo" Congshu Bianji Weiyuanhui. *Dangdai zhongguo de Beijing* (China today: Beijing). Vol. I. Beijing: Zhongguo shehui kexue chubanshe, 1989.

———. *Dangdai zhongguo de Tianjin* (China today: Tianjin). Vol. I. Beijing: Zhongguo shehui kexue chubanshe, 1989.

DeConde, Alexander, ed. *Student Activism: Town and Gown in Historical Perspective.* New York: Scribner's, 1971.

Ding Li. "Yijiu siqi nian shuqi Beiping de zhuxue yundong" (The Assist-Student Movement in Beiping during the summer of 1947), *BDZW*, pp. 331–40.

Ding Sanqing. *Zhongguo qingnian qishilu—Guanyu zhuiqiu minzhu de fansi yu xinshi* (An account of the enlightenment of Chinese youth—Concerning the reflection and the new knowledge of the pursuit of democracy). Fuzhou: Fujian renmin chubanshe, 1989.

Dirlik, Arif. *The Origins of Chinese Communism.* New York: Oxford University Press, 1989.

Disanci guonei geming zhanzheng gaikuang (The general situation of the Third Revolutionary Civil War). Rev. ed. Beijing: Renmin chubanshe, 1983.

Dittmer, Lowell. *Sino-Soviet Normalization and Its International Implications, 1945–1990.* Seattle: University of Washington Press, 1992.

Dong Kunjing et al., eds. *Tianjin tonglan* (An overview of Tianjin). Beijing: Renmin ribao chubanshe, 1988.

Dong Shigui and Zhang Yanzhi. *Beiping hetan jishi* (A factual account of the Beiping peace talk). Beijing: Wenhua yishu chubanshe, 1991.

Dou Aizhi. *Zhongguo minzhu dangpai shi* (A history of the Chinese democratic parties). Tianjin: Nankai daxue chubanshe, 1992.

Du Jianshi. "Cong jieshou Tianjin dao kuatai" (From plundering Tianjin to its collapse), *TLZ*, pp. 1–64.

Duan Zhenkun et al. "Huiyi 'Jixie' " (Reminiscing the work of the "Reporters' Association"), *TJJ*, pp. 266–71.

Dupuy, Trevor Nevitt. *The Military History of the Chinese Civil War.* New York: Franklin Watts, 1969.

Eastman, Lloyd E. *Seeds of Destruction: Nationalist China in War and Revolution, 1937–1949.* Stanford: Stanford University Press, 1984.

Eastman, Lloyd E., et al. *The Nationalist Era in China 1927–1949.* Cambridge: Cambridge University Press, 1991.

Emerson, Donald, ed. *Students and Politics.* New York: Praeger, 1968.

Fairbank, John K. *China: A New History.* Cambridge, Mass.: Harvard University Press, 1992.

Fang Ting. "Jiefang zhanzheng shiqi Beiping dixiadang de douzheng" (The struggle of the Beiping Underground Party during the war of liberation), *BDZW*, pp. 305–20.

———. "Kangri yu jiefang zhanzheng shiqi zhonggong Beijing (Beiping) dang zuzhi gaikuang" (The conditions of the Chinese Communist Beijing [Beiping] party organizations during the periods of the anti-Japanese war and the war of liberation), *Beijing dangshi yanjiu* 6 (1989): 26–32.

———. "Nanwang de zhandou suiyue—Guanyu Beiping dixia diantai de huiyi" (The unforgettable fighting years—Reminiscing the underground radio station in Beiping), in Yondianbu Yondianshi Bianjishi, *Nanwang de zhandou suiye* (q.v.), pp. 234–50.

Fang Xiao, ed. *Zhonggong dangshi bianyilu* (A record of distinguishing the unresolved issues in CCP history). Taiyuan: Shanxi jiaoyu chubanshe, 1991.

Fawubu Tiaochaju, comp. *Zhonggong "funu yundong" yuanshi wenjian huibian* (A compilation of original documents on the Chinese Communist "women's movement"). Vol. I. Taibei: Fawubu tiaochaju, 1981.

Feidang de shentou gongzuo (The infiltration work of the bandit party). Taibei: Zhongyang weiyuanhui disizu, 1953.

Feng Dongsheng. "Dixiadang zai yingjie Tianjin jiefang zhong de gongzuo" (The work of the Underground Party in welcoming the liberation of Tianjin), *TJJ*, pp. 202–5.

Feng Zhi and Dong Lixiang. "Jiefang zhanzheng shiqi Guomindang jiangling qiyi toucheng shulun" (A discussion on the uprisings and defections of GMD generals during the period of the war of liberation), *Shandong yike daxue xuebao: Shekeban* (Shandong Medical University academic journal: Social sciences edition) 2 (1990): 2, 64–67.

Fu Shijun. "Yingjiu Zhao Fan tongzhi" (Rescue Comrade Zhao Fan), *BDDS*, pp. 189–96.

Fu Tao and Zhao Zuchang, eds. *Tianjin gongye sanshiwu nian* (Thirty-five years of the Tianjin industry). Tianjin: Tianjin shehui kexue bianjibu, 1985.

Fu Zuoyi zhi Mao Zedong dian ji qita (The cables and others from Fu Zuoyi to Mao Zedong). N.p., Shidai chubanshe, 1947.

Gao Jun, Wang Guilin, and Yang Shubiao, eds. *Zhongguo xiandai zhengzhi sixiang pingyao* (A critique of the modern Chinese political ideologies). Beijing: Huaxia chubanshe, 1990.

Gao Xinmin. "Shilun chengshi zhongxin lun dui zhongguo gongchandang de yingxiang" (An attempted discussion on the impact of the city-as-the-center concept of the CCP), *Zhonggong dangshi yanjiu* (Research on CCP history) 4 (1988): 75–82.

Goldstone, Jack A. *Revolution and Rebellion in the Early Modern World.* Berkeley and Los Angeles: University of California Press, 1991.

Goldstone, Jack A., Ted Robert Gurr, and Farrokh Moshiri, eds. *Revolutions of the Late Twentieth Century.* Boulder, Colo.: Westview Press, 1991.

Gongfei tegong de lishe (A history of the Communist bandits' special agents). N.p., Shipai xunlianban, 1957.

Gongfei tegong de zuofa (The style of work of the Communist bandits' special agents). N.p., Shipai xunlianban, 1957.

Gongqingtuan Beijing Shiwei Qingnian Yundongshi Yanjiushi. *Beijing qingnian yundongshi* (1919–1949) (A history of the Beijing student movement). Beijing: Beijing chubanshe, 1989.

Gongqingtuan Beijing Shiwei Qingyunshi Yanjiushi, comp. *Beijing qingyunshi lunji* (A collection of essays on the history of the youth movement in Beijing). Hainan: Hainan renmin chubanshe, 1988.

Gongqingtuan Zhongyang Qingyunshi Yanjiushi. *Zhongguo qingnian yundongshi* (A history of the Chinese youth movement). Beijing: Zhongguo qingnian chubanshe, 1984.

Gongqingtuan Zhongyang Qingyunshi Yanjiushi et al., comps. *Jiefang zhanzheng shiqi xuesheng yundong lunwen ji* (Collected essays on the student movement during the war of liberation). Shanghai: Tongji daxue chubanshe, 1988.

Gongren ribao (Workers' daily). Tianjin, 1948.

"Gongrenbu eryuefen gongzuo baogao" (A February work report of the Labor Department), in Zhonggong Beijing Shiwei Dangshi Yanjiushe, *Diyici guogonghezuo zai Beijing* (q.v.), pp. 385–87.

Gray, Jack. *Rebellions and Revolutions: China from the 1800s to the 1980s*. Oxford: Oxford University Press, 1990.

Griggs, Thurton. *Americans in China: Some Chinese Views*. Washington, D.C.: Foundation for Foreign Affairs, 1948.

Gu Shutang et al., eds. *Tianjin jingji gaikuang* (The general situation of the economy of Tianjin). Tianjin: Tianjin renmin chubanshe, 1984.

Guangming bao xunkan (Bright biweekly). Hong Kong, 1945–49.

Guofang Daxue Dangshi Dangjian Zhenggong Jiaoyanshi, *Zhongguo gongchandang de zhanlüe celüe (1921–1949)* (The strategy and tactics of the CCP [1921–1949]). Beijing: Jiefangjun chubanshe, 1991.

Guo Hualun. *Zhonggong shilun* (An analytical history of the CCP). 4 vols. Taibei: Zhonghua minguo guoji guanxi yanjiusuo, 1973.

Guo Lianyu. "He Siyuan gongguan beizha qianhou" (Prior to and after the bombing of the residence of He Siyuan), *Renwu* (Personalities) 4 (1985): 66–68.

Guo Qingshu et al., eds. *Zhongguo renmin jiefangjun lishi jianbian* (A concise history of the Chinese PLA). Shenyang: Liaoning daxue chubanshe, 1985.

Guo Ruokai. "Changxindian jichang jiefang qianhou" (The machine factory of Changxindian prior to and after the liberation), *Beijing dangshi yanjiu* 6 (1989): 42–44.

Guo Tingyi. *Jindai Zhongguo shigang* (A historical outline of modern China). 2 vols. Hong Kong: Zhongwen daxue chubanshe, 1980.

Guo Xiaoping. " 'Guanguo Jiefang Zhanzheng Shiqi Dangshi' Xueshe Taoluhui zongshu" (A summary of the Academic Conference on the Party History during "the Period of the National War of Liberation"), *Henan dangshi yanjiu* (Henan party history research) 5 (1990): 40, 54–59.

————. "Lun Zhonggong gongchandang baiqu gongzuo fangzhen celüe de xingcheng" (A discussion on the formation of the policy and strategy of the CCP's work in White areas), *Zhonggong dangshi yanjiu* 1 (1992): 8, 52–58.

Guofangbu Zhande Zhengwuju, comp. *Beipingshi diqu yanjiu* (Research on the Beiping area). Taibei: Guofangbu zhande zhengwuju, 1964.

Han Mingyang. "Jieshou Beiping Nanyuan Jichang" (Taking over the Beiping Nanyuan Airport), *Zhongheng* (Length and breadth) 31 (1989): 10–13.

Hao Yingde and Shao Pengwen. *Zhongguo xuesheng yundong jianshi, 1919–1949* (A short history of the Chinese student movement, 1919–1949). Hebei: Hebei renmin chubanshe, 1985.

Harding, Harry, and Yuan Ming, eds. *Sino-American Relations, 1945–1955: A Joint Reassessment of a Critical Decade*. Wilmington, Del.: Scholarly Resources Inc., 1989.

Harding, Neil. *Lenin's Political Thought: Theory and Practice in the Democratic and Socialist Revolutions*. 2 vols. London: Macmillan, 1983.

Hartford, Kathleen J., "Step By Step: Reform, Resistance, and Revolution in the Chin-Ch'a-Chi Border Region, 1937–1945." Ph.D. diss., Stanford University, 1979.

Hartford, Kathleen J. and Steven M. Goldstein, eds. *Single Sparks: China's Rural Revolutions*. Armonk, N.Y.: M.E. Sharpe, 1989.

He Dong and Chen Mingxian. *Beiping heping jiefang shimo* (The beginning and the end of the peaceful liberation of Beiping). Beijing: Jiefangjun chubanshe, 1985.

He Lilu. "Huiyi xianfu He Siyuan" (Reminiscing my deceased father He Siyuan), *WZXB* 39 (1990): 146–63.

He Siyuan. "Wo canjia heping jiefang Beiping de huodong" (The activities of my participation in the peaceful liberation of Beiping), *WZXJ* 69 (1979): 73–87.

He Wencheng and Jia Chengzhong. "Guanghui de zhandou licheng—Jiefang zhanzheng qijian dang lingdao Mentougou kuangqu gongren de douzheng" (The glorious fighting experiences—The struggle of the Party-led Mentougou coal mine workers during the time of the war of liberation), *Beijing dangshi yanjiu* 3 (1991): 36–39.

Hebei banyue kan (Hebei bimonthly). N.p., 1946–48.

Hebeisheng Zhengxie Wenshi Ziliao Yanjiu Weiyuanhui and Hebeisheng Difangzhi Bianzuan Weiyuanhui, comps. *Hebei jindai dashiji (1840–1949)* (A record of major modern events in Hebei [1840–1949]). Shijiazhuang: Hebei renmin chubanshe, 1986.

Hershatter, Gail. *The Workers of Tianjin, 1900–1949*. Stanford: Stanford University Press, 1986.

Hong Anqi and He Bufeng. *Zhongguo gongren yundong jianshi* (A concise history of the Chinese labor movement). Xi'an: Shaanxi renmin xiaoyu chubanshe, 1987.

Hong Ze. "Tianjin baoweizhan jianwen" (The scenes of the defense war of Tianjin), parts 1, 2, 3, and 4 in *Shijie ribao*, 19–22 July 1991.

Hooton, E. R. *The Greatest Tumult: The Chinese Civil War 1936–49*. London: Brassey's, 1991.

Hou Renzhi and Jin Tao. *Beijing shihua* (A historical account of Beijing). Shanghai: Renmin chubanshe, 1982.

Hsiung, James C., and Steven I. Levine, eds. *China's Bitter Victory: The War with Japan 1937–1945*. Armonk, N.Y.: M.E. Sharpe, 1992.

Hsü, Immanuel C. Y. *The Rise of Modern China*. 4th ed. Oxford: Oxford University Press, 1990.

Hu Chia. *Peking: Today and Yesterday*. Peking: Foreign Languages Press, 1956.

Hu Kuo-tai. "The Struggle between the Kuomintang and the Chinese Communist Party on Campus during the War of Resistance, 1937–45," *The China Quarterly* 118 (1989): 300–332.

Hu Yaobang. "Speech at the Meeting in Celebration of the 60th Anniversary of Founding of the Communist Party of China," in *Resolution on CPC History (1949–81)* (Beijing: Foreign Languages Press, 1981), pp. 87–120.

Hu Zhixin, ed. *Zhongguo gongchandang tongyi zhanxianshi* (A history of the CCP united front). Beijing: Huaxia chubanshe, 1988.

Hua Binqing, ed. *Wuerling yundongshi* (A history of the May Twentieth Movement). Rev. ed. Nanjing: Nanjing daxue chubanshe, 1990.

Huabei ribao (North China daily). Beiping, 1945–49.

Huabei xinbao (North China news). Beiping, 1945–49.

Huabei Xuesheng Yundong Xiaoshi Bianji Weiyuanhui, comp. *Huabei xuesheng yundong xiaoshi* (A short history of the North China student movement). Part I. Beijing: n.p., 1948.

Huashang bao (Chinese merchant). Hong Kong, 1945–49.

Huebner, Jon W. "Chinese Anti-Americanism, 1946–48," *The Australian Journal of Chinese Affairs* 17 (1987): 115–26.

Hunt, Richard H. *The Political Ideas of Marx and Engels*. Vol. I: *Marxism and Totalitarian Democracy, 1818–1850*. Vol. II: *Classical Marxism, 1850–1895*. Pittsburgh: University of Pittsburgh Press, 1974, 1984.

Huntington, Samuel P. *Political Order in Changing Societies*. New Haven: Yale University Press, 1968.

Israel, John, and Donald W. Klein. *Rebels and Bureaucrats: China's December 9ers*. Berkeley and Los Angeles: University of California Press, 1976.

———. "Reflections on 'Reflections on the Modern Chinese Student Movement,' " in Jeffrey N. Wasserstrom and Elizabeth J. Perry, eds. *Popular Protest and Political Culture in Modern China: Learning from 1989* (Boulder, Colo.: Westview Press, 1992), pp. 85–108.

Jeans, Roger B., ed. *Roads Not Taken: The Struggle of Opposition Parties in Twentieth-Century China*. Boulder, Colo.: Westview Press, 1992.

Ji Gang. "Wo zai *Pingming ribao* dang jizhe" (I worked as a reporter in *Pingming ribao*), *BDDS*, pp. 516–22.

Ji Junbian. "Gongming chui zhubo—Gao Shuxun yu Handan qiyi" (Contribution and fame written on bamboo slips and silk—Gao Shuxun and the Handan uprising), *Zongheng*, part I in 2 (1986): 34–41; part II in 3 (1986): 25–32.

Ji Ruisan et al. "Kangzhan qijian Gongchandang zai Gao Shuxun bu de gongzuo" (The CCP work in the Gao Shuxun corps during the war of resistance), *Gemingshi ziliao* (Materials on the revolutionary history) 15 (1985): 37–54.

Ji Ze. "Ji Beiyang daxue de xuesheng yundong" (A record of the student movement at Beiyang University), *TWZX* 11 (1980): 76–82.

Jiang Huaxuan, Zhang Weiping, and Xiao Shen, eds. *Zhongguo gongchandang huiyi gaiyao* (An outline of CCP's meetings). Shenyang: Shenyang chubanshe, 1991.

Jiang Shaozhen. "Jiefang zhanzheng shiqi Guomindangjun qiyi shulun" (A discussion on the uprisings of the GMD troops during the period of the war of liberation), *Jindaishi yanjiu* (Research on modern history) 4 (1993): 216–32.

Jiang Shuchen. *Fu Zuoyi zhuanlüe* (A concise biography of Fu Zuoyi). Beijing: Zhongguo qingnian chubanshe, 1990.

Jiangguo ribao (National construction daily). Beiping, 1946–48.

Jie Lifu. *Jiefang zhanzheng shilu—Liangzhong mingyun de juezhan* (A factual account of the war of liberation—The decisive battles of two destinies). 2 vols. Shijiazhuang: Hebei renmin chubanshe, 1990.

Jiefang bao (Liberation). Beiping, March–May 1946.

Jiefang ribao (Liberation daily). Yan'an, 1941–49.

"Jin-Cha-Ji Kangri Genjudi" Shiliao Congshu Bianshen Weiyuanhui, comp. *Jin-Cha-Ji kangri genjudi* (The Jin-Cha-Ji anti-Japanese base area). Vol. I: *Wenxian xuanbian* (A compilation of selected materials). 2 vols. Beijing: Zhonggong dangshi ziliao chubanshe, 1988.

———. *Jin-Cha-Ji kangri genjudi*. Vol. III: *Dashiji* (A record of major events). Beijing: Zhonggong dangshi ziliao chubanshe, 1991.

Jin-Cha-Ji ribao (Jin-Cha-Ji daily). Leibao and Zhangjiakou, 1945–49.

Jin-Cha-Ji ribao Bianxiezu, comp. *Jin-Cha-Ji ribao dashiji* (A record of the major events in Jin-Cha-Ji daily news). Beijing: Qunzhong chubanshe, 1986.

Jin Dahai. *Zhonggong tongzhan celüe yanjiu* (A study of the CCP united-front tactics). Taibei: Liming wenhua shiye gongsi, 1983.

Jin Shixuan and Xu Wenshu. *Zhongguo tielu fazhan shi* (The development history of the Chinese railroads). Beijing: Zhongguo tielu chubanshe, 1986.

Jingshi ribao (Statecraft daily). Beiping, 1946–48.

Jishi bao (Record). Beiping, 1946–48.

Johnson, Chalmers. *Revolutionary Change*. 2nd ed. Stanford: Stanford University Press, 1982.

Ka Di. "Zai Liu Ren tongzhi shenbian zuo jiyao yuan" (Serving as a security guard to Comrade Liu Ren), *WZXB* 39 (1990): 58–66.

Kataoka, Tetsuya. *Resistance and Revolution in China: The Communists and the Second United Front*. Berkeley and Los Angeles: University of California Press, 1974.

Kates, George N. *The Years That Were Fat: Peking, 1933–1940*. Intro. Pamela Atwell. Hong Kong: Oxford University Press, 1988.

Kau Ying-mao. "Urban and Rural Strategies in the Chinese Communist Revolution," in John Wilson Lewis, *Peasant Rebellion and Communist Revolution in Asia* (q.v.), pp. 253–70.

Ke Siming. "Lun kangzhan shiqi Zhonggong de 'Qieryi fanzhen'" (Discuss the "7–2–1 Policy" of the CCP during the wartime period), *Jindai zhongguo* (Modern China) 67 (1988): 164–79.

Kiang Wen-han. *The Chinese Student Movement*. New York: King's Crown, 1948.

Kidd, David. *Peking Story: The Last Days of Old China*. New York: Griffin Paperback, 1988.

―――. Letter to the author, 17 Aug. 1989.

Kimura, Yujiro. *A Chronology of the History of the Chinese Labor Movement* (in Japanese). Tokyo: Kyuko shoin, 1978.

Kuai bao (Quick news). Yanjing University, 1947.

Kuo, Warren. *Analytical History of the Chinese Communist Party*. 4 vols. Taibei: Institute of International Relations, 1968–71.

Ladany, Laszlo. *The Communist Party of China and Marxism 1921–1985: A Self-Portrait*. Stanford: Hoover Institution Press, 1988.

Lang Guanying. "Dianxin changtong—Ji Beijing jiefang qianxi de huchang douzheng" (Smooth telecommunications service—Recording the struggle of protecting factories on the eve of the liberation of Beijing), *Beijing ribao,* Beijing, 31 Jan. 1979.

Lao She. *Rickshaw*. Trans. Jean James. Honolulu: University of Hawaii Press, 1979.

Lao Zhuang. *Gudu mengnan ji* (An account of suffering in the old capital). Taibei: Lianheban zong guanlichu, 1953.

Lee Lai To. *Trade Unions in China, 1949 to the Present*. Singapore: Singapore University Press, 1986.

Lenin, V. I. *Collected Works*. 46 vols. Moscow: Foreign Languages, 1960–78.

Levine, Steven I. *Anvil of Victory: The Communist Revolution in Manchuria, 1945–1948*. New York: Columbia University Press, 1987.

Lewis, John Wilson, ed. *Peasant Revolution and Communist Revolution in Asia*. Stanford: Stanford University Press, 1974.

Li Kun. "Jiefang zhanzheng shiqi guotongqu renmin wuzhuang zhi lishi kaocha" (An investigation of the history of the people's armed forces in the GMD-controlled areas during the period of the war of liberation), *Jindaishi yanjiu* 1 (1994): 202–14.

―――. "Yijiu siqi nian Beiping diqu de Fan Jie Fan Neizhan Yundong" (The Antihunger Anti–Civil War Movement in the Beiping area in 1947), *BDYW*, pp. 429–40.

Li, Lincoln. *The Japanese Army in North China, 1937–1941: Problems of Political and Economic Control*. London: Oxford University Press, 1975.

―――. *Student Nationalism in China, 1924–1949*. Albany: State University of New York Press, 1994.

Li Lingyu. "Shilun diertian zhanxian ji qi lishi jingyan" (An attempted discussion on the Second Battlefront and its historical experiences), *Beijing dangshi yanjiu* 6 (1991): 22–29.

Li Ping. "Guanyu wo dang Zhongyang kangri zhanzheng zhong zai Guomindang tongzhiqu gongzuo fangzhen de tifa" (Concerning the wording of our Party's guiding principle of work in the GMD-controlled areas during the anti-Japanese war), in Zhonggong Zhongyang Wenxian Yanjiushi, comp., *Wenxian he yanjiu (Yijiu basan nian huibianben)* (Materials and research [compiled copy of 1983]) (Beijing: Renmin chubanshe, 1984), pp. 463–64.

Li Xue. "Guanyu Beiping dixia diantai de diandi huiyi" (Scattered reminiscences about the underground Beiping radio station), in Youdianbu Youdianshi Bianxieshi, *Nanwang de zhandong suiye* (q.v.), pp. 251–54.

Li Yong and Zhang Zongtian, eds. *Jiefang zhanzheng shiqi tongyi zhanxian dashiji* (A record of major events of the united front during the war of liberation). Beijing: Zhongguo jingji chubanshe, 1988.

Li Yuanchun. "Mianfang sichang chengli chise gonghui qianhou" (Prior to and after the establishment of the red labor union at the 4th Cotton Mills), *Tianjin shizhi* 3 (1987): 60–61.

Li Zhinan. "Tianjin nanxi dixiadang de zuzhi yu huodong" (The organizations and activities of the Tianjin Underground Party's Southern Group), *TJJ*, pp. 195–201.

Liang Jingxiang. *Riben qinlue Huabei shishu* (A historical narrative on the Japanese invasion of North China). Taibei: Chuanji wenxue chubanshe, 1984.

Liang Xianghan and Zhao Gengqi. "Zhang Kexia tongzhi tan canjia geming he ershijiu jun kangri de jingguo" (Comrade Zhang Kexia's talks on his joining the revolution and the anti-Japanese activities of the 29th Army), in Liang and Zhao, eds., *Beijing diqu kangzhan shiliao* (Historical materials on the anti-Japanese war of resistance in the Beijing area) (Beijing: Zijincheng chubanshe, 1986), pp. 30–48.

Liao Yongwu. *Tianjin xiandai geming yundongshi* (A history of the modern revolutionary movement in Tianjin). Tianjin: Tianjin renmin chubanshe, 1985.

Lieberthal, Kenneth. *Revolution and Tradition in Tientsin, 1949–1952.* Stanford: Stanford University Press, 1980.

Lieu, D. K. *China's Economic Stabilization and Reconstruction.* New Brunswick: Rutgers University Press, 1948.

Lin Xingru. "Chuang Tianjinwei zuo teshu de maoyi tanpan" (Going to Tianjin for a special trade negotiation), in Shangyebu Shangye Zhengce Yanjiuhui, comp., *Jianguo qianhou shangye gongzuo shilu* (A factual account of the commerce work prior to and after the establishment of the People's Republic) (Beijing: Zhongguo shangye chubanshe, 1988), pp. 211–20.

Lin Zhida, ed. *Zhongguo gongchandang xuanchuanshi* (A history of the CCP propaganda). Chengdu: Sichuan renmin chubanshe, 1990.

Ling Yaolun et al. *Zhongguo jindai jingjishi* (Modern Chinese economic history). Chongqing: Chongqing chubanshe, 1982.

Liu, F. F. *A Military History of Modern China, 1924–1949.* Princeton: Princeton University Press, 1956.

Liu Hangsheng. "Jiefang qian wozuo fuqin Liu Houtong gongzuo de pianduan" (Scattered reminiscences about the work of my father Liu Houtong prior to the liberation), *BDDS*, pp. 282–83.

Liu Jianqing, Wang Jiadian, and Xu Liangbo, eds. *Zhongguo guomindang shi* (A history of the Nationalist Party of China). Jiangsu: Guji chubanshe, 1992.

Liu Jie. "Shixi 1945–1949 nian Guomindang dui xuesheng yundong de celüe" (An attempted analysis of the Guomindang strategy toward the student movement during 1945–1949), in Gongqingtuan Zhongyang Qingyunshi Yanjiushi et al., *Jiefang zhanzheng shiqi xuesheng yundong lunwen ji* (q.v.), pp. 296–307.

Liu Shaoqi. "Guanyu guoqu Baiqu gongzuo gei Zhongyang de yifeng xin" (A letter to the Central concerning the past work in White areas), in Zhonggong Zhongyang Shujichu, comp., *Liuda yilai: Dangnei mimi wenjian* (Since the Sixth Congress: Party's secret internal documents) (Beijing: Renmin chubanshe, 1981), vol. I, pp. 803–12.

———. *Liu Shaoqi xuanji* (Selected works of Liu Shaoqi). Vol. I. Beijing: Renmin chubanshe, 1981.

———. "Lun gongkai gongzuo yu mimi gongzuo" (A discussion on the open and the secret work), in Zhonggong Zhongyang Shujichu, comp., *Liuda yilai*, vol. II, pp. 215–26.

———. *Selected Works of Liu Shaoqi.* Vol. I. Beijing: Foreign Languages Press, 1984.

Liu Xiao. "Yijiu siqu nian 'Fan jie, fan neizhan, fan pohai' yundong de yixie huigu" (Certain reminiscences on the 'Antihunger, Anti–Civil War, Antipersecution' Movement in 1947), *Dangshi ziliao* (Materials on party history) 3 (1985): 20–33.

Liu Yunjiu. *Guomindang tongzhiqu de minzhu yundong* (The democratic movement in the GMD-controlled areas). Harbin: Helongjiang renmin chubanshe, 1986.

Liu Zehua, ed. *Tianjin wenhua gaikuang* (The condition of culture in Tianjin). Tianjin: Tianjin shehui kexueyuan chubanshe, 1990.

Loh, Pichon P. Y., ed. *The Kuomintang Debacle of 1949: Collapse or Conquest?* Boston: D.C. Heath, 1965.

Lu Yangyuan and Fang Qingqiu, eds. *Minguo shehui jingjishi* (The socioeconomic history of the Republic of China). Beijing: Zhongguo jingji chubanshe, 1991.

Lu Yu. "Zuzhu qilai liliang da, liying waihe ying jiefang—Huiyi Beiping dixiadang gongwei he shizheng gongwei lingdao de douzheng" (Get organized to become powerful, coordinate the interior with the exterior to welcome liberation—Reminiscing the struggle led by the Worker Committee and the Municipal Administration Committee of the Beiping Underground Party), *BDDS*, pp. 129–35.

Lu Yuanchi. "Bianyin *Xinmin ziliao* de qianqian houhou" (Prior to and after the editing and printing of *New Materials*), *BDDS*, pp. 504–15.

Lutz, Jesse G. "The Chinese Student Movement of 1945–1949," *Journal of Asian Studies* 1 (1971): 89–110.

McDonald, Angus W., Jr. *The Urban Origins of Rural Revolution: Elites and the Masses in Hunan Province, China, 1911–1927.* Berkeley and Los Angeles: University of California Press, 1978.

Ma Chaojun, ed. *Zhongguo laogong yundong shi* (A history of the Chinese labor movement). Taibei: Zhongguo laogong fuli chubanshe, 1959.

Ma Demao. "Lun jiefang zhanzheng shiqi de disantiao zhanxian" (A discussion on the Third Battlefront during the period of the war of liberation), *Zhongnan caijing daxue xuebao* (Academic journal of the Central-South Finance and Economics University) 3 (1989): 140–45.

Ma Shitu. *Zai dixia-Baiqu dixiadang gongzuo jingyan chubu zongjie* (Being underground—A preliminary general conclusion of the Underground Party's experiences in White areas). Chengdu: Xichuan daxue chubanshe, 1987.

Mai Xuankun. "Wo xiang dang xian chengfang tu" (I presented the city defense map to the Party), *TJJ*, pp. 298–304.

Mao Tse-tung [Zedong]. *Mao Zedong ji* (Collected works of Mao Zedong). Ed. Takeuchi Minoru. 10 vols. Tokyo: Hokubosha, 1983.

———. *Mao Zedong ji bujuan* (Supplements to collected works of Mao Zedong). Ed. Takeuchi Minoru. 9 vols. Tokyo: Hokubosha, 1983–85.

———. *Mao Zedong shuxin xuanji* (Selected letters of Mao Zedong). Beijing: Renmin chubanshe, 1983.

———. *Mao Zedong xuanji* (Selected works of Mao Zedong). 2nd ed., 4 vols. Beijing: Renmin chubanshe, 1991.

———. *Selected Works of Mao Tse-tung.* 4 vols. Peking: Foreign Languages Press, 1965, 1967, 1969.

Marshall, George C. *Marshall's Mission to China, December 1945–January 1947: The Report and Appended Documents.* Intro. by Lyman P. Van Slyke. 2 vols. Arlington, Va.: University Publications of America, 1976.

Marx, Karl, and Frederick Engels. *Collected Works.* 42 vols. New York: International Publishers, 1975–87.

Meisner, Maurice. *Marxism, Maoism and Utopianism: Eight Essays.* Madison: University of Wisconsin Press, 1982.

Melby, John F. *The Mandate of Heaven: Records of a Civil War, China 1945–49.* Toronto: University of Toronto Press, 1968.

Meng Qingchun. "Guanyu diertiao zhanxian wenti yanjiu de sisuo" (Thoughts on the research concerning the issues of the Second Battlefront), *Qiqihan shifan xueyuan xuebao: Zhesheban* (Qiqihan Normal College academic journal: Philosophy and social sciences edition) 5 (1993): 29–33.

Meng Zhiyuan. "Qianzhu diren junxu houqin de bozi—Beiping junxu beifu xitong dixiadang douzheng jishi" (Grasp the neck of the military and logistical supplies of the enemy—A factual account of the Underground Party struggle in the Beiping military supplies and clothing industry), *BDDS*, pp. 444–63.

Meyer, Alfred G. *Leninism*. Cambridge, Mass.: Harvard University Press, 1957.

Mianhuai Liu Ren tongzhi (Reminiscing Comrade Liu Ren). Beijing: Beijing chubanshe, 1979.

Min Xie. *Zhonggong qunyun yu qingyun pouxi* (An analysis of the Chinese Communist mass movement and youth movement). Taibei: Liming wenhua shiyu gongsi, 1980.

Minguo ribao (Republican daily). Tianjin, 1945–49.

Minzhu zhoukan (The democratic weekly). Beiping, 1945–49.

Mo Wenhua. *Huiyi jiefang Beiping qianhou* (Reminiscing the days prior to and after the liberation of Beiping). Beijing: Beijing chubanshe, 1982.

Moorad, George. *Lost Peace in China*. New York: E.P. Dutton, 1949.

Moore, Stanley. *Three Tactics: The Background in Marx*. New York: Monthly Review, 1963.

Murphey, Rhoads. *The Fading of the Maoist Vision: City and Country in China's Development*. New York: Methuen, 1980.

Myers, Ramon H. *The Chinese Economy: Past and Present*. Belmont, Calif.: Wadsworth, 1980.

Nanfangju Dangshi Ziliao Zhengji Xiaozu, comp. *Nanfangju dangshi ziliao: Dang de jianshe* (Materials on the Party history of the Southern Bureau: Party-building). Chongqing: Chongqing chubanshe, 1990.

Nankai Daxue Xiaoshi Bianxiezu. *Nankai daxue xiaoshi (1919–1949)* (The school history of Nankai University [1919–1949]). Tianjin: Nankai daxue chubanshe, 1989.

Nie Rongzhen. *Nie Rongzhen huiyilu* (The memoirs of Nie Rongzhen). 3 vols. Beijing: Jiefangjun chubanshe, 1984.

Pan Zhiting, ed. *Fadianchang nei wushi nian* (Fifty years inside the Electric Factory). Beijing: Beijing chubanshe, 1959.

Peiping Chronicle. Beiping, 1946–48.

Pelissier, Roger. *The Awakening of China: 1793–1949*. Trans. Martin Kieffer. London: Secker & Warburg, 1963.

Peng Jianhua. "Wo suo liaojie de Beijing he Beifangqu dang zuzhi de yixie qing kuang (jielu)" (Certain situations concerning the Party organizations in Beijing and in the northern area that I know [abridged]), in Zhonggong Beijing Shiwei Dangshi Yanjiushi, *Diyici guogong hezuo zai Beijing* (q.v.), pp. 421–50.

Peng Ming, ed. *Zhongguo xiandaishi ziliao xuanji* (Selected and edited materials on the modern Chinese history). 6 vols. Beijing: Zhongguo renmin daxue chubanshe, 1987–1989.

Peng Zhen. *Guanyu Jin-Cha-Ji bianqu dang de gongzuo he juti zhengce baogan* (A report concerning the work and the concrete policy of the Jin-Cha-Ji Border Region). Beijing: Zhonggong zhongyang dangxiao chubanshe, 1981.

Pepper, Suzanne. *Civil War in China: The Political Struggle, 1945–1949*. Berkeley and Los Angeles: University of California Press, 1978.

———. "The KMT-CCP Conflict, 1945–1949," in John King Fairbank and Albert Feuerwerker, eds., *The Cambridge History of China*, vol. 13: *Republican China, 1912–1949*, part 2 (Cambridge: Cambridge University Press, 1986), pp. 723–41.

Perry, Elizabeth J. *Shanghai on Strike: The Politics of Chinese Labor*. Stanford: Stanford University Press, 1993.

Pingming ribao (Fair and bright daily). Beiping, 1946–48.

Pu Yuhuo and Xu Shuangmi. *Dang de baiqu douzheng shihua* (A historical account of the Party's struggle in White areas). Beijing: Zhonggong dangshi chubanshe, 1991.

Pye, Lucian W. Letter to the author, 6 March 1992.

Qi Mingfu and Zhai Taifeng, eds. *Zhongguo gongchandang jianshe dacidian (1921–1991)* (A large dictionary on the building of the CCP [1921–1991]). Chengdu: Sichuan renmin chubanshe, 1991.

Qi Rushan. *Beiping.* Taibei: Zhengzhong shujiu, 1971. First published 1957.

Qian Siliang. "Nanwang de wangshi—Feichu weicheng Beiping" (The unforgettable past event—Flying out of the besieged city, Beiping), *Zhongwai zazhi* (Kaleidoscope) 5 (1979): 8–10.

Qiao Jinou. "Kangri shiqi balujun zai Huabei de kuozhan zuoda" (The expansion of the 8th Route Army in North China during the period of the war of resistance), *Gongdang wenti yanjiu* (Studies in communism) 1 (1986): 63–70; 2 (1986): 86–103; 3 (1986): 89–104; 4 (1986): 59–78.

Qin Qianmu et al. *Zhongguo zhengdang shi* (A history of the Chinese political parties). Taiyuan: Shanxi renmin chubanshe, 1991.

Qin Xiaoyi et al., eds. *Zhonghua minguo jingji fazhanshi* (A history of the economic development of the Republic of China). 2 vols. Taibei: Jindai zhonguo chubanshe, 1983.

Qingbao Xuexiao Feie Junshi Yanjiuchu, comp. *Guojun dui feiqing zhozhan jingyan yu jiaoxun* (The lessons and experiences of the GMD army in intelligence warfare against the bandits). Taibei: Guofanbu qingbao canmou cichangshi, 1952.

Qinghe Zhinichang Changshi Bianweihui, comp. *Beijing Qinghe Zhinichang wushi nian* (Fifty years of the Beijing Qinghe Woolen Factory). Beijing: Beijing chubanshe, 1959.

Qinghua Daxue Xiaoshi Bianxiezu, comp. *Qinghua daxue xiaoshi gao* (A draft history of the Qinghua University). Beijing: Zhonghua shuju, 1981.

Quanguo Zhengzhi Wenshi Ziliao Yanjiu Weiyuanhui, Gansu Zhengzhi Wenshi Ziliao Yanjiu Weiyuanhui, and Shaanxisheng Zhengzhi Wenshi Ziliao Yanjiu Weiyuanhui, comps. *Deng Baoshan jiangjun* (General Deng Baoshan). Beijing: Wenshi ziliao chubanshe, 1985.

Renmin ribao (People's daily) (overseas ed.). Beijing, Hong Kong, Tokyo, San Francisco, New York, and Paris.

Renmin ribao (People's daily). Pingshan, 1948–49.

Rickett, Allyn, and Adele Rickett. *Prisoners of Liberation.* San Francisco: China Books, 1981.

Sanwu Lingyi Chang Changshi Bianxie Xiaozu. "Baoji huchang, yingjie jiefang" (Secure the machines, protect the factory, and welcome the liberation), *Beijing dangshi yanjiu* 6 (1989): 33–34.

Schram, Stuart. *The Thought of Mao Tse-tung.* Cambridge: Cambridge University Press, 1989.

Selznick, Philip. *The Organizational Weapon: A Study of Bolshevik Strategy and Tactics.* Glencoe, Ill.: The Free Press, 1960.

Seymour, James D. *China's Satellite Parties.* Armonk, N.Y.: M.E. Sharpe, 1987.

Sha Jiansun. "Lun Kangbao Yundong" (Discuss the Antibrutality Movement), *BDYW*, pp. 408–28.

———. "Lun quanguo jiefang zhanzheng shiqi de xuesheng yundong" (A discussion on the student movement during the period of the national war of liberation), in Gongqingtuan Zhongyang Qingyunshi Yanjiushi, *Jiefang zhanzheng shiqi xuesheng yundong lunwen ji* (q.v.), pp. 1–22.

Sha Xiaoquan. "Zhandou zai diertiao zhanxian shang—Huiyi jiefang zhanzheng shiqi Nankai Daxue dixiadang de douzheng" (Struggling on the Second Battlefront—Reminiscing the struggle of the Underground Party at Nankai University during the period of the war of liberation), *Tianjin ribao* (Tianjin daily), Tianjin, 15 Jan. 1979.

Sha Xiaoquan and Liu Yan. "Jiefang qianxi Nankai Daxue de tongzhan gongzuo" (The united-front work in the Nankai University prior to the liberation), *TJJ*, pp. 244–51.

Shanghai xuesheng yundongshi (A history of the student movement in Shanghai). Shanghai: Renmin chubanshe, 1983.

Shao Pengwen and Hao Yingda. *Zhongguo xuesheng yundong jianshi* (A concise history of the Chinese student movement). Shijiazhuang: Renmin chubanshe, 1985.

Shao Weizheng. *Zhongguo gongchandang chuangjianshi* (The founding of the Communist Party of China). Beijing: Jiefangjun chubanshe, 1991.

Shapiro, Sidney. *An American in China: Thirty Years in the People's Republic.* Peking: New World Press, 1979.

Shaw, Chonghal Petey. *The Role of the United States in Chinese Civil Conflicts, 1944–1949.* Salt Lake City: Charles Schlacks, Jr., Publishers, 1991.

Shaw, Henry I., Jr. *The U.S. Marines in North China, 1945–1949.* Washington, D.C.: Headquarters, U.S. Marine Corps, 1962.

She Diqing and Yang Bozhen. "Diertiao zhanxian shang de xianfeng—Huiyi Beiping dixiadang xuewei lingdao de xuesheng yundong" (The vanguard on the Second Battlefront—Reminiscing the student movement led by the Student Committee of the Beiping Underground Party), *WZXB* 5 (1979): 12–33.

She Diqing, Yang Bozhen, et al. "Fan Chiang Fanmei douzheng zhong de xianfeng—Minzhu qingnian lianmeng" (The vanguard in the anti-Chiang anti–United States struggle—the Democratic Youth League), *Beijing dangshi yanjiu* 5 (1991): 22–28.

Shen Bo et al. "Zhongshan Gongyuan Yin Letang Shijian de qianqian houhou" (Prior to and after the Music Hall incident at the Zhongshan Park), *BDDS*, pp. 833–49.

Shi Chongke. "Zai shiliuzi fangzhen zhiyin xia douzheng qianjin—Jiefang zhanzheng shiqi Beiping dixia douzheng de jiben jingyan zhiyi" (Advancing the struggle under the direction of the Sixteen-Character Guideline—One of the basic experiences of the underground struggle in Beiping during the period of the war of liberation), *Beijing dangshi yanjiu* 6 (1989): 14–21.

Shi Jitao. "Huiyi jiefang zhanzheng shiqi de Zhongguo Xuesheng Lianhehui" (Reminiscing the All-China Student Association during the period of the war of liberation), *Zhongguo qingyun* (Chinese youth movement) 2 (1989): 32–38, 4 (1989): 26–28.

Shi Luyi. "Jiefang zhanzheng shiqi de Beiping tielu xitong dixiadang" (The underground Party of the railway system in Beiping during the period of the war of liberation), *BDZW*, pp. 413–23.

Shi Mei. "Yanju Erdui he Zuguo Jutuan" (The Second Theatrical Corps and the Fatherland Theatrical Group), *BDDS*, pp. 218–33.

Shi Ren. "Fu Zuoyi Beiping xianggong jilu" (A record of Fu Zuoyi's defection to the Communists in Beiping), *Shijie ribao*, Los Angeles, 29 Jan. 1992.

———. "Wei Lihuang panbian" (The revolt of Wei Lihuang), *Shijie ribao*, Los Angeles, 15 Nov. 1991.

Shi Weiqun. *Zhongguo xuesheng yundongshi 1945–1949* (A history of the Chinese student movement 1945–1949). Shanghai: Renmin chubanshe, 1992.

Shijie ribao (World journal). Houston and Los Angeles, 1983–

Shijingshan Fadian Zongchang Shizhi Ban(gongshi). "Yingjie jiefang de riri yeye" (The day and night in welcoming the liberation), *Beijing dangshi yanjiu* 6 (1989): 35–38.

Shive, Glenn Landes. "Mao Tse-tung and the Anti-Japanese United Front, a Historical Analysis of a Mixed-Motive Conflict, 1935–1942," Ph.D. diss., Temple University, 1979.

Shum Kui-Kwong. *The Chinese Communists' Road to Power: The Anti-Japanese National United Front (1935–1945).* Hong Kong: Oxford University Press, 1988.

Sifa Xingzhengbu Tianchaju, comp. *Gongfei shentou zhanshu zhi yanjiu* (A study of the Communist bandits' infiltration tactics). Taibei: Sifa xingzhengbu tianchaju, 1962.

———. *Gongfei tongzhan gongzuo de celüe yu yunyong* (The strategy and the practical use of the Communist bandits' united-front work). Taibei: Sifa xingzhengbu tianchaju, 1960.

Sing tao ribao (Singapore island daily) (overseas ed.). San Francisco.

Song Bo, ed. *Beijing xiandai gemingshi* (Modern revolutionary history of Beijing). Beijing: Zhongguo renmin daxue chubanshe, 1988.

Song Chun et al., eds. *Zhongguo guomindang shi* (A history of the Chinese GMD). Jilin: Jilin wenshi chubanshe, 1990.

Song Rufen, Shen Bo, and Xu Wei. "Diyici daji—Huiyi Beiping dixiadang xuewei lingdao de fan zhenshen yundong" (The first attack—Reminiscing the Anti-Examination Movement led by the Student Committee of the Beiping Underground Party), *BDDS*, pp. 34–49.

Spence, Jonathan D. *The Search for Modern China*. New York: W.W. Norton, 1990.

Stranahan, Patricia. "Strange Bedfellows: The Communist Party and Shanghai's Elite in the National Salvation Movement," *The China Quarterly* 129 (1992): 26–51.

Strand, David. *Rickshaw Beijing: City People and Politics in the 1920s*. Berkeley and Los Angeles: University of California Press, 1989.

Su Cheng, ed. "Beiping fan jie fan neizhang dayouxing jishi" (An accurate account of the Antihunger Anti–Civil War great demonstration in Beiping), *Beijing dang'an shiliao* (Historical materials of the Beijing Archives) 2 (1986): 25–28.

Sullivan, Lawrence R. "Reconstruction and Rectification of the Communist Party in the Shanghai Underground: 1931–34," *The China Quarterly* 101 (1985): 78–97.

Sun Lianzhong. *Sun Lianzhong huiyilu* (The memoirs of Sun Lianzhong). Taibei: Sun Fanglu xiansheng guxi huadan choubei weiyuanhui, 1962.

Sun Shuhong. " '*Jiefang*,' '*Jiefang ribao*' he Xinhuashe Beiping fenshe wei dengji beian yu Guomindang dangju douzheng shimo" (The beginning and end of the struggle of the Branch Office of the New China Agency against the Guomindang authorities concerning the registration of *Liberation* and *Liberation daily*), *Beijing dang'an shiliao* 2 (1990): 79–84.

Tan Zhilan. *Cangsang qishi nian* (The seven tumultuous decades). Taibei: Weiju chubanshe, 1989.

Tang Degang and Li Zongren. *Li Zongren huiyilu* (The memoirs of Li Zongren). Hong Kong: Nanyue chubanshe, 1986.

Thomas, S. Bernard. *Labor and the Chinese Revolution: Class Strategies and Contradictions of Chinese Communism, 1928–48*. Ann Arbor: University of Michigan Press, 1983.

Thornton, Richard C. *China: A Political History, 1917–1980*. Boulder, Colo.: Westview Press, 1982.

Tian Ming and Xu Jianchuan, eds. *Gonghui dacidian* (A large dictionary on labor unions). Beijing: Jingji guanli chubanshe, 1989.

"Tianjin de jiaohang" (The transport guilds of Tianjin), *Tianjin lishi ziliao* (Historical materials on Tianjin) 3 (1979): 1–29.

Tianjin Shehui Kexueyuan Lishi Yanjiuzuo "Tianjin Jianshi" Bianxiezu, comp. *Tianjin jianshi* (A concise history of Tianjin). Tianjin: Tianjin renmin chubanshe, 1987.

Tianjin xuelian (Tianjin Student Association). Tianjin, 1946–?.

Tianjinshi Difangzhi Bianxiu Weiyuanhui, comp. *Tianjin jianshi* (A concise history of Tianjin). Tianjin: Tianjin renmin chubanshe, 1991.

Tilly, Charles. *From Mobilization to Revolution*. Reading, Mass.: Addison-Wesley, 1978.

———. "Town and Country in Revolution," in John Wilson Lewis, ed., *Peasant Rebellion and Communist Revolution in Asia* (q.v.), pp. 271–302.

Tong Xiaopeng. "Zhou Enlai zai jiefang zhanzheng shiqi lingdao dier zhanchang douzheng de lishi gongxian" (The historical contributions of Zhou Enlai in leading the

Second Battlefront struggle during the period of the war of liberation), *Dangshi yanjiu yu xiaoxue* (Research and teaching on party history) 3 (1988): 1–9.

Tuanzhongyang Qingyunshi Yanjiushi and Zhongyang Dang'anguan, comps. *Zhonggong zhongyang qingnian yundong wenjian xuanbian (July 1921–September 1949)* (A selection of documents on the CCP CC youth movement [July 1921–September 1949]). Beijing: Zhongguo qingnian chubanshe, 1988.

United States Consulate (and United States Information Service), Peiping, China. *Chinese Press Review.* Peiping and Tientsin, 2 Jan. 1946–27 July 1948.

United States Consulate General (and United States Information Service), Tientsin, China. *Tientsin Chinese Press Review,* 8 Nov. 1945–9 July 1948.

United States State Department. *The China White Paper, August 1949.* Intro. and index by Lyman P. Van Slyke. Stanford: Stanford University Press, 1967.

Van Slyke, Lyman P. *Enemies and Friends: The United Front in Chinese Communist History.* Stanford: Stanford University Press, 1967.

Van de Ven, Hans J. *From Friend to Comrade: The Founding of the Chinese Communist Party, 1920–1927.* Berkeley and Los Angeles: University of California Press, 1991.

Walder, Andrew G. "Comparative Revolution: The Case of China," in Myron L. Cohen, ed., *Asia: Case Studies in the Social Sciences: A Guide for Teaching* (Armonk, N.Y.: M.E. Sharpe, 1992), pp. 429–38.

Waldron, Arthur. "Government Power and the Chinese Student Movement: The Warlords, the KMT, and the CCP," *Chinese Studies in History* 25 (1992): 57–71.

Wan Renyuan and Fang Qingqiu, eds. *Zhonghua minguoshi shiliao changbian* (A long compilation of the historical materials on the history of the Republic of China). Vols. 67–70. Nanjing: Nanjing daxue chubanshe, 1993.

Wang Binglin and Wu Xuguang, "Lun cong nongcun dao chengshi de weida zhanlüe zhuanbian" (A discussion on the great strategic transformation from the countryside to the city), *Zhonggong dangshi yanjiu* 4 (1990): 17–24.

Wang Degui et al. *Bayiwu qianhou de Zhongguo zhengju* (The political situation of China prior to and after 15 August). Jilin: Dongbei shifan daxue chubanshe, 1985.

Wang Fuxuan. "Nongcun baowei chengshi daolu lilun xingcheng de shijian yu biaozhi zhuyao guandian pingxi" (An analysis of the major viewpoints concerning the periodizations and signals of the formation of the theory and the road of the countryside encircling the city), *Shixue yuekan* (Historical studies monthly) 1 (1993): 86–90.

Wang Gan. *Qingyun gongzuo gailun* (A general discussion on the work of the youth movement). Taibei: Taibei zhishi qingnian dangbu, 1970.

Wang Gongan and Mao Lei. *Guogong liangdang guanxishi* (A history of the relationship between the GMD and the CCP). Wuhan: Wuhan chubanshe, 1988.

———, eds. *Guogong liangdang guanxi tongshi* (A general history of the GMD-CCP relationship). Wuhan: Wuhan chubanshe, 1991.

Wang Jianchu and Sun Maosheng. *Zhongguo gongren yundongshi* (A history of the Chinese worker movement). Shenyang: Renmin chubanshe, 1987.

Wang Jianmin. *Zhongguo gongchandang shigao* (A draft history of the CCP). 2 vols. Hong Kong: Zhongwen tushu gongyingshe, 1974–75.

Wang Jie. "Huiyi jiefang zhanzheng shiqi dang zai Tianjin gongwei he shimin xitong de chengshi gongzuo" (Reminiscing the urban work of the Party's Tianjin Work Committee and the Urban Residents System during the period of the war of liberation), *TJJ*, pp. 217–25.

Wang Jingshan. " 'Erzhan' shiqi 'zuo' qing cuowu dui Beijing (Beiping) dang de gongzuo de yingxiang" (The impact of the 'leftist' errors on the Party's work in Beijing [Beiping] during the period of the Second Revolutionary War), *BDZW*, pp. 173–96.

————. "Qianxi jiefang zhanzheng shiqi Beiping xuesheng dui Guomindang fandong benzhi de renshi guocheng" (A simplifed analysis of the understanding process of Beiping's students toward the reactionary nature of the Guomindang during the period of the war of liberation), *Beijing dangshi yanjiu* 6 (1990): 23–27.

Wang Kejun. "Beiping heping jiefang huiyilu" (Reminiscing the peaceful liberation of Beiping), in Zhongguo Renmin Zhengzhi Xieshang Huiyi Quanguo Weiyuanhui Wenshi Ziliao Yanjiu Weiyuanhui, *Fu Zuoyi shengping* (q.v.), pp. 275–97.

Wang Naide. "Tudian geming zhanzheng shiqi Huabei diqu Zhonggong Shun-Zhi Shengwei he Beifangju zuzhi yange gengai" (A general outline of transformations of the Chinese Communist Beijing–Hebei Provincial Committee and the Northern Bureau organizations in northern China during the period of the war of land revolution), in *Zhonggong dangshi ziliao* (Materials on CCP history) 36 (1990): 103–15.

Wang Piji. " 'Beiping fanshi' de chansheng ji lishi yiyi" (The creation and the historical meaning of the "Beiping pattern"), *Junshi lishi* (Military history) 6 (1988): 19–22.

Wang Piji and Xiao Chi. "Beiping heping jiefang" (The peaceful liberation of Beiping), in Zhonggong Zhongyang Dangshi Ziliao Zhengji Weiyuanhui Zhengji Yanjiushi, *Zhonggong dangshi ziliao zhuanti yanjiuji: Di sanci guonei geming zhanzheng shiqi (1)* (q.v.), pp. 1–41.

Wang Qiachuan. "Gongfei panluan shiqi de 'huobian douzheng' " (The 'currency struggle' of the Communist bandits during the period of rebellion), *Gongdang wenti yanjiu* 3 (1975): 92–95.

Wang Qiaoping. "Beiping jiefang qianxi 'Huabei Renmin Heping Cujinhui' daibiao chucheng tanpan de jingguo" (The process of the representatives of the Huabei People's Peace Promotion Association in getting out of the city for peace before the liberation of Beiping), *WZXB* 18 (1983): 21–33.

Wang Qingkui. *Zhongguo renmin jiefangjun zhanyiji* (A compilation of the campaigns of the Chinese PLA). Beijing: Jiefangjun chubanshe, 1987.

Wang Renlin. *Wang Renlin huiyilu* (The memoirs of Wang Renlin). Taibei: Zhuanji wenxue chubanshe, 1984.

Wang Su. "Jiefang qian zuo Zeng Yanji, Liu Houtong gongzuo de pianduan huiyi" (Scattered reminiscences about the work of Zeng Yanji and Liu Houtong prior to the liberation), *TJJ*, pp. 284–85.

Wang Wenhua. "Liming qian de zhandou—Huiyi peihe jiefang Tianjin de dixia douzheng" (The battle before daybreak: Reminiscing the underground struggle that coordinated with the liberation of Tianjin), *TJJ*, pp. 206–16.

Wang Xiaoting and Wang Wenyi, eds. *Zhandou zai Beida de gongchandang ren: (1920.10–1949.2) Beida dixiadang gaikuang* (The Communists who fought at Beijing University: The condition of the Beijing University Underground Party, October 1920–February 1949). Beijing: Beijing daxue chubanshe, 1991.

Wang Xixian. "Huiyi Tianjin Wenhuaren Lianhehui" (Reminiscing the Tianjin Cultural Man Association), *TWZX* 14 (1981): 98–115.

Wang Xueqi and Shi Hansan, eds. *Disi zhanxian—Guomindang Zhongyang Guangbo Diantai duoshi* (The Fourth Battlefront: Getting the truth about the Guomindang Central Broadcasting Radio Station). Beijing: Zhongguo wenshi chubanshe, 1988.

Wang Xuewen. "Zhonggong qieju dalu yiqian cedong xuechao zhi shimo" (The beginning and the end of the CCP's instigation of student tides prior to its stealing of mainland China), *Chintai chung-kuo* (Modern China) 32 (1982): 176–97.

Wang Yuting. "Huabei zhi shoufu yu xianluo" (The recovery and fall of North China), *Zhuanji wenxue* (Biographical literature) 38 (1981), 3: 78–80, 5: 120–28, 6: 69–76; 39 (1981), 1: 117–23, 2: 66–71, 3: 91–97, 4: 54–61.

Wang Zhangling. "Gongdang tewu zuzhi de fenxi" (An analysis of the Communist secret-service organizations). *Gongdang wenti yanjiu* 16 (1990): 1–11.

Wang Zichen. "Wo suo zhidao de qinghongbang zai Tianjin de huodong" (The activities of the Green and Red Gangs in Tianjin that I know), *TWZX* 24 (1984): 206–19.

Wang Zonghua, Li Fuhai, and Wang Ruxian. " 'Dong Sheng Ping' bu pingjing—Jiefang qian yuchiye gongren douzheng de yige cemian" ("Dong Sheng Ping" was not peaceful—One lateral aspect of the struggles of the bathhouse workers prior to the liberation), *BDDS*, pp. 178–88.

Wang Zuo et al. "Jiefang zhanzheng shiqi Yaohua Xuexiao de xuesheng yundong" (The student movement of the Yaohua [Middle] School during the period of the war of liberation), *Tianjin lishi ziliao* 7 (1980): 1–24.

Wasserstrom, Jeffrey N. *Student Protests in Twentieth-Century China: The View from Shanghai*. Stanford: Stanford University Press, 1991.

Wei Hongyun et al., eds. *Zhongguo xiandaishi ziliao xuanbian* (A compilation of selected materials on modern Chinese history). 5 vols. Harbin: Helongjiang renmin chubanshe, 1981.

Wen Hai-kiang. *The Chinese Student Movement*. New York: King's Crown, 1948.

Weng Zhonger. "Guomindang tongzhiqu de aiguo minzhu yundong" (The patriotic democratic movement in the GMD-controlled areas), in Zhonggong Zhongyang Dangxiao Zhonggong Dangshi Jiaoyanshi, *Zhonggong dangshi zhuanti jiangyi: Di sanci guonei geming zhanzheng shiqi (2)* (q.v.), pp. 71–91.

Westad, Odd Arne. *Cold War and Revolution: Soviet-American Rivalry and the Origins of the Chinese Civil War, 1944–1946*. New York: Columbia University Press, 1993.

White, John A. *The United States Marines in North China*. Millbrae, Calif.: n.p., 1974.

Wilbur, C. Martin. "Nationalist China, 1928–1950: An Interpretation," in Chiu Hungdah with Leng Shao-chuan, eds., *China: Seventy Years after the 1911 Hsin-hai Revolution* (q.v.), pp. 2–57.

Wong Young-tsu. "The Fate of Liberalism in Revolutionary China: Chu Anping and His Circle, 1946–1950," *Modern China* 14 (1993): 457–90.

Wu Dongzhi, ed. *Zhongguo waijiao shi: Zhonghua mingguo shiqi 1911–1949*. (A diplomatic history of China: The period of the Republic of China 1911–1949). Henan: Renmin chubanshe, 1990.

Wu Han. "Zhonggong de xueyun gongzuo" (The work of the CCP's student movement). *Gongdang wenti yanjiu* 1 (1987): 10–17.

Wu Jialin. "Beiping dixiadang de douzheng yu Zhongguo geming de daolu" (The struggle of the Beiping Underground Party and the road of the Chinese revolution), *Beijing dangshi yanjiu* 4 (1991): 32–40.

Wu Menghua. "Wo ren Tianjinshi Shehui Juchang sannian" (My three years as the Tianjinshi Social Affairs Bureau Chief), *TLZ*, pp. 82–91.

Wu Mu. "Tianjin xueyun de jiguo wenti" (Several questions concerning the Tianjin student movement), *Qingyunshi yanjiu* (Research on the history of the youth movement) 6 (1986): 11–17.

Wu Peishen and He Jiadong. "Beiping Zhongwai Chubanshe douzheng jishi" (A factual account of the struggle of the Sino-Foreign Publishing Agency), *BDDS*, pp. 207–17.

Wu Tingjun. *Zhongguo xinwenye lishi gongyao* (An outline history of the Chinese news media). Wuchang: Huazhong ligong daxue chubanshe, 1990.

Wu Weiling and Li He, eds. *Beijing gaodeng jiaoyu shiliao: Diyiji (Jinxindai bufen)* (Historical materials on the higher education in Beijing: Vol. I [Modern section]). Beijing: Beijing shifen xueyuan chubanshe, 1992.

Wu Yiguang et al., eds. *Beijingshi jingji dili* (The economic geography of Beijing City). Beijing: Xinhua chubanshe, 1988.

Wu Zhuren. "Wu Zhuren huiyilu zhi liu" (part 6 of the memoirs of Wu Zhuren), *Zhongwai zazhi* 3 (1993): 136–40.

Xi Xionghou. "Beiping dangzuzhi gongkai" (Beiping party organizations' going public), *Beijing dangshi tongxun* (Beijing Party history newsletter) 1 (1989): 43–46.

Xiao Chaoran. "Zhongguo Gongchandang de chuangli yu Beijing daxue" (The founding of the CCP and the Beijing University), *BDYW*, pp. 23–40.

Xiao Chaoran et al., eds. *Beijing daxue xiaoshi (1898–1949)* (A history of the Beijing University [1898–1949]). Rev. ed. Beijing: Beijing daxue chubanshe, 1988.

Xiao Song, Ma Ju, and Song Bo. "Feiteng de Shatan—Jiefang zhanzheng shiqi Beijing daxue dixiadang lingdao Wen, Li, Fa xueyuan xuesheng minzhu yundong de huiyi" (The boiling Shatan—Reminiscing the democratic movement of the students in the Colleges of the Arts, Science, and Law of Beijing University under the leadership of the Underground Party during the period of the war of liberation), *BDDS*, pp. 543–600.

Xie Tianpei. "Jiefang qian Guomindang Tianjinshi difang zuzhi de huodong gaikuang" (The general situation of the Guomindang's Tianjin municipality's local organizations prior to the liberation), *TWZX* 33 (1985): 12–35.

Xie Yinming. "Zhonggong gongchandang lingdao xia de beifang zuoyi wenhua yundong" (The northern cultural movement under the leadership of the CCP), *BDZW*, pp. 224–58.

Xie Zhonghou, Fang Erzhuang, and Liu Gangfan, eds. *Jindai Hebei shiyao* (A historical outline of modern Hebei). Shijiazhuang: Hebei renmin chubanshe, 1990.

Xin Sheng. "Yijiu shiwu nian-yijiu shiba nian 'Beipingshi zonggonghui' de houdong gaikuang" (The general condition of the activities of the 'Beiping Municipal General Labor Union' from 1945 to 1948), *WZXB* 46 (1993): 176–222.

Xinmin bao (New people). Beiping, 1945–49.

Xinsheng bao (New life). Beiping, 1945–49.

Xiong Haiji. *Tiandi you zhengqi: Caolanzi Jianyu douzheng yu "Liushiyi ren an"* (There is upright spirit in heaven and earth: The struggle in the Caolanzi Prison and the "case of the sixty-one people"). Beijing: Beijing chubanshe, 1982.

Xiong Xianghui et al. *Zhonggong dixiadang xianxingji* (An account of the revealed true features of the Chinese Communist Underground Party). 2 vols. Taibei: Zhuanji wenxue chubanshe, 1991.

Xu Zengen et al. *Xishuo Zhongtong Juntong* (Talk about the Central Statistics and the Military Statistics in detail). Taibei: Zhuanji wenxue chubanshe, 1992.

Xu Zhaolin. "Ji jiefang qian Ping-Jin diqu de fengyun renwu Xu Huidong" (A study on Xu Huidong, a prominent personality of the Beiping–Tianjin area prior to the liberation), *WZXB* 28 (1986): 234–37.

Xue Chengye, Li Jieren, and Ji Hong. "Cedong Guomindang jiushier jun quyi de zhuiji" (An account on instigating the Guomindang 92nd Army to revolt), *BDDS*, pp. 821–32.

Xue Shixiao. *Zhonggong meikuang gongren yundongshi* (A history of the Chinese coal miners movement). Henan: Renmin chubanshe, 1986.

Yan Qi et al. *Zhongguo guomindang shigan* (A historical outline of the GMD). Harbin: Helongjiang renmin chubanshe, 1991.

Yan Zhao. "Xu Yeping Shiqing—Fengtai huoche zhan gongren de yici bagong douzheng" (Xu Yeping Incident—The one strike of the railway workers in the Fengtai Railway Station), *BDDS*, pp. 164–71.

Yanda Wenshi Ziliao Bianweihui, comp. *Yanda wenshi ziliao* (Literary and historical materials on Yanjing University). Vol. III. Beijing: Beijing daxue chubanshe, 1990.

Yang, Benjamin. *From Revolution to Politics: Chinese Communists on the Long March.* Boulder, Colo.: Westview Press, 1990.

Yang Guang. "Guomindang jundui huoshao Jinjiao shisan cun zuixing" (The crime of the GMD troops in the burning of thirteen villages in the suburbs of Tianjin), in Zhongguo Renmin Zhengzhi Xieshang Huiyi Tianjinshi Beijiaoqu Weiyuanhui Wenshi Ziliao Yanjiu Weiyuanhui, comp., *Beijiao wenshi ziliao* (Cultural and historical materials in the northern suburbs) (Tianjin: Tianjinshi beijiaoqu weiyuanhui, 1989), vol. II, pp. 64–66.

Yang Guodong. "Jiefang zhanzheng chuqi Dongbei geming genjudi de jianli ji qi lishi tedian" (The construction and the special characteristics of the Northeastern revolutionary base area during the early phase of the war of liberation), *Liaoni shifan daxue xuebao* (Academic journal of the Liaoni Normal University) 2 (1993): 80–84.

Yang Hongyun and Zhao Yunqiu, eds. *Beijing jingji shihua* (A history of Beijing economy). Beijing: Beijing chubanshe, 1984.

Yang Jialuo, ed. *Dalu lunxian qian zhi Zhonghua minguo* (The Republic of China prior to its collapse on mainland China). 5 vols. Taibei: Dingwen shuchu, 1973.

Yang Ruzhou. *Zhonggong qunzhong luxian yanjiu* (A study of the Chinese Communist mass line). Taibei: Liming wenhua shiye gongsi, 1977.

Yang Shuxian and Zuo Zhiyuan. "Shilun Zhonggong baiqu gongzuo de jiguo wenti" (An attempted discussion on the several issues concerning the CCP work in White areas), *Nankai shixue* (Nankai historical studies) 1 (1987): 149–69.

Yang Xuekun. "Wo zai Tanggu jiefang qianxi" (I was in Tanggu prior to the liberation), *TJJ*, pp. 316–19.

Yang Yinpu. *Minguo caizhengshi* (A financial history of the Republic of China). Beijing: Zhongguo caizheng jingji chubanshe, 1985.

Yao Longjing, Li Zhenji, and Xu Shiying, eds. *Zhongguo gongchandang tongyi zhanxian shi (Xin minzhu zhuyi geming shiqi)* (A history of the united front of the CCP [The revolutionary period of New Democracy]). Taiyuan: Shanxi renmin chubanshe, 1991.

Ye Keming. "Pubumie de geming huozhong—Huiyi Beiping dixiadang tiewei lingdao de douzheng" (The inextinguishable revolutionary fire seeds—Reminiscing the struggle led by the Railway Committee of the Beiping Underground Party), *BDDS*, pp. 158–63.

Yen, Maria. *The Umbrella Garden: A Picture of Student Life in Red China*. Westport, Conn.: Greenwood Press, 1978.

Yick, Joseph K. S. "Liu Jen," in Edwin Pak-wah Leung, ed., *Historical Dictionary of Revolutionary China, 1839–1976* (New York: Greenwood Press, 1992), pp. 229–30.

———. "1939–1949, A Decade of Significance: The Ascendancy of the Urban Strategy over the Rural Strategy in the Chinese Communist Movement," *Asian Studies in the Southwest* 2 (1994): 18–25.

———. "The Urban Strategy of the Chinese Communist Party: The Case of Beiping–Tianjin, 1945–1949." Ph.D. diss., University of California, Santa Barbara, 1988.

Yijiu sijiu nian shouce (1949 handbook). Hong Kong: Huashang baoshe, 1949.

Yijiu siqi nian shouce (1947 handbook). Hong Kong: Huashang baoshe, 1947.

Yin Bingyan. "Li Zongren chuzhi Beiping Xingying de qianqian houhou" (Prior to and after Li Zongren took charge of the Beiping Executive Headquarters), *WZXB* 18 (1983): 115–39.

Yin Shubo. " 'Jieshou' dui Guomindang zhengquan shuaibai de yingxiang" (The impact of the "takeover" on the decline of the Guomindang political regime), *Dangshi yanjiu yu jiaoxue* 5 (1990): 45–48.

Yip Ka-Che. "Student Nationalism in Republican China, 1912–1949," *Canadian Review of Studies in Nationalism* 2 (1982): 247–61.

Yishi bao (Social welfare). Tianjin, 1945–49.

Youdianbu Youdianshi Bianjishi, comp. *Nanwang de zhandou suiye—Geming zhanzheng shiqi youdian huiyilu* (The unforgettable fighting years—Memoirs on the telecommunications during the revolutionary war period). Beijing: Renmin youdian chubanshe, 1982.

————. *Zhongguo jindai youdianshi* (A history of the modern Chinese mail and cable service). Beijing: Renmin youdian chubanshe, 1984.

Yu Gan. *Zhongguo ge minzhu dangpai* (The various Chinese democratic parties). Beijing: Zhongguo wenshi chubanshe, 1987.

Yu Heng. *Fenghuo shiwu nian* (The fifteen-year fire). Taibei: Huangguan chubanshe, 1984.

Yu Xueren. *Zhongguo xiandai xuesheng yundongshi changbian* (A long compilation of the modern Chinese student movement). 2 vols. Changchun: Dongbei shifan daxue chubanshe, 1988.

Yuan Beiping Dianxinju Bufen Dixia Dangyuan. "Jiefang qian Beiping dianxin gongren de douzheng" (The struggle of the Beiping telecommunications workers prior to the liberation), *BDDS*, pp. 136–57.

Yuan Lizhou, ed. *Tongzhan zhishi yu zhengce* (The knowledge and the policy of the united front). Beijing: Harbin gongye daxue chubanshe, 1985.

Yuan Lunqu. *Zhongguo laodong jingjishi* (An economic history of the Chinese labor). Beijing: Beijing jingji xueyuan chubanshe, 1990.

Yuan Ping-Jin Qu Tieluju Dixiadang Bufen Dangyuan. "Zhandou zai Tieluju neibu de dixia jianbing" (The underground sharp troops struggling in the interior of the Railway Bureau), *BDDS*, pp. 850–68.

Yuan Qinghua Daxue Dixiadang Bufen Dangyuan. "Zai dizhan chengshi kaibi 'xiao jiefangqu'—Jiefang zhanzheng shiqi Qinghua daxue dixiadang de douzheng" (Establish a "small liberated area" in the enemy-occupied city—The struggle of the Qinghua University Underground Party during the period of the war of liberation), *BDDS*, pp. 338–425.

Yuan Xinqing. *Zai Chianglao zhong* (Inside Chiang's prison). Beijing: Wenshi ziliao chubanshe, 1981.

Yuan Yanjing Daxue Dixiadang Bufen Dangyuan. "Weiminghu pan de fengyun—Ji jiefang zhanzheng shiqi Beiping Yanjing daxue dixiadang de douzheng" (The wind and cloud by the Weiming Lake—A record of the struggle of the Yanjing University Underground Party in Beiping during the period of the war of liberation), *BDDS*, pp. 679–724.

Yue Daiyun and Carolyn Wakeman. *To the Storm: The Odyssey of a Revolutionary Chinese Woman*. Berkeley and Los Angeles: University of California Press, 1985.

Zeng Changning. "Huiyi jiefang qian wozuo fuqin Zeng Yanji de gongzuo" (Reminiscing the work of my father, Zeng Yanji, prior to the liberation), *TJJ*, pp. 272–81.

Zeng Guangshun. *Zhonggong dui qingnian de kongzhi yu yunyong zhi yanjiu* (A study on the CCP's control and use of the youth). Taibei[?]: Haiwai chubanshe, 1972.

Zeng Jingzhong, ed. *Zhonghua minguoshi yanjiu shulue* (A concise account concerning the research on the history of the Republic of China). Beijing: Zhongguo shehui kexue chubanshe, 1992.

Zeng Ruiyan. "Xin zhonggong jianli qianhou huaqiao de aigong yundong" (The overseas Chinese patriotic movement prior to and after the establishment of New China), *Xinan shifan daxue xuebao* (Academic journal of Southwest Normal University) 2 (1991): 35–43.

Zhang Changshan and Wang Yikun. "Liming qian de zhandou—Huiyi Ping-Jin Tieluju Beiping Dianwuduan Dianhuasuo de yici bagong douzheng" (The battle before daybreak—Reminiscing one strike in the Telephone Office, Beiping Telecommunications Section of the Ping-Jin Railway Bureau), *BDDS*, pp. 464–69.

Zhang Chunying. "Lun jiefang zhanzheng shiqi de disantiao zhanxian" (A discussion on the Third Battlefront during the war of liberation), *Zhonggong dangshi yanjiu* 4 (1989): 60–66.

Zhang Dazhong. "Beiping dixia kangri douzheng de huiyi" (Reminiscing the underground anti-Japanese struggle in Beiping), in Zhongguo Renmin Zhengzhi Xieshang Huiyi Beijingshi Weiyuanhui, *Riwei tongzhi xia de Beiping* (q.v.), pp. 16–29.

Zhang Dingchang. *Zhanhou zhonggong "heping minzhu tongyi zhanxian"* (CCP's "peace and democratic united front" in the postwar era). Taibei: Youshi wenhua shiye gongsi, 1987.

Zhang Fan. *Changcheng neiwai* (Inside and outside the Great Wall). 2 vols. Beijing: Zhongguo qingnian chubanshe, 1990.

Zhang Guoqing. "Kangzhan shengli hou Meisu Guogong zai Dongbei de juezhu" (The American-Soviet and GMD-CCP struggles in the Northeast after the victory of the war of resistance), *Minguo dang'an* (Republican archives) 2 (1993): 117–26.

Zhang Guowei. *Fusheng de jingli yu jianzheng* (The experiences and testimony of a floating life). Taibei: Zhuanji wenxue chubanshe, 1980.

Zhang Jingmin. "Ping-Jin chengshi gongzuo mimi jiaotong xian" (The secret communication lines of the urban work in Ping-Jin), *Beijing dangshi tongxun* 2 (1989): 26–32.

Zhang Jingru, ed. *Zhongguo gongchandang sixiangshi* (An intellectual history of the CCP). Qingdao: Qingdao chubanshe, 1991.

Zhang Jinke and Zhou Wenbin. "Ba shengchan gao tanhuan, rang diren tuantuan zhuan—Beiping qishi·binggongchang dixiadang douzheng huiyi" (Disrupt the production, let the enemies circle around—Reminiscing the Underground Party struggle in the Beiping 70th Arsenal), *BDDS*, pp. 869–902.

Zhang Kecheng. " 'Dao' tu" ("Steal" the map), *TJJ*, pp. 305–6.

Zhang Wanlu. "Mao Zedong guanyu Zhongguo zichan jieji de lilun yu shijian" (Mao Zedong's theory and practice on the Chinese bourgeoisie), in Mao Shixin, ed., *Mao Zedong sixiang zhuanti yanjiu* (Topical research on the Thought of Mao Zedong) (Xi'an: Shaanxi renmin xiaoyu chubanshe, 1991), pp. 106–23.

Zhang Wenson and Zhang Qingji. "Jielu diren, huanqi qunzhong—Huiyi Beiping dixiadang wenwei lingdao de douzheng" (Expose the enemy, arouse the masses—Reminiscing the struggle led by the Culture Committee of the Beiping Underground Party), *BDDS*, pp. 197–206.

Zhang Wentian. *Zhang Wentian xuanji* (Selected works of Zhang Wentian). Beijing: Renmin chubanshe, 1985.

Zhang Xianwen, ed. *Zhonghua minguo shigang* (A historical outline of the Republic of China). Henan: Xinhua shudian, 1985.

Zhang Youyu. "Wo zai Tianjin congshi mimi gongzuo de pianduan huiyi" (The scattered reminiscences of my secret work in Tianjin), *TWZX* 10 (1980): 39–68.

———. "Zai Shaoqi tongzhi lingdao xia gongzuo" (Work under the leadership of Comrade Shaoqi), *Geming huiyilu* 2 (1980): 18–24.

Zhang Yuhe. "Wo suo zhidao de Beiping 'Yiji huibao' " (The Beiping "B-grade Conference" that I know), *WZXB* 44 (1992): 52–78.

Zhang Zhenbang et al. *Guogong guanxi jianshi* (A concise history of the GMD-CCP relationship). Taibei: Guoli zhengzhi daxue guoji guanxi yanjiu zhongxin, 1983.

Zhang Zhenglong. *Xuebai xuehong* (Snow is white; blood is red). Beijing: Jiefangjun chubanshe, 1989.

Zhang Zhiyi. "Zai diren xinzang nei—Wo suo zhidao de zhonggong zhongyang Shanghaiju" (Inside the enemy's heart—the CCP Shanghai Bureau that I know), *Gemingshi ziliao* 5 (1981): 9–39.

Zhao Fan and Ji Yuan. "Zhonggong Jizhong Quwei Beiping Gongzuo Weiyuanhui de jianli ji qi huodong" (The establishment and activities of the Beiping Work Committee of the CCP Central Hebei Area Party Committee), *Beijing dangshi yanjiu* 3 (1991): 32–35.

Zhao Fan, Peng Siming, and Xu Ping. "Ranqi laodong renmin douzheng de huoyan—

Huiyi Beiping dixiadang pingwei lingdao de douzheng" (Set the fire of the laboring people's struggle—Reminiscing the struggle led by the Commoner Committee of the Underground Party in Beiping), *BDDS*, pp. 172–77.

Zhao Gengqi and Liang Xianghan. "Kangzhan qianxi Liu Shaoqi tongzhi zai Ping-Jin gongzuo qijian de zhongda gongxian" (The major achievements of Comrade Liu Shaoqi in the Ping-Jin work on the eve of the anti-Japanese war of resistance), in Liang and Zhao, *Beiping diqu kangzhan shiliao* (q.v.), pp. 3–15.

———. " 'Qiqi Shibiao zhi yijiu sanba nian zai Beiping congshi dang de dixia douzheng de qingkuang—Louping tongzhi tanhua jilu" (An account on the work of the underground struggle of the Party from the July Seventh Incident to 1938—A record of Comrade Louping's talks), in Liang and Zhao, *Beiping diqu kangzhan shiliao* (q.v.), pp. 76–81.

———. "Yijiu sanba nian de zhi yijiu siyi nian zai Beiping congshi dang de dixia douzheng de qingkuang—Zhou Bin tongzhi tanhua jilu" (An account on the work of the underground struggle of the Party from the end of 1938 to 1941—A record of Comrade Zhou Bin's talks), in Liang and Zhao, *Beiping diqu kangzhan shiliao* (q.v.), pp. 82–86.

Zhao Shenghui. *Zhongguo gongchandang zuzhishi ganyao* (An outline of the organizational history of the CCP). Wuhu: Anhui renmin chubanshe, 1987.

Zhao Xihua. *Minmeng shihua 1941–1949* (A historical account of the Democratic League). Beijing: Zhonggong shehui kexue chubanshe, 1992.

Zhao Yongtian. "Yijiu siliu nian Beiping 'Sisan' Shijian shimo" (The beginning and the end of the "April Third Incident" in Beiping in 1946), *BDYW*, pp. 395–407.

Zheng Deyong and Zhu Yang, eds. *Zhongguo gemingshi changbian* (A long compilation of the Chinese revolutionary history). 2 vols. Changchun: Jilin renmin chubanshe, 1991.

Zheng Guang and Lo Chengquan, eds. *Zhongguo qingnian yundong liushi nian (1919–1979)* (The sixty years of the Chinese youth movement [1919–1979]). Beijing: Zhongguo qingnian chubanshe, 1990.

Zheng Mengping. "Wie jieguan jiu Beiping fayuan zuo zhunbei" (In preparation for taking over the old law courts in Beiping), *BDL*, pp. 148–54.

Zheng Weishan. *Cong Huabei dao Xibei*. (From North China to the Northwest). Beijing: Jiefangjun chubanshe, 1985.

Zhong Wen. "Guanyu Fu Zuoyi de 'Huabei Jiaozong' " (Concerning Fu Zuoyi's North China Bandit-Suppression General Headquarters), in Zhongguo Renmin Zhengzhi Xieshang Huiyi Quanguo Weiyuanhui Wenshi Ziliao Yanjiu Weiyuanhui, *Fu Zuoyi shengping* (q.v.), pp. 340–49.

"Zhonggong Beijing diwei guomin yundong gongzuo baogan" (A work report of the CCP Beijing Local Committee on the national movement), in Zhonggong Beijing Shiwei Dangshi Yanjiushi, comp., *Diyici guogonghezuo zai Beijing* (q.v.), pp. 361–84.

Zhonggong Beijing Shiwei Dangshi Yanjiushi, comp. *Beijing dangshi yanjiu wenji* (Collected essays on the research in Beijing party history). Beijing: Beijing chubanshe, 1989.

———. *Beijing dangshi zhuanti wenxuan* (Selected essays on the special topics in Beijing party history). Beijing: Beijing daxue chubanshe, 1989.

———. *Beijing gemingshi dashiji* (A record of the major events in Beijing revolutionary history). Beijing: Zhonggong dangshi ziliao chubanshe, 1989.

———. *Beijing gemingshi jianming cidian* (A concise dictionary on the Beijing revolutionary history). Beijing: Beijing chubanshe, 1992.

———. *Diyici guogonghezuo zai Beijing* (The first GMD-CCP cooperation in Beijing). Beijing: Beijing chubanshe, 1989.

———. *Kangri meijun zhuhua baoxing yundong ziliao huibian* (A compilation of materials on the protest movement against the brutality of the American military personnel in China). Beijing: Beijing daxue chubanshe, 1989.

Zhonggong Beijing Shiwei Dangshi Yanjiushi, Wu Jialin, and Xie Yinming, *Beijing dang zuzhi de chuangjian huodong* (The founding activities of the Party organizations of Beijing). Beijing: Zhongguo renmin daxue chubanshe, 1991.

———. *Fan jie fan neizhan yundong ziliao huibian* (Compiled materials on the Antihunger Anti–Civil War Movement). Beijing: Beijing daxue chubanshe, 1992.

Zhonggong Beijing Shiwei Dangshi Ziliao Zhengji Weiyuanhui, comp. *Yier jiu yundong* (The December Ninth Movement). Beijing: Zhonggong dangshi ziliao chubanshe, 1987.

Zhonggong Beijing Shiwei Dangshi Ziliao Zhengji Weiyuanhui Bangongshi, "Wei jiefang wenhua gudu fendou de Beiping dixiadang" (The struggle of the Beiping Underground Party in liberating the old cultural capital), in Zhongguo Renmin Jiefangjun Lishi Ziliao Congshu Bianshen Weiyuanhui, *Ping-Jin zhanyi* (q.v.), pp. 671–81.

Zhonggong de tewu huodong (The activities of the Chinese Communist secret services). Hong Kong: Aertai chubanshe, 1984.

Zhonggong Hebei Shengwei Dangshi Yanjiushi, Zhonggong Liaoning Shengwei Dangshi Yanjiushi, Zhonggong Beijing Shiwei Dangshi Yanjiushi, Zhonggong Tianjin Shiwei Dangshi Ziliao Zhengji Weiyuanhui, Zhonggong Neimenggu Zizhiquwei Dangshi Yanjiushi, comps. *Yiqie weiliao qianxian—Ping-Jin zhanyi zhiqian ziliao huibian* (Everything for the front—Compiled materials on supporting the front during the Battle of Beiping–Tianjin). Beijing: Zhonggong dangshi chubanshe, 1992.

Zhonggong Shanghai Shiwei Dangshi Ziliao Zhengji Weiyuanhui, *Jiefang zhanzheng shiqi de Zhonggong Zhongyang Shanghaiju* (The CCP CC Shanghai Bureau during the war of liberation). Shanghai: Xuelin chubanshe, 1989.

Zhonggong Tianjin Shiwei Dangshi Ziliao Zhengji Weiyuanhui, *Tianjin jiefang jishi* (A factual account on the liberation of Tianjin). Beijing: Zhonggong dangshi ziliao chubanshe, 1988.

Zhonggong Tianjin Shiwei Dangshi Ziliao Zhengji Weiyuanhui Bangongshi, "Yingjie Tianjin jiefang—Ji Ping-Jin zhanyi zhong de Tianjin dixiadang" (Welcome the liberation of Tianjin—A record of the Tianjin Underground Party in the Battle of Beiping–Tianjin), in Zhongguo Renmin Jiefangjun Lishi Ziliao Congshu Bianshen Weiyuanhui, *Ping-Jin zhanyi* (q.v.), pp. 682–93.

Zhonggong Zhongyang Dangshi Yanjiushi. *Zhongguo gongchandang lishi* (CCP history). Vol. I. Beijing: Renmin chubanshe, 1991.

———. *Zhongguo gongchandang lishi dashiji* (A record of the major events in CCP history). Beijing: Renmin chubanshe, 1989.

———, comp. *"Zhongguo gongchandang lishi" (shangjuan) ruogan wenti shuoming* (A clarification of certain issues in "CCP history" [vol. I]). Beijing: Zhonggong dangshi chubanshe, 1991.

Zhonggong Zhongyang Dangshi Yanjiushi and Wu Sheng, comps. *Zhongguo gongchandang de qishi nian* (The seventy years of the CCP). Beijing: Zhonggong dangshi chubanshe, 1991.

Zhonggong Zhongyang Dangshi Ziliao Zhengji Weiyuanhui Zhengji Yanjiushi, comp. *Zhongong dangshi ziliao zhuanti yanjiuji: Di sanci guonei geming zhanzheng shiqi (1)* (Compiled CCP historical materials on special researched topics: The period of the Third Revolutionary Civil War [1]). Beijing: Zhonggong dangshi ziliao chubanshe, 1989.

Zhonggong Zhongyang Dangxiao Dangshi Jiaoyanshi. *Zhongguo gongchandang qishi nian de licheng he jingyan* (The seventy-year historical process and experience of the CCP). Beijing: Zhonggong zhongyang dangxiao chubanshe, 1991.

Zhonggong Zhongyang Dangxiao Lilunbu, comp. *Zhongguo gongchandang jianshe quanshu 1921–1991* (A complete work on the CCP building). 9 vols. Taiyuan: Shanxi renmin chubanshe, 1991.

Zhonggong Zhongyang Dangxiao Zhonggong Dangshi Jiaoyanshi, comp. *Zhonggong dangshi zhuanti jiangyi: Di sanci guonei geming zhanzheng shiqi (2)* (Lecture notes on special topics concerning the Chinese Communist party history: The period of the Third Revolutionary War [2]). Beijing: Zhonggong zhongyang dangxiao chubanshe, 1989.

Zhonggong Zhongyang Shujichu, comp. *Liuda jilai—Dangnei mimi wenjian* (Since the Sixth Congress—Secret internal party documents). 2 vols. Beijing: Renmin chubanshe, 1980.

Zhonggong Zhongyang Tongyi Zhanxian Gongzuobu and Zhonggong Zhongyang Wenxian Yanjiushi. *Zhou Enlai tongyi zhanxian wenxuan* (Selected works of Zhou Enlai on the united front). Beijing: Renmin chubanshe, 1984.

Zhonggong Zhongyang Wenxian Yanjiushi, ed. (under the direction of Jin Chongji). *Zhou Enlai chuan 1898–1949* (A biography of Zhou Enlai, 1898–1949). Beijing: Renmin chubanshe, Zhonggong zhongyang wenxian chubanshe, 1989.

"Zhongguo Gongchandang Jianshe Dacidian" Bianji Weiyuanhui, comp. *Zhongguo gongchandang jianshe dacidian* (A large dictionary on the CCP building). Chengdu: Sichuan renmin chubanshe, 1991.

"Zhongguo Gongchandang Lishi Dacidian" Bianji Weiyuan, comp. *Zhongguo gongchandang lishi dacidian: Xinminzhu zhuyi geming shiqi* (A dictionary of CCP history: The period of the New Democratic Revolution). Beijing: Zhonggong zhongyang dangxiao chubanshe, 1991.

Zhongguo gongchandang lishi dacian: Zonglun, renwu (A dictionary of CCP history: General discussion, personalities). Beijing: Zhonggong zhongyang dangxiao chubanshe, 1991.

Zhongguo Guomindang Zhongyang Weiyuanhui Dangshi Weiyuanhui, comp. *Zhonghua minguo zhongyao shiliao chubian—dui Ri kangzhen shiqi* (A preliminary compilation of important historical materials on the Republic of China: The period of the war of resistance). *Diwu bian: Zhonggong huadong zhen xiang* (Vol. V: The true face of CCP activities). 4 vols. Taibei: n.p., 1985.

Zhongguo Mao Zedong Sixiang Lilun Yu Shijian Yanjiuhui Lishihui, comp. *Mao Zedong sixiang cidian* (Mao Zedong Thought dictionary). Beijing: Zhonggong zhongyang dangxiao chubanshe, 1989.

Zhongguo Renmin Daxue Gongye Jingjixi, comp. *Beijing gongye shiliao* (Historical materials on the Beijing industry). Beijing: Beijing chubanshe, 1960.

Zhongguo Renmin Jiefangjun Lishi Ziliao Congshu Bianshen Weiyuanhui. *Ping-Jin zhanyi* (The Battle of Beiping-Tianjin). Beijing: Jiefangjun chubanshe, 1991.

Zhongguo Renmin Jiefangjun Nanjing Zhengzhi Xiaoyuan Lishi Xuexi. *Zhongguo xiandaishi zhengminglu: Shijianbian* (A compilation of contentious events in modern Chinese history: Compiled events). Nanjing: Jiangsu jiaoyu chubanshe, 1990.

Zhongguo Renmin Jiefangjun Zhengzhi Xueyuan Dangshi Jiaoyanshi, comp. *Zhonggong dangshi cankao ziliao* (Reference materials on CCP history). 11 vols. Beijing[?]: n.p., n.d.

Zhongguo Renmin Zhengzhi Xieshang Huiyi Beijingshi Weiyuanhui Wenshi Ziliao Yanjiu Weiyuanhui, comp. *Beijing de liming* (Beijing's daybreak). Beijing: Beijing chubanshe, 1988.

———. *Beiping dixiadang douzheng shiliao* (Historical materials on the struggle of the Beiping Underground Party). Beijing: Beijing chubanshe, 1988.

———. *Riwei tongzhixia de Beiping* (Beiping under the control of the Japanese and the puppets). Beijing: Beijing chubanshe, 1987.

———. *Wenshi ziliao xuanbian* (Selected and compiled materials on culture and history). Beijing, January 1979–.

Zhongguo Renmin Zhengzhi Xieshang Huiyi Quanguo Weiyuanhui Wenshi Ziliao Yanjiu Weiyuanhui, comp. *Fu Zuoyi shengping* (The life of Fu Zuoyi). Beijing: Wenshi ziliao chubanshe, 1985.

———. *Ping-Jin zhanyi qinliji (Yuan Guomindang jiangling de huiyi)* (Personal participation in the Battle of Beiping-Tianjin [The reminiscences of the Guomindang generals]). Beijing: Zhongguo wenshi chubanshe, 1989.

———. *Wenshi ziliao xuanji* (Selected materials on culture and history). Beijing, January 1960– .

Zhongguo Renmin Zhengzhi Xieshang Huiyi Tianjinshi Weiyuanhui Wenshi Ziliao Yanjiu Weiyuanhui, comp. *Tianjin lishi de zhuanzhe* (The turns in the course of events in Tianjin history). Tianjin: n.p., 1988.

———. *Tianjin wenshi ziliao xuanji* (Selected materials on the culture and history of Tianjin). Tianjin, December 1978– .

Zhongguo xiandaishi ziliao xuanbian (A selected compilation of materials on modern Chinese history). 10 vols. Beijing: Renmin chubanshe, 1979–84.

Zhonghua Chuango Funu Lianhehui. *Zhongguo funu yundongshi: Xin minzhu zhuyi shiqi* (A history of the Chinese women's movement: The period of New Democracy). Beijing: Chunqiu chubanshe, 1989.

Zhonghua Minguo Kaiguo Wushinian Wenxian Bianzuan Weiyuanhui and Guoli Zhengzhi Daxue Guoji Guanxi Yanjiu Zhongxin, comps. *Gongfei huoguo shiliao huibian* (A compilation of historical materials on the Communist bandits' destruction of the nation). 6 vols. Taibei: Zhonghua minguo kaigo wushinian wenxian bianzuan weiyuanhui, 1976, 1978.

Zhonghua minguo guomin zhengfu gongbao (Public announcements of the National Government of the Republic of China). Reprinted by Chengwen chuban gongsi, Taibei, 1981.

Zhonghua minguo zongtongfu gongbao (Public announcements of the Presidential Office, Republic of China). Reprinted by Chengwen chuban gongsi, Taibei, 1981.

Zhonghua Quanguo Funu Lianhehui, comp. *Cai Chang Deng Yingchao Kang Keqing funu jiefang wenti wenxian (1938–1987)* (Selected articles of Cai Chang, Deng Yingchao, and Kang Keqing on the question of women's liberation). Beijing: Renmin chubanshe, 1988.

Zhonghua Quanguo Zonggonghui Zhongguo Gongren Yundongshi Yanjiushi, comp. *Zhongguo gonghui lici daibiao dahui wenxian* (Materials on the various representative assemblies of the All-China Labor Union). Vol. I. Beijing: Gongren chubanshe, 1984.

Zhongyang Dang'anguan, comp. *Zhonggong zhongyang wenjian xuanji* (A selection of CCP Central Committee documents). 14 vols. Beijing: Zhonggong zhongyang dangxiao, 1982–87.

Zhongyang Tongzhanbu and Zhongyang Dang'anguan, comps. *Zhonggong zhongyang jiefang zhanzheng shiqi tongyi zhanxian wenjian xuanbian* (A selected compilation of CCP CC documents on the united front during the period of the war of liberation). Beijing: Dang'an chubanshe, 1988.

Zhou Enlai. *Selected Works of Zhou Enlai*. Vol. I. Peking: Foreign Languages Press, 1981.

———. *Zhou Enlai xuanji* (Selected works of Zhou Enlai). Vol. I. Beijing: Renmin chubanshe, 1980.

Zhou Ruijing. "Shilun 1944 nian 4 yue zhi 1949 nian 3 yue Zhonggong gongzuo zhongxin de zhubu zhuanyi" (An attempted discussion of the gradual shifting of the center of gravity of work of the CCP from April 1944 to March 1949), *Dangshi yanjiu yu xiaoxue* 1 (1991): 38–46.

Zhu Baoshan et al. "Jiefang zhanzheng shiqi dang lingdao Tianjin Jiqichang de douzheng" (The struggle led by the Party in the Tianjin Machinery Factory during the war of liberation), *TJJ*, pp. 226–36.

Zhu Cishou. *Zhongguo jindai gongyeshi* (A history of modern Chinese industry). Chongqing: Chongqing chubanshe, 1989.

Zhu De. *Zhu De xuanji* (Selected works of Zhu De). Beijing: Renmin chubanshe, 1983.

Zhu Hanguo, Xie Chungtao, and Fan Tianshun, eds. *Zhongguo gongchandang jiansheshi* (A history of the CCP building). Chengdu: Sichuan renmin chubanshe, 1991.

Zhu Meiduan. "Yanyuan jiefangshi de riji" (The diary during the liberation of Yanjing University campus), in Yanda Wenshi Ziliao Bianweihui, *Yanda wenshi ziliao* (q.v.), vol. III, pp. 222–25.

Zhu Qihua and Liu Yongze. *Tianjin quanshu* (A complete book on Tianjin). Tianjin: Tianjin renmin chubanshe, 1991.

Zhu Wenlin. "Dalu zhong guojia anquan fangju jiqi chengxiao zhi yanjiu" (An analytical study of the Republic of China's national security work during the suppression of the Communist rebellion), *Dongan jikan* (East Asia quarterly), part I in 18 (1987) 1: 1–24; part II in 18 (1987) 4: 1–22.

Zhu Zhuying. "Wo he Wu Daren laoshi de jiaowang" (The contact between me and the teacher, Wu Daren), *TJJ*, pp. 252–56.

Ziyuan weiyuanhui dang'an shiliao Chubian (A preliminary compilation of the archival historical materials of the Natural Resources Committee). Taibei: Guoshiguan, 1984.

Zuo Jian and Qin Ge. "Jiefang zhanzheng shiqi de Tianjin xuesheng yundong" (The Tianjin student movement during the period of the war of liberation), *TWZX* 22 (1983): 1–40.

Index

Joseph K. S. Yick is assistant professor of history at Southwest Texas State University. He received his Ph.D. from the University of California at Santa Barbara.